Musicology and Dance

Long treated as peripheral to music history, dance has become prominent within musicological research, a prime and popular subject for an increasing number of books, articles, conference papers and special symposiums. Despite this growing interest, there remains no thorough-going critical examination of the ways in which musicologists might engage with dance, thinking not only about specific repertoires or genres, but about fundamental commonalities between the two, including issues of embodiment, agency, subjectivity and consciousness. This volume begins to fill this gap. Ten chapters illustrate a range of conceptual, historical and interpretive approaches that advance the interdisciplinary study of music and dance. This methodological eclecticism is a defining feature of the volume, integrating insights from critical theory, film and cultural studies, the visual arts, phenomenology, cultural anthropology and literary criticism into the study of music and dance.

DAVINIA CADDY writes about the interrelations between music, the visual arts and gesture. She is the author of *The Ballets Russes and Beyond* (Cambridge University Press, 2012), and is currently working on projects related to contemporary musical culture, archival theory and practice.

MARIBETH CLARK is Associate Professor of Music at New College of Florida. Her articles on theatrical and social dance in mid-nineteenth-century Paris have appeared in *Journal of Musicology, 19th-Century Music, Musical Quarterly* and several edited volumes. She is currently writing a monograph on the cultural history of whistling.

Musicology and Dance

Historical and Critical Perspectives

Edited by DAVINIA CADDY
MARIBETH CLARK

CAMBRIDGE
UNIVERSITY PRESS

University Printing House, Cambridge CB2 8BS, United Kingdom

One Liberty Plaza, 20th Floor, New York, NY 10006, USA

477 Williamstown Road, Port Melbourne, VIC 3207, Australia

314-321, 3rd Floor, Plot 3, Splendor Forum, Jasola District Centre, New Delhi - 110025, India

103 Penang Road, #05-06/07, Visioncrest Commercial, Singapore 238467

Cambridge University Press is part of the University of Cambridge.

It furthers the University's mission by disseminating knowledge in the pursuit of education, learning and research at the highest international levels of excellence.

www.cambridge.org
Information on this title: www.cambridge.org/9781108469951
DOI: 10.1017/9781108567947

© Cambridge University Press 2020

This publication is in copyright. Subject to statutory exception and to the provisions of relevant collective licensing agreements, no reproduction of any part may take place without the written permission of Cambridge University Press.

First published 2020
First paperback edition 2022

A catalogue record for this publication is available from the British Library

Library of Congress Cataloging in Publication data
Names: Caddy, Davinia, 1980– editor author. | Clark, Maribeth, editor author.
Title: Musicology and dance : historical and critical perspectives / edited by Davinia Caddy and Maribeth Clark.
Description: [1.] | New York : Cambridge University Press, 2020. | Includes bibliographical references and index.
Identifiers: LCCN 2019059935 (print) | LCCN 2019059936 (ebook) | ISBN 9781108476188 (hardback) | ISBN 9781108567947 (ebook)
Subjects: LCSH: Dance music – History and criticism. | Music and dance – History. | Ballet – History.
Classification: LCC ML3400 .M87 2020 (print) | LCC ML3400 (ebook) | DDC 781.5/5409–dc23
LC record available at https://lccn.loc.gov/2019059935
LC ebook record available at https://lccn.loc.gov/2019059936

ISBN 978-1-108-47618-8 Hardback
ISBN 978-1-108-46995-1 Paperback

Cambridge University Press has no responsibility for the persistence or accuracy of URLs for external or third-party internet websites referred to in this publication, and does not guarantee that any content on such websites is, or will remain, accurate or appropriate.

Contents

List of Figures [*page* vii]
List of Tables [viii]
List of Music Examples [ix]
List of Contributors [xi]
Acknowledgements [xiv]

Introduction [1]
DAVINIA CADDY AND MARIBETH CLARK

PART I CONCEPTUAL STUDIES

1 Bach and the Dance of Humankind [19]
JOHN BUTT

2 Dance as 'Other': Contrasting Modes of Musical Representation [49]
SUZANNE ASPDEN

3 Thinking on Our Feet: A Somatic Enquiry into a Haydn Minuet [71]
JOSEPH FORT

4 Making Moves in Reception Studies: Music, Listening and Loie Fuller [91]
DAVINIA CADDY

PART II CASE HISTORIES

5 The 'Splendid and Shameful Art': Dancing in and around the Wagnerian *Gesamtkunstwerk* [121]
THOMAS GREY

6 Hymnody, Dance and the Sacred in the Illustrated Song [151]
MARIAN WILSON KIMBER

7 Pavanes and Passepieds in the Age of the Cancan [172]
CARLO CABALLERO

PART III CRITICAL READINGS

8 Nijinsky, Modernism, Repression: The Faun Ballet – Once Again – Under Analysis [207]
DAVID J. CODE

9 Choreographing Mahler Songs at the Centenary [231]
WAYNE HEISLER JR

10 Embodied Heritage: English Country Dance in Austen Screen Adaptations [259]
MARIBETH CLARK

Select Bibliography [280]
Index [302]

Figures

0.1 Jules Chéret, 'La pantomime' (1891); courtesy of the Getty Images Historical Picture Archive [*page* 2]
3.1 Z-figure (Feldtenstein, 1772, Fig. 67) [78]
3.2 Hasty's diagram showing projection from the standpoint of durational products C and C'; courtesy of Oxford University Press [85]
3.3 Bass rhythm and step rhythm [87]
4.1 Frederick W. Glasier, *Loie Fuller*, c. 1902; courtesy of the Library of Congress, Washington DC [96]
4.2 R. Moreau, *Loïe Fuller dansant* (à la Carrière), c. 1904; courtesy of the Musée Rodin, Paris [99]
4.3 Anonymous, *Loie Fuller as Blurred Figure in Room*, c. 1900; courtesy of the New York Public Library [106]
4.4 Anonymous, *La Loïe*, c. 1893; courtesy of the Musée des Arts Décoratifs, Paris [112]
6.1 Pose for 'Still, all my song shall be / Nearer, my God, to Thee', in 'Nearer, My God, to Thee'; Grace B. Faxon, *Favorite Pantomimed Songs and Poses* (Danville, NY: F. A. Owen, 1917), 69 [153]
6.2 Pose for 'Religious Devotion', in R. Anna Morris, *Physical Education in the Public Schools: An Eclectic System of Exercises, Including the Delsartean Principles of Execution and Expression* (New York: American Book Company, 1892), 98 [169]
9.1 Lawrence Rhodes as the 'lonely boy' in Eliot Feld's *At Midnight*; photo by Martha Swope [238]
9.2 Christine Sarry and John Sowinski's *pas de deux* in Feld's *At Midnight*; photo by Martha Swope [241]
10.1 'Mr Beveridge's Maggot' from *The Dancing Master* (1695) [272]

Tables

3.1   Minuet step distribution   [*page* 80]
3.2   Executing the Z-figure to Haydn's minuet   [81]
7.1   The pavane returns, 1878–1910   [173]
7.2   So-called passepieds   [174]
10.1 English country dances performed in *Pride and Prejudice* (dir. Langton, BBC 1, 1995)   [270]
10.2 English country dances performed in *Emma* (dir. Lawrence, ITV, 1996)   [270]
10.3 English country dances in *Pride and Prejudice* (dir. Wright, 2005)   [275]

Music Examples

1.1 J. S. Bach, Cantata 57, no. 3, Aria, 'Ich wünschte mir den Tod', bars 1–20 [*page* 32]
1.2 J. S. Bach, Cantata 57, no. 3, Aria, 'Ich wünschte mir den Tod', bars 21–60 [33]
1.3 J. S. Bach, Cantata 63, no. 5, Duet, 'Ruft und fleht den Himmel an', bars 1–20 [36]
1.4 J. S. Bach, Cantata 63, no. 5, Duet, 'Ruft und fleht den Himmel an', bars 23–40 [37]
1.5 J. S. Bach, Cantata 63, no. 5, Duet, 'Ruft und fleht den Himmel an', bars 104–32 [39]
1.6 J. S. Bach, Brandenburg Concerto no. 1 in F, BWV1046, movement 3, bars 1–17 [41]
1.7 J. S. Bach, Brandenburg Concerto no. 1 in F, BWV1046, movement 3, bars 80–4 [45]
3.1 Joseph Haydn, Minuet Hob. IX: 11, no. 1, keyboard version (minuet only) [81]
5.1a–b Main 'Allegro theme' (a) and chromaticized transition theme (b) from overture to *Tannhäuser* (1845 Dresden version) [132]
5.2 Presto 6/8 variant of 'Allegro theme' from Venusberg Bacchanal, *Tannhäuser*, Act 1, scene 1 (1845 Dresden version) [133]
5.3 'Aural dissolve' and transition from conclusion of Venusberg Bacchanal, *Tannhäuser*, Act 1, scene 1 (1845 Dresden version) [134]
5.4 Flower Maidens scene, main (slow, waltz-like) theme, *Parsifal*, Act 2 [138]
7.1 Paladilhe, Pavane from *Patrie*, bars 1–9 [178]
7.2 Fauré, Pavane in F♯ minor, op. 50, bars 27–30 [179]
7.3 Ravel, 'Pavane pour une infante défunte', bars 1–6 [184]
7.4 Chabrier, 'Idylle' from *Dix pièces pittoresques*, bars 1–5 [184]
7.5 Debussy, Passepied from *Suite bergamasque*, bars 1–6, with harmonic analysis [185]
7.6 Delibes, Pavane from *Le roi s'amuse*, arr. piano, bars 1–8 [188]
7.7 Delibes, Lesquercarde from *Le roi s'amuse*, arr. piano, bars 1–4 [188]
7.8 Delibes, Passepied from *Le roi s'amuse*, arr. piano, bars 1–5 [190]

x *List of Music Examples*

7.9 Ravel, 'Pavane de la Belle au bois dormant', no. 1 from *Ma mère l'oye*, bars 1–4 [197]
7.10 The descending tetrachord (a) and its contrapuntal realizations by (b) Paladilhe, (c) Fauré and (d) Messager in their pavanes [198]
7.11 Messager, Pavane from *Isoline*, bars 1–5 [199]
7.12 Ravel, 'Pavane pour une infante défunte' comparing bars 3–6 and bars 62–5 [200]
7.13 (a) Saint-Saëns, Pavane from *Etienne Marcel*, arr. piano, bars 1–4 and (b) its contrapuntal modelling, showing the combination of the descending tetrachord (alto) and the minor-mode *romanesca* [201]
8.1 Reduced short score of Claude Debussy, *Prélude à l'après-midi d'un faune* [216]

Contributors

SUZANNE ASPDEN is Associate Professor at the Faculty of Music, University of Oxford, and Fellow of Jesus College, Oxford. She specializes in eighteenth-century opera and dramatic music, identity politics, performance aesthetics and performativity. Publications include *The Rival Sirens: Performance and Identity on Handel's Operatic Stage* (Cambridge University Press, 2013) and the edited volume, *Operatic Geographies* (Chicago, 2019), as well as a co-edited volume on word–music interrelationships. Her current book projects concern music and national identity in eighteenth-century Britain and the culture of country-house opera in twentieth- and twenty-first century Britain.

JOHN BUTT is Gardener Professor of Music at Glasgow University and Music Director of Edinburgh's Dunedin Consort. He has published widely in the field of Bach, seventeenth- and eighteenth-century music, the culture of historically informed performance and musical modernity. He also has a large discography as both organist (Harmonia Mundi) and conductor (Linn). His recordings have received two Gramophone awards: Handel's *Messiah* in 2007 and Mozart's *Requiem* in 2014 (which also received a Grammy nomination); four further discs have received Gramophone award nominations. Recent discs include Bach's *Magnificat*, *Brandenburg Concertos* and *Christmas Oratorio*, together with the complete *Well-Tempered Clavier* (on harpsichord).

CARLO CABALLERO is Associate Professor of Music at the University of Colorado, Boulder. He is the author of *Fauré and French Musical Aesthetics* and has published essays in *Victorian Studies*, *19th-Century Music*, *The Journal of the American Musicological Society* and many edited collections. His current projects include studies of social continuities in French music from the eighteenth to twentieth centuries, the historiography of nineteenth-century ballet, and a second monograph on Fauré. His new critical edition of Fauré's two piano quintets for *The Complete Works of Gabriel Fauré* is in press at Bärenreiter-Verlag.

DAVINIA CADDY has taught at the universities of Oxford, Oxford Brookes and Auckland. She is the author of *The Ballets Russes and Beyond: Music and Dance in Belle-Époque Paris* (Cambridge University Press, 2012), articles in *Cambridge Opera Journal, Journal of the Royal Musical Association, 19th-Century Music* and *The Opera Quarterly*, as well as the general-interest guide *How to Hear Classical Music* (Awa Press, 2013). She is currently working on projects related to contemporary musical culture, archival theory and practice.

MARIBETH CLARK is Associate Professor of Music at New College of Florida in Sarasota. Her articles on theatrical and social dance in mid-nineteenth-century Paris have appeared in *Journal of Musicology, 19th-Century Music* and *Musical Quarterly*. She is currently writing a monograph on the cultural history of whistling in the United States.

DAVID J. CODE is Reader in Music at the School of Culture and Creative Arts, University of Glasgow. Previously, he taught at Stanford University, on a Mellon Postdoctoral Fellowship, and at Bishop's University in Québec. He has published on Debussy, Stravinsky, Mallarmé and Kubrick in leading journals including *Journal of the American Musicological Society, Journal of the Royal Musical Association* and *Representations*, and he has contributed a Debussy biography to the Reaktion Press 'Critical Lives' of key modern figures.

JOSEPH FORT is the College Organist and Director of the Chapel Choir, and Lecturer in Music at King's College London. He completed a PhD at Harvard University in 2015, with a thesis on dance-music relationships in Joseph Haydn's minuets, and has published in the *Eighteenth-Century Music* journal. As a conductor, he has broadcast on BBC Radio 3, and records for the Delphian label.

THOMAS GREY is Professor of Music at Stanford University. He is the author of *Wagner's Musical Prose: Texts and Contexts* (Cambridge University Press, 1995), as well as editor and co-author of the Cambridge Opera Handbook on Wagner's *Flying Dutchman* (2000), the *Cambridge Companion to Wagner* (2008) and *Wagner and his World* (Princeton University Press, 2009). He has also written on Beethoven, Mendelssohn and the history of nineteenth-century opera. Recent projects include a study of the paintings of Hans Makart in relation to Wagner reception in the late nineteenth century, essays on the idea of 'absolute music', eco-critical perspectives on landscape and nature in nineteenth-century music, and the entry on

Richard Wagner for Oxford Bibliographies Online. New fields of interest include American musical theatre and relations between music and the 'Gothic' in theatre and fiction.

WAYNE HEISLER JR is Professor of Historical and Cultural Studies in Music at The College of New Jersey. His publications include *The Ballet Collaborations of Richard Strauss* (University of Rochester Press, 2009), an article on 'Antony Tudor's *Dark Elegies* and the Affirmation of Mahler's Body, 1937–1947' in *Dance Chronicle* (2013), an essay 'Dancing Lieder Singing' for a 2014 colloquy in the *Journal of the American Musicological Society* ('Studying the Lied: Hermeneutic Traditions and the Challenge of Performance'), as well as an essay on choreographies of Strauss's *Vier letzte Lieder* as 'total art' (Berghahn, 2016). He guest-edited a recent issue of *Opera Quarterly* focusing on Strauss; he is also Reviews Editor of *Opera Quarterly* and serves on its Editorial Board.

MARIAN WILSON KIMBER is Professor of Musicology at the University of Iowa. She has published widely on Felix Mendelssohn and Fanny Hensel, investigating issues of biography, gender and musical reception. Her book, *The Elocutionists: Women, Music, and the Spoken Word* (University of Illinois Press, 2017) explores the combination of elocution and music by women in American musical life. As a reciter, she has revived the performance of women's spoken-word compositions, appearing with pianist Natalie Landowski.

Acknowledgements

With a keen interest in dance, we both chose early in our careers to inhabit the margins of our discipline – a treacherous place, it appeared initially, where loneliness and frustration danced hand in hand with opportunity, excitement and a certain intensity of feeling. In recent years, our company on the periphery has grown substantially – in size, status and critical clout. Rather than being overlooked or else rejected entirely, the body in motion is nowadays considered a pivotal and productive thematic across many of musicology's subfields, from theory and analysis to history, anthropology and aesthetics. To further explore this idea, we enlisted contributors to this volume who, for the most part, examine well-known works in the European tradition with a view to how dance engages the music, and an ear to how music engages the body. This volume, then, recognizes the centrality of both dance and the body to the multiple processes and mediating factors intertangled with music-making, even in Europe. Indeed, this may be the volume's strongest and most enduring outcome: the promotion of the visceral, the fleshy and the ephemeral alongside a musical corpus with which many of us are deeply familiar – at times, perhaps, unthinkingly at ease.

Another outcome is of the human kind. Volumes like this one – featuring multiple authors of different disciplinary backgrounds and from different international institutions – tend to function as a kind of preservative; that is, they record and result from scholarship first presented at conferences, annual meetings, roundtables or special symposiums. Ours emerged differently. Working at opposite ends of the globe, one of us some fourteen hours ahead of the other, we had to start from scratch, with no institutional backing, no funds, no planned get-together, no fixed deadlines, no promises and no pre-existing papers to tweak or expand. We say this not to congratulate ourselves, but to acknowledge and applaud whole-heartedly those contributors with whom we have worked, steadily and with shared determination, over these past six or seven years. Without their generosity of spirit and kindness of heart, their intellectual curiosity and acuity of perception, their enthusiasm, commitment and super-human patience (especially when faced with a battery of emails from us both), this volume would simply not exist. To us, they represent the good in musicology: John, a genius in prose as in performance; Suzanne, our initial and lasting stimulus; Joe, a daring to do something different; Carlo, an unsurpassed level of professionalism; Tom, a colossal intellect; Marian, an archival gold-standard; David, a lyric poeticism; and Wayne, a rare capacity to show, interpretively speaking, just how far open the door can be flung. Our thanks must also extend to those colleagues who shared conversations, perspectives and/or paragraphs in the early stages of this project; in particular, Vicki Cooper, Arnie Cox, Jamie Currie, Sarah Hibberd, Yvonne Kendall, Roger Parker, Marian Smith, Helena Kopchick Spencer and Lawrence Zbikowski.

On a practical note, we would like to express our gratitude to all those involved in bringing this volume to its current form, particularly Kate Brett, Eilidh Burrett and the crew at Cambridge University Press. Kate took a punt on this project quite early on in the proceedings: she has proved remarkably understanding and patient, despite our several false starts, somehow knowing when to give us time to think and write, and when to hurry us along. Eilidh has been a pleasure to work alongside over the last year or so: her efforts in relation to the front cover of the volume, in particular, are very much appreciated. This is not to mention our anonymous reviewers, who read first our proposal and then various portions of the manuscript, offering crucial advice and alternative angles to consider. Simon Morrison, our not-so-anonymous clearance reader, deserves special mention: the warmth and understanding that shone through his comments, when reporting on our final draft of the manuscript, could not have been more thankfully received.

A few words, in turn:

I owe a debt of gratitude to many colleagues, friends, and family members who have made my contributions to this volume possible. My mother, Barbara Hosterman Clark, an artist and an illustrator, helped me see the motion of the crossing diagonal lines in 'La pantomime', the Chéret poster that introduces the volume. Katherine Brion, my colleague in art history at New College, shared her essay on Jules Chéret with me, coincidentally illustrated with that same poster. Danielle Fosler-Lussier and Marian Wilson Kimber have provided invaluable friendship and mentoring at critical moments. Numerous colleagues at New College, past and present, continue to develop my sense of what it means to be an embodied intellectual, including Michelle Barton, Mark Dancigers, K. E. Goldschmidt, Heidi Harley, Sarah Hernandez, Sonia Labrador-Rodríguez, Susan Marks, Steve Miles, Julie Morris, Hugo Viera-Vargas, Alina Wyman and Queen Meccasia Zabriskie. My sister, Crissi, supported me with swimming pools and fishing trips. Sonja Jaffee and the O'Jaffens provided escape in New York City and southwestern Vermont. I owe my husband, Andrew Jaffee, more than I can express, while our children, Esther and Toby, continue to reveal life's richness to me in unexpected ways. (Maribeth Clark, Sarasota, Florida)

As ever, I owe thanks to Roger Parker, who taught me so much about how to think and how to write, even when jogging along the cobbled streets of Cambridge. To Suzanne Aspden, I am also grateful: it was while sitting in on Suzanne's undergraduate lectures on music and dance, soon after the two of us had started new positions within the Faculty at Oxford, that I first entertained the possibility of an edited volume such as this. My friends here in New Zealand have also proven instructive, showing me how to walk tall, along the sands of our seaside suburb, even when dark clouds gather. Chris and Hazel have weathered all storms besides me: it is difficult to put into words what their love and devotion has meant. (Davinia Caddy, Mission Bay, Auckland)

Introduction

DAVINIA CADDY AND MARIBETH CLARK

In 1891, the Parisian artist Jules Chéret (1836–1932) designed a poster titled 'La pantomime', a copy of which adorns the cover of this volume (see Figure 0.1). Most of Chéret's lithographs were fashioned as advertisements, but he intended this one and many others like it as a plan for the painting of wall decoration in the home.[1] Art historian Katherine Brion describes the resulting murals as providing bourgeois city dwellers with a means of recovery from, but also connection to, the frenetic pace encountered in public spaces, both relaxing and recharging them for their re-entrance into public life. This effect arose from the sexual, jubilant and (for some) excessive bodily energy that characterizes the four *commedia dell'arte* figures in 'La pantomime', suspended in space.[2]

The bourgeois Parisian viewers of 'La pantomime' could have engaged with its content in a number of ways, as can we today. They might decipher the symbolic meanings of objects such as the folds of the fan and the phallic pole pointed at it, the juxtaposition of gendered bodies, the dramatic role associated with each figure, the costumes, as well as the loose comic plots that *commedia dell'arte* characters in general suggest. They might also consider the image's resonance with present and past artistic traditions such as that of early eighteenth-century French painter Jean-Antoine Watteau (1684–1721), or with the many other public posters designed by Chéret and his contemporaries that advertised theatrical events. Yet Brion's analysis advances a mode of reception distinct from decipherment or imaginative gap-filling. She posits a reflexive relationship between art object and viewer that grants the poster itself, separate from the artist, some agency – efficacious or agentive qualities. While viewers may make sense of its content, the imagery can also act on them. In other words, Chéret's

---

[1] 'La pantomime' comes from a set of four posters representing the performative arts. The other three are titled 'La musique', 'La danse' and 'La comédie'. For a collection of Chéret's posters, see Réjane Bargiel and Ségolène le Men, eds., *Catalogue: La Belle Époque de Jules Chéret de l'affiche au décor* (Paris: Bibliothèque nationale de France, 2010), which features the set from 28–31.
[2] Katherine Brion, 'The *Fin-de-siècle* Poster: A Healthy Modern Stimulus in the French Interior', in *Designing the French Interior: The Modern Home and Mass Media*, ed. Anca I. Lasc, Georgina Downey and Mark Taylor (London: Bloomsbury, 2015), 111.

Figure 0.1 Jules Chéret, 'La pantomime' (1891); courtesy of the Getty Images Historical Picture Archive

design potentially engaged the viewer's body as tactile (touching), kinaesthetic (moving) and proprioceptive (positional). These concepts complicate Laura Mulvey's conception of the unidirectional gaze and introduce more complex models for physically, psychologically and intellectually experiencing what one sees – the mind inseparable from the experience of the body.[3]

And yet, given the subject of pantomime, this image inspires – almost requires – interpretation: what story do these costumed, moving, gendered bodies enact? A plot emerges with some resistance. The woman could well be Columbine, clad in a yellow-and-white striped dress, dark blue stockings and mustard-coloured shoes. Her body, bent at the knees, the hips and the elbows, provides a zigzag of motion as well as a central focus. Harlequin, identifiable by the black-and-white diamond pattern of his costume, is positioned suggestively close behind her, their lower torsos overlapping. He seems to share Columbine's legs, positioned as they are where his would appear, suggesting a unity between the two figures. While he looks at her face through his black mask, his stick, parallel and below the line of his gaze, points suggestively at her fan. In contrast to Harlequin, Pierrot shadows Columbine, occupying the space behind Harlequin and her. His legs hidden from view, he seems more like a ghostly double than a physical partner to the woman. His eyes angle towards her fan as his right hand echoes hers in the curve of its light-blue fingers, his pale-orange left arm outstretched to further emphasize the parallel diagonal axes of the composition. His face floats like a full moon shining benevolently over the scene, which defies specification of time and location. The relationship between the three heads suggests the three points of a triangle – perhaps a love triangle. A narrative then begins to emerge.

The details of this story, however, remain elusive, and are perhaps even undermined by the fourth figure, a Zanni (clown), identified by his baggy outfit, whom Chéret placed towards the front in the lower half of the poster. Compositionally, he is both separated from and connected with the other three bodies. If Pierrot doubles Columbine, then the Zanni echoes Harlequin while subtly connecting with Columbine through the repetition of the green and burnt orange of his costume in the flowers of her dress and the floral print of her fan, his arm positioned at the edge of her skirt. Unlike the other three, whose faces seem passive except for their eyes, the Zanni seems to giggle if not laugh, his eyes squinted, his face wrinkled, his head positioned so that his

---

[3] Laura U. Marks might call the experience that Brion attributes to Parisians viewing Chéret's interiors 'haptic', seeing that results in an embodied physical reaction to an object of performance, touching with one's eyes, as opposed to 'optic' visuality, a process of seeing that results more in decipherment than in physical connection and reaction. See Laura U. Marks, *The Skin of the Film* (Durham and London: Duke University Press, 2000), 162–3. For Mulvey's influential essay that conceptualized the male gaze, see Laura Mulvey, 'Visual Pleasure and Narrative Cinema', in *Visual and Other Pleasures: Language, Discourse, Society* (London: Palgrave Macmillan, 1989), 14–26.

attention appears to move simultaneously backward, towards the other three figures in the poster, and forward, inviting the viewer's engagement – but also blocking it, pushing the viewer away with his flat, open palms at shoulder level. He emphasizes the theatrical 'fourth wall', paradoxically articulating the separation of the viewer from the scene of the poster as he seems to connect with the audience. This connection and separation finds duplication in the idea of his laughter, which animates his body and potentially ours despite our inability to hear sounds associated with the performance.

For a book that focuses on musicology and its relationship to dance, laughter as sound and motion combined, issuing from a performing body, begins to articulate a framework for engaging with music and dance from the past: it suggests a world of possibility in regard to noise or music, ephemeral and unheard yet foundational to the idea of performance referenced by the poster. Mikhail Bakhtin posited that laughter generates a human connectedness that resonates with procreative and degenerative, decaying and renewing bodily energies.[4] In performances involving gesture and music, these relationships raise questions about the interconnectedness of sound and motion, music and dance – performance, life and death.[5] At the same time, the image raises many questions about how musical performances, especially those involving dance, construct meaning and escape meaning, belong to a historical moment and geographical locale and challenge the notion of time and place.

I

Despite the aesthetic appeal of posters, their potential physical effect on viewers, and the skill with which they were designed, for the most part Chéret's works escaped the critical attention of art historians until recently. Once seen as too low, functional or commercial to merit attention, the art historical work of Robert L. Herbert and T. J. Clark during the 1970s provided art historians with models for social histories. Such approaches encouraged examination of the artwork as evidence of how individuals lived and how human bodies engaged in the world around them.[6] These new

---

[4] Bakhtin discusses carnivalesque laughter in *Rabelais and His World*, trans. Helene Iswolsky (Bloomington and Indianapolis: University of Indiana Press, 1984), 11–12.

[5] For a discussion of the capture of sound through the gesture of silent film, see Carolyn Abbate, 'Overlooking the Ephemeral', *New Literary History* 48, no. 1 (2017), 85–7.

[6] Joel Isaacson acknowledges the role of Robert L. Herbert and T. J. Clark in approaching art in its cultural context in his review of Herbert's *Impressionism: Art, Leisure, and Parisian Society* in *Art Journal* 49, no. 1 (1990), 63–8.

critical possibilities raised questions that ultimately allowed commercial work such as Chéret's to become a focus of art-historical discourse. Ruth Iskin's monograph, for example, examines the poster's aesthetic force as well as its role in the development of advertising, design and collecting.[7]

For many of the same reasons that art historians once avoided the study of posters, before the 1980s musicologists rarely approached dance and the music associated with it as a field of inquiry. In an article about European attitudes towards dance music of the nineteenth century, music theorist Lawrence Zbikowski articulated the double bind of music associated with dance that led to this marginalization: 'the very basis for the effectiveness of dance music – the thoroughly embodied knowledge with which music is associated – dooms it to a subhuman status'. During the second half of the nineteenth century, the period when musicology was established as a discipline, 'knowledge of the body and the ways it shaped musical practice was expunged from the appreciation of music'.[8]

Scholars of music have been struggling productively against this stigma now for over thirty years, so much so that, in recent decades, musicologists have taken what Emily Dolan has called a 'material turn'. Dolan calls attention to how, despite its seeming newness, this turn resonates with founding father of musicology Guido Adler's vision for the discipline that he penned in 1885. Although Dolan's essay discusses materiality in its broadest sense, an interest in the human body's role in music-making and music reception is part of the expanded terrain she outlines for musicologists.[9] Following Dolan, musicologists Holly Watkins and Melina Esse have pointed to the necessity of considering the body's role in the experience of music, since human bodies are a central 'natural resource' for the musical encounter.[10] This materialist turn has allowed music associated with dance as well as human bodies in motion to come to the fore in musicological research, and has to a large extent inspired this volume.

---

[7] Ruth E. Iskin, *The Poster: Art, Advertising, Design, and Collecting, 1860s–1900s* (Hanover, NH: Dartmouth College Press, 2014). See also Karen L. Carter, 'The Spectatorship of the *Affiche Illustrée* and the Modern City of Paris, 1880–1900', *Journal of Design History* 25 (2012), 11–31.

[8] Lawrence Zbikowski, 'Music, Dance, and Meaning in the Early 19th Century', *Journal of Musicological Research* 31 (2012), 147–65. Susan McClary shares similar sentiments focusing on sixteenth- and seventeenth-century music in 'Music, the Pythagoreans, and the Body', in *Choreographing History*, ed. Susan Leigh Foster (Bloomington and Indianapolis: Indiana University Press, 1995), 82–104.

[9] Emily I. Dolan, 'Musicology in the Garden', *Representations* 132 (2015), 88.

[10] Holly Watkins and Melina Esse, 'Down with Disembodiment; or, Musicology and the Material Turn', *Women and Music: A Journal of Gender and Culture* 19 (2015), 161.

Scholarship published during the 1980s began to point towards dance as a potential field of study, as part of an expanded cultural terrain for musicologists and music theorists alike. Readers may recall, for instance, Wye J. Allanbrook's inspirational 1983 study of rhythmic gesture in Mozart opera.[11] Trained under music theorist Leonard Ratner, Allanbrook espoused a historically informed approach to musical analysis, one that was based on *topoi*, specific musical gestures known for their ability to conjure images, suggest moods and evoke social circumstances outside the realm of 'the music itself'.[12] Allanbrook argued that these musical topics, many of which related to dance, helped to constitute the meaning of Mozart's operas, exposing ways in which music could communicate not only the dramatic content and expressive messages of opera, but also the complexity of human character.

Allanbrook's work inspired a long line of scholars, including Zbikowski (mentioned above) and opera expert Mary Ann Smart, who credits the existence of her book *Mimomania: Music and Gesture in Nineteenth-Century Opera* to Allanbrook's foundational work.[13] Ballet-pantomime scholar Marian Smith owes Allanbrook a similar debt, and has generated her own disciplinary following: her book *Ballet and Opera in the Age of 'Giselle'* has been widely acclaimed as pivotal in musicological and dance research, acknowledged by Maribeth Clark as a 'primer' for anyone interested in ballet and lyric theatre more generally.[14] Other prominent scholars include Bruce Alan Brown, Rebecca Harris-Warrick, Natalie Jenne, Yvonne Kendall, Meredith Little, Carol Marsh, Tilden Russell and Roland John Wiley: their careful archival research has unearthed new choreographic, iconographical and musical sources, opening innumerable avenues for music-historical and performance practice-based investigation.[15] Then there is Stephanie Jordan, a dance

---

[11] Wye J. Allanbrook, *Rhythmic Gesture in Mozart: 'The Marriage of Figaro' and 'Don Giovanni'* (Chicago: University of Chicago Press, 1983; 2nd edn 2016).

[12] Leonard Ratner, *Classic Music: Expression, Form and Style* (New York: Simon and Schuster, 1980).

[13] Mary Ann Smart, *Mimomania: Music and Gesture in Nineteenth-Century Opera* (Berkeley and Los Angeles: University of California Press, 2004).

[14] Marian Smith, *Ballet and Opera in the Age of 'Giselle'* (Princeton: Princeton University Press, 2000); Maribeth Clark, 'Review: Marian Smith, *Ballet and Opera in the Age of 'Giselle*. Princeton: Princeton University Press, 2000', *Cambridge Opera Journal* 13, no. 2 (2002), 191–6.

[15] Musicological work in this vein includes Tilden Russell, *Theory and Practice in Eigtheenth-Century Dance: The German-French Connection* (London: Rowman & Littlefield, 2018); Sarah Gutsche-Miller, *Parisian Music-Hall Ballet, 1871–1913*, Eastman Series in Music (Rochester, NY: University of Rochester Press, 2015); G. Yvonne Kendall, *The Music of Arbeau's 'Orchesographie'*, The Wendy Hilton Dance and Music Series, no. 17 (New York: Pendragon Press, 2013); Meredith Little and Natalie Jenne, *Dance and the Music of J. S. Bach* (Bloomington and Indianapolis: Indiana University Press, 1991; expanded edition 2009);

specialist known for her so-called 'choreo-musical' analysis, moment-by-moment close reading of small- and large-scale 'structural categories' between audio and visual parameters.[16] Jordan's work, which has focused on twentieth-century ballet and modern dance (especially that of George Balanchine and Mark Morris), is important not only for its acknowledgement of the interrelationship between musical sound and bodily gesture, but also for its historical scrutiny of the working relations between specific composers and choreographers.

Despite the long-standing intellectual aversion to the body (a theme underpinning several chapters of our volume), academics across a range of disciplines are now finding ways (methods, approaches) and words (terminology and modes of discourse) to comment critically on what is universally regarded as fallacy: the distinction between mental and physical spheres.[17] In film studies, this has involved dismantling a basic theoretical principle – the metaphor of the disembodied eye. Attentive to cinema's inherent sensuous qualities, scholars now recognize the human body as the material ground of film spectatorship and proceed to study both the phenomenological and the cognitive aspects of the cinematic experience.[18] Dance studies has tended towards the phenomenological – what is often called somatics, a first-person process of enquiry (purportedly 'self-reflexive' and 'self-enacted') into the ways in which consciousness inhabits the body. This enquiry, which has its basis in theories of embodiment developed by the likes of Heidegger and Merleau-Ponty, is often subsumed within a 'cultural studies' framework: scholars aim to explore how choreographic practice negotiates the slippery terrain between

---

Roland John Wiley, *Tchaikovsky's Ballets: Swan Lake, Sleeping Beauty, Nutcracker* (Oxford: Clarendon Press, 1985). A number of recent publications demonstrate collaboration between musicologists and dance historians. See, for instance, Rebecca Harris-Warrick and Bruce Alan Brown, eds., *The Grotesque Dancer on the Eighteenth-Century Stage: Gennaro Magri and His World* (Madison: University of Wisconsin Press, 2005), which includes work by musicologists Harris-Warrick, Brown, Carol Marsh and Kathleen Kuzmick Hansell alongside dance scholars such as Moira Goff, Sandra Noll Hammond and Linda Tomko. A similar collaboration can be observed
in the work of Michael Burden and Jennifer Thorpe in editions such as *Ballet de la Nuit: Rothschild B1/16/6* (Hillsdale, NY: Pendragon Press, 2009).

[16] See, for example, Stephanie Jordan, 'Choreomusical Conversations: Facing a Double Challenge', *Dance Research Journal* 43, no. 1 (2011), 43–64.

[17] See, for example, Suzanne Cusick, 'Feminist Theory, Music Theory, and the Mind/Body Problem', *Perspectives of New Music* 32, no. 1 (1994), 8–27; and Amy Cimini, 'Vibrating Colors and Silent Bodies. Music, Sound and Silence in Maurice Merleau-Ponty's *Critique of Dualism*', *Contemporary Music Review* 31, nos. 5–6 (2012), 353–70. Placing importance on artists' lived experiences has led to important recent scholarship such as Daniel Callahan, 'The Gay Divorce of Music and Dance: Choreomusicality and the Early Works of Cage-Cunningham', *Journal of the American Musicological Society* 71, no. 2 (2018), 439–525.

[18] Marks, *The Skin of the Film*, 162–3.

somatic experience and cultural representation – the latter tied to identity politics, issues of gender, ethnicity and community.[19]

Dance is key to this volume's critical musicological reassessment: its combination of visual, gestural and sonorous parameters has the potential to destabilize ingrained ways of thinking about well-worn issues of musical meaning and significance. The contributing authors explore how a focus on dance might shed new light on musical works (the conditions of their invention, realization and reception), on critical orthodoxy (the ideas and attitudes underpinning our thoughts about artworks) and on the means by which choreographic musical repertoire can sustain itself and undergo revision and transformation. Contributors aspire to stage animated encounters between bodies seen and suggested. Music plays many roles in this context. These writers propose ways to approach music and dance, with an emphasis on the *and* – in other words, on the interrelations between the two. This volume adopts a deliberately self-reflexive stance: individual chapters tug and push at the boundaries between different scholarly working methods, guiding principles and modes of discourse. Indeed, our 'dance-attentive musicology' (as contributor Wayne Heisler calls it) acts as a laboratory of sorts, a privileged site for studying some of the most polemical tropes within musicology and its sister disciplines: issues of agency, subjectivity, transcendence, textuality, presence, voice and cultural value, and embodiment. In this regard, our volume contributes to burgeoning cross-disciplinary conversations, providing a testing ground for some of the critical ideas and assumptions at the heart of historical and hermeneutical traditions.

Musicology, it might be said, has variously embraced embodiment. Certainly, the cognitive aspect has been explored. Borrowing from the psychological sciences, a wave of scholars has conceptualized the music-listening experience as 'perceptive', 'attentive', 'interpretive' and, what's more, 'mimetic' – in the words of Arnie Cox, dependent on 'a kind of physical empathy that involves imagining making the sounds we are listening to'.[20] Attention to the body's relationship to musical representation – on stage, on screen and in what we might describe as regular performance – has also played

---

[19] See, for example, Sondra Fraleigh's philosophical explorations of dance in *Dance and the Lived Body: A Descriptive Aesthetics* (Pittsburgh: University of Pittsburgh Press, 1987) and *Dancing Identity: Metaphysics in Motion* (Pittsburgh: University of Pittsburgh Press, 2004).

[20] Arnie Cox, 'Embodying Music: Principles of the Mimetic Hypothesis', *MTO: A Journal of the Society for Music Theory* 17, no. 2 (2011), paragraph 3, www.mtosmt.org/issues/mto.11.17.2/mto.11.17.2.cox.php.

a large role in the pathbreaking scholarship of Susan McClary and Suzanne Cusick, scholars who have inspired legions of musicological fans. Interest in opera, performance and film (the work of Carolyn Abbate and of Michal Grover-Friedlander comes to mind) has provided additional models for musicologists to consider how physical expression might inform musical experience – as well as how music might inscribe new meanings onto the moving body.[21] Over the last two decades, moreover, there has been a trickle of highly sophisticated studies of embodiment as related to historical musical performance: one might think especially of Dana Gooley, Elisabeth Le Guin and James Davies.[22] Each of these helps demonstrate how musicologists might broach the ontological, physical and sensorial gap between music and the moving body, thus suggesting ways in which music and dance – as two creative practices and two interpretive metaphors – might be conceptualized as a whole, a goal of the collection of essays gathered here.

Our contributors focus on dance as an enabling or animating force, a means through which European musics might be newly conceived, realized, de-familiarized, enlivened – perhaps even revalorized. Indeed, we should like to suggest how dance might be implicated in what is often looked upon unfavourably in modish musicological circles – namely, to quote Richard Taruskin, our 'fetishization' of musical texts.[23] Following Lawrence Kramer, we aim to take seriously our personal choices related to dance.[24] We seek to embrace ideas of musical pleasure, rapture and allure. To keep an eye on the dancing body, we argue, might be to listen more attentively – certainly, more imaginatively – to our music and to ourselves.

II

On first glance, readers will encounter ten separate chapters, each individually coherent – with its own statement of purpose, carefully delineated subject area

---

[21] Carolyn Abbate's focus on performance might be best articulated in *In Search of Opera* (Princeton: Princeton University Press, 2001). Michal Grover-Friedlander explores similar themes in '"The Phantom of the Opera": The Lost Voice of Opera in Silent Film', *Cambridge Opera Journal* 11, no. 2 (2008), 179–92.

[22] Dana Gooley, *The Virtuoso Liszt* (Cambridge: Cambridge University Press, 2004); Elisabeth Le Guin, *Boccherini's Body: An Essay in Carnal Musicology* (Berkeley and Los Angeles: University of California Press, 2005); James Davies, *Romantic Anatomies of Performance* (Berkeley and Los Angeles: University of California Press, 2014).

[23] Richard Taruskin, 'Setting Limits', in *The Danger of Music and Other Anti-Utopian Essays* (Berkeley and Los Angeles: University of California Press, 2009), 450.

[24] Lawrence Kramer, *Music as Cultural Practice, 1800–1900* (Berkeley and Los Angeles: University of California Press, 1990), especially 'Tropes and Windows', 1–20.

and chosen method or approach. Each author situates a topic within a broader disciplinary context, reflecting critically on the ways in which the contribution relates to current scholarly wisdom both inside and outside musicology. In practical terms, this individual coherence allows chapters to be read independently by readers of different specialties and interests. Yet the extent to which chapters are independent is matched by the extent to which each fits into the whole.

It should also be noted that each chapter reads not as a chronicle, a chronologically ordered and essentially descriptive account of events, compositions, performances and reception histories. Instead, our collective impetus is narrative: we put forward carefully structured arguments, ones that seek to explore various interrelations between the arts, society and the larger world of ideas – whether strict causes and effects, lines of influence, or looser, more proximate connections.

With a focus on issues of ontology, chapters explore the salience or meaning of dance across a range of musical contexts: art music or so-called 'absolute' music; dramatic music for the stage; sacred vocal music; and music for social dancing. In addition, chapters demonstrate ways in which dance can be variously conceptualized within musicological enquiry: as a genre (ballet, waltz, pavane); a social activity or religious ritual; a form of popular entertainment; a folk tradition; a literary symbol or philosophical conceit; a type of bodily labour; and a music-stylistic topic of the kind envisaged by Ratner and Allanbrook, referring to a set of characteristics (involving metre, rhythm, motif) identifiable both in music for actual dancing and in music inspired by but conceived of as separate from that physical act.

The collective aim of these chapters is thus to explore different horizons for the concepts of music and dance. In so doing, contributors engage in a variety of scholarly approaches, from traditional close reading or analysis to a looser and more speculative brand of hermeneutics. Contributors also negotiate a set of common and deep-rooted themes. These include creative agency, autonomy, transcendence, subjectivity, consciousness and cultural value – in particular, the labelling and separation of 'high' and 'low', self and 'Other', mind and body.

Part I: Conceptual Studies

The four chapters of Part I are geared towards concepts, ideas and abstractions – different ways of thinking about music and dance, as well as thinking *through* music and dance, as interpretive metaphors.

The first chapter of the collection, by **John Butt,** raises questions about J. S. Bach and his relationship to dance. As Butt describes it, the standard musicological way of thinking about Bach and his music turns on ideas of compositional authority and control, aesthetic abstraction and religiosity, and a music-stylistic complexity that betrays the composer engaged in intricate motivic working-out. Butt envisages something different, steering us away from the mental or cerebral sphere towards the physical, the material and the bodily. Drawing on the phenomenology of Merleau-Ponty, Butt ponders the applicability of the notion of embodiment to Bach's music, not only to pieces labelled 'bourée' or 'gigue', but also to music with more oblique dance associations. The provocations embedded in Butt's argument – that there is no mental sphere without the physical, no music without dance – suggest lines of enquiry that later contributors actively pursue.

The concept of 'Otherness' – specifically, dance as 'Other' (and its concomitant associations) – lies at the heart of Chapter 2, a deliberately wide-ranging, pan-historical and provocative piece by **Suzanne Aspden.** With reference to an impressive range of examples from across genres and repertoires, Aspden illustrates some of the various ways in which dance has been embodied within Western 'art' music. Exploding the myth of 'the music itself', Aspden notes a significant historical swing in both aesthetics and compositional practice at roughly the turn of the nineteenth century, as musical representations of dance gradually morphed from being overtly ornamental and elaborate to more straightforwardly transparent in their dependence upon a long-established vocabulary of musical topics. While tracing this historical shift, Aspden offers a nuanced critical commentary on some of the shop-worn assumptions about dance that have marked traditional textbook histories of European music, especially negative associations between dance and the anti-intellectual, the 'low', the feminine and the 'Other'.

In Chapter 3 **Joseph Fort** ponders a specific case of late eighteenth-century musical embodiment, one that has its origins in social and popular dance. Fort focuses on a particular minuet by Joseph Haydn (Minuet in D major, Hob. IX/11, no. 1), emblematic not of contemporary concert-hall music, but of the music performed in front of a living – and physically mobile – audience at the charity ball held at the Hofburg Redoutensäle in Vienna, 25 November 1792. Reconstructing both the music and the dancing, Fort offers a revealing account of the Vienna dance scene, as well as the minuet's position within it. More than this, though, he presents a close reading of the interrelations between music and dance from a specifically somatic perspective – one that is deeply intuitive, subjective and sensorial. Realizing his innovative approach alongside similar scholarly attempts at 'live' musical embodiment (particularly the work of

Elisabeth Le Guin), Fort offers a compelling analysis of the movement that reveals sharp insights into not only the musical score, but also the intrinsically musical and gestural experience of dancing to it.

In Chapter 4, **Davinia Caddy** examines the role of music and music listening in the stage shows and reception histories of dancer Loie Fuller. A midwestern American, Fuller found fame across Western Europe and the United States with her theatrical dance-and-light effects that seemed to transform her body into a flower, fire, waves or the sun: to her Symbolist observers, into pure metaphor or idea. Music, Caddy notes, was often incorporated into this abstract mélange, thought to symbolize a sphere of influence or aesthetic condition that text and visuals (dance, set design, props) could only aspire to. Yet Caddy considers this now-notorious reception history ripe for questioning: with reference to little-known source material, she offers a revisionist reading of Fuller's musical initiative and her spectators' attention to it. Drawing analogies with early modernist visual art and advertising, Caddy suggests new and different ways of envisaging music, and music listening, in relation to Fuller's dance shows and the copy-cat craze they inspired.

Part II: Case histories

In this section, contributors prioritize historical enquiry. Chapters address canonic works and historical characters, exploring interrelations not only between music and dance, but also between music, dance and the written word (opera libretti, poetic texts, pedagogic literature). Difficult questions are put forward: What did it mean, historically, to bring together different art forms? How was 'togetherness', as a principle, variously conceived, realized and received? And what are the possible determining factors and underlying motivations, the ways in which historical specifics might resonate with broader aesthetic ideologies and debates? Building on recent historiographical thinking, each chapter gently critiques the notion of context as a singular, static backdrop. Focusing on issues of reciprocity, process and mediation, authors present carefully nuanced views of the social, political, religious, national and institutional milieus within which dance and musical practices were situated. In addition, they address the 'anti-dance' rhetoric pervasive within Western intellectual culture (introduced in Part I), suggesting ways in which music might help transcend the negative associations that have long accumulated around dance.

Chapter 5 presents a focused yet far-reaching account by **Thomas Grey** of the significance of dance to Richard Wagner. Grey's chapter is essentially comparative. First, he explores ways in which Wagner theorized the roles of dance, music and text in his 'total artwork', then he considers historical practice – examples of the actual dances (and also what Grey calls the 'sublimated choreography') in several Wagnerian music dramas, especially *Tannhäuser*, with its infamous Venusberg Bacchanal. Wagner's feelings towards dance, Grey explains, were double-edged. On the one hand, the composer acknowledged the importance of movement and gesture in the creation of his ideal artwork. Indeed, as Grey suggests, Wagner sought to play up the two, emphasizing the role of the erotic, sexualized body onstage. On the other hand, Wagner liked to ridicule contemporary ballet. But, to Wagner, ballet's problematic status did not relate to its explicitly bodily and human aspects. Instead, it was the genre's association with an institutional context – ballet as produced and consumed at the Paris Opéra – that troubled the composer. The chapter also examines the attitudes of the poet Heinrich Heine towards ballet, and his creation of the 'dance poem', a literary genre that allows dance to aspire to the superior condition of poetry. Heine's attitudes parallel Wagner's for and against ballet as experienced in European urban centres during the mid-nineteenth century. Grey explores how Wagner and Heine distanced themselves from this context, while also reforming ballet through their artistic endeavours. For both Wagner and Heine this resulted in the realigning of the 'sister arts' while developing a new kind of balletic-musical expression that would pave way for *fin-de-siècle* creative experiments.

In Chapter 6, **Marian Wilson Kimber** outlines another historical realignment, exploring the relation between music, dance and poetry in late nineteenth-century amateur dance practices in the United States. With reference to little-known archival sources (musical scores, photographs, programme leaflets and educational guides), Wilson Kimber examines how elocutionists combined their recitation with posing in imitation of ancient Greek statuary. These performances grew from the expressive physical fitness movement known as Delsarte (after the nineteenth-century French musician and teacher), itself rooted in elocution, the American practice of public speaking that was a common form of entertainment on programmes with chamber music throughout the United States. To the accompaniment of hymns, women recited and posed to entertain one another, but also with the goal of self-improvement. Describing these practices, Wilson Kimber articulates another historical case of what we might call choreographic legitimization, considering ways in which dancers sought to elevate the seemingly suspect status of their art with reference to ancient Classical values and sacred music.

Carlo Caballero paints a contrasting historical picture in Chapter 7. While noting the usual scholarly snubbing of 'excessive' and 'insubstantial' dance tunes, Caballero explores dance's significance and popularity – not only with audiences, but also with 'serious' composers. Writing about late nineteenth-century French musical culture, Caballero examines a vogue for the sixteenth-century pavane (with reference to examples by Saint-Saëns, Delibes, Fauré, Ravel and Debussy, amongst others), considering how and why the genre of the pavane became emblematic of a constellation of contemporary cultural strains of influence. As Caballero recounts, far from a debased signifier (of the kind deplored by Wagner) or an irreligious evil (as thought the American Protestants), dance took on new significance during the period, aligned with historical prestige, antique exoticism, the French aristocracy, musical nationalism and modernity itself. Guided by this case history, Caballero reminds us of the cultural embeddedness of both dance and musical practices, and why we need ways of understanding these practices as both socially conditioned and conditioning.

Part III: Critical Readings

In this third and final section, contributors also engage with local historical specifics and broader cultural conditions; moreover, like Caballero in Part II, they trace a revivalist impulse, emphasizing transience and transformation over time. Yet whereas Caballero investigates musical re-workings of a traditional genre of dance, contributors here address choreographic re-workings of music (individual pieces or repertoires). At issue, principally, is the process of revision – but not the outmoded notion of revision as a singular, purposeful and definitive act undertaken by an author in pursuit of perfection. These three chapters suggest the opposite: uncertainties, instabilities and multiple challenges to authorial control. Influenced by recent musicological scholarship on the business of 'setting limits', as well as a long tradition of literary and critical theory, authors offer historically grounded accounts of music's gestural afterlife, steering us towards a series of astute and, indeed, optimistic critical readings.[25] Instead of lamenting a lost, irreplaceable original, or else a lack of interpretive resolution, they celebrate various hermeneutical conundrums. These can offer new sources of pleasure and intrigue, new ways to appreciate the most familiar music – opportunities that might speak more generally to present-day interest in hyper-textuality and the interactive potential of new media and the internet.

---

[25] Taruskin, 'Setting Limits', 447–66. The essay asserts that 'social mediation inevitably changes whatever it mediates' (449), and celebrates fresh, creative approaches to performances of what we might call Western 'art' or 'classical' music.

In Chapter 8, **David J. Code** explores Vaslav Nijinsky's *L'après-midi d'un faune*, a 1912 choreographic reworking of Claude Debussy's orchestral *Prélude* (completed in 1894). Peeling away layers of historical reference, Code presents a nuanced yet wide-ranging interpretation of Nijinsky's danced design, situating the ballet within new and vivid historical and critical contexts. Developing insights from the latest scholarly studies of the ballet, as well as the earliest journalistic reviews, Code invites us to open our eyes and ears to the sensuous aspect of both music and dance, an aesthetic realm of experience long denied ('repressed') within the ballet's now-notorious reception history. Through analysis of music and gesture, his new reading demonstrates the importance of reassessing the ballet's much-discussed disjunction between angular or 'Cubist' choreography and fluid, expressive music. The author casts a wider net, exploring how our understanding of the Faun has been symptomatic of that of aesthetic modernism more generally: an unexpected analogy between the ballet and a painting by French artist Henri Matisse (*Le bonheur de vivre*) highlights ways in which we might refresh and refocus our usual ways of engaging with the ballet.

Chapter 9, by **Wayne Heisler Jr**, strikes a chord with Chapters 5 and 7, by Grey and Wilson Kimber: all three explore interrelationships between music, dance and the written word. In addition, like Grey and Wilson Kimber, Heisler pursues the historical implications of his subject matter, considering social, cultural and philosophical discourses, and their appeals to music and the body. But Heisler tells a different kind of story: his chapter addresses a series of new choreographies of canonic vocal-instrumental repertoire – 'song-ballets' from the 1960s and 1970s, set to the music of Gustav Mahler. Heisler's aim is to open interpretive pathways, suggesting ways in which dance can refuel Mahler's music, repurposing its expressive vocabulary. In a series of vivid critical readings of both live and recorded performances, Heisler projects additional meanings onto Mahler's danced songs, suggesting their resonance with the composer's biography and musical personality (with emphasis on 'universal' and 'transcendental' qualities), as well as their impact on characterization, drama and musical structure. In doing so, Heisler acknowledges the interdisciplinary methods underpinning his analysis, noting in particular the relevance of both performance studies and phenomenology.

In Chapter 10, **Maribeth Clark** adds to the interdisciplinary toolbox, drawing on film studies and social anthropology. Addressing recent screen productions of Jane Austen's 1813 novel *Pride and Prejudice* (dir. Langton, BBC 1, 1995; dir. Wright, 2005), and 1815 novel *Emma* (dir. Lawrence, ITV, 1996; dir. McGrath, 1996) Clark explores the function of music, dance, drama and visuals in specific danced divertissements. Her focus, like that of fellow contributors to this section, is on variation: namely, choreographed versions of picturesque social dance scenes set to the late seventeenth-century music of Henry Purcell and his contemporaries up to the late eighteenth century. Whereas the authors of earlier chapters trace a historical narrative of mutation and transgression, her chapter describes an impulse towards unity and congruence, towards the establishment of a stable repertoire, a conservative tradition – a canon, as Clark suggests, building on the work of those involved in the twentieth-century English country dance revival. The author goes on to explain how English country dancing in Austen's period was marked by instability and flux: changing social structures, habitation patterns and communal leisure activities led to a multiplicity of dance practices of different popular appeal. In depicting this phenomenon, as Clark observes, film and TV directors in line with broader audio-visual ambitions sought to create a coherent, idealized and seemingly universal aesthetic for social dance of the period – and a stable interpretive framework within which this dance could be designed and understood. In her analysis, Clark reminds us of 'invented traditions', to quote Eric Hobsbawm's classic phrase.[26] Exorcising the myth of the singular, stable canon, while emphasizing its enduring embodiment, Clark's chapter brings into sharper focus the myriad interpretive possibilities that may challenge persistent intellectual tropes and patterns of thought.

In summary, this volume provides models for a historically grounded musicology that recognizes relationships between gestures and words, music and dance, sounds and noises, human bodies and social acts over time. We examine dance as a multifaceted and rich experience in contexts where the value of the material has often been denied. Many challenges arise in the study of European music and dance together: the ephemerality of performance, the fuzzy boundaries between theatrical and social dance, the legacies and inequalities associated with colonialism and imperialism and the complexity of the sources. We also grapple with the divides among related areas, disciplines and fields (including, but not limited to, performance studies, theatre and dance history, comparative literature, film studies, philosophy, cognitive psychology, music theory, history, anthropology and sociology as well as musicology – the list could go on). In order to grasp our shared humanity more deeply, however, we attempt to stretch our integrated minds and bodies, observing and listening with sensitivity to otherness as well as to the vibrations, like laughter, that potentially reveal our common ground.

---

[26] Eric Hobsbawm, 'Introduction: Inventing Traditions', in *The Invention of Tradition*, ed. Eric Hobsbawm and Terence Ranger (Cambridge: Cambridge University Press, 1983), 1.

PART I

Conceptual Studies

1 | Bach and the Dance of Humankind

JOHN BUTT

> In ... suites [of Bach's time] there were ... many French character pieces and dance tunes, in which the rhythm was the most important object. The composers were therefore obliged to make use of a great variety of metre, measure, and rhythm ... and become very adept therein, if they wished to give each dance melody its prescribed character and rhythm. Bach carried this branch of the art also much farther than any of his predecessors or contemporaries. He tried and made use of every kind of metre to diversify, as much as possible, the character of his pieces. He eventually acquired such a facility in this particular [art] that he was able to give even to his fugues, with all the intricate interweaving of their single parts, striking and characteristic rhythmic proportions in a manner as easy and uninterrupted from the beginning to the end as if they were minuets.[1]
>
> J. N. Forkel, 1802

Bach's music is saturated with dance idioms and these have provided the focus for a broad range of study, from the metaphysical considerations of Wilfred Mellers's *Bach and the Dance of God* to historically grounded studies of the steps used in actual dance practice. It is indeed not difficult to discern the shards of dances such as gavottes or gigues in even the most theologically weighty of arias and choruses,[2] and as Forkel suggests, even

---

[1] Translation adapted and completed from Hans T. David and Arthur Mendel, eds., *The New Bach Reader*, revised edn ed. Christoph Wolff (New York and London: W. W. Norton, 1999), 488. Johann Nikolaus Forkel, *Ueber Johann Sebastian Bachs Leben* (Leipzig: Hoffmeister und Kühnel, 1802; ed. Axel Fischer; repr Kassel: Bärenreiter, 1999), 32–3: 'In ... Suiten kamen ... viele Französische Charakterstücke und Tanzmelodien vor, bey welchen es vornehmlich auf den Rhythmus ankam. Die Componisten mußten also von einer großen Menge Takt-Arten, Tonfüen und Rhythmen ... Gebrauch machen, und sehr gewandt darin werden, wenn sie jeder Tanzmelodie ihren bestimmeten Character und Rhythmus geben wollten. Auch dieser Zweig der Kunst hat Bach viel weiter getrieben als irgend einer seiner Vorgänger oder Zeigenossen. Keine Art von Zeitverhältniß ließ er unversucht und unbenutzt, um den Charakter seiner Stücke dadurch so verschieden als möglich zu modificiren. Er bekam zuletzt eine solche Gewandtheit darin, daß er im Stande war, sogar seinen Fugen bey allem künstlichen Gewebe ihrer einzelnen Stimmen ein so auffallendes, charactervolles, vom Anfange bis ans Ende ununterbrochenes und leichtes rhythmisches Verhältniß zu geben, als wenn sie nur Menuetten wären.'

[2] For a systematic study, see Doris Finke-Hecklinger, *Tanzcharaktere in Johann Sebastian Bachs Vokalmusik* (Trossingen: Hohner-Verlag, 1970).

fugues can be examined for their dance characters. Nevertheless, attempts at using Bach's music in actual dance practice are surprisingly rare (beyond whatever is generated by various jazz and pop arrangements of certain pieces)[3] – perhaps there is even a sense that dancing to this music somehow violates its undoubted cultural value as music from one of the most prestigious composers in the Western tradition. Classical music is – the stereotype might affirm – designed for passive and silent contemplation, whether in a privileged private venue or in the concert hall, the latter a customized space which traditionally seems to straddle the roles of holy temple and sterile laboratory. Moreover, as Forkel's commentary makes explicit, the most essential evidence of dance in Bach's music is rhythmic and metrical, and not specifically melodic and harmonic. These latter aspects are those that have tended to be privileged above rhythm in the criticism and analysis of Western art music.

There is no doubt that Bach's 'pure' dances, like those from the four Orchestral Overtures could have served as the vehicles for baroque dance, just as is the case with many similar works by Bach's contemporaries. The more 'modern' dance genres here, such as minuets, gavottes and bourrées, display the regular phraseology that is conducive to the physical activity of dancing. But perhaps the repeated allusions to dance elsewhere in Bach's vocal and instrumental music are generally too far removed from regular dance structure to serve for practical dancing.[4] It is precisely this sense of Bach's music implying a position both within and outside dance practice that might account for its special quality as somehow 'about dance' rather than merely a vehicle for movement; it might well offer us a nuanced insight into the potentials for the embodied subject in Bach's time. Indeed, the apparent distancing from 'pure', practical dance in Bach's overall style could imply a level of reflection on the embodied experience that might run simultaneously with or slightly separated from any participation in actual dance. Perhaps one of the things that Forkel implies is that this music can actually transcend its origins and practical function and perform a new role in our appreciation of music. This, of course, plays back into one of the standard narratives about Western 'art' music: that its quality is often judged

---

[3] Another exception might be the application of Bach as dance to a specialist style of education such as Eurhythmics in the Waldorf tradition. See Alan Stott, ed., *Bach and the Dance of Heaven and Earth* (Weobley: Anastasi, 2003).

[4] As Johann Mattheson notes in *Der vollkommene Kapellmeister* (Hamburg: Herold, 1739), the minuets very familiar in keyboard suites are not well suited for actual dancing or singing (225). For a thorough study of the relationship of Bach's music to actual dance patterns, see Meredith Little and Natalie Jenne, *Dance and the Music of J. S. Bach* (Bloomington and Indianapolis: Indiana University Press, 1991).

as directly proportional to its autonomous nature, and thus as somewhat removed from any of the practical functions in which it originated. The drift of this chapter may well lead us in such a 'retrogressive' direction, but if it does, it is important to show that any apparent autonomy this music might imply is strictly conditional on its ongoing relationship with the world in which it was (and continues to be) situated.

Most commentators tend to gravitate towards the notion of music as disembodied *thought* when contemplating Bach's achievements. After all, this music is so contrapuntally complex and motivically integrated that our inherited view of Bach is perhaps not that far from the caricature of the calculating, Leibnizian God who would have appealed to so many in the intellectual milieu of Bach's Leipzig. As the various anecdotes attest, Bach was able to perceive the potential in a musical theme almost instantaneously, working out its various combinations and permutations within the harmonic possibilities at hand. Some writers have tried to humanize the composer by noting the ways in which some considerable creative effort is required to generate a finished composition: not only is a degree of experimentation required in generating the productive material for a piece in the first place, but also once this has been selected, we can often imagine how the composer had to sift through the possibilities for further combination or extension, throwing out the poorer possibilities, mending the flawed ones and somehow working out a plausible sequence for the music in time.[5] Study of Bach's copying processes suggests that his compositional thinking was never dormant and that he was constantly on the lookout for new possibilities or refinements, even within music that was to all intents and purposes 'finished'. So, we already have models by which to imagine Bach as a critical and creative human being, one with whom we can share something in our own encounters with the world through his music.

But there is surely more to it than critical mental activity tempering an outstanding talent for instantaneous calculation. We also share a sense of physicality with our ancestors that is arguably just as important, if not more so, than the mental processes. Indeed, some would suggest that our very concept of the mental and intellectual is embedded in our physicality and our experience of the space and time around us. Since at least the development of phenomenology, particularly that of Maurice Merleau-Ponty, there has been a growth in awareness of the importance of embodiment and corporeity. Merleau-Ponty even suggests that objects from the past

---

[5] Most striking here is the work of Laurence Dreyfus, *Bach and the Patterns of Invention* (Cambridge, MA: Harvard University Press, 1996).

retain something of the physical presence of their originators, reflecting traces of their experience of inhering, intending and moving within the physical world.[6] Therefore dance, as stylized movement, might tell us much about the way subjects of the past honed their own physical consciousness.

If we apply something of this to Bach's music, what is there to be gained? Is it just a matter of extending some of the mental modelling that we already imagine within his compositional style, supplementing this with the inference of 'ways of moving' or inhering in space? It is, after all, relatively easy to find out about baroque dance, and there are many current practitioners who could help us. Dance is also something that is hardly common just to Bach, and virtually all his contemporaries wrote music that had choreographic potential. But perhaps what Bach might have to offer is something richer and more complex than this. If his attitude to the mental side of composition is partly one of critical assessment and observation, might the same not be true of his attitude towards embodiment? To test this hypothesis, we first need to have some idea of the role that dance might have played in Bach's environment, and particularly the degree to which it was viewed as a civilizing and regulating art, associated with particular mental and physical states. Only then will we be in a better position to gauge the ways in which Bach may have manipulated dance as observer, participant and reflecting composer. Through this it may become plausible to propose a specifically 'Bachian embodiment', one that may have been ignored by most of the generations that have encountered his music.

Dance in Lutheran Thought and Culture

What, then, is the place of dance in the understanding and value systems of Bach's society? After all, it is often popularly associated with religious proscription, and particularly with the puritanical view that it leads to lascivious, anti-spiritual, carnal behaviour. It is not difficult to find such attitudes within Bach's culture, not least within the Pietist wing of the Lutheran confession, which tended to eschew the cultivated arts in general.[7] Pietism's attitude towards dance was very similar to that which it held towards the complex church music of the type that Bach produced. Indeed, this negative coupling of the high arts of music and dance is itself telling, paralleling a similar pairing

---

[6] Maurice Merleau-Ponty, *Phenomenology of Perception* (Paris: Gallimard, 1945), esp. 405–6.
[7] By far the most notorious publication against dance was Johann Christian Lange's *Vernunfft-mässiges Bescheidenes und Unparteyisches Bedencken* (Frankfurt and Leipzig, 1704).

on the part of those who supported them, not least Luther himself. Indeed, Luther – well known for his intense love of music – was obviously not the type of Protestant who automatically condemned dance and he clearly had little difficulty in understanding the frequent biblical references to dance as an element of religious celebration.[8] Although Luther did not write at all extensively about dance, when he did, he used similar arguments to those with which he justified music and its appropriate use. In his sermon on the Wedding at Cana, for the second Sunday of Epiphany, he notes that dance for the purposes of celebration is no different from eating and drinking; in other words, it is no bad thing in itself, and only problematic if taken to excess.[9] Even more striking is his explicit linking of dance with polyphonic music in his introduction to Georg Rhau's *Symphoniae Iucundae* of 1538:

But where the natural music is refined and developed through art, then at last it is possible to taste with wonder (yet not to comprehend) God's absolute and perfect wisdom in his wondrous work of music. Here it is most remarkable that one single voice sings the tenor, while at the same time three, four or five other voices play around it exulting and adorning it in exuberant strains and, as it were, leading it forth in a divine roundelay, so that those who are the least bit moved know nothing more amazing in this world.[10]

Here it is clear that dance, like music, is to be an essential part of the heavenly experience. Arts and their cultivation are clearly gifts from God

---

[8] Orthodox Lutheran writing makes frequent reference to dance during Bach's age. For instance, Zedler's mention of dance in his *Grosses vollständiges Universal-Lexicon aller Wissenschafften und Künste*, vol. 41 (Halle and Leipzig, 1747) refers to Miriam the prophet leading the women in dancing with her tambourine (Exodus 15:20) in celebration of the escape from Egypt and also to David after the victory over Goliath (1 Samuel 18:6-7) when the women sang and danced to celebrate Saul's 1000 slain enemies and David's 10,000.

[9] *Sermons by Martin Luther*, vol. 2, trans. and ed. John Nicholas Lenker, 43-4, www.martinluthersermons.com.

[10] Translation adapted from *Luther's Works*, vol. 53, ed. Ulrich S. Leupold (Philadelphia: Fortress Press, 1965), 324. See *D. Martin Luthers Werke – Weimarer Ausgabe*, vol. 50, ed. Joachim Karl Friedrich Knaake (Weimar, 1883-1929), 372-3: 'Wo aber die natürliche Musica durch die Kunst gescherfft und polirt wird, da sihet und erkennet man erst zum teil (denn gentzlich kans nicht begrieffen noch verstanden werden) mit grosser verwunderung die grosse und volkomene weisheit Gottes in seinem wunderbarlichen werck der Musica, in welcher vor allem das seltzam und wol zu verwundern ist, das einer eine schlechte weise oder Tenor (wie es die Musici heissen) her singet, neben welcher drey, vier oder fünff andere stimmen auch gesungen werden, die umb solche schlechte weise oder Tenor, gleich als mit jauchtzen gerings herumbher, umb solchen Tenor spielen und springen und mit mancherley art und klang dieselbige weise wunderbarlich zieren und schmücken und gleich wie einen Himlischen Tantzreien füren. Also das die jenigen, so solches ein wenig verstehen und dadurch bewegt werden, sich des hefftig verwundern müssen und meinen, das nichts seltzamers in der Welt sey, den ein solcher Gesang mit viel stimmen geschmückt.'

that in turn reveal the beauty and joy of his creation. It is interesting that the satisfying patterning of polyphonic music is seen as part of an ordered 'Tantzrei[h]en' (round-dance or roundelay), as if each art implies the other, at least at the divine level. Although it is not certain whether all musicians of Bach's age, some two centuries later, were familiar with this statement (but Bach himself possessed the works of Luther, twice over), Luther's use of the term within his Bible translation would clearly have been very familiar.[11] Indeed, the notion of the round dance features very strongly in the alto and tenor duet within Bach's Christmas cantata 'Christen, ätzet diesen Tag' (BWV63), most likely first performed on Christmas Day in Weimar, 1714: 'Ruft und fleht den Himmel an, Kommt, ihr Christen, kommt zum Reihen, Ihr sollt euch ob dem erfreuen, Was Gott hat anheut getan!' ('Call and beseech heaven; Come, you Christians, come to the [round- or line-]dance; you shall rejoice over that which God has done today!').

Here the allusion to a dance celebrating Jesus's birth, in which all are encouraged to participate, is irresistibly stirred up by Bach's rustic-sounding music. As with Luther's comments on dance and music, there seems to be no hint of disapproval, and voices, text and music run seamlessly together, just as they might have done for Miriam, David and Saul.

Not only did the combination of dance with music and text within the Reigen/Reihen genre have strong biblical resonance in Bach's time, but it also relates to his contemporaries' understanding of ancient Greek practice. Johann Mattheson, ever alert to the possibilities of categorizing music according to classical categories, relates the 'Reigen' both to the 'high' style of dancing (the 'hyporchematic' style, which the Greeks used around their altars) and, more directly, to the 'choraic' style, which specifically links singing and dancing.[12]

Although Mattheson's understanding seems generally both confused and confusing, it is clear that the ancient Greek concept of choraic dance was seen as a justification for the beneficial use of both music and dancing. Athenaeus had, after all, stressed the general belief that music and dancing were analogues of the human soul, so that its inner virtues could be judged

---

[11] Zedler associates 'Reigen' with singing and instrumental participation, linking it to various biblical expressions of dance, such as Miriam's celebrations, in *Lexicon*, vol. 31, 229–30.

[12] Mattheson, *Der vollkommene Kapellmeister*, Part 1, Ch. 10, paragraph 85, 87: 'Und wo dieses Wort das Reihen-Lied der alten Griechen, darnach sie um den Altar tantzten, bedeutet hat; so ist es demselben nur in Ansehung des erhöheten Ortes beigeleget worden: denn sonst gehören die Reihen-Täntze zum choraischen Styl.' Paragraph 114, 92: 'Er führt seinen Nahmen vom Chor oder Reihen, wo ihrer viele zusammen tantzen, und die Glieder der choraischen Melodie sind zwar etwas schwächer, als der hyporchematischen.'

externally in the quality of the art. Choraic dance also served to cultivate discipline and military physique.[13] Plato's *Laws* link the arts of rhythm and harmony specifically to the human condition (as opposed to the disposition of animals), but Plato insists that they require specific discipline and education in order to cultivate inner and outer virtue together. He also notes that the choraic art is a form of representation, involving the imitation of many different types of character, which appear in all kinds of situation and action. This implies that the disciplines of music and dance function as a sort of rehearsal for life.[14]

So far, then, we gain a sense of dance being closely yoked to music and of the two arts embedded in the human condition, inherited from both Christian-Judaic and Greek traditions. The correct use and cultivation of the arts seems to relate to virtue and discipline (and, by extension, incorrect use leads to its opposite), with the assumption that the perfection of the physical can directly benefit the mental and moral disposition. It is precisely this range of claims that is frequently used in defences of the practical arts against Pietist attack, whether from the founder of the movement, Jacob Spener, and most particularly from J. C. Lange's 1704 tract against dance.[15] The most illuminating justification comes in the principal German dance manual of Bach's age, written by the Leipziger Johann Pasch in 1707: *Beschreibung wahrer Tanz-Kunst*. As Christina Thurner has observed, Pasch's defence of dance is remarkably thorough and firmly grounded in the intellectual traditions of the late seventeenth century.[16] Typical for its early modern, pre-Enlightenment approach is the balance it sees between nature, human reason and art, all three working together to further the human condition. Art is the method of regulating and refining what is inherited naturally and is therefore supremely useful in giving the human a lively and compelling spirit.[17] The foreword makes the analogy with God's gift of ore: ore lies inside the earth, just as does the disposition for dance lie

---

[13] Andrew Barker, *Greek Musical Writings* (Cambridge: Cambridge University Press, 1984), 287–9.

[14] Barker, *Greek Musical Writings*, 141–9.

[15] Zedler notes the antipathy to dance from the founder of the Pietists, Jacob Spener and J. C. Lange, Lexicon, vol. 41, 1755. For Lange, see note 7 above.

[16] Christina Thurner, *Beredte Körper – bewegte Seelen: Zum Diskurs der Doppleten Bewegungen in Tanztexten* (Bielefeld: transcript Verlag, 2009), 55–8.

[17] Johann Pasch, *Beschreibung wahrer Tanz-Kunst* (Frankfurt, 1707), 11: 'Alle Künste wann wir sie recht genau betrachten sind an und vor sich selbst nichts anders als die eigene natürliche Geschicklichkeit des Menschen seine Gemüth und Nachsinnen nebst dem Verstande in Regeln gebracht und kommen also die Künste denenjenigen zu Hülffe welch nicht mit einem so glücklichen Naturel lebhafften und dringenden Geiste und einem versichernden judicio gebohren werden als wie diejenigen welch durch eine lange Erfahrung und vieler reflexion das

within the body; and just like ore, the art of dance needs to be refined and separated from its impurities.[18]

Following classical precedents, the physical art of dance has a particular effect on the internal disposition, especially the passions. Here Pasch also makes reference to the relatively modern theory of Descartes, by which the movement of animal spirits within the body is shown clearly in the outward disposition of the passions.[19] His two main bodies of authority are contemporary French dancing masters and Quintilian's rhetoric. The former reflects the centrality of contemporary French practice to dance in Europe around 1700, namely, as a vehicle for the regulation of the body and as an analogue for the regulation of court and society; much of this was closely emulated by the many courts of the German lands. The importation of classical rhetoric is something that is very familiar within the music theory and criticism of the German Baroque. Not only does it imply an attitude towards the satisfactory invention and disposition of a composition, but it also takes into account the attitude of the performer and listener/viewer, in order to render the presentation as convincing as possible. Rhetorical theory enables Pasch to separate the art of dancing into two areas: ethical and bodily skills, on the one hand, and a study and internalization of theatrical gesture and action, on the other.[20] Particularly striking is the way the description of the art of dance parallels other fields: the fundamental steps parallel the five vowels (and also the concept of long and short syllables), which can be combined in countless permutations, something which is very reminiscent of music theorists' outline of the countless permutations of just a few notes of music.[21] Following French practice, the various dances are coupled with their appropriate affects (from serious – e.g., sarabande – to very lively – e.g., gigue or bourrée). What is especially interesting is the way dance training is seen to enhance one's own sense of being and identity: by understanding the integrity of one's inner and outer dispositions, passions and movements of the soul, one then takes account of those who are present, those with whom one dances and also the requirements of the occasion. In all, then, this provides the basis not

---

vollkommene in der Nature sind gewahr worden: Dieses weiset klar daß die Künste nicht nur in eine confusen Phantasie bestehn sondern aus der Vernunfft fliessen.'

[18] Pasch, *Beschreibung wahrer Tanz-Kunst*, Vorrede (by 'Borckmann').
[19] Pasch, *Beschreibung wahrer Tanz-Kunst*, 9.
[20] Pasch, *Beschreibung wahrer Tanz-Kunst*, 17. This latter field then is precisely that area of representation specified by Plato's *Laws*; see note 13, above.
[21] Pasch, *Beschreibung wahrer Tanz-Kunst*, 27. Wolfgang Caspar Printz notes, for instance, that a single crotchet beat can be varied nearly 3000 ways through permutations of various subdivisions. See his *Phryis Mytilenaeus oder Satyrischer Componist*, vol. 2 (Quedlinburg, Dresden and Leipzig, 1676–7/1696), 61.

only for a reasonably complex understanding of the self but also of the way this self is regulated in a social situation.[22]

Pasch's influence is strongly felt in Saxony and beyond over the coming decades, with much of his theory and moral justification of dance quoted in Zedler's *Lexicon*.[23] His reliance on Quintilian's rhetoric is directly paralleled in the musical field, not least by Johann Mattheson, whose *Der vollkommene Kapelmeister* (1739) provides the most thorough rhetorical theory of music. It is immediately clear that Mattheson integrates the notion of physical movement with music, initially through the rhetorical category of gesture and gesticulation: 'Gesticulation, words and sounds form a three-part braid, and should perfectly harmonize with each other to the goal that the feeling of the listener be stirred.'[24] In good Lutheran fashion, this enhanced emotion is to be directed towards the praise of God. While this would most simply refer to the actual gesture one might add to a musical performance, Mattheson also suggests that such physicality can be embodied within the written notes of music, as achieved by the composer Conti:

Conti ... was uncommonly experienced in the portrayal of gestures through musical notes (where is this a loss to art?) and his ideas have about the same charming effect merely on paper as if one were to see all sorts of pleasant, vivacious postures in the flesh.[25]

While Mattheson gives his greatest attention to categorizing different types and levels of music, in relation to dance as to all other genres, he offers some very interesting observations along the way, including the notion that a composer who pays attention to all the subtleties and relationships that are implicit in dance composition will most likely achieve a richer style:

We should consider all French dance-songs and melodies ... attentively, to find the proper ordering, uniformity and correct divisions therein as I am sure one will discover that these very types of dance (be they hyporchematic as well as the choraic)

---

[22] Pasch, *Beschreibung wahrer Tanz-Kunst*, 24–44.   [23] Zedler, *Lexicon*, vol. 41, 1762.

[24] Mattheson, *Der vollkommene Kapelmeister*, Part 1, Ch. 6, p. 37, paragraph 22: 'Meinung mit dieser gantzen Wissenschafft zielet dahin, daß Geberden, Worte und Klang eine dreifache Schnur machen, und zu dem Ende mit einander vollkommen übereinstimmen sollen, daß des Zuhörers Gemüth beweget werde.' Translation from Ernest C. Harriss, *Johann Mattheson's Der vollkommene Capellmeister: A Revised Translation with Critical Commentary* (Ann Arbor: UMI Research Press, 1981), 137.

[25] Mattheson, *Der vollkommene Kapelmeister*, Part 1, Ch. 6, p. 40, paragraph 46. Translation adapted from Harriss, *Johann Mattheson's Der vollkommene Capellmeister*, 142: 'Conti ... war in solchen Abbildungen der Geberden durch musicalische Noten (wo ist den der Kunst-Verlust?) ungemein erfahren, und seine Einfälle führen auf dem blossen Papier fast eben die ergetzliche Wirckung mit sich, als ob man mit Augen allerley lächerliche, lebendige Posituren vor sich sähe.'

are full of unusual richness and all sorts of beautiful inventions of composition. I know great composers who have drawn more out of this choraic style than out of all other styles of writing and who have drawn numerous ideas therefrom.[26]

This seems to parallel directly the comments that Forkel later made about Bach, by which the implications of dance heavily inform even the most distant of musical genres. What lies latent in much of Mattheson's writing on dance is not just the detailed exposition of the different affective qualities of the individual dance but the notion that the best music seems to contain a sense of the movement and relationships in space that are implied by dance. In just the same way that dance makes physically manifest the inner disposition of the dancer, having itself worked towards regulating the spiritual and emotional balance of the self, music on its own evokes the quality of movement in dance, even without the necessary movements taking place. This point is made explicit a few years later by the Lübeck cantor, Caspar Rüetz, when explaining the advantages of dance rhythms in the context of church music: 'if we should not bring into the church even the least thing that belongs to dancing, we would have to leave feet and hands, indeed the whole body, at home'.[27] Following Pasch, Rüetz considers dancing as an important art for cultivating both bodily and mental discipline and he also reiterates the biblical uses of dance to express joy. So, if church music promotes 'hopping and jumping in the hearts of upright Christians', why should such devices be avoided? In any case, if all rhythms pertaining to dance were removed, nothing would remain but pure chorales, which would be just as absurd as confining the preacher to words that were not used in everyday life or the theatre.[28] In all, far from the

---

[26] Mattheson, *Der vollkommene Kappelmeister*, Part 1, Ch. 10, p. 92, paragraph 113: 'Man betrachte endlich alle Französische Tantz-Lieder und Melodien, so klein als sie auch sey mögen, bis auf die Menuetten, die eben sowol, als die grössesten Ouvertüren, ihre eigne Schreib-Art erforden; man betrachte sie, sage ich, mit Aufmercksamkeit, welche feine Ordnung, Gleichförmigkeit und richtige Abschnitte darin zu finden sind, ich weiß, man wird erfahren daß eben diese Tantz-Style (den hyporchematischen bey dem choraischen mit eingeschoffen) voller ungemeinen Reichthums sind, und allerhand schöne Erfindungen im Setzen an die Hand geben. Ich kenne grosse Componisten, die aus diesem choraischen-Style mehr, als aus allen andern Schreib-Arten gesammlet, und häuffige Einfälle daraus geschöpffet haben.' Translation adapted from Harriss, *Johann Mattheson's Der vollkommene Capellmeister*, 223.

[27] Caspar Rüetz, *Widerlegte Vorurtheile von der Beschaffenheit des heutigen Kirchenmusic und von der Lebens-Art einiger Musicorum* (Lübeck, 1752), 35: 'Wenn wir nicht das geringste, was zum Tantzen gehöret, in die Kirche bringen, sollen, müsten wir Füsse und Hände, ja den gantzen Leib zu Hause lassen.' Translation from Joyce Irwin, 'Bach in the Midst of Religious Transition', in *Bach's Changing World: Voices in the Community*, ed. Carol K. Baron (Rochester, NY: University of Rochester Press, 2006), 121.

[28] Rüetz, *Widerlegte Vorurtheile*, 41–2, 'so könte doch eine solche Music, die hin und wieder mit tantzenden Klangfüssen einhergehet, das Hüpfen und Springen aufrichtiger Christen Hertzen vorstellen und befördern ... Solten sie aber all Rhithmos, welche in diesen Melodey

Pietist or Puritan view of dance as a distraction from religion, the notion of embodied movement connected to spiritual emotion seems to render dance entirely positive within church practice.

Bach's Integration of Dance into His Musical Language

Turning to Bach's own use of dance idioms, this study begins with the relatively straightforward cases in both church and courtly vocal works where the strong affective connotations of an actual dance complement or double the emotion of the text concerned. The mutual inflection between the various elements might parallel various combinations of mental and physical experience, ones that we might imagine were those observed, experienced or modelled by the composer himself. After this, I examine movements that have clear dance elements but which depart in some respect from the regular phraseology that dance customarily brings. Here the notion of a counterpoint between dance elements and other compositional factors takes us towards the notion of a productive distancing from dance in its purest, functional form. Such music begins to acquire an uncanny sort of autonomy implying reflection on the world and its beliefs while still being embedded within it. Finally, I attempt to take this type of analysis one stage further, by which the interruptions of dance allusions almost seem to model an individual's experience, where various forms of attention seem to develop during the course of the piece, as if it were duplicating an actual occasion. This might also imply forms of 'corporeal polyphony' by which different virtual personages interact within the temporal and spatial flow of the music.

Although we do not have any direct evidence of Bach himself dancing, it is difficult to doubt that he did, both in the context of the many court appointments he held (and the visits he made) and as a citizen of relatively high status within the upwardly mobile mercantile and intellectual environment of Leipzig. In any case, the saturation of dance idioms within his music renders the question of his own dancing prowess redundant: one way or another he clearly had close experience of dance practice. More important perhaps is the fact that there is vivid testimony that Bach took the physical element of performance very seriously and could use his entire

Arten zu finden, vermeiden, dürfte sie nicht vielmehr als ein blosser Chorale übrig bleiben. Diese Forderung wäre eben so seltsam, als wenn man von einem geistlichen Redner verlangte, er solte kein Wort gebrauchen, daß im gemeinen Leben, oder wohl gar auf dem Schauplatze üblich.'

body in communicating as a director.[29] He clearly associated music with both movement and communication, and this could work at the virtual level as well as the outwardly physical.

It is relatively easy to identify various dances used in Bach's vocal music, and to infer a kind of mood that these might be intended to evoke in conjunction with the text. Both of the surviving Passions end with choruses of mourning (that of the John Passion is followed by a chorale): 'Ruht wohl' from the John Passion is cast in a sort of rondo form and 'Wir setzen uns' of the Matthew Passion is a particularly clear example of an orthodox binary sarabande. This forms the A section of a da capo structure (i.e., ternary form, ABA) and in shape can easily be compared with sarabandes from Bach's instrumental music, such as the opening rhythmic shape of that from the A major English Suite no. 1, BWV806 or, even closer in pitch, that from the C minor Lute Suite, BWV997. The two halves are twelve bars each (comprising three regular four-bar phrases and modulating to the relative major at the end of the first half, returning to C minor in the second) and what would normally have been the repeat of each half of the binary form is indeed the same music but now with the text added. It fits both the affect and the gesture of the text extremely well, since it literally 'sits down' on the second bar (to the text 'Wir setzen uns mit Tränen nieder'), and the word 'Tränen' ('tears') coincides directly with sighing paired quavers. It is hardly controversial to suggest that the text seems to confirm what we hear in the instrumental version (particularly given the context of this chorus within the piece as a whole). The latter part of the text ('Sanfte ruh, ruhe sanfte!') cuts across the triple pulse, as if caressing and rocking Jesus's body, and giving a little metrical subtlety to the regular tread of the dance.

On the whole, it is surely likely that one's assimilation of this connection today is not so tremendously different from the experience of Bach's own listeners. We are invited to be possessed by a specific mood for the duration of the music. A contemporary listener might well have felt something of the original physical gestures of the sarabande as an actual dance, which would imply a doubling of experience (a physical feeling, a particular mood together with whatever spiritual meaning evolves). What might be especially important physically is the implication of a type of gait, a way of walking and holding the limbs that interacts both with the implied emotion of the text and with the gestural notion of sitting down in sorrow.

---

[29] The most striking anecdote comes from Johann Matthias Gesner in 1738. See David and Mendel, *The New Bach Reader*, 328–9.

Other examples of literal dances in Bach's texted music are relatively rare, although rather more common in the secular repertory, which was normally dedicated to a royal personage or to the honour of aspirational citizens. The gavotte at the end of the cantata celebrating the young Saxon crown prince's eleventh birthday in 1733, choosing the way of virtue over pleasure in Cantata 213 ('Laßt uns sorgen, laßt uns wachen'), seems in this context to confirm his royal, 'well-bred' status, and perhaps a similar courtliness is implied for the couple celebrated at the end of the wedding cantata, BWV202 ('Weichet nur, betrübte Schatten'). The sprightly bourrée at the end of 'Schweigt stille, plaudert nicht', BWV211 (the 'Coffee Cantata'), seems to evoke both the lightness of mood and perhaps contributes a comic, mock-courtly character to the bourgeois drama that has just been played out.

All these examples are fairly straightforward and conform to the traditional expectation that at least some dances could be coupled with singing, an appropriate text and an implied affect. However, the vast majority of Bach's dance idioms in vocal music occur not with literal dances but with allusions to dance. Here the implications for movement and embodiment are more subtle because the dance is itself distanced, as one component among several within a larger musical representation. One excellent example to compare with the closing chorus of the Matthew Passion is the soprano aria from the cantata, BWV57, 'Selig ist der Mann, der die Anfechtung erduldet' (1725), which is cast as a dialogue between Jesus (bass) and the Soul (soprano). The Soul's first soliloquy concerns the comfort offered by Jesus, and the tribulations that she would face if he were to abandon her. It ends with the line 'Ach! Jesu, wüßte ich hier nicht Trost von dir, So müßte Mut und Herze brechen, Und voller Trauren sprechen' ('Ah! Jesus, if I knew no comfort from you here, then my courage and heart must break and, full of sadness say'). And what is to be said is the text of the Soul's ensuing aria: 'Ich wünschte mir den Tod, den Tod, Wenn du, mein Jesu, mich nicht liebtest. Ja wenn du mich annoch betrübtest, So hätt ich mehr als Höllennot' ('I would wish upon myself death, death, if you, my Jesus, did not love me. Indeed, if you still grieved me, I would have more than Hell's anguish').

The aria is built around a wonderfully stylized sarabande-like idiom to encapsulate the potential sorrow. The entirety of the model dance is presented as the ritornello for strings that is played before the singer enters: two regular four-bar phrases leading to the dominant chord (what might be considered the first half of a 'real' binary sarabande) and twelve more bars (one four-bar sequential phrase, then two that are elided) (Example 1.1).

Example 1.1 J. S. Bach, Cantata 57, no. 3, Aria, 'Ich wünschte mir den Tod', bars 1–20

This short piece, complete in itself, goes through its own trajectory: the first part presents a sort of matching of phrases, antecedent and consequent, while the second (bar 9) begins with a strong sense of sequential movement which gets 'stuck' on a dominant pedal four bars later. The final, elided phrase resolves this hiatus and provides a conclusion to the piece as a whole. In other words, not only is this a balanced, strongly phrased piece that activates its own doleful dance, almost without players or listeners trying, but it also tells its own story: its movement away from the opening gesture, a sense of being detained in one mood, as if damming up the emotion, which is both confirmed and reiterated in the final phrase. It is relatively easy to imagine this as the modelling of a particular mental state drawn out in time, greatly inflected by implicit posture and gesture, and one which the putative soul might be experiencing.

Rather than directly doubling the 'dance' with the first vocal entry, the first four bars of the soprano's first line present a new phrase (although very much of a piece with the overriding mood), as if placing her at a distance from the representation of mood so strongly gestured in the opening ritornello (Example 1.2). Only her second entry at bar 25, rhetorically

Example 1.2 J. S. Bach, Cantata 57, no. 3, Aria, 'Ich wünschte mir den Tod', bars 21–60

Example 1.2 (cont.)

repeating the opening line, doubles the dance, and she follows it through for the first twelve bars. But, instead of the next phrase – the one with the 'stuck' dominant pedal – she repeats the text (bar 37) to her opening, independent first four bars, now in the dominant, G minor, and then continues, as before, with the actual dance, now complete and now itself in the dominant. All this essentially completes the A section of a modified da capo aria, something which is achieved with very typical Bachian efficiency: the ritornello is used in both complete and incomplete forms, and the new interjection is itself reused. In effect, the singer is entirely 'built-in' to the opening dance.[30] But, if we consider the dance at the opening to represent the personage's essential state of mind, we might well gain the sense of the singer taking charge, first by distancing herself from the actual musical material and then by developing this material in a new tonal direction.

The middle section (i.e., the B section of a da capo, ABA form) is also free with a new and complementary text: 'Ja wenn du mich annoch betrübest, So hätt ich mehr als Höllennot' ('Indeed, if you still grieved me, I would have more than Hell's anguish'), and the final, modified da capo section presents the opening in shortened form. This last section repeats the singer's own opening, continues to the built-in ritornello, which is now heard complete, without modulation, in C minor. In other words, we might imagine the singer now fully reconciled to whatever it is that the dance represents, back in the home key and without diversion to G minor.

Even without detailed study, this aria presents the notion of a singer who, like us, hears the opening, and then adapts it to her own text and ideas, only fully embracing it as a complete entity in the closing section. It is not difficult to imagine, once the text is heard, that the dance, heard then joined, represents the longing for death that the Soul would have if Jesus did not love her. In other words, this curiously touching proto-sarabande is a representation of the subjunctive mood: it represents what *would* be the case in different circumstances, not what actually *is* the case from the point of view of this cantata as a whole (i.e., Jesus's enduring love for the Soul, and his dialogic partnership with it). Dance, together with its associated gestures and affective content, is both imagined and potentially directly modelled by the attentive listener, but its melancholic implications, however strongly felt, are kept at a distance. We are imagining what the singer herself is imagining the situation to feel like were the circumstances to be tragically different. Rather than giving the impression of an ever-fainter carbon copy of a real emotion and situation, the distancing surely offers us a sort of intensification of the feeling and a more nuanced contemplation of the ways in which our physical disposition relates to our emotional state.

---

[30] The notion of the vocal part of an aria or chorus being 'built-in' ('Vokaleinbau') to a pre-existing musical structure was greatly explored by Alfred Dürr's concept of *Einbau*. See Alfred Dürr, *The Cantatas of J. S. Bach*, trans. and ed. Richard Jones (Oxford: Oxford University Press, 2005), 19–20. Bach uses this technique to produce an efficient but never entirely predictable or routine structure.

Example 1.3 J. S. Bach, Cantata 63, no. 5, Duet, 'Ruft und fleht den Himmel an', bars 1–20

Bach uses very similar techniques of joining, hearing and distancing the singers from dance in one of the few pieces that actually mentions dance as part of its text,[31] namely the alto and tenor duet from the Christmas cantata, 'Christen, ätzet diesen Tag', BWV63, with its invitation to Christians to join the 'Reihen'. Bach's Reihen is a swift dance in 3/8, notated with a secondary barring every two bars, thus showing a pairing of groupings. In terms of its rhythm and shape it has been described as a hybrid 'gigue-passepied',[32] something with the flowing triple groupings of the gigue (together with its associated joyful affect), coupled with typical passepied rhythms (namely, one quaver followed by four semiquavers and, later, one quaver followed by a dotted quaver and two closing demisemiquavers). Again, the dance is complete in its own right, albeit slightly unusual in shape (the opening four-bar phrase is answered by a closing four-bar phrase, separated by a twelve-bar internal phrase) (Example 1.3).

Also similar to BWV57/3 is the way that the singers do not enter with a full statement of the opening, but rather with repetitions of the opening phrase, as if trying to encourage the other virtual participants to dance: 'Ruft und fleht den Himmel an, Kommt, ihr Christen, kommt zum Reihen, Ihr sollt euch ob

---

[31] Finke-Hecklinger, *Tanzcharaktere in Johann Sebastian Bachs Vokalmusik*, 128. The only other example she gives of an explicit reference to dance within an aria text is Pan's aria, no. 7, from Cantata 201 (*Phoebus und Pan*), 'Zu Tanze, zu Sprunge', which in this case is a parody of unrefined art.
[32] Finke-Hecklinger, *Tanzcharaktere*, 102.

Example 1.4 J. S. Bach, Cantata 63, no. 5, Duet, 'Ruft und fleht den Himmel an', bars 23–40

dem erfreuen, Was Gott hat anheut getan!' ('Call and beseech heaven; Come, you Christians, come to the dance; you shall rejoice over that which God has done today!'). Equally similar is the way the vocal parts are eventually 'built-in' to a complete iteration of the ritornello-dance, in the dominant in the first section (bar 33) and back in the tonic in the modified da capo (bar 153).

In other respects, this aria works in almost the opposite way to the one from BWV57. Rather than treating the dance as a representation of what *would* have been the case, this one is an attempt to stir up immediate joy and communal movement in celebration of the Incarnation. Particularly interesting is the way the two complete iterations of the dance within the vocal sections (i.e., bar 33 and bar 153) begin by cutting across the vocal lines, marked *pianissimo* and therefore entering almost surreptitiously (Example 1.4). The effect is of a dance that is going on anyway, regardless of what the singers say and what we may choose to do. Only after the first four bars in each of these instances do the singers seem to notice that the dance has begun, and they then literally 'join the dance' themselves, often providing rhythmic dialogue with the figures in the instrumental parts.

Another point to note here, again in contrast to BWV57 (where the dance phrases are almost relentless in their regularity), is the fact that we frequently hear fragments of the dance elsewhere in the piece. First the tenor presents the opening four bars and the instrumentalists respond with the first two bars, but now beginning on the 'weak' bar (bar 24), the fourth bar of the tenor's entry. A similar pattern is heard for the ensuing alto entry. It is almost as if we hear a succession of beginnings, two of them slightly displaced, the repetition of which acts like a corporeal rhetoric, inviting us to join in.

The central section (i.e., the B section of a modified da capo form) presents a new, closely related text: 'Da uns seine Huld verpfleget Und mit so viel Heil beleget, Daß man nicht g'nug danken kann' ('For his favour takes care of us and showers us with so much well-being that we cannot thank him enough'). Much of the material for this central section is new, like the text, but very much in the same idiom. Most interesting though is a passage with two interrupted fragments of the ritornello, with the first two bars in C major (bar 112) and then the original bars 5–8 in E minor, at bars 122–8. In other words, these two fragments match in a sense, although the first lacks its last two bars and the second is in the wrong key, thus giving them a doubled sense of distortion (interruption, transposition) (Example 1.5).

This almost seems to suggest a partial hearing of the dance that is going on in the background, as if one missed a whole section of the music and joined together two disparate bits in one's consciousness; or perhaps it represents a recollection of the experience, partly misremembered. Either way, there is surely an uncanny sort of effect here, as if we have taken a further step from the experience (which was already doubled: a dance that goes on regardless of the personal inclinations of the duetting singers; then their joining of that dance). This might also be the moment that we feel ourselves as particularly separated from both the instrumental dance and the duetting singers who invite us to join. The memory and distortion distribute the subjectivity of the piece further and perhaps encourage us to be aware of our own duration and varied attention over the course of the dance. Moreover, if we were sympathetic to the notion of Luther's round-elay in heaven, we might interpret this experience in a spiritual sense as an intuition of the dance which we believe to be real and continuous in heaven, just impinging on the edges of our earthly consciousness.

Example 1.5 J. S. Bach, Cantata 63, no. 5, Duet, 'Ruft und fleht den Himmel an', bars 104–32

It is this sense of memory or fragmentary recollection embedded into what seems like a direct experience of a dance that also characterizes some of Bach's purely instrumental uses of dance. The extended fourth movement of the first Brandenburg Concerto consists of a binary minuet, which is played four times, with three trio movements interspersed. The very long sequence of minuet music is very appropriate for a dance with a long and complex range of steps, and in which music and steps do not normally become synchronized and the dance completed until a considerable number of repetitions (at least 100 bars of music); it was normal practice to use at least two bipartite pieces, repeating the first one as necessary.[33] The first trio, in the relative minor, plays in well to the sense of continuous minuet music, but both the Polonaise and the final march for horns and oboes cut rudely across the minuet metre (by being in 3/8 and 2/4, respectively). Thus, assuming this sequence of movements is listened to in a court performance, we might be reminded of another type of courtly event, but one which is interrupted and undermined by other fragments of music that might have been more appropriate at different moments in the evening. The listener is perhaps encouraged to remember, and thus internally assimilate, different stages, and thus different physical dispositions, within a piece that cultivates a deceptive sense of continuity.

At one further stage removed from actual dance is the procedure in the third movement of the same concerto, a movement that has, like the duet from BWV63, been described as a sort of 'gigue-passepied', since it is a gigue in terms of its metre and a passepied in most of its component rhythms and hemiola references.[34] Yet, as is typical of countless movements by Bach and his contemporaries, the dance elements are integrated into a concerto structure based on an alternation of ritornelli and soloistic episodes. This particular movement is a rather complex case, since the solo line for piccolo violin is not particularly idiomatic for a violin concerto and the structure of the movement is cast in the 'free da capo' form that is common in Bach's arias and choruses but very unusual in his concertos. These features suggested to Malcolm Boyd that both this movement and the later parody of it as the chorus opening Cantata 207 in fact go back to a lost choral original.[35] Whatever the truth behind this conjecture, the amalgam of different generic references is particularly rich, even by Bach's standards.

---

[33] See Little and Jenne, *Dance and the Music of J. S. Bach*, 65.
[34] Finke-Hecklinger, *Tanzcharaktere in Johann Sebastian Bachs Vokalmusik*, 102.
[35] Malcolm Boyd, *Bach: The Brandenburg Concertos* (Cambridge: Cambridge University Press, 1993), 67–70.

Example 1.6 J. S. Bach, Brandenburg Concerto no. 1 in F, BWV1046, movement 3, bars 1–17

The opening ritornello is typical of a concerto-style movement, with its opening gesture, sequential centre and closing section. The opening gesture can be heard as essentially the opening half of a passepied (four bars of 6/8, therefore eight for a dance in 3/8), but after this the dance structure is clearly violated, with the interpolation of a three-bar Fortspinnung (a sequential section, bars 5–7). The passepied seems to resume, with another four-bar section (but coming one 6/8 bar too early, bar 8), followed by a cadential section full of hemiolas in very typical passepied style. Yet this final section is based on 3+3 bars, ending on the downbeat of the next bar. To someone familiar with the rhythms and phraseology of the passepied, then, this whole ritornello might be heard as a skewed version of the dance, seemingly cut out of a real dance and pasted into a concerto ritornello (Example 1.6).

Very strong, but discontinuous, elements of the dance are therefore taken from one place and replayed in another, as if one were remembering something of the sensations of an actual experience and recalling them elsewhere. If we were familiar with the dance steps, we would be aware of the cross-beat

Example 1.6 (cont.)

nature of the passepied, which takes the syncopated steps of the minuet to a more extreme level. It would also – if we are to believe Mattheson and others – bring connotations of the pastoral, frivolity and light-heartedness (like a 'female who, though she is a little inconstant, nevertheless does not therewith lose her charm', he helpfully suggests).[36] Assuming one possesses the belief that formal dance is a regulator of society and one's own deportment, it may be that one should both contemplate but also model the movement, character and specific regulatory quality of this dance within a performance context similar, but not identical, to that of an actual dance.

The sense of a dance, relived but also somewhat defamiliarized, is made even stronger by the fact that the opening phrase with a new extension reappears in a *piano* form (from bar 21). Ritornello fragments are virtually never notated to be repeated at a different dynamic in Bach's concertos and here there is the effect of distancing, as if the dance is heard from afar, while we might hear the discourse

---

[36] Mattheson, *Der vollkommene Kapellmeister*, Part 2, Ch. 13, p. 229, paragraph 113: 'so wie manch Frauenzimmer, ob es gleich ein wenig unbeständig ist, dennoch ihren Reitz dabey nicht verliert.'

Example 1.6 (cont.)

of the piccolo violin at a much closer range. Then there is the solo part itself, which, unusually for a concerto, begins with a reiteration of the opening phrase – exactly as would be the expected process in a vocal piece, where the opening text usually has a close relation to the shape of the opening gestures. With a background in vocal, instrumental and dance music then, a listener might well hear the solo sections as implying some sort of discourse or discussion of the implications of the opening material, as if the intellectual and the physical are counterpoised and compared to one another. The notion of discourse is taken further by the fact that the closing (C major) ritornello of the A section is undertaken not by the full tutti with horns but led by the first of the ripieno violins, as if in conversation with the piccolo violin (bars 40–53). Whether or not we personally identify with the solo violin piccolo, there is clearly more than one subjectivity involved in this discourse. Then, further subverting the expectations of the central ritornello of a free da capo movement, this closing ritornello is finished off without woodwind and therefore with a sort of orchestrated *diminuendo*. This is a shading away, as if we are tuning out of the immediacy of the experience, something again that is unusual within the normally uniform dynamic progress of baroque concerto movements.

Example 1.6 (cont.)

The idea of a conversation with the soloist is taken further in the central section, with dialogues between the oboe, the horns and the other violin soloist. Following vocal practice, the solo material in this central section is largely new and no longer connected with the opening gestures – in other words, one might imagine this section to have a new text or sense. Most striking of all is the sudden interpolation of an Adagio (bars 82–3), as if some point of profundity had been reached at the end of the B section and heralding the condensed da capo of the essential material of the A section (beginning with the violin's first solo, now adapted to remain in the tonic key, and ending with a complete reiteration of the opening ritornello) (Example 1.7).

From the point of view of dance, this moment is even more remote from the continuity of movement in an actual ball. It is rather like a private moment experienced as completely abstracted from the proceedings. This is the point at which one might contemplate the implications of the dance mood and movement, in relation to the further process of one's existence. While there

Example 1.7 J. S. Bach, Brandenburg Concerto no. 1 in F, BWV1046, movement 3, bars 80–4

are elements of a doubling of one's varied attention at an actual dance, together with an awareness of others (e.g., the dividing of the violin line between two players), what is perhaps most significant is a kind of *digestion* of past experience, physical and mental, combined with some sort of contemplation and discussion of how this could be used, processed or somehow assimilated into one's ongoing being. The music in concerto style thus works in performance as a means of recalling another artificial means of regulating and refining movement and emotion – dance – and inviting us to draw something from this restaged memory.

Much of this, of course, presupposes that the physical allusions and memories are somehow felt in the body of the listener rather than merely intellectualized. The music may function to stir up a range of moods, gestures and memories, provide extension and commentary on these, and also help to draw these towards a central synthesizing point. The listener is perhaps invited both to identify with the various forms of subjectivity created in the music (most obviously the solo piccolo violin) and to hear the individual from the outside and perhaps belong to a larger group of participants. Such a construction does not necessarily imply any specific semantic content, more an extended experience over the duration of the movement. But such an experiential framework could potentially serve a range of texts or scenarios, which may or may not complement the range of experiences the listener draws from it. So what of the earliest surviving text for this movement, adapted as the first chorus for Cantata 207, and performed several years later, in 1726? In fact, this complements the sort of experience I have suggested remarkably well, particularly since it invites reflection on the music and festive sonorities that we are experiencing:

Vereinigte Zwietracht der wechselnden Saiten,
Der rollenden Pauken durchdringender Knall!
Locket den lüsteren Hörer herbei,
Saget mit euren frohlockenden Tönen
Und doppelt vermehretem Schall
Denen mir emsig ergebenden Söhnen,
Was hier der Lohn der Tugend sei.[37]

[(United discord of changing strings,/ penetrating sound of rolling drums./ Draw hither the desirous listener,/ speak with your cheerful tones,/ and the doubly augmented sound,/ to my diligently dutiful sons,/ about what is here the reward of virtue.)]

---

[37] Translation adapted from Boyd, *Bach: The Brandenburg Concertos*, 66.

This text substantiates much of what the purely instrumental movement seems to be about: the notion of uniting dissonance (and, by association, cross-rhythms and the disjointed elements of a dance), bringing all together; attracting thereby a number of attentive listeners and together drawing towards the overall point (articulated precisely at that Adagio moment) about the rewards of virtue. Such virtue is therefore actualized in the regulation and coordination of all the varied elements of the music, solo and communal, dance and concerto.

Conclusion

If I am right in suggesting that Bach was unusually perceptive in linking dance to a contemplation of embodied human experience over time, he is not doing something beyond the bounds of possibility during his age. Indeed, towards the end of his life, and just beyond it, Etienne Bonnot, Abbé de Condillac, was developing a theory that linked embodiment to modern subjectivity, in strikingly similar ways. In his *Essai sur l'origine des connaissance humaines*, 1746, Condillac places gesture at the very origin of human communication and language, through a fanciful theory of kinaesthetic sympathy between people.[38] For him primitive language was a 'language of action' recognizable in physical gesture accompanied by vocal utterances, which only later was accompanied and eventually replaced by language as we understand it today. However, he believed that spoken language is still most effective in inducing sympathy when it is accompanied by physical gesture. Within this putative history of human language, dance (developed within two genres, one to express thoughts and the other feelings) becomes a crucial development and refinement of the fundamentals of gesture and is therefore prior to verbal language. Condillac sees ancient Greek and Hebrew expression in dance as crucial to the communication of their culture, government and religion, and as something that it sadly lacking in modern culture.[39]

At the next stage of historical development, as verbal language took over from the physical, it encapsulated the residue of the physical gesture in spoken language through the application of music (and poetry for written language). So music, like dance, is prior to spoken language. In all, then, for Condillac the

---

[38] See Joshua M. Hall, 'Core Aspects of Dance: Condillac and Mead on Gesture', *Dance Chronicle* 36, no. 3 (2013), 357–61.

[39] Susan Leigh Foster, 'Choreographing Empathy', *Topoi* 24, no. 1 (2005), 84.

very foundations of language lie in a historical hierarchy beginning with gesture, which is later organized into dance, and which then evolves into music and poetry as the basis of modern spoken and written language. In his later treatise on the human senses, *Traité des sensations* (1754), Condillac places touch at the forefront of human self-awareness. His hypothetical statue, which is confined to each sense one by one in order to determine the essence of each, finds its fundamental feeling in touch. Only through touch does it become aware of the space in which it resides, and also of the difference between touching and being touched. Condillac also evokes the sense of a being as aware of persisting both inside and outside the physical body, finding the possibilities of space through touch but also reflecting back iteratively on the discovered self. As Elisabeth Le Guin has noted, Condillac's statue not only discovers the self through the interaction of touch and space, but also through duration and the interaction of memory with the succession of bodily sensory impressions. It is here that music becomes a crucial aspect of self-constitution by which it provides a sense of persistence over time.[40]

While it is highly unlikely that Bach would have had any knowledge or encounter with an obscure French abbot's thoughts, it is clear that their respective interpretations of movement, dance and duration come from common roots. Such roots can be traced both to Greek and Hebrew traditions but receive an increased emphasis in an age when issues of social and personal cultivation and order become particularly vital. Within the history of Western music, Bach's contribution is not only to encapsulate various forms of physical movement within his notated music, but also to suggest several levels of reflection on this movement through durational extension and staged memory. The myth of Bach as the disembodied purveyor of perfected counterpoint is unlikely to disappear, but his insights into the embodied human are surely a crucial aspect of his contribution to the Western tradition. Indeed, Forkel's observation of a specific dance-like quality in Bach's music could be applied not only to many of Bach's contemporaries but also specifically to the composers who took him as a fundamental model. We should surely be exploring the rhythmic quality of 'dance-ness' in much music that has hitherto been prized primarily for its pitch content, and also the possibility that such rhythmic issues can open up a substantial field concerned with the contemplation of both self and community.

---

[40] Elisabeth Le Guin, *Boccherini's Body: An Essay in Carnal Musicology* (Berkeley and Los Angeles: University of California Press, 2005), 7–11.

2 | Dance as 'Other': Contrasting Modes of Musical Representation

SUZANNE ASPDEN

Music for dance is surely one of the oldest and most ubiquitous functional forms, and yet, partly because of this status, its place within discourse about so-called 'art' music has often been problematic. Indeed, when in 1976 dance scholar Judith Lynne Hanna complained that there remained a 'conceptual plague besetting the understanding of dance' deriving from 'a misguided separation of dance from intelligence', she might have added 'dance music' to that complaint – both dance and dance music have until recently been largely excluded from university syllabi (if not from academic study).[1] As Hanna's observation implies, dance and dance music are still often conceptualized within a strict mind–body dualism. Writing in 1999, Jeremy Gilbert and Ewan Pearson suggested similarly that state anxiety about electronic dance music derived from fear of its expression of bodily pleasure.[2] And in 2003, anthropologist Ruth Finnegan observed it still to be the case that 'popular and "other" music, in the past often stereotypically categorized as solely of the body, [is pitted] against the classical Western canon with its assumed intellectual quality'.[3]

The binarism that Hanna and Finnegan identify suggests dance and dance music fall on one side of a network of traditionally interrelated dualities: mind/body, self/'Other', high-art/popular, male/female. That is to say, just as the gendering of the mind/body duality has long been

---

[1] Judith Lynne Hanna, *Dance, Sex and Gender* (Chicago: University of Chicago Press, 1988), 9; paraphrasing Curtis Carter, 'Intelligence and Sensibility in the Dance', *Arts in Society: Growth of Dance in America* 13, no. 2 (1976), 210–21. For similar complaints, see Andrew Ward, 'Dancing Around Meaning (and the Meaning around Dance)', in *Dance in the City*, ed. Helen Thomas (Basingstoke: Macmillan, 1997), 7; Eric McKee, *Decorum of the Minuet, Delirium of the Waltz* (Bloomington and Indianapolis: Indiana University Press, 2012), 129; David Gramit, 'Between *Täuschung* and *Seligkeit*: Situating Schubert's Dances', *Musical Quarterly* 84 (2000), 221–37; Maribeth Clark, 'The Quadrille as Embodied Musical Experience in 19th-Century Paris', *The Journal of Musicology* 19 (2002), 503–26, esp. 505.

[2] Jeremy Gilbert and Ewan Pearson, *Discographies: Dance Music, Culture and the Politics of Sound* (London: Routledge, 1999), 38.

[3] Ruth Finnegan, 'Music, Experience, and the Anthropology of Emotion', in *The Cultural Study of Music*, ed. Martin Clayton, Trevor Herbert and Richard Middleton (New York and London: Routledge, 2003), 362.

recognized and the body feared, so too has dance been associated with the female/body/'Other' nexus.[4] Of course, dance has often been regarded as an activity suitable for men – even specifically associated with men – and has at times been accorded respect as a physical expression of intellectual and moral conditioning, as in humanist-influenced, fifteenth-century Italy and early modern courtly France.[5] And women, too, have been admired for their prowess as dancers or enlightened patrons of dance, as studies such as Lynne Matluck Brooks's *Women's Work: Making Dance in Europe before 1800* show.[6] However, when dance has been viewed negatively (from the earliest times), criticism has often been couched in gendered terms, linking fear of the body with fear of the female 'Other'; for example, the story of Salome was used by the Church fathers and again in medieval times as a warning of the dangers of dancing.[7] And while courtly dance flourished in the early modern period (as noted above), criticism was also plentiful: Christian attacks on the immorality of dance increased during the Reformation and Counter-Reformation, and women were a particular object of reproach.[8] Even the French dance theorist and historian Thoinot Arbeau, in his well-known dance treatise *Orchésographie* (1588), mused on women's susceptibility to the intoxicating effects of music: the volta, he felt, was a dance that would leave a woman's 'brain confused, her head full of giddy whirlings', and he asked male dancers to 'consider if it be a proper thing for a young girl to make such large steps and separations of the legs; and whether both honour and health are not concerned and threatened'.[9] Equally, those

---

[4] On gender and the body, see Sherry B. Ortner, *Making Gender: The Politics and Erotics of Culture* (Boston: Beacon Press, 1996). On the nineteenth-century association of inferior mass culture with women, see Andreas Huyssen, 'Mass Culture as Woman', in *After the Great Divide: Modernism, Mass Culture, Postmodernism* (Basingstoke: MacMillan, 1986), 44–62. On the early association of female/body/'Other' with dance, see Louise K. Stein, '"La musica de dos obres": A Context for the First Opera of the Americans', *The Opera Quarterly* 22 (2006), 433–58.

[5] Jennifer Nevile, *The Eloquent Body: Dance and Humanist Culture in Fifteenth-Century Italy* (Bloomington and Indianapolis: Indiana University Press, 2004); Kate van Orden, *Music, Discipline, and Arms in Early Modern France* (Chicago: University of Chicago Press, 2005).

[6] Lynne Matluck Brooks, *Women's Work: Making Dance in Europe before 1800* (Madison: University of Wisconsin Press, 2007).

[7] Linda Hutcheon and Michael Hutcheon, 'Staging the Female Body', in *Siren Songs*, ed. Mary Ann Smart (Princeton: Princeton University Press, 2000), 204–21, at 280–1.

[8] Alessandro Arcangeli, 'Dance under Trial: The Moral Debate, 1200-1600', *Dance Research* 12, no. 2 (1994), 127–55, at 128–33. I infer a focus on women from the literature Arcangeli cites.

[9] Thoinot Arbeau, *Orchésographie* (1588), trans. Mary Stewart Evans, *Orchesography* (New York: Dover, 1967).

who wished to impugn men for a lack of appropriately 'manly' behaviour incorporated dance into their invective, the English Puritan William Prynne complaining in 1633 of 'effeminate cinque-pace coranto-frisking gallants'.[10]

While, from today's position of radical pluralism and post-structuralist hermeneutics, we might lament a history of bias against dance and the binaries with which it has been aligned, this mode of understanding might invite careful attention to the representation of dance in 'art' music. Dance music, with its nexus of associations with the body, physicality, femininity and the 'Other', as well as its widespread recognizability, enjoyed the function of a musical signifier – or a musical 'topic' – long before the period (the eighteenth and nineteenth centuries) we traditionally associate with the use of topics: well-known dances have always possessed what Kofi Agawu has called 'intuitive adequacy' to communicate meaning beyond that of the musical form itself, allowing composers to deploy dance topics as recognizable vehicles of social discourse. Thus Agawu's explanation of the function of topics (with regard to those Leonard Ratner delineated for the eighteenth century) might also stand for the way dance music operates within 'art' repertoires more generally:

Ratner's topics form part of the listening environment of composers and listeners alike, so that an analysis that takes this condition as its point of departure satisfies the empiricist's demand for a verifiable point of departure. We might even invoke the notion of implicit contractual values between composer and audience in order to argue not only that a topical approach is intuitively adequate, but also that it constitutes a necessary ... analytical preliminary.[11]

Inspired by these music-analytical ideas, this chapter proposes two ways in which dance (in the broadest sense) functioned topically, suggesting a fundamental shift from the first to the second, one that occurred during the nineteenth century and was closely related to the increasing prominence of dance's function in representing the (feminized) 'Other' within musical Orientalism. Indeed, I will suggest that, in some ways, the nineteenth century's new understanding of dance within the context of Orientalist discourse encouraged a reversal of earlier musical practice, which tended to sublimate or disguise dance's most recognizable elements. In the nineteenth century, I argue, dance and the dancing body were variously foregrounded in representations of the 'Other'.

---

[10] William Prynne, *Histrio-mastix* (London: E. A. and W. I. for Michael Sparke, 1633), 232.
[11] Kofi Agawu, *Playing with Signs: A Semiotic Interpretation of Classical Music* (Princeton: Princeton University Press, 1991), 19.

Sublimation

Examining the use of the *contredanse* in the finales of 'classical' instrumental works, David Neumeyer has identified an 'active and expressive opposition' between dance music, created for physical enjoyment, and instrumental music, created for listening and contemplation; this opposition, he proposed, is observed in the musical language of the larger forms derived from dances, which demonstrate 'a well-developed expressive dialectic between hypermetric clarity and ambiguity'.[12] Others have also remarked on the ways in which musical representations of dance seem to toy with and even obscure their origins: speaking of the French dance suites by J. S. Bach, Eric McKee has observed that older forms no longer in fashion as dances were 'subject to greater stylisation', while the relatively novel dance form of the minuet was more closely adhered to by the composer.[13] In the later eighteenth century, when the minuet no longer represented novelty in either dance or art music, Franz Joseph Haydn (among others) was keen to 'thwart' expectations associated with the minuet's dance characteristics.[14] Indeed, Agawu has observed that the eighteenth-century use of topics tends to 'defamiliarise "ordinary" materials such as fanfares, hunt-calls, brilliant-style effects, and so on, therefore making them properly and self-consciously artistic'.[15]

It seems, indeed, that popular dances absorbed into 'art' music from the sixteenth century onwards were regularly subjected to a degree of elaboration that removed them from their practical origins.[16] There might have been several reasons for this. One explanation might lie with the highly prized nature of complex ornamentation. In the Renaissance, for example, dancers delighted in cross-rhythms and syncopation, including gestural intertextuality, by which the characteristic steps (and rhythms) of one dance reappeared within another.[17] Dance music, too, which traditionally featured simple and

---

[12] David Neumeyer, 'The Contredanse, Classical Finales, and Caplin's Formal Functions', *Music Theory Online* 12, no. 4 (2006), paragraph 29.

[13] Eric McKee, 'Influences of the Early Eighteenth-Century Social Minuet on the Minuets from J. S. Bach's French Suites, BWV812–17', *Music Analysis* 18 (1999), 235–60, at 241.

[14] Bryan Proksch, 'Vincent d'Indy as Harbinger of the Haydn Revival', *Journal of Musicological Research*, 28 (2009), 162–88, at 181.

[15] Agawu, *Playing with Signs*, 137.

[16] The English pavan represents an early example of this pattern; see Peter Holman, *Dowland: 'Lachrimae' (1604)* (Cambridge: Cambridge University Press, 1999), 31–2.

[17] See, e.g., Antonio Cornazano, *The Book on the Art of Dancing* (1455), trans. Madeleine Inglehearn and Peggy Forsyth (London: Dance Books, 1981); Arbeau, *Orchésographie* (1588); Carlo Negri, *Le gratie d'Amore* (1602). See also van Orden, *Music, Discipline, and Arms*, 88–104,

highly repetitive patterns, was designed for improvised elaboration by its professional performers, who could thus extend a dance for as long as required by the dancers.[18] This perhaps helps explain why, when instrumental tutors' popularity grew in the seventeenth century, these formerly improvised patterns were written out in extensive variations for the amateur to learn. *Greensleeves* in *The Division Violin* (1686), for example, uses a formulaic, improvisatory tune over a bass combining the *passamezzo antico* and *romanesca* formulae, and then provides the basis for multiple variation movements.[19] In this context, dance and music might offer a complementary commentary on one another. And, indeed, in performance, dancer and musician might spur one another to greater heights, as Thomas Morley – here writing on the instrumental pavan – seems to suggest:

In this you may not so much insist in following the point [musical subject] as in a Fantasy, but it shall be enough to touch it once and so away to some close. Also in this you must cast your music by four, so that if you keep that rule it is no matter how many fours you put in your strain for it will fall out well enough in the end, the art of dancing being come to that perfection that every reasonable dancer will make measure of no measure, so that it is no great matter of what number you make your strain.[20]

Of course, besides the tradition of elaboration, another possible reason for the stylization of dance music (and dance itself) concerns the long-standing unease about the relationship between 'high' and 'low' cultural forms, and between mind and body.[21] Although we might now problematize the division

---

on the galliard; and for the eighteenth century, Jennifer Thorp, 'In Defence of Danced Minuets', *Early Music* 31 (2003), 101–8.

[18] On improvization and memorization in early repertoires, see Timothy J. McGee, ed., *Instruments and their Music in the Middle Ages* (Aldershot: Ashgate, 2009), and his *The Sound of Medieval Song: Ornamentation and Vocal Style according to the Treatises* (Oxford: Clarendon Press, 1998), 1–4; Keith Polk, 'Instrumentalists and Performance Practices in Dance Music, c. 1500', in *Improvisation in the Arts of the Middle Ages and Renaissance*, ed. Timothy J. McGee (Kalamazoo, MI: Medieval Institute Publications, Western Michigan University, 2003), 98–114, esp. 98.

[19] J. M. Ward, 'And Who But Ladie Greensleeues?', in *The Well Enchanting Skill: Essays in Honour of F. W. Sternfeld*, ed. J. A. Caldwell, E. D. Olleson and S. Wollenberg (Oxford: Oxford University Press, 1990), 181–211.

[20] Thomas Morley, *A Plaine and Easie Introduction to Practicall Musicke* (1597; Westmead, Farnborough, Hants, UK: Gregg International Publishers, 1971). See also Thorp, 'In Defence of Danced Minuets'.

[21] Alexandra Carter notes the 'fundamental' nature of assumptions about the 'evolution' of dance from 'primitive' and 'folk' forms to 'high' art, with ballet as 'the apex of civilized Western achievement'; Alexandra Carter, 'Locating Dance in History and Society', in *The Routledge Dance Studies Reader*, ed. Alexandra Carter (London and New York: Routledge, 1998), 193–5, at 193–4; see also Andrée Grau, 'Myths of Origin', in *The Routledge Dance Studies Reader*, 197–202.

between 'low' and 'high', noting the ways in which they interpenetrate, the historical discourse (itself generated by 'high' culture[22]) tended to perpetuate the division, delineating the characteristically cautious ways in which practitioners of 'high' culture were seen to appropriate the 'low'.[23] So, for example, the mid-fifteenth-century Italian dancing master Antonio Cornazano mentioned the 'country' origins of the piva (the 'dance from which all the others are developed') only in order to compliment aristocratic society: 'nowadays intellects have developed and flowered into greater refinement and amongst the nobility and good dancers it [the piva] has been discarded and has fallen from use'.[24] Strikingly similar is Italian choreographer Gennaro Magri's late eighteenth-century narrative about the minuet: 'born among the Peasants of Anjou ... little by little it was improved and under Louis the Great ... it was put into better order and, by degrees, perfected'.[25] The temporal and cultural distance separating these two commentators only underscores dance scholar Alexandra Carter's assessment that one of the long-standing 'fundamental beliefs' about dance is the evolutionary narrative 'that dance has progressed from the "primitive" through to the "civilized"'.[26]

For music, such narratives were further complicated by distinctions maintained until at least the seventeenth century between, on the one hand, 'learned' musicians and singers of liturgical music – who could read and theorize about music – and, on the other, professional instrumentalists, street musicians who 'merely' performed from memory and improvised.[27] Moreover, it might not be unreasonable to imagine that, given the opprobrium traditionally attached to music-making for 'licentious pleasures', such as dance, and to practical rather than theoretical musicians more generally, those engaged in formal composition would have taken pains to distance themselves from their lowly cousins and from the physicality and sensuality of dance.[28] Perhaps this might

---

[22] Skiles Howard, *The Politics of Courtly Dancing in Early Modern England* (Amherst: University of Massachusetts Press, 1998), 5, 160–1.

[23] On 'high'/'low' connections in Renaissance dance, see Julia Sutton, introduction to Fabritio Caroso, *Nobilità di dame* (Venice, 1600), ed. and trans. J. Sutton, music ed. F. Marian Walker (Oxford: Oxford University Press, 1986), 29; Ingrid Brainard, *The Art of Courtly Dancing in the Early Renaissance. Part II: The Practice of Courtly Dances* (West Newton, MA: n.p., 1981), 4.

[24] Antonio Cornazano, *The Book on the Art of Dancing*, 23, 20. The 'Other' dances he mentions are the saltarello, quaternia and bassadanza.

[25] Magri (1779), 179; cited in Eric McKee, 'Mozart in the Ballroom: Minuet-trio Contrast and the Aristocracy in Self-portrait', *Music Analysis* 24 (2005), 383–434, at 393.

[26] Carter, 'Locating Dance in History and Society', 193.

[27] For example, see Christopher Page, 'German Musicians and their Instruments: A 14th-Century Account by Konrad of Megenberg', *Early Music* 10 (1982), 192–200, at 196.

[28] The quotation is from Thomas de Chobham, *Summa Confessorum* (c. 1215), cited in John Stevens, *Words and Music in the Middle Ages: Song, Narrative, Dance and Drama, 1050–1350* (Cambridge: Cambridge University Press, 1986), 235. Hostility to secular instrumentalists who played for

be one reason why, whether through metrical or formal games, or through various kinds of musical embellishment, the effect of 'art' music's elaboration on dance motifs has sometimes been to make the music (seemingly) undanceable.[29]

Musical Representations of Dance in the Nineteenth Century

The obfuscation of dance in 'art'-music representation, together with the long-standing ingrained unease about dance, might seem to point towards the avoidance of dance music as an artistic topic altogether. Such, according to Lawrence Zbikowski, seems to have been the case in the nineteenth century, when 'two things specific to social dance of the nineteenth century – its association with the bourgeoisie and its manifest physicality – placed it outside the pantheon of musical works deemed worthy of sustained attention' in artistic terms.[30] In this hypothesis, Zbikowski may be following Hanna's observation that the 'French and industrial revolutions ... dealt serious blows to the prestige of dance, sending it from the epitome of royal male performance to the nadir of "inferior" female performance'.[31] If true, this may help explain why dancing reputedly lost favour amongst men in the period.[32] However, as the remainder of this chapter will show, 'art' music's re-imaginings of dance continued unabated. Indeed, as Neumeyer's observation of a dialectical process suggests, these later treatments of dance in 'art' music seem to have derived much of their power from the play between the embrace and disavowal of dance's forbidden pleasures. As such, we might want to reappraise Zbikowski's proposal that dance's topical role in the nineteenth century disappeared because 'the very basis for the effectiveness of dance music – the thoroughly embodied knowledge with which dance is associated – doom[ed] it to a subhuman status'.[33]

---

dancing was primarily religious, as many have pointed out; see, e.g., James McKinnon, 'The Meaning of the Patristic Polemic against Musical Instruments', *Current Musicology* 1 (1965), 69–82. But the lowly status of such musicians was also reinforced on other grounds. John Baldwin has suggested that *jongleurs* only salvaged their social status (and, in the eyes of the Church, their souls) through moving from a focus on bodily movement or dance to one on music; see John W. Baldwin, *Masters, Princes, and Merchants: The Social Views of Peter the Chanter and His Circle*, 2 vols. (Princeton: Princeton University Press, 1970), 198–204.

[29] For differing views on the feasibility of dancing to 'art' music, see Christopher Hogwood, 'In Defence of the Minuet and Trio', *Early Music* 30 (2002), 236–51; and Jennifer Thorp, 'In Defence of Danced Minuets', *Early Music* 31 (2003), 101–8.

[30] Lawrence M. Zbikowski, 'Music, Dance, and Meaning in the Early Nineteenth Century', *Journal of Musicological Research* 31, nos. 2–3 (2012), 147–65, at 162.

[31] Hanna, *Dance, Sex and Gender*, 123.   [32] Clark, 'The Quadrille', 507–8.

[33] Zbikowski, 'Music, Dance and Meaning', 163.

Instead, I would like to suggest that dance music's 'Otherness' (which, in any case, had been associated with dance's physicality long before the nineteenth century[34]) facilitated a different kind of topical resonance in the nineteenth century from the elegant social associations which coloured the reception of (high-class) dance music during the eighteenth century. Indeed, in an era of political and social upheaval across Europe, we might suspect that art forms such as dance, which traversed the boundary between 'low' and 'high', would attract particular interest. In the nineteenth century, I will suggest, dance served as a marker for all that was troubling: 'low' social class, physicality over intellect, and the (female) body.

Evidence for growing interest in the non-normative within late eighteenth- and early nineteenth-century society emerges in a variety of ways. Perhaps the earliest was nostalgia for a rural, 'folk' authenticity, of which Marie Antoinette's masquerades as a shepherdess are only the best known: if aristocratic and then bourgeois society did indeed refine and distinguish their dances and their 'art' music away from popular or country origins (as the 'fundamental' narrative identified by Carter has suggested), at the same time there lingered a fascination with those lowly beginnings – a fascination already evident in the popularity of publisher John Playford's 'country dances' of seventeenth-century England.[35] Such nostalgic interests perhaps intensified as urbanization and then industrialization took hold.[36] The reification of popular music as 'folk' art, from at least the eighteenth century, and its gathering pace in the nineteenth as part of various nationalist movements, is well known;[37] dance and its music were surely part of this process. At eighteenth-century courts, masquerades acquired increasing popularity: in Germany they were known as *Wirthschaften*, rustic balls at which courtiers performed peasant dances in peasant attire.[38]

---

[34] Treatises such as Thomas de Chobham's *Summa Confessorum* of c. 1215 make the primitive status of dance clear; see note 28, above.

[35] On Playford's expression of an aristocratic nostalgia for country dance, see Christopher Marsh, *Music and Society in Early Modern England* (Cambridge: Cambridge University Press, 2010), 329.

[36] On industrialization and nostalgia, see Raymond Williams, *The Country and the City* (Oxford: Oxford University Press, 1973); John Barrell, *The Dark Side of the Landscape: The Rural Poor in English Painting, 1730–1840* (Cambridge: Cambridge University Press, 1980); Karen Sayer, *Women of the Fields: Representations of Rural Women in the Nineteenth Century* (Manchester: Manchester University Press, 1995).

[37] Matthew Gelbart, *The Invention of 'Folk Music' and 'Art Music': Emerging Categories from Ossian to Wagner* (Cambridge: Cambridge University Press, 2007).

[38] Franz Magnus Böhme, *Geschichte des Tanzes in Deutschland* (Wiesbaden: Breitkopf und Härtel, 1967), I: 144–5; cited in Meredith Little, 'Courtly, Social and Theatrical Dance', in *The Worlds of Johann Sebastian Bach*, ed. Raymond Erickson (New York: Amadeus Press, 2009), 207–28, at 216. See also Mosco Carner, cited in Robert Samuels, *Mahler's Sixth*

Other nineteenth-century developments further assisted the shift in dance's social meaning and use in 'art' music away from the eighteenth century's polite and high-class associations towards the (multiply) transgressive and seemingly problematic. A heady mix of industrialization (or mechanization), nationalism and imperialist Orientalism/exoticism all infused and helped re-configure dance's meaning. The impact of each factor is worth exploring a little here, because the associations they developed in theatrical representation (particularly concerning women) seem to have influenced the way dance and dance music were re-framed within 'art' music as objects worthy of attention.

Interest in the rural past and the 'folk' was balanced by (and coupled with) fear of industrial progress and the 'masses' in ways that could also be expressed in dance. Teresa Magdanz has suggested that the waltz's associations with technology (the mechanical action of perpetual revolution) may have conditioned both the long-lived fascination with spinning dances and our metaphorical understanding of the dance.[39] The conjunction of Magdanz's emphasis on non-human technology in the waltz and Zbikowski's on 'sub-human' physicality in nineteenth-century understandings of dance generally is suggestive: though the mechanical and the embodied may seem antithetical, both can stand for the physical in its opposition to the intellectual in ways that recall issues of class and gender.[40] In other words, just as women were feared for their artifice (and increasingly for their artificiality), 'mechanical' (as a noun, rather than an adjective) was used pejoratively to describe 'people engaged in manual work, esp. regarded as a class, artisanal; vulgar, coarse'.[41] In both instances, the opposition to the 'natural' is expressive of ideological concerns. Tellingly, Magdanz's association between technology and the waltz

---

Symphony: A Study in Semiotics (Cambridge: Cambridge University Press, 1995), 129. On the ballroom craze for 'national' dancing, see Lisa C. Arkin and Marian Smith, 'National Dance in the Romantic Ballet', in *Rethinking the Sylph: New Perspectives on the Romantic Ballet*, ed. Lynn Garafola (Hanover, NH: Wesleyan University Press, 1997), 11–68.

[39] Teresa Magdanz, 'The Waltz: Technology's Muse', *Journal of Popular Music Studies* 18, no. 3 (2006), 251–81, at 251–2.

[40] On the dangers of female musical artifice, see Felicia Miller Frank, *The Mechanical Song: Women, Voice, and the Artificial in Nineteenth-Century French Narrative* (Stanford: Stanford University Press, 1995); and Heather Hadlock, *Mad Loves: Women and Music in Offenbach's 'Les Contes d'Hoffmann'* (Princeton: Princeton University Press, 2000).

[41] 'Mechanical, adj. and n.', OED Online, September 2012, Oxford University Press, www.oed.com/view/Entry/115544?redirectedFrom=mechanical. The earliest example the *Oxford English Dictionary* provides for this definition, from John Lyly in 1584, emphasizes the old mind/body duality: 'There is no reasoning with these Mechanical doltes, whose wits are in their hands, not in their heads.'

hinges on the hurdy-gurdy or barrel organ and the fairground carousel – purveyors of popular entertainment of the 'lowest' kind.

As Magdanz's appraisal of the fascination engendered by the mechanized waltz suggests, the physical realm assumed new significance in the nineteenth century, not only as the point of contact between the non-human and the human, but also (particularly in the uncanny realm of automata) for its connection to the sub- or unconscious.[42] 'Art' music demonstrated this fascination variously – not only in representations of dreams and fantasies of automata, but also in according dance psychological significance in dramatic and programmatic works.[43] Perhaps most notably, the liminality of a physical activity such as dance, with its perceived connection to the unconscious (through the rational mind's relaxation), facilitated the ready association of dance and its music with the elucidation of national identity – itself represented as an authentic expression of mass consciousness.[44] During the early to mid-nineteenth-century craze for 'national' dance, the genre was privileged over 'artificial' conventional ballet because, as one English critic put it, 'the sounds of feet echo the feelings in the heart'.[45] National dance music also came to represent a kind of compositional authenticity, examples of which are legion across a range of genres, from the Spanish fandangos composed by Fernando Sor for Parisian salons in the late eighteenth century or the supposedly Portuguese minuets of the mid-eighteenth century, to Chopin's polonaises or, indeed, Astor Piazzolla's tangos.[46]

Of course, the 'national' in musical terms was always 'Other' to a perceived mainstream (central European) norm.[47] The 'Otherness' of national music was particularly pronounced when expressed in dance and, indeed, dancing became strongly associated with the depiction of exotic 'Others', as nineteenth-century balletic developments demonstrate. Scholars have recently observed

---

[42] On automation's perceived challenge to human agency, see Jane Goodall, 'Transferred Agencies: Performance and the Fear of Automatism', *Theatre Journal* 49, no. 4 (1997), 441–53.

[43] On automata, see Carolyn Abbate, *In Search of Opera* (Princeton: Princeton University Press, 2001), 194–213. Most obvious examples are the use of dance in Berlioz's *Symphonie fantastique* and (particularly the waltz and ländler) in Mahler's symphonies, on which see Stuart Feder, *Gustav Mahler: A Life in Crisis* (New Haven: Yale University Press, 2004), 229–30.

[44] Arkin and Smith, 'National Dance in the Romantic Ballet', discuss the perceived authenticity of such dances, 30ff.

[45] *Read's Characteristic National Dances* (London, 1853); cited in Arkin and Smith, 'National Dance in the Romantic Ballet', 27.

[46] Vanda de Sá Martins da Silva, 'Avondano's Lisbon Minuets: The Establishment of a Cosmopolitan Model', *Ad Parnassum* 8, no. 15 (2010), 79–92, at 87, 91. Representative national dances of course appear also in earlier periods, but assume nationalist cultural valence in the nineteenth century.

[47] Richard Taruskin, 'Nationalism', *Grove Music Online*, Oxford Music Online, Oxford University Press, www.oxfordmusiconline.com/subscriber/article/grove/music/50846.

how important 'national' (including, by modern terms, 'folk') dance was to ballet and opera of the early to mid-nineteenth century, helping to cement famous dancers' reputations and becoming a theatrical staple. So, for example, Mozart's *Don Giovanni*, Donizetti's *La favorite*, Rossini's *Guillaume Tell* and Auber's *La Muette de Portici* (to name but a few) all included national dances.[48] But the 'national' dances concerned were almost invariably seen as in some way alien, even if only from Spain, Sicily or Poland.

Dance's articulation of national identity also facilitated the exploitation of the association pointed out by Hanna (above) of dance with the (often low-class) female body, in various colourful fantasies caricaturing a plethora of exotic 'Others'. Susan Leigh Foster explains that Romantic ballet characteristically paired 'a noble if confused male lead with one of two female character types: the supernatural creature or the exotic foreigner'.[49] Both women facilitated a danced narrative:

> As some form of exotic, whether foreign or supernatural, her character could easily be construed as one predisposed to dancing. Or even better, dancing might figure as the character's very mode of being in the world. Rather than a walking, talking, gesturing person, she knew best how to float, gambol, suspend, and disappear ... Her pressing desire to dance thus facilitated an easy transition from story to spectacle and back again.[50]

But other forms of narrative reliant on spectacle – opera, most notably – also exploited this heady conjunction: nineteenth- and early twentieth-century operas on exotic themes almost invariably interpolated dances, whether necessary to the plot or not.[51] Thus (sampling of the well known and the more obscure) Meyerbeer's *L'Africaine* (1865), Verdi's *Aida* (1871), Karl Goldmark's *Die Königen von Saba* (1875), Bizet's *Carmen* (1875), Saint-Saëns's *Samson et Dalila* (1877), Jules Massenet's *Hérodiade* (1881) and *Cléopâtre* (1914) and Franco Alfano's *La leggenda di Sakùntala* (1921) all included dancing girls (and sometimes boys) as an evocation of their exotic locale. In each of these instances (as part of the tradition of grand opera), the dancers were incorporated into

---

[48] Arkin and Smith, 'National Dance in the Romantic Ballet', 13–14; Marian Smith, 'Dance and Dancers', in *The Cambridge Companion to Grand Opera*, ed. David Charlton (Cambridge: Cambridge University Press, 2003), 93–106, at 97–8.

[49] Susan Leigh Foster, 'The Ballerina's Phallic Pointe', in *Corporealities*, ed. Susan Leigh Foster (New York: Routledge, 1996), 1–24, at 4.

[50] Foster, 'The Ballerina's Phallic Pointe', 4.

[51] In Parisian grand opera, they were a theatrical requirement; Wagner complained in 1861: 'Opera itself had there become a mere excuse for Ballet'; 'A Report on the Production of *Tannhäuser* in Paris', in *Prose Works*, ed. and trans. W. A. Ellis, vol. 3, The Theatre (London: Kegan Paul, Trench, Trübner & Co. Ltd., second impression, 1907), 351.

scenes of grand spectacle – processions, temple scenes, banquets and the like – often accompanying themselves on appropriately 'Oriental' instruments, whether cymbals, harps or castanets, to emphasize their 'national' credentials. Such dances often served (Marian Smith suggests), as 'extension[s] of the elaborate *mise-en-scène*'.[52]

Yet dance scenes figured in these operas not simply to provide *couleur locale*; as Foster's analysis suggests, the exotic dancing woman (whether non-European or supernatural) was also an irresistible erotic spectacle. Indeed, in 1848, dance theorist August Bournonville characterized dance families along broad racial-regional types. The clear distinction between a rational, 'civilized' and overtly masculine central and eastern Europe, and a physical and feminized 'south' makes Bournonville worth quoting at length:

The native or so called national dances with which we are familiar may be divided into three types: the chaste, the voluptuous, and the martial. Among the first ought to be classed the earlier Italian, Spanish, and French dances which, like the Nordic, were performed to the accompaniment of romances, heroic poems, and elegies. They moved quite slowly and demanded great dignity on the part of both the man and woman. These dances were those of civilized nations ... I would call them *classical*. The second kind stems from Hindustan, where female dancers are raised in temples ... from them come the Egyptian *almées*, the Moorish and later Spanish and Italian dances whose central motif is the ecstasy of love and whose performance is, for the most part, left to women. This is the *Indian* genre. Lastly, those dances wherein the masculine grace and strength are particularly displayed, and where the female dancer is more subordinate, have their origins in northern Asia and are known throughout Russia, Poland, Hungary, and Bohemia, to Germany and the entire north, by the names of polska and waltz ... These are the *Slavic* dances.[53]

Bournonville reflected wider thinking: his observation that the 'Indian' dances were left mostly to women underlines a similar association with Orientalist music. For example, Paul Robinson notes that all *Aida*'s conventional 'exotic music' is linked to women, 'to the point that the antithesis between exotic and non-exotic music in *Aida* comes to seem a code as much for gender difference as for ethnic difference'.[54] Indeed, the connection of chromatic or highly ornamental music with the exotic seems to reflect a long-standing link with female seductiveness.[55]

---

[52] Smith, 'Dance and Dancers', 101.

[53] August Bournonville, *My Theatre Life*, trans. Patricia N. McAndrew; cited in Arkin and Smith, 'National Dance in the Romantic Ballet', 36–7.

[54] Paul Robinson; 'Is *Aida* an Orientalist Opera?' *Cambridge Opera Journal* 5 (1993), 133–40, at 138.

[55] See Thomas Ravenscroft, *A Briefe Discourse of the True (but Neglected) Use of Charact'ring the Degrees* [...] (London: Printed by Edw: Allde for Tho. Adams, 1614), sig. A3v., and

Not surprisingly, many of the most popular operas of the period were those exploring the 'voluptuous' regions' dangerous fascinations, in both music and dance. To give one well-known example, Saint-Saëns's *Samson et Dalila* relies on an antagonistic binary between the God-fearing Hebrew (European) male and the God-hating Philistine woman, and seems specifically to contrast the male voice in the Hebrew presence onstage (at the beginning of Act 1) with the female bodies of the Philistine dancers who appear with Dalila.[56] The dancers' sensuality is emphasized in the stage direction for the Act 1 'Danse des prêtresses de Dagon', which describes 'leurs poses et ... leurs gestes voluptueux'. A similar sensuality is implied in the 'Bienentanz der Almeen' (Almeen bee's dance) from Goldmark's *Die Königen von Saba* – stolen from the infamous 'Pas de l'abeille' (bee dance) in the ballet *La Péri* (1843), and carefully narrated in the scenic description: a girl 'wrapped in a veil which forms part of her upper clothing' starts to dance around a bee, half playfully, half fearfully, stripping off her veil when the bee crawls into her clothing (her fear undoubtedly intended to add to the unwitting striptease's titillation). Salome's 'Dance of the Seven Veils', performed for her stepfather Herod at the climax of Richard Stauss's opera, is one logical culmination of such scenes; Elektra's *Totentanz*, at the end of another eponymous Strauss opera, is another.

As Thomas Grey investigates in this volume, so accepted was dance's association with the representation of female eroticism that even Richard Wagner, resistant as he was to the inclusion of a ballet in *Tannhäuser* on its Paris premiere, waxed lyrical about dance's role in the earlier Venusberg scene:

I could not possibly disturb the course of just this second act by a ballet, which must here be senseless from every point of view; while on the other hand I thought the first act, at the voluptuous court of Venus, would afford the most apposite occasion for a choreographic scene of amplest meaning, since I myself had not deemed [it] possible to dispense with dance in my first arrangement of that scene. Indeed I was quite charmed with the idea of strengthening an undoubtedly weak point in my earlier score, and I drafted an exhaustive plan for raising this scene in the Venusberg to one of great importance.[57]

William Prynne, *Histrio-mastix* (London: E. A. and W. I. for Michael Sparke, 1633), 275, for this association; both cited in Amanda Eubanks Winkler, 'From Whore to Stuart Ally: Musical Venuses on the Early Modern English Stage', in *Musical Voices of Early Modern Women: Many-Headed Melodies*, ed. Thomasin La May (Aldershot: Ashgate, 2005), 171–85, at 174.

[56] Ralph P. Locke, 'Constructing the Oriental "Other": Saint-Saëns's *Samson et Dalila*', *Cambridge Opera Journal* 3 (1991), 261–302, at 271.

[57] Wagner, 'A Report on ... *Tannhäuser*', III: 351–2.

Even where scenic directions do not explicitly point to an erotic aspect, costume designs (and, no doubt, the highly sexualized idea of the *danseuse*) would often have suggested this quality.[58] Thus, in the early stages of the 'national' dance fashion, one commentator ogled the ballerina Fanny Elssler in the *cachucha* that helped make her famous (noting that his fellows did likewise), not only for 'Those swayings of the hips ... those provocative gestures', but also for 'that seductive music, those castañets, that unfamiliar costume, that short skirt, that half-opening bodice'.[59] Similarly, the French sisters Lise and Félicité Noblet, dancing 'El Jaleo de Jerez', excited anticipation by appearing in 'the whole fantastic costume of Dolores Serral' (a famed Spanish dancer), and then 'danced the most daring and brazen *pas* ever to have been seen at the Opéra ... swaying hips, spines arching back, arms and legs thrown into the air, the most provocatively voluptuous movements, a hot-blooded fury, and a diabolical attack'.[60] In similar vein, the illustrations for both the original 1871 Cairo production of *Aida* and the 1880 Paris staging show that suggestively transparent (and highly impractical) clothing was part of the visualization of such scenes (even if photographs of the costumes prove their realization to be much more conventional).[61] Such was the strength of the association between irresistible eroticism and the female dancer that in operas such as *Samson et Dalila*, Bizet's *Carmen*, Strauss's *Salome* and Berg's *Lulu* this irresistibility was itself thematized.

Dance as Topic

As the foregoing discussion suggests, in the context of the fascination with uncanny automata or the erotic/exotic female, there was a transformation in the way in which 'art' music represented dance: where previously (with the possible exception of the theatre[62]) 'art' music had tended to obscure dance's embodied origins by complicating musical lines and rhythms, now

---

[58] Prostitution was an accepted *corps de ballet* sideline at the Paris Opéra, largely because their pay was derisory; Smith, 'Dance and Dancers', 106.

[59] Smith, 'Dance and Dancers', 106; Lisa Arkin, 'The Context of Exoticism in Fanny Elssler's *Cachucha*', *Dance Chronicle* 17, no. 3 (1994), 303–25.

[60] Arkin and Smith, 'National Dance in the Romantic Ballet', 15–16.

[61] Knud Arne Jürgensen, *The Verdi Ballets* (Parma: Istituto Nazionale di Studi Verdiani, 1995), plates 50–1, 68–9, 71–7.

[62] Wendy Heller, 'Dancing Desire on the Venetian Stage', *Cambridge Opera Journal* 15 (2003), 281–95, at 291, points out that 'libidinous creatures' are characterized by music that 'values rhythm and movement above other sorts of expression'.

that embodied-ness was frequently highlighted (albeit in diverse musical ways) through emphasis on the physicality of the dance in the structures of the music. Certainly, when interest in 'national' (exotic) dance first became fashionable, one reason cited was the greater opportunity for physical expression.[63] And the first clear manifestation of Orientalism in music, through the 'Turkish' march, similarly emphasized physicality, via the simplicity of a combined bass tattoo on a tonic pedal and a melodic line that also emphasized the tonic triad.[64]

The physicality of dance was given expression in nineteenth-century 'art' music in various ways. One approach derived from the pantomimic conventions of the mid-eighteenth-century *ballet d'action*, which transformed (via Jean Jacques Rousseau and others) into the nineteenth-century *ballet-pantomime*.[65] *Ballet-pantomime*'s musical gestures, conveyed through a range of mimetic conventions (underpinned by spatial and kinetic metaphor), had a significant impact on dance's representation in musical terms, outside the theatre as well as in – allowing it even some sense of rationality.[66] For example, Carl Maria von Weber's famous *Aufforderung zum Tanz* (Invitation to the Dance, op. 65, 1819) prefaces its rondo concert waltz with a musical mimic representation of a young couple negotiating the opening to their dance. Yet while singing and mute characters sometimes 'conversed' in a few early grand operas, relying on their shared language of musical gesture, later opera-ballets, as Smith points out, 'tended to cast ballet dancers as other-worldly spirits, or birds, or shades; as creatures incapable of and uninterested in language'.[67]

Taking up balletic conventions, dancers in operas on 'exotic' themes also used pantomimic gesture to help advance the action or convey a message.[68] But here, pantomime may have contributed not to a sense

---

[63] See *Histoire chronologique, philosophique et morale du Canan*; cited in Arkin and Smith, 'National Dance in the Romantic Ballet', 18. Arkin and Smith note that the physical contrast such dances provided to the traditional ballet *pas* and its pantomimic passages must have added to their attractions in a theatrical context (28–30).

[64] Derek Scott, 'Orientalism and Musical Style', *The Musical Quarterly* 82, no. 2 (1998), 309–35, at 312.

[65] Smith, 'Dance and Dancers', 93.

[66] Pantomime may have lent an aesthetic air to the viewing of female bodies, seen as simulacra of Greek statues; Maribeth Clark, 'Bodies at the Opéra: the Hermaphrodite in the Dance Criticism of Théophile Gautier', in *Reading Critics Reading: Opera and Ballet Criticism in France from the Revolution to 1848*, ed. Roger Parker and Mary Ann Smart (Oxford: Oxford University Press, 2001), 237–53.

[67] Smith, 'Dance and Dancers', 102, 103.

[68] French dancer-choreographer-teacher Jules Perrot was influential in this regard; see Arkin and Smith, 'National Dance in the Romantic Ballet', 44–5.

of the rationality of dance, but rather to the distinction between the physical expressivity of the dancers and the verbal authority of the singers. Pantomimic (or figurative) dance seems to have been particularly associated with 'Eastern' dancers: Verdi's 'Danza sacra delle sacerdotesse' (Sacred Dance of the Priestesses) in the consecration scene (Act 1) of *Aida* was intended to be of this figurative type; so, too, was Salome's dance in Strauss's opera, for which Strauss designed 'menacing steps or lively paces' to illustrate different moments in the music – mimic gesture that was without linguistic signification.[69] In Alfano's *Sakùntala*, stage directions indicate that the female dancers who perform for the king at the opening of Act 3, 'advancing from within the scene, will accompany the three essential movements of the "Dance of the Bee"'.[70] The 'Dance of the Bee' presumably expressed the text of the accompanying chorus, which presented the 'restless bee, wandering bee' as a metaphor for the lustful king who 'through new desire always seek[s] new honey', and which was itself characterized as 'gloomy, solemn, insidious – intermixed with languid and poignant accents', and was set to music that prominently thematized that well-known Orientalist trope, the interval of the augmented second.[71]

As a Rousseauian optimism about dance's ability to communicate via pantomime soon faded, and (Smith's observation suggests) such gestures became another means of differentiating the carnality of the female dancer from the rational and verbally competent (male) singer, interest in representing dance's embodiment in 'art' music also took other guises. Stripping dance back to its essentials and foregrounding rather than masking dance elements – rhythm, in particular – could help highlight associations of class or physicality. A well-known example is the waltz in Weber's *Der Freischütz* (1821). Music critic A. B. Marx used it to illustrate the 'genuine waltz motive' because of its transparency as a dance:

It is a fact that this rustic dance contents itself with ... the unaltered primitive material of the three-step motive, without elaborating clear groupings for the complete motion of twice three steps, as would be appropriate in a nobler, more perfect conception of the waltz. Apart from this, it should be noted [that] in [*Der Freischütz*] auxiliary notes are placed before the merely chordal ones in

---

[69] Jürgensen, *The Verdi Ballets*, 117–20; Hutcheon and Hutcheon, 'Staging the Female Body', 215–6.

[70] 'avanzando dall'interno accompagneranno i tre momenti essenziali della "Danza dell' Ape"'.

[71] 'dapprima cupo, grave, insidioso – frammezzato da accenti languidi e pungenti – salirà man mano di tono, fino a raggiungere una espressione di sferzante ironia'.

order to bring out the beginning [of the bar] and that every other melodic, harmonic or rhythmic accentuation serves the same end. The accompaniment for these essential elements should be as simple and as clear in marking the beat as possible.[72]

Marx's contrast between the 'unaltered primitive material' of rustic dance and the 'elaborations' of a 'nobler, more perfect conception of the waltz' strongly suggests that the dance's musical simplicity was a correlate of its lowly origins in Marx's – and presumably Weber's and his audiences' – minds (as it had been for the earlier dance writers, Cornazano and Magri, cited above).

Although Marx felt that Weber's stylization of the waltz in *Der Freischütz* was predicated on class differentiation, highlighting the simple physicality of the dance clearly had strong gender associations. Again, what underpinned this connection in the nineteenth century was the assumption that in women, as in the exotic 'Other' and the lower classes, physical impulse dominated rationality. This entrenched belief manifested itself in medicalized concern for female dancers, even from advocates of dance such as Donald Walker who, writing *Exercise for Ladies* in 1836, opined that women should 'abandon waltzing, on account of its causing too violent emotions or an agitation which produces vertigo and nervous symptoms. [The waltz's] rapid turnings, the clasping of the dancers, their exciting contact, and too quick and too long continued succession of lively and agreeable emotions [was likely to damage] women of an irritable constitution.'[73] Similar complaints were expressed by other social commentators in dance manuals, newspapers and novels of the period.[74]

---

[72] Adolph Bernhard Marx, *Die Lehre von der musikalishen Komposition*, vol. 2 (Leipzig: Breitkopf und Härtel, 1842), 59–60, cited in Sevin H. Yaraman, *Revolving Embrace: The Waltz as Sex, Steps, and Sound* (Hillsdale, NY: Pendragon Press, 2002), 20: 'Allein dieser bäurische Tanz begnügt sich mit den ersten, gleichsam noch rohen Stoffe, dem Motiv von drei Schritten, ohne daraus deutlichere Klauseln für die vollendete Bewegung von zweimal drei Schritten zu bilden, wie es einer vollkommern und edelern Auffassung des Tanzes ziemen würde. Abgesehen hiervon sehen wir in obigen Sätzen Hülftöne in der Melodie den blossen Akkordtönen vorgesetzt, um den Autritt hervorzuheben; jede andre melodische, harmonishe, rhythmische Schärfung, auch allenfalls aus die Aushülfe eines *forzato*, eines vorschlagenden Basse u.s.w. dient zu gleichem Zwecke. Diesem wesentlichen Inhalte nun gesellt sich die Begleitung möglichst einfach und taktbezeichnend.'

[73] Donald Walker, *Exercise for Ladies: Calculated to Preserve and Improve Beauty* (London: Thomas Hurst, 1836).

[74] See, e.g., Charles Burney, 'Waltz', in *Rees's Cyclopaedia* (London, 1819); Mme. Celnart, *The Gentleman and Lady's Book of Politeness* (Boston, 1833); and Anon., *The Illustrated Manners Book* (New York, 1855); Sevin H. Yaraman, *Revolving Embrace*; Elizabeth Aldrich, 'Social Dancing in Schubert's World', in *Schubert's Vienna*, ed. Raymond Erickson (New Haven and London: Yale University Press, 1997), 119–40.

The anarchic dangers of female dance – to the woman herself, as much as to society in general – are highlighted in a range of operas and ballets, from *Giselle* to *Wozzeck*, through an emphasis on the overpowering, narcotic effects of rhythm. Strauss's *Salome* and *Elektra* are particularly potent examples. Elektra's *Totentanz*, a pounding waltz, forms the climax of the opera, as music (the orchestra) triumphs over language – music which Elektra claims emanates from herself ('Ob ich die Musik nicht höre? Sie kommt doch aus mir' ('Do I not hear music? It is coming from me')). The inherent femininity of the insistent waltz has already been asserted in *Elektra*'s association of the dance not only with Elektra, in her anticipation of revenge (scene two), but also with Elektra's sister Chrysothemis, when she sings of her desire for 'a woman's lot', marriage and childbearing (scene 3), and when Elektra herself evokes such a hopeful vision for her sister (scene 5). It is telling of twentieth-century attitudes to dance in general, as well as to dance in *Elektra*, that musicologist Derek Puffett suggested in 1989 that, as one of the 'longest and most powerful' of Strauss's many waltzes, the *Totentanz* recalls Adorno's criticism that Strauss 'wrote display music on a worldwide scale – World's Fair Music'.[75]

The (gendered) essentialization of dance through emphasis on its rhythmic aspect lent itself especially to theatrical representations of national dances (including exotic dances), as these were often conditioned by a nominal interest in 'authenticity'. Because this 'authenticity', of course, was always determined by overarching Orientalist cultural narratives, such apparently distinctive local touches (in *Aida* or in *Carmen*, for example) were selected according to the imperative to distinguish the exotic 'Other' from the European norm. In pursuit of this Orientalist 'authentic', emphasis on rhythm was particularly important in works such as *Aida*.[76] Although musicologist Ralph P. Locke has recently taken to task students of *Aida* for oversimplifying the musical representation of Egyptian aspects of the plot (particularly the ballets), it is easy to see why these moments attract attention, for they also attracted the attention of historical spectators: the critic Filippo Filippi observed at the opera's premiere that 'the

---

[75] Derrick Puffett, *Richard Strauss: 'Elektra'* (Cambridge: Cambridge University Press, 1989), 37, 158.

[76] For similar observations on the idea of 'Spain' in nineteenth-century France, see James Parakilas, 'How Spain Got a Soul', in *The Exotic in Western Music*, ed. Jonathan Bellman (Boston: Northeastern University Press, 1997), 137–93, at 143.

Oriental hues of the dances' were generally admired, but he expressed particular interest in the dances' 'rhythmic motives', which 'are still heard today here [in Egypt] in the traditional manner'.[77] Similarly, rhythmic ostinati in, for example, the overture to Etienne-Nicolas Méhul's *Les deux aveugles de Tolède* (1806) or Chopin's A minor Bolero (1834) served to emphasize the 'Otherness' of the Spanish dance. As James Parakilas points out, Méhul's representation of the bolero rhythm also mimics guitar strumming in its repeated chords, an effect that produces a revolutionary 'movement with no line' that in itself represents the exoticist cliché of combined 'energy and stasis'.[78] Such characterization might well be traced back to the earliest instances of musical Orientalism in which, as noted above, 'Turkish' music was represented through the combination of an energetic bass iteration of the march rhythm and the harmonic sterility of tonic emphasis in both the bass and a melodic line centred on the tonic triad.

This seemingly paradoxical admixture of rhythmic energy and melodic or harmonic stasis can be understood as an ideological construction – a musical representation of the sensual irrationality and unchanging nature of the 'Other' as imagined by Europeans – and characterized stagings of the Orient more generally. *Aida*, for example, is replete with this sort of contrast: at the close of Act 1, the simultaneous representation of Egyptian religious belief in the sinuous vocal and physical gestures of the dancing priestesses and in the modal choral singing of the male priests emphasizes the ideological instability of this society, both theologically rigid and sensually lax.[79] Dance and Eastern eroticism are again associated at the beginning of the next act, when, as Locke has pointed out, Amneris's swooning melismatic vocal line ('Ah! Vieni, amor mio, m'inebria, fammi beato il cor' ('Ah! Come my love, bring madness and blessed peace to my heart')) is both framed by the accompanying slave dances as an outpouring of desire and is stimulated by them.[80] In this sense, musical representation of dance played into Orientalist fantasies of the irrational, feminized 'Other', implicitly in need of the order and stability offered by European hierarchies of melody and harmony.

---

[77] Filippo Filippi, review in *La perseveranza*, 13 January 1872; cited in Ralph Locke, 'Beyond the Exotic: How "Eastern" Is *Aida*?' *Cambridge Opera Journal* 17 (2005), 105–39, at 105.
[78] Parakilas, 'How Spain Got a Soul', 143–4.
[79] On the 'ancient' choral style of the priests' choruses as a critique of imperialist authoritarianism, see Locke, 'Beyond the Exotic', 113, 116.
[80] Locke, 'Beyond the Exotic', 122.

This juxtaposition of stasis and energy was frequently articulated not only in general narrative structure, but also through dance itself, particularly in representations of Egypt and the 'Near East' in operas of the late nineteenth and early twentieth centuries, as examples from *Aida* (1871), Massenet's *Cléopatre* (1914) and Strauss's *Salome* might demonstrate. Verdi's annotations to the priestesses' 'Danza sacra' in *Aida* (for the 1872 Milan production) show that 'immobilità' (immobility) was required at certain points, an 'immobilità coreografica' (choreographic immobility) that had also characterized the dances in a previous 'Egyptian' ballet (*Le figlie di Chèrope*) by *Aida*'s choreographer, Hyppolyte Monplaisir.[81] When dancing, however, the priestesses played finger cymbals to accentuate their steps.[82] Massenet's *Cléopatre* introduces the queen to Marcus Antonius at the beginning of Act 1 with a similar use of immobility, here designed to be titillating: '*Cléopatre, dans une tunique transparente qui laisse deviner les splendeurs de son corps, est là, immobile au milieu de ses suivantes*' (Cleopatra, in a transparent tunic which reveals the splendours of her body, is there, motionless in the midst of her followers).[83] Cleopatra's opening address, 'Je suis venue', is also remarkable for its melodic and harmonic stasis, the presiding monotone thrown into relief by a sinuous ascending and descending scale. Despite Cleopatra's own immobility, the music that accompanies the first mention of her and the arrival of the (female) Egyptian slaves (presaging Cleopatra's appearance) adopts a triple metre suggestive of dance. As for Strauss's opera, Salome's dance music swerves between the wild and the slow and seductive, with waltz music intermixed with 'Oriental' effects (including castanets) and Salome's dancing (at least in Strauss's choreographic outline) matched to the music – yet often characterized by what Linda and Michael Hutcheon describe as 'almost static swaying'.[84] In outlining his aspiration for the dance, Strauss drew connections between immobility and Orientalism, asserting that 'Salome, being a chaste virgin and an oriental princess, must be played with the simplest and most restrained of gestures'.[85]

An emphasis on rhythm in operatic dance was nothing unusual, of course, as it helped to provide mimetic underpinning to the performance of dance onstage – as in *Aida*'s dancing priestesses. Yet, as the previous discussion indicates, highlighting the rhythms of exotic dance also foregrounded its embodiment in ideological terms, providing, like the use of

---

[81] Jürgensen, *The Verdi Ballets*, 118–19.   [82] Jürgensen, *The Verdi Ballets*, 120.
[83] Similarly, Cleopatra's conquest over Mark Antony later in the scene is achieved '*sans un geste*'.
[84] Hutcheon and Hutcheon, 'Staging the Female Body', 285.
[85] Strauss, 'Reminiscences', 151, cited in Hutcheon and Hutcheon, 'Staging the Female Body', 216.

musical and physical stasis, a concomitant opposition of the physical to the rational and the intellectual. Given such exoticist connotations, it is hardly surprising that the musical rhythms seem to encourage the physical entrainment of the dancers. Nonetheless, given those same, politically unsavoury connotations, it is somewhat surprising that modern choreographies seem to take up the invitation to bodily entrainment with such gusto. For example, the famous 'Bacchanale' in Act 3 of *Samson et Dalila* underpins the Philistines' decision to 'prolongeons la fête' of debauchery – as Locke puts it, 'urged on by hypnotic rhythms in the castanets, timpani and low strings'.[86] It is notable that productions of the opera often exploit the rhythmic tattoos as they are introduced in the 'Bacchanale' for choreographic mimicry.[87] In *Aida*'s Act 2 'Ballabile', the Egyptian celebration descends from the majesty of the triumphal march into a rapid, excitable and rhythmically unstable ballet; again, rhythmic mimicry of the orchestral writing is a notable feature of modern choreographies.[88] Bizet's Carmen is characterized by dance from the first: as Susan McClary notes, since Don José sums her up by invoking her 'swaying hips', it is to be expected that her 'Habañera' and 'Seguidilla' should 'routinely inspire choreographers to demand sensual hip motion' from their Carmens.[89] The frequent turns to waltz material in Salome's dance have also been exploited in productions of Strauss's opera, contributing to the sensualization of performances of the dance in ways that shocked critics and even Strauss himself.[90]

If modern choreographers willingly (and perhaps naively) embrace the opportunities offered by the rhythmicized representation of the 'Other' in order to enliven their stage representations, scholarly unease at the representation of dance and dance music in 'art' music suggests continuity with the long-lived suspicion of both dance and the feminized, 'Othered' body. In

---

[86] Locke, 'Constructing the Oriental "Other"', 266.
[87] See, e.g., the 1981–2 San Francisco Opera production, choreography by Margo Sappington (Art Haus Musik, 100 202, 1981), second kettledrum tattoo; the 1998 Metropolitan Opera production, choreography by Graeme Murphy (Deutsche Gramaphon, 00440 073 0599, 1998), at various points, including the second kettledrum tattoo, with actions including simulated sexual pelvic thrusts.
[88] For example, the 2009 Taormina production at the Teatro Antico, under the direction of Fabio Mastrangelo (choreography, Rita Colosi), which was danced exclusively by women, some topless. The more classical Rome 1993 (Zeffirelli) and Metropolitan Opera (Sonja Frisell) productions (designed in 1988 and revived regularly since then) also embody the shifts in musical rhythm.
[89] Susan McClary, *Georges Bizet: 'Carmen'* (Cambridge: Cambridge University Press, 1992), 55.
[90] The 2008 Covent Garden production (choreographed by Andrew George) uses the waltz tellingly, reflecting societal anxiety about the dance's effects in the nineteenth century, as the near-delirious Salome swoons around the dance floor in the incestuous clutches of her stepfather, Herod.

language strikingly reminiscent of Puffett's observation (following Adorno) that Elektra's *Totentanz* was 'World's Fair Music', Robin Holloway has suggested that the culmination of Salome's dance in a thirty-two-bar waltz represents 'sustained, masterly, deeply-thrilling kitsch [which] here comes into its own as the absolutely right level and intonation for this particular situation in this particular work'.[91] As Holloway's observation hints, the disquiet engendered by this essentialization of dance as an emanation of the body (through rhythm, gesture and Orientalism) expressed itself in the narratives surrounding those dances as well: from Victor Hugo's *Les orientales* (1829) and Hans Christian Anderson's *The Red Shoes* (1845) to *Elektra, Salome* and even *Le sacre du printemps*, male anxiety about the bacchanalian powers of the *danseuse* was fulfilled in stories of wayward women who danced themselves to death. The increased interest in depicting the physicality of dance in music and on the stage thus betrayed a fear of the 'Other' (erotic Woman included, of course), which was partly managed by narratives that reasserted the moral and physical subjugation of that 'Otherness'.

---

[91] Robin Holloway, '*Salome*: Art or Kitsch?', in *On Music: Essays and Diversions 1963–2003* (Cambridge: Cambridge University Press, 2003), 112.

3 | Thinking on Our Feet: A Somatic Enquiry into a Haydn Minuet

JOSEPH FORT

On 25 November 1792, over two thousand people filed into the Hofburg Redoutensäle in Vienna, the opulent dance hall of the principal Habsburg residence. The occasion was a charity ball for the new Gesellschaft bildender Künstler (the Artists' Society), founded in 1788 to provide pensions for aging artists. The guest list included the Habsburg Archduchesses Marie Anna and Marie Clementina, as well as Princess Maria Anna Esterhazy; even the Emperor was expected, but was kept away by illness. Noted patrons of the arts were also present, such as Count Fries, Countess Würbna and Baron Waldstätten; and the city's most celebrated artists turned out, too, including the painter and frescoer Franz Anton Maulbertsch, the poet Franz Anton Schrämbl and the composer Franz Joseph Haydn. In total, some 2181 tickets were sold for this ball at two Gulden apiece: 509 were bought in batches by subscribers, listed by name on a document retained by the Gesellschaft; the remainder were bought individually and anonymously by members of the public.[1] This public, along with the subscribers and notable invitees, were to enjoy music for the evening's dancing – twelve minuets and twelve *Deutsche Tänze* – all composed by Haydn, at the Gesellschaft's request: two *Wiener Zeitung* advertisements proclaimed in advance that 'for the minuets and *Deutsche Tänze* the famous Kapellmeister Herr Joseph Haiden has crafted original music out of love for his artistic kinsfolk and for the benefit of our institution'.[2]

There was nothing particularly remarkable about this event: balls formed a staple part of cultural life in late eighteenth-century Vienna. Particularly during the Carnival season (*Fasching*), the Viennese were gripped by dancing.[3] As writer and actor Johann Friedel stated boldly in

---

[1] This ticket list is held in the Wiener Stadt- und Landesarchiv, under folder classification A1/5 – Pensionsgesellschaft des Vereines bildender Künstler in Wien – Aufzeichnungen über die Ausgegebenen Redoute Billets 1792–1827.

[2] 'Der berühmte Kapellmeister Herr Joseph Haiden, zu den Menueten und deutschen Tänzen aus Liebe zur Kunstverwantschaft und zum Besten des Institutes eine originelle Musik verfertigt.' *Wiener Zeitung*, 14 November 1792, 3080; repeated 21 November 1792, 3144–5.

[3] *Fasching* lasted from Epiphany until the beginning of Lent.

1784, 'better not to live than not to dance'; another writer, Johann Pezzl, echoed the idea in 1786, claiming that during the Carnival 'the chief pursuit is the dance and whatever belongs to it and is connected with it'. Indeed, by the 1780s, the Austrian capital seemed 'dancing mad', to quote the Irish tenor Michael Kelly.[4] The dance hall formed a focal point of Viennese society: much of the city's social and cultural life revolved around this institution.

As primary sources reveal, the 1770s had witnessed the opening up of Vienna's ballrooms to anyone who could afford admission. New Habsburg legislation decreed that 'any person, regardless of class, is to be admitted to these balls in the Redoutensaal'.[5] No longer was access restricted solely to the nobility: the emergent bourgeoisie could now participate in public balls.[6] These changing demographics entailed changes to contemporary dance practice: old dance types were retained, but adapted for their new participants. In the case of the minuet, the focus of this chapter, the dance was still performed, but no longer by only one couple at a time, with the rest of the assembly looking on; now, numerous couples danced simultaneously, normally lined up in rows. Perhaps because of these innovations, not to mention the seeming democratization of dance, Vienna saw an influx of dancing masters in the final decades of the century, come to satisfy a growing public demand for their services, prompting the popular satirist Joseph Richter to remark that dancing masters 'give instruction to the kitchen workers in the morning and to the noble ladies in the afternoon'.[7] In her study of the *Ländler*, the Austrian scholar Reingard Witzmann recognizes that 'even at the turn of the century, the minuet was taught alongside the *Deutsche Tänze* in the dance schools, which were attended by all classes'.[8] The minuet was no longer the sole preserve of

---

[4] 'Ja lieber nicht leben, als nicht tanzen.' Johann Friedel, *Galanterien Wiens: Auf einer Reise gesammelt, und in Briefen geschildert* (1784), 145; Historisches Museum der Stadt, Wien, 'Die Hauptbeschäftigung ist der Tanz und was dazugehört und damit verbunden ist', in *Fasching in Wien: der Wiener Walzer 1750-1850* (Vienna: Historischen Museum der Stadt Wien, 1979), 5; Michael Kelly and Roger Fiske, *Reminiscences* (Oxford: Oxford University Press, 1975), 102.

[5] 'Werden zwar zu diesen Bällen in dem Redoutensaal: jede Person ohne Unterschied des Standes.' 'Ballordnung', *Wienerisches Diarium* 103 (Vienna, 1772), 17–18.

[6] See Joonas Korhonen, 'Urban Social Space and the Development of Public Dance Hall Culture in Vienna, 1780-1814', *Urban History* 40, no. 4 (2013), 606–24.

[7] 'in der Früh den Kuchelmenschern und am Nachmittag der gnädigen Frau Unterricht'. Gerhard Tanzer, *Spectacle müssen seyn: die Freizeit der Wiener im 18. Jahrhundert* (Vienna: Böhlau, 1992), 233.

[8] 'Auch um die Jahrhundertwende wird das Menuett neben dem Deutschen in den Tanzschulen gelehrt, die von allen Ständen besucht warden.' Reingard Witzmann, *Der Ländler in Wien: ein Beitrag zur Entwicklungsgeschichte des Wiener Walzers bis in die Zeit des Wiener Kongresses* (Vienna: Arbeitsstelle für den Volkskundeatlas in Österreich, 1976), 81.

the nobility; other social classes could learn and perform this dance, which was at the heart of Vienna's dance culture in the late eighteenth century.[9]

This chapter constitutes an attempt to rehabilitate a dancer's perspective on the minuet. More specifically, I offer a somatic enquiry into a short musical passage from one of the minuets danced at the Hofburg on 25 November 1792: Haydn's Minuet in D major, Hob. IX/11, no. 1, bars 1–24. Putting myself in the shoes of an attendee at this ball, I dance a portion of the minuet and ask how my somatic knowledge and kinaesthetic undertaking of the dance affects and informs my experience of Haydn's music. I also consider the converse relationship: how my sonic experience of the music impacts my kinaesthetic experience of the dance. Let us remember: an integral feature of social life in late eighteenth-century Vienna, the steps and music of the minuet were familiar to the nobility and much of the middle class. Putting some critical pressure on this idea, we might say that these eighteenth-century bodies *contained the minuet*; 'minuet', to them, meant a set of defined bodily movements, as much as any characteristic musical patterning or structure. With two centuries of sedentary, stationary listening behind us, present-day listeners tend to forget that, for Haydn's audiences, the minuet must have summoned not just an array of aural and social connotations, but also intense somatic, kinaesthetic feelings and associations. These audiences would not have considered the music of the minuet apart from its associated dance, or the dance apart from its music. Even when they attended a musical concert, rather than a social ball, they did so in bodies engrained with the dance of the minuet, and they would not simply forget or deactivate their somatic knowledge when listening to concert minuets.[10] Dance and music were intrinsically tied together, inconceivable without one another.

---

[9] The question of just who danced the minuet has previously been the subject of some debate. Contrast the recent claim of David Wyn Jones that 'by the middle of the [eighteenth] century, it was the most common social dance in Austria, at all levels of society' with Melanie Lowe's claim that the minuet belonged solely to the nobility, and that its 'courtly status and association with nobility was affirmed at every public ball by the effective exclusion of all but those dancers'. In contrast, the late eighteenth-century German-language dance treatises and contemporaneous descriptions of balls, which I explore in my dissertation, all attest to the group dancing of the minuet. See David Wyn Jones and Otto Biba, *Haydn* (Oxford: Oxford University Press, 2002), 234; Melanie Lowe, *Pleasure and Meaning in the Classical Symphony* (Bloomington and Indianapolis: Indiana University Press, 2007), 109; and Joseph Fort, 'Incorporating Haydn's Minuets: Towards a Somatic Theory of Music', PhD diss., Harvard University (2015).

[10] See Gretchen Wheelock, *Haydn's Ingenious Jesting with Art: Contexts of Musical Wit and Humor* (New York: Schirmer, 1992), 56, for an account of a 1770s listener judging a keyboard minuet in relation to the dance steps.

My efforts in this chapter – which are both practical-empirical and conceptual-reflexive – are directed towards two principal goals. The first is to explore whether knowing how to dance the minuet can sensitize a listener towards any facets of minuet composition; in other words, whether experiencing this music as a dancer can reveal and highlight musical features that would otherwise go unnoticed. The second goal is to consider the somatic nature of musical experience more generally, thus taking seriously composer David Lidov's 1987 assertion that 'music is significant only if we identify perceived sonorous motion with somatic experience'.[11] Theorizing a dancer's relationship with musical sounds may also shed light on other forms of listening experience.

This line of enquiry has precedents in Haydn scholarship. Musicologists Gretchen Wheelock and Danuta Mirka both argue that a somatic understanding of the entire minuet genre, they maintain, was defined by the danced minuet, such that 'patterns of steps and gestures guided expectations of eighteenth-century listeners not only in danced but also in heard minuets'.[12] Both writers also assert the power of engrained somatic knowledge to heighten one's musical interpretation. Wheelock asserts that 'when expectations are grounded as habits and tendencies in patterned motions and gestures, discontinuities of motion and disturbances in metric and phrase structures can have a visceral impact'.[13] Mirka suggests some such kinaesthetic examples, where 'a missing beat in a minuet feels like stepping into a hole', and where 'a surprisingly strong event falling on a weak beat feels like stumbling against a stone'.[14] In a similar manner, Lawrence Zbikowski analyses the finale of Haydn's op. 76, no. 4 as a disrupted bourrée, noting how the movement starts by exhibiting the characteristic rhythms of this dance, and then subverts them.[15]

For these writers, dance behaves or functions in a certain way: it establishes a set of expectations, which Haydn then subverts in his compositions.[16] Wheelock explicitly equates artfulness with deviation,

---

[11] David Lidov, 'Mind and Body in Music', *Semiotica* 66, nos. 1-3 (1987), 70.

[12] Danuta Mirka, *Metric Manipulations in Haydn and Mozart: Chamber Music for Strings, 1787-1791* (Oxford: Oxford University Press, 2009), 297.

[13] Wheelock, *Haydn's Ingenious Jesting*, 89.   [14] Mirka, *Metric Manipulations*, 297.

[15] Lawrence M. Zbikowski, 'Dance Topoi, Sonic Analogues and Musical Grammar: Communicating with Music in the Eighteenth Century', in *Communication in Eighteenth-Century Music*, ed. Danuta Mirka and Kofi Agawu (Cambridge: Cambridge University Press, 2008), 283-309.

[16] A further example comes with Melanie Lowe's early notion of a 'minuet filter', according to which audience members would hear any minuet in relation to the dance. See Melanie Lowe, 'Falling from Grace: Irony and Expressive Enrichment in Haydn's Symphonic Minuets', *Journal of Musicology* 19, no. 2 (2002), 171-221.

describing minuets as 'engaging a double awareness – of the dance as a basis for physical expectations and of artfulness in departures from them'.[17] Yet the danger with this approach is surely that it risks characterizing the dance as a stable collection of movements, and the dancer's body as little more than a repository of entrained movements, the value of which lies mostly in their eventual disruption in the undanced repertoire.[18] My enquiry here adopts a different attitude towards dance and dancer. Put simply, dance forms the focal point of this study, the locus of interpretation; it does not merely provide the patterns and norms that set up later interpretation. Moreover, the somatic analysis that follows should not be restricted to explaining moments of deviation; rather, it should be able to deal with passages that contain no such subversion of expectation.

Elisabeth Le Guin's now-seminal study *Boccherini's Body: An Essay in Carnal Musicology* offers a musicological model for this undertaking. Playing the sonatas that Luigi Boccherini composed for himself to play, Le Guin finds herself in a 'physically reciprocal relationship' with the dead cellist-composer:

As this composer's agent in performance, I do in this way become him, in much the same manner as I become myself. And my experience of becoming him is grounded in and expressed through the medium of the tactile.[19]

Similarly, dancing the minuet allows us to establish something of a historically reciprocal relationship with the original audiences of this music, in that they, too, embodied the music physically, often dancing to minuets at balls and other social events. Of course, we must not overestimate the proximity we can attain here: our bodies differ from eighteenth-century bodies in manifold ways. Moreover, numerous errors might persist in our present-day reconstruction of the earlier steps, and the dance patterns had considerable flexibility, anyway. Yet dancing the minuet affords opportunity to engage the music with a similar mode of attentiveness to that which its original audiences might have bestowed. Just as Le Guin attempts to inhabit Boccherini's body through the tactile sensations of playing his music, through dance I attempt to come closer to the body of an eighteenth-century listener. This analytical approach treats dance as

---

[17] Wheelock, *Haydn's Ingenious Gesting*, 56.
[18] See also Sevin Yaraman, *Revolving Embrace: The Waltz as Sex, Steps and Sound* (Hillsdale: Pendragon Press, 2002), 71–90, where she presents the concert waltzes of Chopin, Brahms and Tchaikovsky as 'liberated from the steps'.
[19] Elisabeth Le Guin, *Boccherini's Body: An Essay in Carnal Musicology* (Berkeley and Los Angeles: University of California Press, 2005), 24.

a form of listening; it posits the dancer as a listener in possession of a very particular technical apparatus. Yet dance also conflates the traditional musicological categories of listener and performer, with its kinaesthetic performance of a listening experience.

This somatic enquiry is fundamentally an exercise in imagination. Just as a music theorist sits at a desk, holding a score and imagining its sounds, I imagine being present in the Hofburg Redoutensäle on 25 November 1792, hearing the music and dancing to it. I imagine my surroundings: the sawdust on the floor, the light of the candles, the other couples nearby, and my partner coming towards me and then retreating. And I imagine the temporal unfolding of the music, with its potential both to surprise and to fulfil the expectations of a score-less dancer. Musical analysis rarely attempts to reconstruct an historical scene in this way, but it is vital for the purposes of this kind of enquiry. The latter is highly conjectural, and there are few (if any) absolute guarantees of accuracy; after all, more than two centuries separate us from this historical moment. But research allows us at least a glimmer of the scene: we can know the guest lists, walk the extant spaces, see the pictures, try on the costumes, wear the shoes, read the accounts, study the treatises and hear the music. Striving for historical sensitivity both aids fidelity to the experience and stimulates the imagination. Moreover, dancing the minuet offers an unusually concrete way of experiencing an eighteenth-century body: to learn the minuet is to inscribe on my body the very movements that were practised by the bodies of two centuries ago. Dance scholar Isabelle Ginot draws a parallel between the bodily incorporation of prosthetic instruments and the bodily entrainment of somatic movement, arguing that 'somatics itself is a technique of fabricating the body'.[20] While I acknowledge the gulf between my body and the bodies that I study, I trust in the potency of dance to bridge this gap to some degree.

The following somatic enquiry comprises three sections. It starts with an introduction to the specific steps and figures of the minuet, in which I outline the main bodily motions that I will perform. My version of the dance is reconstructed from various eighteenth-century German-language dance treatises, and particularly from the 1772 publication *Erweiterung der Kunst nach der Chorographie zu tanzen* by the German dancing master Carl Joseph von Feldtenstein.[21] Next, I turn to the chosen Haydn minuet and

---

[20] Isabelle Ginot, 'From Shusterman's Somaesthetics to a Radical Epistemology of Somatics', *Dance Research Journal* 42, no. 1 (2010), 24.

[21] Carl Joseph von Feldtenstein, *Erweiterung der Kunst nach der Chorographie zu tanzen: Tänzen zu erfinden, und aufzusetzen; wie auch Anweisung zu verschiedenen National- Taenzen, als zu*

observe how the dance maps onto the music in question. I present this from my first-person perspective as a dancer, describing my own experience of dancing to this music. Finally, I interrogate certain facets of this experience, showing how somatic enquiry can inform interpretation of the musical sound. In addition, I differentiate between the kinaesthetic and sonic aspects of the experience, probing their relationship whilst attempting to account for the intensity and vitality of the embodied musical-gestural practice.

Choreographing the Minuet

The complete minuet can be divided into several sections or, in choreographic parlance, 'figures'. These include bowing figures, the so-called 'giving of hands' and the Z-figure.[22] The Z-figure forms the minuet's defining shape, so named because the dancing partners follow a Z-like path across the dance floor. Figure 3.1 illustrates this figure from above. The semicircle in the upper-left corner of the diagram denotes the starting position of the male dancer, while the two nested semicircles in the lower-right corner show the female dancer's starting position. According to the diagram, the male dancer follows the path of the continuous line, moving first from the upper-left to the upper-right corner, then following the continuous line that curves around the diagonal line from the upper-right to the lower-left corner, and finally moving along the bottom of the figure from the lower-left to the lower-right corner. Meanwhile, the female dancer simultaneously follows the dotted line, moving from the lower-right to the lower-left corner, then following a curving route from the lower-left to the upper-right corner, and finally moving from the upper-right to the upper-left corner. Following these paths brings each dancer to the other's starting position, at which point they follow the same paths back in reverse, arriving where they began.

As mentioned previously, Figure 3.1 shows the dancers' movements from above. From the dancers' own perspective, however, the experience of movement and contour is quite different.[23] When standing at opposite

---

Englischen, Deutschen, Schwaebischen, Pohlnischen, Hannak- Masur- Kosak- und Hungarischen; nebst einer Anzahl englischer Tänze (Braunschweig, 1772).

[22] The 'giving of hands' figures entail holding hands with one's partner while walking around him/her, following a prescribed path.

[23] The reader is advised to walk the path being explained here, reading from the diagram in Figure 3.1, to gain an 'on the ground' sense of this figure.

Figure 3.1 Z-figure (Feldtenstein, 1772, Fig. 67)

ends of the Z-shape, about to begin the characteristic figure, both dancers face in towards the middle of the dance floor. The first long linear movement for each dancer, then, goes leftwards. The dancers continue to face inwards throughout this first part of the figure, stepping sideways to their respective lefts. Next, they wind across the diagonal, first with a curve out to their left and then one out to the right; they pass right shoulders with each other in the centre of the floor. For this part of the figure, the dancers orient themselves forwards, turning their body in the direction of the step. They pass each other in the middle. As they arrive at the other side of the diagonal, a fast turn – of about 225 degrees anti-clockwise (i.e., a little more than 180 degrees) – is necessary in order to bring the body around so that it is again facing into the middle of the dance floor. Following this turn, the dancers perform right-ward sidesteps, ultimately arriving in the location from which their partners started the figure.

As the dancers trace the path of the Z-figure across the floor, they continually execute the 'minuet step', a series of movements that together combine to create the characteristic look and feel of the dance. The symbols marked along the continuous and dotted lines on Figure 3.1 denote these movements. As Feldtenstein describes it, the minuet step consists of four component steps, two 'bent' and two 'straight'.[24] The two bent steps come first, the first onto the right foot and the second onto the left. This step, the *demi coupé*, consists of three stages, which for our purposes here can be termed BEND, PLACE and RISE.[25] For the *demi coupé* onto my right foot, I first BEND both legs; next, I PLACE my right foot forward, keeping the weight back on my left leg; then, I RISE onto my right leg, transferring the weight onto this leg. I then repeat the above with the opposite feet, for the *demi coupé* onto the left foot. The BEND and PLACE stages are regarded as somewhat preparatory to the RISE. The two straight steps that follow are more straightforward: termed an *élevé*, each step is essentially a plain walking step, taken with a straight leg, swung from the hip. The first of these steps is onto the right foot, and the second is onto the left. Combined, these two *demi coupés* and two *élevés* form the idiomatic minuet step.

Even without going into great detail, it is easy to identify the *demi coupés* and *élevés* on Figure 3.1. Each of the step symbols has a very short line attached to the mid-point of its longest line. The short lines that extend out diagonally denote *demi coupés*, while those that are perpendicular show *élevés*. Recalling that a minuet step comprises two *demi coupés* and two *élevés*, we can deduce that each portion of the Z-figure – the first horizontal line, the curving around the diagonal and the second horizontal line – consists of eight component steps in total, or two minuet steps. We should also bear in mind that a minuet step is always enacted over two bars of music. Although different writers and dancing masters advocate different rhythmic distributions, the most frequently cited example recommends executing the first *demi coupé* over the first bar, and then the remaining three component steps (*demi coupé*, *élevé*, *élevé*) over the second bar, as shown in Table 3.1. (Note: The BEND and PLACE stages of the *demi coupé* occur in the previous beat to that on which the *demi coupé* is actually designated to begin; the beat on which it is marked denotes the moment and duration of its RISE. The second *élevé* runs immediately into the BEND and PLACE stages of the following *demi coupé*.) If each portion of the

---

[24] Different German-language dancing treatises from the period suggest slightly different forms of the minuet step. The version given here seems to have been the most popularly adopted. For a more detailed explanation of this notation, see Philippa Waite and Judith Appleby, *Beauchamp-Feuillet Notation: A Guide for Beginner and Intermediate Baroque Dance Students* (Cardiff: Consort de Danse Baroque, 2008).

[25] These particular terms are my invention, for clarity in describing the component parts of a *demi coupé* to a non-dancing audience.

Table 3.1 Minuet step distribution

Bar	1			2		
Beat	1	2	3	1	2	3
Step	demi coupé (R)			demi coupé (L)	élevé (R)	élevé (L)

Z-figure requires two minuet steps, or four bars of music, one complete Z-figure takes twelve bars, in total. A further twelve bars would then be needed for the dancers to retrace their steps in order to arrive where they started.

Dancing Haydn

As mentioned above, for this somatic enquiry I imagine myself at the Gesellschaft bildender Künstler's charity ball at the Hofburg Redoutensäle, 25 November 1792. I am eager to dance with my partner, and we are standing in place in time for Haydn's first minuet of the evening (given in Example 3.1). The following account offers a description of the imaginary experience of dancing the Z-figure outlined above to bars 1–24 of the minuet (Example 3.1). As is also mentioned above, this entire exercise is one of creative conjecture and speculation, and it offers just one of countless possible scenarios. The extant primary sources show considerable variability in some of the most basic aspects of the dance, such as the chosen rhythm for the steps, the length of the figures and the number of Z-figures danced. These matters were all to be determined by the dancers in the moment; there was no one, single way in which the minuet was always danced. Across all the couples dancing on that night in 1792, numerous different versions of the minuet were probably enacted, each aligning somewhat differently with Haydn's music. The account that follows thus offers merely one hypothetical set of possibilities.

If the initial bows of the dance were completed during the first playing of bars 1–8, the Z-figure could begin on the repeat of this section and continue into bars 9–24. Table 3.2 shows how the Z-figure lines up with the music in this way. The sections of music and dance do not seem to fit particularly closely: the start of the second section of the music (at bar 9) comes during the first Z-figure, instead of coinciding with the start of the second Z-figure, as we might expect. Yet a somatic enquiry into the experience of dancing to this music actually demonstrates some interesting correspondences generated by this alignment – more the product of happy chance than of careful design. In

Table 3.2 Executing the Z-figure to Haydn's minuet

Bars	Figure	Part of Z-figure
1–8	Bows	N/A
1–4	First Z-figure	Leftwards steps
4–8		Diagonal steps
9–12		Rightwards steps
13–16	Second Z-figure	Leftwards steps
17–20		Diagonal steps
20–24		Rightwards steps

Example 3.1 Joseph Haydn, Minuet Hob. IX: 11, no. 1, keyboard version (minuet only) bars 1–32

fact, the interplay between musical sounds and dance steps in this passage comes to account significantly for the sheer pleasure of dancing to it.

The overriding sensation I experience while dancing this minuet is a consciousness that *the music is carrying my body*. Bars 1–4 provide a solid foundation on which to plant the first stage of the Z-figure – the leftward sidesteps. The clearly articulated crotchets establish a dependable pulse with which my step can easily slot right in time. The move to the dominant at bar 3 happens concurrently with the start of my second minuet step; indeed, the slow rate of harmonic change over bars 1–4 befits a stately but unadventurous leftwards motion along a straight line. This effect changes with bar 5. Over bars 5–8, as I weave my way around the diagonal of the Z-figure, and around my partner who approaches from the other direction, new music supports this very different motion. The chromatic contour and legato lilt of the melodic line encourage the liquid quality of my winding path across the middle of the floor. Moreover, this passage contains a harmonic *progression* to a D major cadence, precisely at the point when I progress to the other side of the space. This harmonic motion, with its increased rate of harmonic change, imbues my moving body with a sense of *travelling*, in a way that the music of bars 1–4 does not. Next in the dance, with the music of bars 9–12, comes the sharp, fast 225-degree turn anti-clockwise, followed by the rightward sidesteps to finish the first iteration of the Z-figure. The thrill of the fast (but graceful) turn is heightened by the striking B minor chord of bar 9, driven by the quavers in the bass. The same motivic cell that supported my leftward sidesteps over bars 1–4 returns for the similar rightward sidesteps over bars 9–12, with a new harmonization.

For my return journey through the Z-figure, during bars 13–24, the music continues to carry my body in ways that are conducive to the particular motions in question. The first part of the return Z-figure, the leftward sidestep back along the line that I traced immediately prior, has a quality of 'rewinding' to it, and feels the least venturesome part of the entire dance over bars 1–24. The same impression is also made by the music here, which simply prolongs an A major harmony throughout bars 13–16, securing the dominant as the local tonic prior to the perfect authentic cadence in the following phrase. Next, just as bars 5–8 carried my winding, travelling motion over the diagonal with a legato phrase and a harmonic progression leading to a conclusive perfect authentic cadence, bars 17–20 support my return motion over the diagonal in just the same way, the cadence now affirming A major as the local tonic. Then, just as my sharp turn into the rightward sidestep coincided with a sudden B minor chord at bar 9, bar 21 greets this parallel moment in the return journey with a sudden, *forte* D minor interjection, energized by the semiquaver anacrusis of bar 20. Finally, at the very moment when I arrive back where I started in bar 1, so too does the music: bars 25–32 offer a literal repeat of the opening bars 1–8.

Once More, with Some Detail

The above is a somewhat superficial analysis of the relation between music and dance during bars 1–24; while it highlights some features of my somatic awareness, it does not delve into the potential phenomenological reasons for the experiences that I describe. To explore some of these reasons more fully, I should like to focus on a few specific aspects of the experience of dancing to bars 1–8, beginning with one of my first impressions of this passage: namely, that bars 5–8 support a fundamentally different type of motion to that of bars 1–4.[26] Dancing the minuet step during bars 1–2 of this music feels fundamentally different from dancing the minuet step during bars 5–6. This feeling is not only a result of the changed motion of the Z-figure itself; it also relates to the changed musical accompaniment. In other words, my felt experience of bars 5–6 differs from my felt experience of bars 1–2, and this difference impacts upon my kinaesthetic experience of dancing the minuet. What makes my experience different in these two passages of music?

Kinaesthetically alone, regardless of the music, winding over the Z-figure's diagonal feels radically different from the sideways step in the first part of the figure. Stepping sideways while the body remains oriented forwards is far less natural than dancing through the curved diagonal, with the body rotating to follow the direction of the step. This is not only because the body is more accustomed to walking in the direction that it is facing, but also because executing the minuet step leftward requires passing through fifth position, planting the toes of my right foot carefully behind the heel of my left, in a series of small, intricate steps. A more pronounced disparity between the two experiences arises from differences between the sense of destination or direction in each. Dancing the leftward sidestep, I have only some sense of where I will arrive by the end of the second minuet step (in bar 4). I set out on the leftwards journey aware of my partner's own leftwards journey, and we expect to cross sightlines around the middle of the two-step passage, as the first step

---

[26] Of course, when I claim that bars 1–4 just happen to support the motion I wish to enact to them remarkably well, and that bars 5–8 then support my new motion just as well, the question immediately arises: does the music just seem to support the particular motions because I want it to? Would any music in triple metre with a clear pulse and the right tempo support these steps and figures? No. This is not the case. This is illustrated if we reverse the combination of music and dance steps: if I try to dance the second part of the Z-figure to bars 1–4, and the first part of it to bars 5–8, the relationship between my sonic and kinaesthetic experiences is simply nowhere near as congruent in this latter combination as it was when I previously danced to this music.

flows into the second. Beyond this, however, there is little sense of goal orientation: simply put, I arrive where I do at the end of it more out of inevitability than anything else. Dancing across the diagonal, in contrast, is a more goal-oriented enterprise. As I set off on this second part, I visually note the point from which my partner is leaving. This visual orientation is necessary: she will no longer be there as a target when I arrive, so I need to aim for it now. In order to execute well-shaped, symmetrical curves across the diagonal, I need to calculate them according to my arrival point. Moreover, movement towards a goal generally feels more natural when travelling forwards with the body than when stepping sideways. Perhaps, then, the kinaesthetic movement of the second part of the Z-figure, traversing the diagonal over bars 5–8, simply *flows* more easily than the first. My body moves more readily and more smoothly when its motion is directed towards a goal, when the positions through which the feet will pass are comfortable and straightforward, and when the body is oriented towards the direction that it is travelling.

The music of bars 1–4 and 5–8 also contains some significant differences. Bars 1–8 espouse a sentential structure: bars 1–2 present the basic idea in the tonic, which is then repeated in the dominant over bars 3–4; bars 5–6 constitute the fragmentation; and the cadential material comes in bars 7–8.[27] Listening to the music, seated, my gut reaction is that bars 1–4 *feel* much more stationary bars 5–8. This is largely a result of the harmony. Bars 1–4 consist solely of a move from I to V^6, each chord leisurely spanning two bars. Bars 5–8, on the other hand, constitute a faster I^6–ii^6–V^7–I progression, with the harmony changing each bar. It is not only the accelerated rate of harmonic change that gives bars 5–8 a greater sense of travel and direction than bars 1–4, but also the harmonic destination of each. While bars 1–4 open out onto the dominant, bars 5–8 return conclusively to the tonic. Moreover, this tonic return engenders a sensation of goal-directedness considerably before the tonic's actual arrival in bar 8: I feel it from the start of bar 5, in the same way that I set out on the corresponding part of the Z-figure aiming for its final destination. In conjunction with this greater sense of harmonic flow over bars 5–8, the melody of the later bars is considerably less angular in contour and more legato in articulation. In the orchestral version of this minuet, the emphatic block chords of the brass and tympani in bars

---

[27] I adopt the concept and terminology of sentential structure from William Caplin, *Classical Form: A Theory of Formal Functions for the Instrumental Music of Haydn, Mozart, and Beethoven* (New York: Oxford University Press, 1998), 10.

Figure 3.2 Hasty's diagram showing projection from the standpoint of durational products C and C'; courtesy of Oxford University Press

1–4 drop out suddenly in bar 5, and the bass line loses its heavy downbeat. These factors all contribute to the greater sense of flow that I hear in the music of bars 5–8, compared with bars 1–4.

Yet there is a further factor at issue here, one that – arising out of the interaction between my sonic and kinaesthetic experiences – can be explored further with reference to the work of music theorist Christopher Hasty.[28] Central to Hasty's thesis is the notion of metre as *projection*, an idea which he introduces along with the etymological root 'throwing forth'. With the visual aid of a diagram (see Figure 3.2), Hasty explains that events A and A' create duration C, which itself *projects* duration C'.[29]

In the immediate context of this project, Hasty's work offers fertile terrain. There is a significant link to be made between Hasty's basic notion of projection and the practical experience of dance: 'throwing forth', of course, is precisely what the body does, physically, when dancing. To put this in other words, dancing itself is to throw *the body* forth. Indeed, both music and body project together, in dance.

With this idea in mind, the music of bars 1–2 and 3–4 seems to fully support and in fact bolster the muscular effort required of this step. I feel inflated, not just in my calves but also in my torso, and particularly by the bass line. It is this process that causes the change in somatic experience at bar 5, and the subsequent sensation of instability. On the final beat of bar 4, I BEND into the coming *demi coupé*, expecting the bass line on the downbeat of bar 5 to constitute something similar to that of bars 1 and 3 to propel my RISE. I project my body into this RISE, but the music fails me at this point. It gives me nothing of the ballast that the *demi coupés* of bars 1 and 3 enjoyed, and which they had set me up to expect, with the bass not even

---

[28] Christopher Hasty, *Meter as Rhythm* (New York: Oxford University Press, 1997). Drawing on Hasty's work to account in greater phenomenological depth for the somatic experience of bars 1–8 seems apt, since in *Meter as Rhythm* he makes the case for a kinaesthetic interpretation of a musical sentence, describing a sentential scheme that 'acquires some "kinetic energy" at its end' (113). To dance the minuet to Haydn's sentence is to feel precisely that kinetic energy, and indeed to liberate it from the quotation marks in which Hasty carefully encapsulates it.

[29] Hasty, *Meter as Rhythm*, 84.

coming in until the second beat of bar 5. The projection of bar 5, for which I was preparing over bars 3–4, is fundamentally different from that which I had been expecting. This unfulfilled expectation, on which I had acted by way of physical preparation, strengthens the impact of the somatic sensation. The instability caused when, for want of a better expression, the musical rug is pulled out from under me at bar 5 is not limited to that one moment: its effects are felt for the entirety of the minuet step of bars 5–6, and even beyond. Without the heavy crotchets and slow harmonic pace anchoring my step, my body acquires a new forward intent as well as a lightness, motivated by a desire for a return to stability. As such, it latches readily onto the goal-oriented harmonic progression of the music, with its promise of a destination. I throw my body forth *onto the music* to carry me in this way. Not only has my kinaesthetic experience of the minuet step changed between bars 1–2 and bars 5–6 but also the dynamic relationship between my kinaesthetic and sonic experiences has shifted.

Having asserted the potency of the music of bars 1–2 to support the minuet step as a whole, I want to investigate this relationship in a little more detail, considering the four component parts of the minuet step. Speaking generally, and from my perspective at least, it is easier to dance minuets that begin with an anacrusis than it is to dance those beginning on a downbeat. In part, this experience is likely a result of the simple fact that hearing the upbeat aids my enactment of the BEND and PLACE components of the *demi coupé* occurring during this beat. Yet the effect goes beyond practical considerations like these: even when I know precisely when the upbeat is implied, and can thus perfectly time the BEND and PLACE of the *demi coupé*, the motion is somehow different – easier, more fluid – when the upbeat is audibly present. In fact, dancing to a phrase that starts on the downbeat, the *demi coupé* feels jerkier and abrupt. Certainly, whether or not this effect is measurable, I *feel* more of a 'down-up' sensation through the BEND–PLACE–RISE stages of the downbeat *demi coupé* than in an upbeat *demi coupé*. Upbeat *demi coupés* tend to feel more connected to the overall direction (forwards, sideways and so on) in which I am travelling for the figure I am executing at the time. Put another way, I am more aware of the vertical aspect of the *demi coupé* when the phrase starts on the downbeat, and more aware of its horizontal orientation across the dance floor when it starts on an upbeat. As a result, a *demi coupé* usually feels more connected to the rest of the minuet step when it has an upbeat. In Haydn's minuet here, the upbeat prior to bar 1 demonstrably aids the *demi coupé*. There is a ready analogue between the ascending perfect 4th of the melody's A–D motion and my own kinaesthetic rising motion through the stages of BEND–PLACE–RISE. Yet the sonic-kinaesthetic correlation goes much further. To BEND in the *demi coupé* is to introduce the need to RISE – to introduce an elastic tension that needs to be released. This process of tension-release that occurs over the course of BEND and RISE is matched by the tension-release of dominant to tonic with the A–D melody. Not only does the sonic dominant–tonic motion coincide with the kinaesthetic motion of my BEND and RISE but also the energy of the dominant, willing its move to the tonic, seems to infuse my body's physical motion with a like energy, lifting my RISE out of the BEND.

Nonetheless, if the dominant upbeat provides the charge for the initial RISE into the minuet step, the real ballast for the step's motion comes from the entrance of the other parts on the downbeat of bar 1. To feel the impact exerted on my movement by the bass line and the inner parts requires just a simple thought experiment, one in which I first dance to bars 1–8 hearing the melody alone, and then dance a second time whilst hearing all the parts. While the melody alone suffices for my enactment of the minuet step, the accompaniment *buoys* my movement. Indeed, the rhythm of the bass line defines the rhythmic shape of bars 1–2 (and those that follow) overall. The inner parts also carry the same rhythm, and the melody only differs from it by way of an upbeat, some grace notes and an additional crotchet on the second beat of bar 2, elided onto the previous crotchet by a slur. The weighty accompaniment grounds the melody, in the same way that in the RISE I assume the weight of my body.

The rhythm of the bass line complements that of the dance steps remarkably well, with the crotchets interlocking neatly across the two domains, as Figure 3.3 shows. In a pragmatic sense, the bass line's crotchets in bar 1 set up the crotchet steps of bar 2: the music of bar 1 establishes a clear triple-metre crotchet pulse to which I will dance the three steps in bar 2. Yet this is by no means a purely mechanical exercise, in the sense that the music's crotchets merely 'set the tempo' for the dance steps. Rather, the music's crotchets in bar 1 *inflate* the RISE of my *demi coupé* in that bar, and *propel* the three crotchet steps that follow. To describe the RISE as being 'inflated', I refer to my bodily sensation,

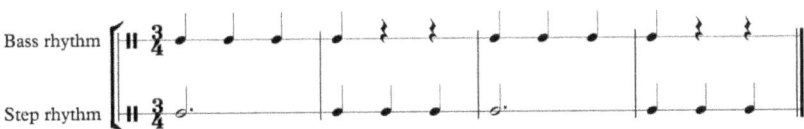

Figure 3.3 Bass rhythm and step rhythm

primarily around my torso, of feeling lighter as I come up out of the BEND, as if filled with air. Surely this feeling is in part a result of the ascending crotchet arpeggio in the bass line, with its own concomitant feeling of weight loss. A musical performance of this melodic cell would also hopefully be imbued with a dynamic shape whereby the first crotchet of bar 1 is strong, and the next three progressively lighter. Finally, the fact that bars 1–2 (and then bars 3–4) consist of a single chord imbues my kinaesthetic sensation of the step with continuity. It fuses the individual component parts of the step into one, so that the entire minuet step here feels like a single entity.

One other moment in the minuet brings us to a different aspect of somatic experience. Earlier, I briefly mentioned the 'thrill' of performing the rapid turn at bar 9, coinciding with the B minor chord of that bar. This being one of the most striking emotional sensations of dancing during bars 1–24, I should like to interrogate it a bit further. The question is: what constitutes or causes the thrill at bar 9? This fast turn gives rise to distinct sensations in several different areas of my body. Although the aim throughout the minuet is to keep all movement contained within the bounds of gracefulness, this turn is surely the most vigorous and energetic moment in the Z-figure. For me, the most pleasurable sensation of this movement in fact comes at the very end of the motion, in the feeling of momentum that the initial impetus of the turn causes, and which follows the body into the rightward sidesteps that follow. I feel this in my eyes: my glance wants to continue in the anti-clockwise motion, out to the left. Perhaps related to this feeling, the left side of my neck feels very free, as if my head could continue the turn. My left arm has been slightly thrown out to the side by the turn, and takes the entire duration of bar 9 to fall back in towards my body; I feel its weight particularly in the palm of my left hand, which faces up, and which I lifted slightly during the RISE of the *demi coupé*. I also feel strongly aware of the base of my spine, carrying the weight of my upper body, as the front of my torso re-orients its openness to the space in front of it. This overall bodily momentum imbues a strong sense of flow into this particular minuet step: the *demi coupé* onto the left foot, which takes us into bar 10, feels as if it catches the body, still in motion from the thrust of bar 9. My sonic experience of bar 9 also contributes to this thrill. Although B minor is by no means a remote chord for D major, this is the boldest harmonic move of the composition so far, and the quavers in the bass charge the texture with new energy. This chord sends a surge into the RISE of my *demi coupé*, which carries into the body. Performing a *demi coupé* also charges my engagement with the music at this point, energizing my sonic experience with vitality and intensity.

On reflection, describing the sensation of performing a turning *demi coupé* at bar 9 as a 'thrill' might seem too glib a summary of the experience, but one aspect that it does successfully capture is the emotional nature of the fast turn. Moving the body is not merely a functional, mechanical exercise; it is also an emotional activity. Of course, movement has the capacity to cause us considerable pleasure, as well as pain. Neuroscientist Jonathan Cole and philosopher Barbara Montero have together coined the term 'affective proprioception' in their discussion of movement as a means of causing pleasure – that is, 'the ineffable pleasure of, and of being in, action'.[30] They consider dancers, musicians and sports players as practitioners who gain pleasure from the movement associated with their tasks, regardless of whether that movement is typically considered as the means to an end, such as the swing to hit a golf ball into a hole, or as the end in itself, as in a dancer's step. While the reasons for the connection between bodily movement and psychological pleasure might be little known, even to medical specialists, this is surely a factor that needs to be acknowledged in any somatic enquiry. In the present case, the fact remains: dancing the minuet is typically an intensely pleasurable experience. All kinds of pleasure can arise from the act of dancing the minuet, be it the satisfaction of executing the steps well and in time, the erotic desire of dancing with a partner, or the egocentric delight in parading one's body. The specific kind of pleasure I am interested in here is that which arises out of movement itself: the plain, basic joy of kinaesthetic activity. Yet it is not kinaesthetic activity alone that gives me this pleasure: dancing the minuet feels particularly pleasurable because it gives me a ready means of bodily engagement with the music that I am hearing. The music not only supports and propels the movements of the dance but also intensifies them. It lifts my body and, with vigour, carries it forwards.

Contemplating the Generic, the Body Now Still

If nothing else, the foregoing analysis demonstrates the capacity for somatic enquiry to enhance musical experience. The minuet considered above would rarely feature in any music-analytical discussion; indeed, it

---

[30] Jonathan Cole and Barbara Montero, 'Affective Proprioception', *Janus Head* 9, no. 2 (2007), 303.

has received very little attention from scholars, save as a model of generic convention and regularity. Indeed, the very features that make this minuet so danceable render it of little interest to analysts: there is no 'stumbling against a stone' or 'stepping into a hole' here; the music moves readily and easily. Analytical modes geared towards revealing puzzling aspects or anomalous moments in the music are not particularly suited to this repertoire. Yet this enquiry demonstrates that dancing the minuet can be a rich experience, intensely pleasurable and intellectually stimulating. It also shows how analysis that focuses on the musical *experience* rather than on 'the music itself' can also be revelatory.

As I made clear at the outset, my interpretive foray into the dance is highly specific: it pertains to just one possible version of the minuet step, applied to a single minuet composition, and is considered entirely through the lens of my own personal experience. The correspondences and moments of coherence come about more through chance than by design, and there is no guarantee that they will recur. However, some general implications can be considered, some broader insights drawn. For starters, this method of enquiry can be applied to other minuets, as a means of heightening engagement with this music. Performing a turning *demi coupé* with the B minor chord of bar 9 imbues this moment with a vitality and intensity that it previously lacked, for example. Indeed, listening kinaesthetically in this way – *listening as a dancer* – has the capacity to intensify one's sonic experience of the music. Crucially, this opens up analytical involvement beyond those passages where expectations are subverted or disrupted, passages to which previous minuet analysis has often been drawn. Most importantly, though, this mode of enquiry attempts to account for actual musical experience. Listening as a dancer forces the analyst out of the score, closing the gap between analysis and music as it actually happens, music made and received by humans, in the real world. Let us remember: dance in eighteenth-century Vienna was largely a joyous affair; people elected to dance less for show than ever before, and more for their own personal investment and enjoyment. The music to which they danced sought to enhance this pleasure; as musicologists, we should recognize this state of affairs, and analyse accordingly.

4 | Making Moves in Reception Studies: Music, Listening and Loie Fuller

DAVINIA CADDY

Broadly speaking, this chapter aims to reconfigure a historiographical specialism across the humanistic disciplines, one that is nowadays synonymous with the not-so-New Musicology of decades past.[1] Reception studies, brought forth from a constellation of literary theory, sociology, cultural history and anthropology, remains a busy and burgeoning field:[2] witness the seemingly endless stream of musicological literature on critics, audiences, politics and the press – that is, on people of the past and their historical habits of listening.[3] Within this literature, nineteenth-century Paris has emerged as a focal point, as has music theatre: seminal studies by Katharine Ellis, Sarah Hibberd and Mary Ann Smart (to name three of the most frequently cited) recount spectators' perceptions as recorded in print, exposing underlying aesthetic biases, institutional allegiances and prominent strands of social and

---

[1] Perennial favourites include Carl Dahlhaus, *Foundations of Music History* (Cambridge: Cambridge University Press, 1983); Richard Leppert and Susan McClary, eds., *Music and Society: The Politics of Composition, Performance and Reception* (Cambridge: Cambridge University Press, 1987); and Scott Burnham, *Beethoven Hero* (Princeton: Princeton University Press, 1995).

[2] The impulse towards reception is often dated back to Roland Barthes's now-classic essay 'The Death of the Author', *Image–Music–Text*, trans. Stephen Heath (New York: Hill and Wang, 1977), 142–8; also see Hans Robert Jauss, *Toward an Aesthetic of Reception*, trans. Timothy Bahti (Brighton: Harvester, 1982); and Robert Holub, *Reception Theory: A Critical Introduction* (London: Methuen, 1984).

[3] A representative selection, across musical repertoires and genres, includes Alexandra Wilson, *The Puccini Problem: Opera, Nationalism and Modernity* (Cambridge: Cambridge University Press, 2002); Joseph Lanza, *Elevator Music: A Surreal History of Muzak, Easy-Listening and Other Moodsong* (Ann Arbor: University of Michigan Press, 2004); Matthew Riley, *Musical Listening in the German Enlightenment: Attention, Wonder and Astonishment* (Aldershot: Ashgate, 2004); Mark Evan Bonds, *Music as Thought: Listening to the Symphony in the Age of Beethoven* (Princeton: Princeton University Press, 2006); Kevin Karnes, *Music Criticism and the Challenge of History: Shaping Modern Musical Thought in Late Nineteenth-Century Vienna* (Oxford: Oxford University Press, 2008); Daniel Cavicchi, *Listening and Longing: Music Lovers in the Age of Barnum* (Middletown: Wesleyan University Press, 2011); Gianmario Borio, *Musical Listening in the Age of Technological Reproduction* (Aldershot: Ashgate, 2015); Alessandra Campana, *Opera and Modern Spectatorship in Late Nineteenth-Century Italy* (Cambridge: Cambridge University Press, 2015); and Christian Thorau and Hansjakob Ziemer, eds., *The Oxford Handbook of Music Listening in the 19th and 20th Centuries* (Oxford: Oxford University Press, 2018).

cultural influence.[4] Yet print material – critics' articles and reviews – provides only one category of evidence, if the most sizeable and ostensibly promising, given the rapid press digitization of recent years. As media theorists have not tired of telling us, there are other 'discourse networks' to explore, ones that recall the lived dimensions of musical experience, its sensual 'thickness' and perceptual variations.[5] With these in mind, I should like to propose a broadening of scope – variegated interconnections between text and act – that offers new historical and interpretive insights into Parisian music listening, both inside and outside the theatre. Inspired by the recent groundswell of interest in performativity and embodiment, as well as by attempts across the newly minted 'cognitive humanities' to explode the concept of listening as a purely cerebral–textual affair, my project juxtaposes critics in the stalls with performers on stage, words in print with bodies in motion, cultural studies with art history and aesthetics.[6]

Dancers active in late nineteenth- and early twentieth-century Paris make for an excellent workshop on this methodological manoeuvre, primarily because they preached an intimate sensory response to

---

[4] See Katharine Ellis, 'Paris, 1866: In Search of French Music', *Music & Letters* 91, no. 4 (2010), 536–54; and her 'Opera Criticism and the Paris Periodical Press', *Revue belge de Musicologie* 66 (2012), 127–31; Sarah Hibberd and Richard Wrigley, eds., *Art, Theatre, and Opera in Paris, 1750–1850: Exchanges and Tensions* (Aldershot: Ashgate, 2014); Sarah Hibberd, *French Grand Opera and the Historical Imagination* (Cambridge: Cambridge University Press, 2009); her 'Cherubini and the Revolutionary Sublime', *Cambridge Opera Journal* 24, no. 3 (2012), 293–318; and Mary Ann Smart, 'Mourning the Duc d'Orléans: Donizetti's *Dom Sébastien* and the Social Meanings of Grand Opéra', in *Reading Critics Reading: Opera and Ballet Criticism in France from the Revolution to 1848*, ed. Roger Parker and Mary Ann Smart (Oxford: Oxford University Press, 2001), 188–212.

[5] See Friedrich A. Kittler, *Discourse Networks: 1800/1900* (Stanford: Stanford University Press, 1990); and his *Gramophone, Film, Typewriter* (Stanford: Stanford University Press, 1999). For nuanced reflections on Kittlerian themes, see Stephen Sale and Laura Salisbury, eds., *Kittler Now: Current Perspectives in Kittler Studies* (Cambridge: Polity, 2015); and Maria Teresa Cruz, ed., *Media Theory and Cultural Technologies: In Memoriam Friedrich Kittler* (Newcastle upon Tyne: Cambridge Scholars Publishing, 2017).

[6] I have taken particular inspiration from Vivian Sobchack, *The Address of the Eye: A Phenomenology of Film Experience* (Princeton: Princeton University Press, 1991); Laura U. Marks, *The Skin of the Film: Intercultural Cinema, Embodiment and the Senses* (Durham, NC: Duke University Press, 2000); Eve Kosofsky Sedgwick, *Touching Feeling: Affect, Pedagogy and Performativity* (Durham, NC: Duke University Press, 2002); Mary Ann Smart, *Mimomania: Music and Gesture in Nineteenth-Century Opera* (Berkeley and Los Angeles: University of California Press, 2004); Elisabeth Le Guin, *Boccherini's Body: An Essay in Carnal Musicology* (Berkeley and Los Angeles: University of California Press, 2005); Carrie Noland, *Agency and Embodiment: Performing Gestures/Producing Culture* (Cambridge, MA: Harvard University Press, 2009); and Peter Garratt, ed., *The Cognitive Humanities: Embodied Music in Literature and Culture* (London: Palgrave Macmillan, 2016).

music.⁷ Take the American 'barefoot' dancer Isadora Duncan, who confessed (with characteristic hyperbole): 'I am not a dancer. I am here to make you listen to the music.'⁸ On witnessing Duncan's performances in the French capital, most seemed to agree:⁹ according to the conductor Franz Ruhlmann, 'Isadora Duncan est la Musique même, son incarnation, sa réalisation plastique. Elle est la Musique qu'on regarde';¹⁰ ballet critic and historian Valerian Svétlow spoke similarly, extolling 'l'union de la pure plastique et de la pure musique', besides 'une impression artistique complète'.¹¹ Similar applause was extended to the Russian dancer Natalia Trouhanova. The so-called 'Concerts de danse' performed by the Ballets-Russes principal at Paris's Châtelet theatre in April 1912 were thought to offer 'des synthèses remarquables':¹² Trouhanova embodied 'une fidélité absolue' to her music's internal genetics (themes, rhythms, accents and instrumentation), as well as 'une interprétation psychologique'.¹³

Comments like these, repeated throughout the specialist press and the large-distribution dailies, are more than a piquant source of interest. For they prompt us to envisage a new and different kind of reception history, one that asks what we might learn about listening – and about music (even, 'la Musique même') – by looking at these dancers: what their aural receptivity, soma-sensory experience and physical shape-shifting might tell us about the history of attention and musical aesthetics. Focusing here on a single case study, I will suggest how a dancer could stage – literally, embody and enact – models of listening emblematic of early modernism, thus bringing into the theatre the sensory-perceptual dynamics of the city

---

[7] For a summary account, see my essay 'Representational Conundrums: Music and Early Modern Dance', in *Western Music and Representation*, ed. Joshua Walden (Cambridge: Cambridge University Press, 2013), 144–64.

[8] Quoted in Fredrika Blair, *Isadora: Portrait of the Artist as a Woman* (New York: McGraw-Hill, 1986), 187–8. Also see *Isadora Speaks*, ed. Franklin Rosemont (San Francisco: City Lights Books, 1981), 38: 'Music touches the heart, makes it vibrate with emotion. The dance is only at is beginnings, in its infancy. Music is like a great strong goddess which leads the dance by the hand like a little child.'

[9] But not all. Here is the French poet and critic René Chalupt, writing in the periodical *L'Occident* 115 (June 1912), 'elle dansa tout à tort et à travers avec le discernement d'une corneille abattant des noix' (230).

[10] Franz Ruhlmann, n.d.; clipping, Paris, Bibliothèque nationale de France, département des Arts du spectacle (hereafter F-Pn), Fonds Rondel (Ro) Rés 12073, 'Isadora Duncan, Biographie, Critique'.

[11] Valerian Svétlow, *Le Ballet contemporain* (Paris: Brunoff, 1912), 71.

[12] Robert Brussel, 'De la Musique et de la danse', *Revue Musicale S.I.M.*, n.d.; clipping, F-Pn, Ro 12777.

[13] Brussel; and Georges Haller, 'En marge d'un concert de danse', *La Phalange*, 20 June 1912; clipping, F-Pn, Ro 12776.

outside. My argument, I hope, will shed light on histories of listening, spectatorship and sensory perception; in addition, it might prompt us to rethink the nature of the decisions we make about how music can carry meaning – in performance as well as in print.

On this last point, the old chestnut about musical meaning, I need to acknowledge a specific stimulus from recent scholarship: a 2007 book by literary historian Anne-Lise François. Titled *Open Secrets: The Literature of Uncounted Experience*, François's study explores literary moments in which, to quote the author, 'nothing happens'.[14] Inconspicuous, inconsequential, these are moments of 'eventless experience' that do not advance plot or characterization, do not register, even, in the overall structural design.[15] For François, these moments are doubly significant: not only do they provide ample subject-matter for her study, but their spirit or character also insinuates her critical method, as well as her mode of discourse. To put this in other words, François shifts the interpretive axis from traditional hermeneutics to what she calls (somewhat paradoxically) 'recessive action', essaying a type of critical phenomenology that attends to the diegetic reality of literary experience – the everyday, the commonplace, the indifferent – without reading for meaning or truth, mining hidden depths or disclosing covert ideologies.[16] Part of a recent rush of literary criticism aimed at questioning the demystifying protocols of the infamous 'hermeneutics of suspicion', François's study aims simply to address what is 'there for the taking'.[17] On the surface, that is. To François, literary surfaces – rendered invisible by so-called 'symptomatic reading' or else cast off as superficial and/or deceptive – insist on being looked at, rather than seen through. This looking, moreover, demands a literal-mindedness that, in terms of critical attitude and methodology, gives priority to surface description: noticing, measuring, articulating – what François calls 'the act of bearing witness to the given'.[18]

---

[14] Anne-Lise François, *Open Secrets: The Literature of Uncounted Experience* (Stanford: Stanford University Press, 2007), xv.

[15] François, *Open Secrets*, 47. She goes on to describe the open secret as 'a trope for secondary, supplemental, naturalized revelation – revelation that one is free to take for granted'.

[16] See François, 'Toward a Theory of Recessive Action', in *Open Secrets*, 1–65.

[17] Of particular importance, to me at least, is Sedgwick's essay 'Paranoid Reading and Reparative Reading, or You're So Paranoid, You Probably Think This Essay Is About You', in *Touching Feeling*, 123–51; and Anne Anlin Cheng, *Second Skin: Josephine Baker and the Modern Surface* (Oxford: Oxford University Press, 2010). This is not to forget the 2009 special edition of *Representations* 108, no. 1, dedicated to 'The Way We Read Now'; and the essay that gave the kick to its titular directive, 'Against Interpretation', in Susan Sontag, *Against Interpretation and Other Essays* (New York: Farrar, Straus and Giroux, 1966), 4–14.

[18] François, *Open Secrets*, 35.

There is much to address here, not least the author's intertwined aims: to find interest and sufficiency in ostensibly non-promising places, while offering respite from the dominant critical compulsion to extricate and elaborate on meaning. What follows in this chapter might be interpreted similarly; that is, as an attempt 'to define the relations on the very surface of discourse'; 'to make visible what is invisible only because it is too much on the surface of things'.[19] These words, from a little-known interview with Michel Foucault, will help focus a searchlight on the various source materials I go on to explore, materials that benefit, not from further critical heroics, but from a willed and sustained proximity to the musical and choreographic surface.

I

Certainly, this more modest programme of criticism is almost entirely absent from the accumulation of literature on my chosen case study. The American Loie Fuller – or 'La Loïe', as she was known affectionately to the Parisian public – remains a favourite subject of deconstruction, an invitation to the kind of incessantly productive hermeneutics that tends to make music and dance pregnant with interpretive possibility. Consider the words of Jacques Rancière. In his recent book *Aisthesis*, a philosophical reverie-turned-rewriting of the history of art and aesthetics, Rancière presents Fuller as an emblem of pure potentiality: 'the poetic operation of metaphoric condensation and metonymic displacement'.[20] Indeed, the dancer graces the front cover of Rancière's book (see Figure 4.1), a photograph of Fuller in characteristic costume-cum-camouflage, an empty stage draped in black. As is well known, Fuller made her name in an ostensibly new and inventive style of abstract, non-narrative dance, performing at the *fin de siècle* in music-halls across Western Europe and the United States to captivated audiences of literary and artistic elites, as well as the working classes. Her 'modern' manner of dancing formed a stark contrast to the representational mandate of classical ballet, as Fuller sought to free the physical form from its staged reliance on pantomimic gestures and virtuosic display. To this end, she devised and depended on props: huge swaths of silk (attached to bamboo sticks that she waved around) and coloured light

---

[19] Quoted in *Foucault Live: Interviews, 1961–84*, ed. Sylvère Lotringer, trans. John Johnston (New York: Semiotext(e), 1989), 46.

[20] Jacques Rancière, *Aisthesis: Scenes from the Aesthetic Regime of Arts*, trans. Zakir Paul (London: Verso, 2013), 99.

Figure 4.1 Frederick W. Glasier, *Loie Fuller*, c. 1902; courtesy of the Library of Congress, Washington DC

projections (emanating from the rear of the theatre as well as from underneath the stage) accompanied her performances, while she swirled and spun around, seeming to depict a butterfly, a lily, waves, fire – objects or, rather, apparitions in constant metamorphosis.[21]

In his cover image, Rancière appears to have chosen wisely, for Fuller is a fitting embodiment of his book's principal thesis: the eclipse, across the nineteenth century, of the so-called 'representative regime of art' – that by which different art forms were recognized as distinctive and autonomous, identifiable by their established hierarchies, generic specificities and transparent representational logic. But 'embodiment' might be the wrong word. To Rancière, Fuller's performance gave prominence to a 'new body', one that was 'relieved of the weight of its flesh, reduced to a play of lines and

---

[21] There is an accumulation of secondary literature on Fuller and her artistry. Rhonda Garelick's work, at least to me, is among the most compelling; see her *Electric Salome: Loie Fuller's Performance of Modernism* (Princeton: Princeton University Press, 2007). Other historically sensitive studies include Giovanni Lista, *Loïe Fuller: Danseuse de la Belle Époque* (Paris: Stock, 1994); Tom Gunning, 'Loïe Fuller and the Art of Motion: Body, Light, Electricity, and the Origins of Cinema', in *Camera Obscura, Camera Lucida: Essays in Honour of Annette Michelson*, ed. Richard Allen and Malcolm Turvey (Amsterdam: Amsterdam University Press, 1995), 75–89; Guy Ducrey, 'La Danseuse Loïe Fuller et L'Art nouveau', *Mélange* 1 (2000), 119–31; and the exhibition catalogue *Loïe Fuller, danseuse de l'art nouveau*, ed. Valérie Thomas and Jérôme Perrin (Paris: Éditions de la Réunion des Musées Nationaux, 2002).

tones, whirling in space'.[22] As such, Rancière continues, Fuller forecast 'a new paradigm of art', one in which reality would blur, images would metamorphose and dance would entirely disengage from corporeality, the dancer using her body to absent its very bodiliness from the stage: in Rancière's words, 'to institute the place of its becoming metaphorical'.[23]

In this assessment, Rancière of course echoes a long line of French literary heavyweights, the first and most famous of which was the poet and theatre enthusiast Stéphane Mallarmé. Scribbling inside the Folies-Bergère during Fuller's first run of Paris performances (1893), Mallarmé observed not only the indistinction of the arts (he spoke of 'l'harmonieux délire'), but the complete disembodiment of the dancer.[24] His 1896 text – with the oft-cited statement 'la danseuse *n'est pas une femme qui danse*' – extends this line of argument, the author denying the dancer's personhood, corporeality, gender, earthliness, humanity, literacy and even her limbic movement, not to mention the established conventions of theatrical staging and perspective.[25] Conceptualizing Fuller by her impersonality and intrigue, meaning by its concealment and mystery, and language by its inability to encode, Mallarmé reveals himself as full-on symptomologue – a reader obsessed with latent, repressed content. Indeed, his various writings seem as genre-bending and elusive as Fuller's dances themselves. Turning the established theatre review into a piece of intellectual criticism, Mallarmé shirked from technical dance vocabulary (although sources say he knew it well), instead preferring to call upon vague examples and loose allusions to 'beauty', 'silence' and 'shadow'. The poet appeared to concentrate less on the dancing before him, or on the dancer herself, than on the process of critical thinking the two set in motion: he brought this critique to the forefront of his discussion, asking his readers to ask themselves: 'Que peut signifier ceci?' ('What can this signify?')[26]

As even a cursory glance through the period press reveals, this throwing up of critical hands was a common occurrence: it gestured to a broader cultural context that linked Fuller, Mallarmé and their Parisian

---

[22] Rancière, *Aisthesis*, 94. [23] Rancière, *Aisthesis*, 103.
[24] See Stéphane Mallarmé, 'Considérations sur l'art du ballet et la Loïe Fuller', *National Observer*, 13 May 1893; reprinted (with some revisions) in 'Autre étude de danse: Les fonds dans le ballet', in *Œuvres complètes*, ed. Georges Jean-Aubry and Henri Mondor (Paris: Gallimard, 1945), 307–9.
[25] Mallarmé, 'Ballets' (1896); reprinted in *Œuvres complètes*, ed. Mondor and Jean-Aubry, 303–7, at 304.
[26] Mallarmé, 'Ballets', 307. Martin Puchner provides a highly readable account of Mallarmé's notoriously oblique theatrical musings in his *Stage Fright: Modernism, Anti-Theatricality, and Drama* (Baltimore and London: Johns Hopkins University Press, 2002), 59–80.

contemporaries to the defining principles and practices of artistic modernism.[27] As Rancière reminds us, the late nineteenth and early twentieth centuries witnessed more than a simple shift from representational art to abstraction. The powers of representation were themselves put through their paces, as artists tended towards what one recent scholar calls 'potential images' – ambiguous, absorbing and dependent in meaning and effect on the creative contribution of the beholder.[28] Examples embrace not only visual art (by Moreau, Degas, Monet, Cézanne) but also literature, most famously the Symbolist poetry of Mallarmé himself, for whom the pleasures of suggestion, the enigma of the 'Idée' and the depersonalization of the 'auteur' found their ultimate incarnation in Fuller herself.[29] Occupying this same sphere of influence, the sculptor Auguste Rodin (known in fact for his friendship with Fuller) confessed similar thoughts, acknowledging the obscurity and ambiguity of his sculptures, as well as their appeal to the observer. To Rodin, this appeal encapsulated the inner essence of art: suggestiveness was privileged for its ability to awaken the imagination, expand its creative capacity and press upon the borders of meaning and signification.[30]

Figure 4.2, dating from 1904, epitomizes and encapsulates this ideal. Dedicated to the French artist Eugene Carrière, the original image – a calotype, an early photographic negative dipped in silver nitrate and gallic acid – depicts Fuller's characteristic swirling motion and voluptuous

---

[27] Ducrey explores the specific influence of Mallarmé's 'théories sur la danse' on the contemporary press, citing in particular the writings of the Belgian Georges Rodenbach: see Guy Ducrey, 'La Danseuse et *Le Figaro*', *Littérature et nation* 2, no. 14 (1995), 161–72.

[28] See Dario Gamboni, *Potential Images: Ambiguity and Indeterminacy in Modern Art* (London: Reaktion, 2002). Gamboni's study begins with a 1902 diary entry by the French artist Odilon Redon – *À soi-même: journal (1867–1915)* (Paris: Floury, 1922), 97 – that sums up the contemporaneous aesthetic of indeterminacy: 'Le sens du mystère, c'est d'être tout le temps dans l'équivoque, dans les double, triple aspects, des soupçons d'aspect (images dans images), formes qui vont être, ou qui le seront selon l'état d'esprit du regardeur. Toutes choses plus que suggestives, puisqu'elles apparaissent.' Gamboni also links the phenomenon of 'potential images' to concurrent trends in the philosophy and psychology of perception, as well as the modernist 'subjectivization' of the observer described by Jonathan Crary in his *Techniques of the Observer: On Vision and Modernity in the Nineteenth Century* (Cambridge, MA: MIT Press, 1990).

[29] See Mallarmé, 'Crise de vers', in *Œuvres complètes*, ed. Mondor and Jean-Aubry, 360–8.

[30] On his sculptures, Rodin maintained: 'Ils éveillent sans aucun secours étranger l'imagination des spectateurs. Et cependant, loin de l'encercler dans les limites étroites, ils lui donnent de l'élan pour vagabonder à sa fantaisie. Or c'est là, selon moi, le rôle de l'art.' See Auguste Rodin, *L'Art: entretiens réunis par Paul Gsell* (Paris: Bernard Grasset, 1911), 213. Redon, equally enthused by 'le monde ambigu de l'indéterminé', described the role of art in similar terms: 'd'obtenir chez le spectateur, par un attrait subit, toute l'évocation, tout l'attirant de l'incertain, sur les confins de la pensée'. See Odilon Redon, 'Confidances d'artiste' (1909), in *À soi-même: journal (1867–1915)* (Paris: José Corti, 1961), 11–30, at 27–8.

Figure 4.2 R. Moreau, *Loïe Fuller dansant* (à la Carrière), *c.* 1904; courtesy of the Musée Rodin, Paris

veils. But it also conveys its own ambiguities. Despite celebrations (and accusations) of mechanical reproduction, the medium of photography contributed many 'potential images': techniques of photomontage, multi-exposure and gum-bichromate printing enabled the 'blurring' of photographed objects, foregrounding visual indeterminacy while engaging the observer in the creative process.[31] Here, the blurred effect – which owes in

---

[31] See Heinz K. Henisch and Bridget A. Henisch, *The Photographic Experience, 1839–1914: Images and Attitudes* (University Park, PA: Pennsylvania State University Press, 1994); Michel Frizot,

part to the calotype process – dissolves the outline of Fuller's veils, as well as her facial features. The resulting impression of movement, swift yet gentle, draws the observer into continuously reconstructing the visual scene. But look closely and, ironically, we are told to look from afar ('Regardez de loin'). Fuller's body becomes vaguer still, devoid of all detail and reference points. Eventually she/it disappears, a blotch of white on a non-descript background, a random smudge.

The effect is that which Fuller set out to achieve. In newspaper articles and published interviews, Fuller gushed at length about her guiding principle, an aesthetic of obliquity in which dance was a free-floating signifier, one that compelled the spectator's 'reading in'.[32] Certainly, this line of argument underscored her thoughts on music. Unlike several of her dancing contemporaries, Fuller chose not to advocate pseudo-scientific theories of specific alignments or equivalences (of beat, rhythm, motif, metre and so forth) between music and gesture.[33] Instead, she spoke sweepingly of the mobility of musical meaning, the indeterminacy of the orchestra and a special symbolic quality that made music replete with imagined metaphoricity. The role of the imagination was key. Fuller exalted the interpretive endeavour and the creative agency of the observer – that of the spectator inside the theatre and that of herself, 'observer' of music. While advocating an impromptu style of dancing based on individual intuition and a musical invitation to experience, she encouraged those in her audience to 'read your own story into a dance, just as you … read it into music'.[34]

---

ed., *A New History of Photography* (Cologne: Könemann, 1998); and, most recently, Kaja Silverman, *The Miracle of Analogy, or The History of Photography*, vol. 1 (Stanford: Stanford University Press, 2015).

[32] Readers might wish to consult the voluminous files of press clippings, programmes and iconographical material housed at the Bibliothèque-Musée de l'Opéra (Dossier d'artiste, Loie Fuller); the Bibliothèque nationale de France, département des Arts du spectacle (Fonds Rondel); the Houghton Library, Harvard University (Theatre Collection, Loie Fuller Research Files and Clippings); the New York Public Library for the Performing Arts (Loie Fuller Papers and Robinson Locke Collection); as well as the Musée Rodin Archives. To pick one clipping almost at random, see Fuller's interview with 'Covielle', 'Danse, musique, lumière chez Loie Fuller', *L'Éclair*, 5 May 1914; F-Pn, Fonds Rondel 12124.

[33] For more on contemporary dance theories and theorists, see my 'Representational Conundrums'. In Fuller's words, 'Oh, des doctrines! Il n'y a pas de doctrines, pas de règles, pas de formules, pas de théories, pas de discipline': see Fuller's interview with André Arnyvelde, 'Écoles de beauté', *Je sais tout*, 15 November 1913, 599–614, at 610.

[34] Fuller, quoted in 'Lois [sic] Fuller in a Church', n.d.; clipping, Houghton Library, Harvard University (hereafter US-CAh), TMC, HTC, Clippings 1. She continued: 'No one can tell you what Beethoven thought when he wrote the "Moonlight Sonata"; no one knows Chopin's point of view in his nocturnes, but to each music lover there is in them a story, the story of his own experience and his own explorations into the field of art … You can put as many stories

As Rancière observes, few of Fuller's critics mentioned music in their reviews, besides listing the repertoire Fuller used as accompaniment – mostly pre-existing instrumental pieces, likely familiar to spectators.[35] But those who did dwelt not on specific repertoire choices, prominent pictorial allusions or musical motifs: like Fuller, reviewers tended to invoke music in the abstract, as an aesthetic condition or sphere of influence that text and visuals (dance, set design, props) could only aspire to. French writer Anatole France – the author of a preface for Fuller's 1908 autobiography – described 'une musique pour les yeux' ('music for the eyes').[36] Critic and novelist Leo Clarétie – the nephew of Jules, a prominent literary figure who urged Fuller to write that autobiography – gushed in similar terms:

Music is the joy of the ears; it is also the joy of the eyes. She makes the music pictorial; she sees it and makes it seen; she evokes the otherworldly; she embodies the intangible.[37]

The touchstone for some critics was a proto-Wagnerian concept of synesthesia: Fuller, it was said, had fulfilled Wagner's ambition, creating an enticing audio-visual unity. For Camille Mauclair, this new paradigm of art was understood not as a confluence or fusion of disparate art forms but as the re-emergence of a 'homogenous essence' (the term is from British literary critic Frank Kermode) underlying each.[38] Fuller, to Mauclair, embodied this shared, singular substance:

There is no show, no song, no dance, but there is Art, nameless, radiant, estranged from all theories, offering the soul, the mind and the senses the pleasure that comes from a complete and homogenous zone.[39]

---

as you wish to music, but you may be sure that no two people will see the same story. So every dance has its meaning, but your meaning is not mine, nor mine yours. Dancing is movement made beautiful. You must in it express your own true self.'

[35] Rancière, *Aisthesis*, 96–7.

[36] Anatole France, cited in Louis Schneider, 'La Loie Fuller et son école de danse', 10 November 1912; clipping, F-Pn, Ro 12124.

[37] 'La musique est la joie des oreilles; elle fut encore la joie des yeux. Elle rend la musique picturale; elle voit et fair voir; elle est évocatrice de l'iréel; elle matérialise l'insaisissable.' Clarétie's acclamatory words appeared, alongside those of other critics, within the programme that accompanied Fuller's appearance at the Théâtre du Châtelet, May 1914; housed at US-CAh.

[38] Frank Kermode, 'Poet and Dancer before Diaghilev', in *Puzzles and Epiphanies: Essays and Reviews 1958–1961* (New York: Chillmark Press, 1962), 1–28, at 2.

[39] 'Il n'y a là, ni pièce, ni un chant, une danse, mais il y a de l'Art, innommé, radieux, étranger aux théories, donnant à l'âme, à l'intelligence et aux sens la jouissance qui resulte d'un lieu homogène et complet.' Mauclair's comments were also printed in the 1914 programme described in note 37.

Mallarmé, Mauclair's literary crush, also spoke of the emergence of 'Art', singling out 'Musique' as the sonorous equivalent of one of Fuller's billowing sheets of silk.[40] Like a veil, a medium of both concealment and suggestion, 'Musique' helped further deny the material reality of Fuller's danced theatre. It signalled an immaterial milieu, one that Fuller, 'une apparition magique', made visible on stage.

Here we might pause for a moment and hazard a hypothesis: if music is elusive and inscrutable, saturated with ever-shifting meaning, then listening is subjective and speculatory, something akin to the French custom of *flânerie*. This hypothesis is not new. Speaking in general terms of music listening as an interpretive experience, Lawrence Kramer invokes the everyday lifestyle of the *flâneur*: the keen-eyed, casual wanderer who strolls the city streets, making detour after detour, observing and delighting in the transitory surrounds and the excitement of the city's sensory attractions. To Kramer, these characteristics offer a useful actualization of the listening experience, suggesting a mode of attention and an interpretive awareness – as well as a sense of freedom from real or imagined constraints – that resonates with the mechanics of musical perception and understanding, besides their performative aspects.[41] In the present case, the analogy seems particularly apt. As is well known, the *flâneur* has its origins in a specific type or category of nineteenth-century Parisian, one that signified a way of seeing, feeling, knowing and behaving in an urban culture based increasingly on visual spectacle and performance. The *flâneur* was known to idle and saunter; a kind of bourgeois urban explorer, he was a man of leisure and imaginative licence not only to observe but also to command and participate in city life. With overdeveloped sensibilities and individualistic tastes, the *flâneur* fancied himself as both a connoisseur of the arts and an amateur detective. He was fascinated by the bursting metropolis, drawn to investigate the mysteries of the urban scene and to intensify his experience when confronting, and partaking in, the city's sensualized delights.[42]

---

[40] See Mallarmé, 'Considérations sur l'art du ballet et la Loïe Fuller', *Œuvres complètes*, ed. Mondor and Jean-Aubry, 309.

[41] Lawrence Kramer, *The Thought of Music* (Berkeley and Los Angeles: University of California Press, 2016), 149–50.

[42] As is well known across the humanistic disciplines, there exists a huge literature on the *flâneur*, the concept dating back to Charles Baudelaire's mid-nineteenth-century essay 'The Painter of Modern Life' (1863), famously brought to scholarly consciousness by Walter Benjamin in his unfinished magnum opus *The Arcades Project*. Studies I have found especially stimulating include Susan Buck-Morss, *The Dialectics of Seeing: Walter Benjamin and the Arcades Project* (Cambridge, MA: MIT Press, 1989); Priscilla Parkhurst Ferguson, *Paris as Revolution: Writing the Nineteenth-Century City* (Berkeley and Los Angeles: University of California Press, 1994);

Pondering the mysterious, extending the imaginative reach, actively engaged in the interpretive process: according to the standard nineteenth-century taxonomy, the *flâneur* is not unlike the theatrical spectator – at least, the spectator at Loie Fuller's performance. *Flânerie*, it follows, might be a salutary metaphor: the practice can furnish the terms and dynamics of the spectator's engagement with Fuller, thus helping us appreciate and articulate the interpretive ethos of contemporary critics and visual artists, as well as Fuller herself. Perhaps the alignment is to be expected. Theatrical experience, then as now, is constructed and mediated by a mirage of subjective sensory impressions that relate as much to life outside the theatre as to the goings-on inside: the theatre and the city might function as one boundless and continually negotiated environment, filtered through text, image, gesture and sound. As for this sound, we might conceive of *flânerie* as an aural experience too, listening as a mode of creative conjecture, confabulation, speculation, extrapolation, pursuit, coaxing, modelling, imagining – an act of critical productivity that seeks to recover and disclose hidden metaphorical content.

II

Yet this argument surely bears further scrutiny. Why? Not least because, as literary theorist Anne Anlin Cheng reminds us in her recent 'surface archeology' of skin: 'Sometimes it is not a question of what the visible hides, but how it is that we have failed to see certain things on its surface.'[43] In the present context it is tempting to wonder whether blanket endorsements of *flânerie* might eclipse the surface complexities and historical contingencies of audio-visual spectatorship.

As recent scholars have shown, *flânerie* can be easily exposed as a pseudo-historical fiction, a convenient yet potentially misleading umbrella-term for a range of sensory-perceptual regimes and human relations – interpersonal relations as well as an individual's relations with contemporary technologies of sight, sound and mechanical reproduction. Revisionist scholarship tends to identify alternative modes of urban spectatorship, particularly towards the end of the century, during the formative period of the French mass press (roughly 1860 to 1910), modes that reveal

and Vanessa Schwartz, *Spectacular Realities: Early Mass Culture in fin-de-siècle Paris* (Berkeley and Los Angeles: University of California Press, 1998).
[43] Anne Anlin Cheng, 'Skins, Tattoos, and Susceptibility', *Representations* 108, no. 1 (2009), 98–119, at 101.

something of the larger socio-cultural fabric of the period, of which *flânerie* was but one tangled and tattered thread.[44]

Contemplating Fuller's Parisian reception with this revisionist impulse in mind, a number of events, reports, objects and images flash red. (Or, rather, *should* flash red, for these bits and pieces of evidence, readily available across digital platforms, are rarely cited in the secondary literature, even though – or perhaps because – they offer insights that would appear to undermine our usual perceptions.) For starters, it is difficult to look past the incident that occurred at the newly renovated Théâtre des Arts, Paris, 9 November 1907. During the evening entertainment, the *répétition générale* of Fuller's production of *La Tragédie de Salomé* (set to a score by the French composer Florent Schmitt), the stage lights went out. According to a reporter for the theatrical daily *Comœdia*, Fuller immediately stalled:

The great artist stopped, shocked, furious, devastated; she pointed accusingly toward the electricians leaning over the stage curtains and moaned, her sadness expressed in a strange foreign accent: 'I've failed! I've failed!'[45]

Afterwards, the article continues, no one in the audience dared laugh; and Fuller took a turn for the worse, becoming ill – 'toute impressionnée, toute nerveuse' – from the stress of it all. Perhaps she had read the review in the fortnightly *Le Monde musical*, written by editor and dance enthusiast André Mangeot. While Mangeot chose not to mention the electrical mishap, he was far from complementary about Fuller, 'la pseudo-danseuse':

Stripped of her serpentine dances, Loïe Fuller is no longer anything. Not a single gesture is beautiful, not a single pose is gracious ... She is neither a mime nor a dancer, she is, in the snake or peacock dance, nothing but a clothes horse, clumsy and ugly.[46]

---

[44] Susan Buck-Morss, 'The Flâneur, the Sandwichman and the Whore: The Politics of Loitering', *New German Critique* 39 (1986), 99–140; Keith Tester, *The Flâneur* (London and New York: Routledge, 1994); Schwartz, *Spectacular Realities*; Mary Gluck, 'The Flâneur and the Aesthetic: Appropriation of Urban Culture in Mid-Nineteenth-Century Paris', *Theatre, Culture and Society* 20, no. 5 (2003), 53–80; and her *Popular Bohemia* (Cambridge, MA: Harvard University Press, 2005).

[45] G. Davin de Champclos, 'Théâtre des Arts', *Comœdia*, 10 November 1907, 2–3: 'La grande artiste s'arrêta, interloquée, furieuse, désolée; elle tendit des bras chargés d'imprécations vers les électriciens penchés dans les frises et gémit, avec un indéfinissable accent de tristesse et d'outre-Manche: "Je suis manquée! Je suis manquée!"'

[46] André Mangeot, '*La Tragédie de Salomé*', *Le Monde musical*, 15 November 1907, 318: 'Dépouillée de ses danses serpentines, la Loïe Fuller n'est plus rien. Pas une geste n'est beau, pas une attitude n'est gracieuse ... Elle n'est ni une mime, ni une danseuse, elle n'est, dans la danse des serpents ou du paon, qu'un porte-accessoire, maladroit et laid.'

Mangeot's are harsh words, but not necessarily surprising: *Salomé* was a drawn-out dramatic piece, quite unlike Fuller's usual abstract and autonomous offerings. Moreover, his entirely negative summation, coupled with the technical short-circuiting and general fiasco, paints a curious picture of Fuller and her Parisian reception, yet one that resonates with a later article by the well-known music critic Louis Laloy. Published in *La Revue Musicale*, Laloy's review offers a lengthy explanation of something that he – and, it seems, Mangeot – regards as fact: Fuller is not a dancer. With reference to Fuller's acquisition of a dance school and her recent undertaking as a teacher, Laloy offers a series of unflattering comparisons, exalting the talent and artistry of the ballet master Leo Staats, the inimitable Vaslav Nijinsky and the dance queen Anna Pavlova, but finding only fault with Fuller. More specifically, it is the perceived vulgarity of the American's stage effects that so offends Laloy, together with the brutal reality of Fuller's physical form. In a telling inversion of Mallarmé's famous line, Laloy quips: 'Ce que nous voyons n'a plus rien de fictive: c'est la femme' ('That which we see no longer has anything fictive about it: it is a woman').[47] In sum: a woman emptied of metaphor, of the imaginary, of the inexhaustible richness of meaning. Ballooning across the stage is someone weighty and corpulent, fleshy and kitsch, as real as faulty wiring, as crude as industrialized effects.

Something of this same idea emerges from the extant visual evidence. Certainly, Fuller's picture-album contains plenty of illustrations *à la* Carrière: photographs, such as Figure 4.2 by Moreau, that convey a sense of ethereality and suggestiveness; sculptures, such as the gleaming bronzes by Raoul François Larche, that appear to transcend the conventional body; and drawings, such as Rodin's roughly sketched watercolour, that depict only a vivid, hallucinogenic swirl. But there are also visual representations that call to mind a contrasting surface aesthetic. Consider Figure 4.3, an unsigned photograph dating from around 1900. On first glance, this photograph might look familiar: with Fuller reduced to a dissolvable blur, the image resembles Figure 4.2. But instead of the usual black backdrop and empty visual scene, Fuller-in-motion is photographed in an artist's studio, the interior decoration as distinctive as the dancer herself. Large framed posters, sculpted busts, decorative plates, jugs, vases, figurines: all are crammed into this room, the two large posters on the left vying for space; and all are material manifestations of the American – memorabilia or else promotional material for her shows, miscellanies of Brand Fuller.

[47] Louis Laloy, 'To dance or not to dance', *La Revue musicale SIM*, 1 June 1914, 56–8, at 57.

Figure 4.3 Anonymous, *Loie Fuller as Blurred Figure in Room*, c. 1900; courtesy of the New York Public Library

That Fuller put considerable effort into creating and sustaining her public image, continually seeking to capitalize on her shows, her teaching initiatives, her pseudo-scientific inventions and the success of her students, is well known. Hence the accumulation of souvenirs, from decorative tins to brass bookends, fabric scarves and jewellery. These were largely functional items, for personal or domestic use; manufactured en masse, they were designed to pictorialize the object in question – the scarved, swirling and (unusually) svelte dancer – and throw a spotlight on Fuller's signature appearance. Compared to the standard iconography, though, they should give us pause. Presenting Fuller as an airbrushed icon or graphic likeness while compacting her pictorial significance into concrete, tangible form, the souvenirs reveal a change in attitude, a Gestalt-switch, according to which the dancer becomes a highly marketable inventory. This shift in perception – from free-wheeling interpretive reverie (i.e., from regarding Fuller as a unique and irreplaceable form of creative wealth) to consumerist insatiability (eying her image for its assets and iterability) – situates Fuller squarely within the technology of industrial production. As a result, the souvenirs attest to a form of cultural reprogramming or restructuring of the aesthetic object: they are not aiming to exalt ambiguity, suggestiveness or any potentially boundless metaphoricity; neither are they designed to convey the imaginative side of seeing, to 'subjectivize' the observer. The latter, indeed, is downgraded in status, reduced to a function of fandom; the keepsakes themselves short-circuit the representational mode and collectively normalize Fuller's once-radical stage pictures.[48]

Were they, though, radical? Fuller's assimilation into a culture of commodity production – a culture based on the industrialization of artisanal practice, on stereotyping, banalizing, multiplication and unlimited simulacra – casts new light on the theme of originality. Clearly, Fuller was driven to promote the perceived novelty of her theatrical methods and her manner of dancing, upholding the originary purity and autographic character of the resulting 'art'. Yet she happily stepped aside and gave over that 'art' to an afterlife of mechanical reproduction. This begs the question: was there ever an original, a unique or authentic exemplar, or was Fuller's dancing an art of reproduction from its very beginning, an art for which no one could claim the patent?

History offers clues. In 1892, Fuller filed an infringement suit against a chorus girl called Minnie Renwood Bemis who was offering her own version of the 'Serpentine Dance' at the Casino Theatre, New York. In brief, Fuller lost the case: Judge E. Henry Lacombe refused to award her an injunction against Bemis or to grant copyright protection to the Serpentine number. The dance, the judge explained, was:

a series of graceful movements, combined with an attractive arrangement of drapery, lights and shadows, telling no story, portraying no character, depicting no emotion. The merely mechanical movements by which effects are produced on the stage are not subjects of copyright where they convey no ideas whose arrangement makes up a dramatic composition. Surely those described and practiced here convey, and were designed to convey, to the spectator no other idea than that

---

[48] Garelick identifies Fuller's 'odd position between high modernist art and "low" popular or mass culture' in her interpretive tour-de-force *Electric Salome*, 17.

a comely woman is illustrating the poetry of motion in a singularly graceful fashion.[49]

No story, no character, no emotion. No idea. While 'graceful', 'attractive' and 'pleasing', Fuller's were 'merely mechanical movements', her small footsteps and more vigorous *baguette*-twirling seemingly mass-produced and commodified, divested of dramatic content and any kind of expression. The 'Serpentine Dance' was thus from the outset divided and multiple, entangled with prior exemplars – including skirt-dancing, vaudeville skits, Indian Nautch dancing and the ancient tradition of veil-dancing from Tanagra, Greece.[50] And it went on to be copied, circulated widely across the United States and Western Europe by Fuller herself (in repeated acts of self-imitation), besides Bemis and countless others. The most well-known spin-off was perhaps the 1896 short film by Louis and Auguste Lumière (it was one of their earliest cinematic attempts): a one-minute sequence of silk-swirling by a convincing Fuller look-alike.[51] That this person was not Fuller was seemingly of no concern, for the dancing body was exchangeable, the 'Serpentine Dance' firmly ensconced in the public domain. Like the souvenirs and promotional posters mentioned earlier, these silent sixty seconds of colourful, wave-like transformations function to capture and enframe the dancer. That is, they pictorialize her moving figure, quite literally: the Lumière brothers tinted the veils of each frame by hand, attempting to depict with some precision Fuller's multi-coloured light effects.[52]

Picturing, I would argue, is also the dominant effect of Figure 4.3, Fuller *à l'intérieure*, the function not only of the massive posters and shelved souvenirs, but also of the photograph itself. The latter, of course, comes with its own mechanism of enframing, the perpendicular angles helping structure and encase the visual field. Yet the boundary lines of the photo also draw attention to the various acts of enframing within it (or is it the other way around?): the hefty-looking constructions that delimit the size of

---

[49] *Fuller v. Bemis*, Circuit Court S. D. New York, 18 June 1892; quoted in *Federal Reporter* 50, no. 989 (1892), 929.

[50] Anthea Kraut offers a detailed account of Fuller's legal case in her book *Choreographing Copyright: Race, Gender, and Intellectual Property Rights in American Dance* (New York and Oxford: Oxford University Press, 2015), 43–90.

[51] Louis and Auguste Lumière, *Danse serpentine* (1896), Archives du Film du Centre National de la Cinématographie, Lumière Catalogue Number 765; also see the film *Loïe Fuller et ses imitatrices*, a short montage produced by Giovanni Lista in collaboration with the Cinémathèque de la Danse, Paris (1994) and, an extended version, with CNRS, Paris (2006).

[52] On the role of colour in the emergence of silent film, see Joshua Yumibe, *Moving Color: Early Film, Mass Culture, Modernism* (New Brunswick: Rutgers University Press, 2012).

the posters; the invisible frames that capture and collapse the dancer into token or memento – that is, into pure, transparent objecthood. To me at least, all this framing points to the bottomless pit of reduplication, to the ongoing objectification of Fuller as – is it foolish to suggest? – a kind of inverse-Readymade.

The creation of French artist-provocateur Marcel Duchamp, the Readymade was designed to offer a private viewing experience and was originally exhibited in Duchamp's home studio. A foreboding of the death of painting according to some commentators, the genre appeared to renounce the conventional principle and model of mimesis in favour of straightforward if unusual physical placement and an attitude of visual indifference. For the most glaring feature of the Readymade was its material content: ordinary, manufactured items (a bicycle wheel, a shovel, a urinal) were displayed as art, their ontological status completely re-envisaged by their selection, rehoming and exhibition, as well as the mode of spectatorship they now seemed to demand.[53] It is this feature that constitutes the obvious point of difference with Figure 4.3, in which the Readymade logic is inversed: Fuller, that ethereal incarnation of Art-with-a-capital-A, is presented here as 'found object', as an ordinary, manufactured item. Relegated to the status of a domestic commonplace, she is divested of symbolic or metaphorical content, her dancing body evacuated of meaning. Together with the material items photographed, Figure 4.3 shares a set of cultural coordinates with the evidence already presented – the copyright saga, the technical hitch, the negative reviews by Mangeot and Laloy. There is, it seems, an emerging counter-narrative to the usual scholarly wisdom about Fuller, one that swaps authorship for objecthood, quiddity for multiplicity, opacity for transparency and a metaphorical draining of the dancer in question.

---

[53] The art and aesthetic of Marcel Duchamp have attracted a good deal of scholarly attention in recent decades; indeed, attention itself – as a historical phenomenon and theoretical problematic – comes to the fore in many studies, alongside issues of visual perspective, mechanical reproduction and indeterminacy within modern art. I have found the following particularly engaging: Martha Buskirk and Mignon Nixon, eds., *The Duchamp Effect* (Cambridge, MA: MIT Press, 1996); Hans Belting, *Looking Through Duchamp's Door: Art and Perspective in the Work of Duchamp, Sugimoto, Jeff Wall* (Cologne: W. König, 2009); Thomas Deane Tucker, *Derridada: Duchamp as Readymade Deconstruction* (Lanham: Lexington, 2009); Herbert Molderings, *Duchamp and the Aesthetics of Chance: Art as Experiment* (New York: Columbia University Press, 2010); John Moffitt, *Alchemist of the Avant-Garde: The Case of Marcel Duchamp* (New York: State University of New York Press, 2012); and Adina Kamien-Kazhdan, *Remaking the Readymade: Duchamp, Man Ray and the Conundrum of the Replica* (London and New York: Routledge, 2018).

III

If we are to ask what music has to do with this alternative viewpoint, we might point to the commodification, multiplication and stereotyping that characterized Fuller's method; that is, her dancing to pre-existing 'classical favourites', well-known extracts by Wagner, Debussy, Mendelssohn, Chopin, Grieg, Schubert and others. Clearly, this ethos of reproduction would help promote and extend the counter-narrative suggested, off-setting mystical visions of 'Music' (boundless, imaginary) and listening ('symptomatic', conjectural) with the cultural reality of commercialization. But there is more to it than this, I think; more to do with that Readymade connection.

Another feature of Duchamp's specimens was their signatory inscription, sometimes false and fictitious (say, that of an alter-ego), sometimes linked to a title, dedication or cryptic comment. An obvious example is the men's urinal titled *Fountain* by Duchamp. Exhibited for the first time at the Grand Central Palace, New York City, where it was placed on its side (at 90 degrees from its normal position), the porcelain object carried the signature 'R. Mutt 1917', a possible reference to one of Duchamp's friends or collaborators, or even to the generic designation Readymade. Equally curious (and notorious) was the snow shovel Duchamp had bought from a local hardware store and hung from the ceiling of his studio two years earlier. At a time when the Readymade was still a private experience, a type of parlour game between the artist and his friends, the shovel offered a prophetic insight: Duchamp added the line 'In advance of the broken arm', signing the structure as himself on this occasion. Certainly, his black painted scrawl could indicate an 'authentic' artistic presence, the aura of singularity and uniqueness conferring a warrant of authorization or origination. But it could also function as a marker of commodification, trivialization and potentially endless reproduction, betraying the essential iterability of the convention of signatures and so endorsing the status of the objects exhibited not as artworks but manufactured goods.[54]

It is irresistible to imagine, in Fuller's moving theatre, this signatory function assigned to music. Admittedly, dance might be the more obvious possibility. Dance critics, historians and practitioners have long conceptualized dance as an art of inscription: consider, for example, the notion of dance-as-physical-graffiti

---

[54] On the function of Duchamp's signatures and inscriptions, see Dalia Judovitz, *Unpacking Duchamp: Art in Transit* (Berkeley and Los Angeles: University of California Press, 1998); and her *Drawing on Art: Duchamp and Company* (Minneapolis: University of Minnesota Press, 2010).

(an analogical principle used by Sally Banes to describe emerging hip-hop styles);[55] or the critical trope dance-as-apparatus-of-capture (for André Lepecki, the working definition of Western choreography).[56] Even in the late nineteenth century, and in relation to Fuller specifically, the idea of dance as a form of corporeal writing gained special salience, not least from Mallarmé, for whom dance was the supreme theatrical form of poetry, the body a source of living symbols.[57] An anonymous lithograph dating from c. 1893 (Figure 4.4) appears to suggest something similar. Depicting a radiant, frizzy-haired Fuller, her body not human but serpentine, the image underscores what was a common theme in contemporary popular culture: Fuller-as-snake implicated her famous 'Serpentine Dance', with its characteristic snaking movements, as well as her exoticist cultural baggage (interrelated themes of seduction, decadence and the mythological femme-fatale). But then there is another implication, equally obvious: Fuller-as-snake is an instrument of writing. Besides the mini-snakes outlining each letter of Fuller's nickname, Fuller-as-snake is in possession of long white scrolls, reams of uncoiling paper. The analogy, it seems, could not be clearer: dance-as-writing, body-as-tool, with Fuller in control of her critical reception.

Yet the paper is blank. That not a single word is inscribed on the scrolls makes explicit – in purely visual terms – the draining of content described, repeatedly, in this chapter. We might argue that Fuller-as-snake indexes an absence of signification, a lack of ideational value: she/it forgoes any representational function and appears to 'sign' like a footprint in the snow, a doorbell ringing, thunder, smoke – that is, like a paradigmatic index, a trace left by a physical presence.

So to repeat my earlier hypothesis: when transposed to the theatre, Brand Fuller emanates from the pit. The facts of production can be recalled in support. Fuller's soundtracks, far from hermeneutical conundra, were often chosen for her by theatre directors, entrepreneurs with an eye to box-office receipts; others were tried and tested, for she could dance the same number (say, the 'Fire Dance') to different musical choices (first, to an

---

[55] Sally Banes, 'Physical Graffiti: Breaking is Hard to Do', *Village Voice*, 22 April 1981; also see her edited volume *Writing Dancing in the Age of Postmodernism* (Hanover, NH: Wesleyan University Press, 1994).

[56] André Lepecki, *Exhausting Dance: Performance and the Politics of Movement* (London and New York: Routledge, 2006).

[57] On the historical context from which Mallarmé's dance-themed writings emerged, see Terri A. Mester, *Movement and Modernism: Yeats, Elliot, Lawrence, Williams and Early Twentieth-Century Dance* (Fayetteville: University of Arkanas Press, 1997); and Mary Fleischer, *Embodied Texts: Symbolist Playwright-Dancer Collaborations* (London and New York: Rodopi, 2007).

Figure 4.4 Anonymous, *La Loïe*, c. 1893; courtesy of the Musée des Arts Décoratifs, Paris

extract from Gabriel Pierné's 1895 *Salomé* suite, later, to Wagner's 'Ride of the Valkyries'). As Fuller biographer Giovanni Lista has noted, it was Rud Aronson, impresario at the Casino Theatre in New York City, who came up with the name 'Serpentine Dance' and decided upon the associated music: 'Loin du bal', by French composer Ernest Gillet, Fuller's first signature tune.⁵⁸ 'Ride of the Valkyries' quickly became another, associated less with Wagner and his ideological agenda than with the newly designed system of under-lighting that Fuller invented and employed to convey the illusion of being engulfed by flames.⁵⁹

In Fuller's theatre, then, music could be a form of inscription or branding: in true indexical fashion, it could serve as an empty signifier, could operate on a sub-symbolic level. As a handful of critics noted, across a decade-or-so of Fuller productions, there seemed to be little synchrony or parallelism between music and movement;⁶⁰ as mentioned earlier, most reports failed to note anything of interest about the chosen musical extracts, merely listing their titles and composers.⁶¹ Music, we might conclude, functioned as a sonorous signature-stroke, as well as an aide-mémoire: a then-familiar tune such as 'Ride of the Valkyries', incised from Wagner's music-drama, could be attached to Fuller and her flames, and could then circulate in a kind of repetitive orbit, bearing and gathering the authenticating weight, not of origination, consent or any kind of cultural heritage, but of illusion, consumption, capital.

IV

To pursue this premise of the indexical model might be to press the point about music and/as advertising, sketching the history of the two in the mid- to late nineteenth century, a period of significant expansion in Parisian consumer culture and one in which the boundary lines between art, entertainment and advertising were increasingly eroded.⁶² We need only glance at front-cover illustrations of the satirical magazine *Le Courrier*

---

[58] Lista, *Loïe Fuller: Danseuse de la Belle Époque*.

[59] See *Loie Fuller's Fire Dance: Reconstruction and Performance*, produced by John Mueller, performed by Jessica Lindberg (Columbus: Dance Film Archive, Ohio State University, 2003).

[60] While Fuller would rhapsodize about music's essential role in her performance ('Something in a bar of music suggests a movement or an attitude to the mind, and accordingly the body shapes itself and moves in sympathy with that idea'), others were unconvinced: see 'Loie Fuller on Dancing', 1 January 1910; clipping, TMC HTC Clippings 1. Laloy, for example, described how she taught her students absolutely nothing, except how to walk and run out of time: Laloy, 'To Dance or Not to Dance', 58. Mangeot spoke similarly, implying a rhythmic discrepancy, in the 'Fire Dance', between music and movement, one that brought to mind an image of flames rising from a log fire while a Chopin waltz was played at the piano: see his article 'L'École de danse de Loïe Fuller', *Le Monde musical*, 30 May 1914, 173.

[61] See Rancière, *Aisthesis*, 96–7.

[62] H. Hazel Hahn offers a stimulating account of the emergence of so-called 'commercial modernity' within the French capital in her *Scenes of Parisian Modernity: Culture and Consumption in the Nineteenth Century* (London and New York: Palgrave Macmillan, 2009).

français to see how music – most often trumpet, gong and drum – was incorporated into the iconography of *Réclame*, used to represent untrustworthiness, danger, materialism and irrationality (noise); namely, the unsavoury side of the advertising industry.

For now, though, let us return to Fuller on stage, tossing her veils and swirling around, while kaleidoscopic colours are projected onto her enormous drapery, and while Wagner roars from the orchestra. If this music could function as mere postulate, an over-familiar signature tune that formed part of a massive flooding of the senses, listening might correlate, not to any inspired interpretive contemplation, but to a wondrous incredulity dubbed 'a lowest-common-denominator culture of the street'.[63] The French term is *badauderie*, after the *badaud* (the gawker), a city-dweller identified by his open, gaping mouth, his involuntary staring and easy, guileless amazement. As mentioned earlier, the nineteenth century witnessed considerable variation in the nature of spectatorship, variation that was represented as much in newly emerging paradigms and patterns of social behaviour and urban planning as in contemporary artistic representations (literature, poetry, painting). The nineteenth-century literary critic Victor Fournel draws a stark comparison between the idealized *flâneur* – Master-and-Commander of the city – and the astonished, overwhelmed *badaud*:

> The simple *flâneur* is always in full possession of his individuality. The individuality of the gawker, on the other hand, disappears and is absorbed by the outside world which delights him to the point of delirium and ecstasy. Under the influence of spectacle, the gawker becomes an impersonal being: no longer a man, he is the public, the crowd.[64]

---

[63] See Gregory Shaya, 'The *Flâneur*, the *Badaud*, and the Making of a Mass Public in France, circa 1860–1910', *The American Historical Review* 109, no. 1 (2004), 41–77, at 51. Shaya offers a revisionist account of late nineteenth-century crowd theory – epitomized by Gustave LeBon's 1895 study *Psychologie des foules* – and the splattering of secondary literature that emerged from the 1970s: see Robert A. Nye, *The Origins of Crowd Psychology: Gustave LeBon and the Crisis of Mass Democracy in the Third Republic* (London: Sage, 1975); Susanna Barrows, *Distorting Mirrors: Visions of the Crowd in Late Nineteenth-Century France* (New Haven and London: Yale University Press, 1981); and Serge Moscovici, *L'Âge des foules: Un traité historique de psychologie des masses* (Paris, 1981).

[64] Victor Fournel, *Ce qu'on voit dans les rues de Paris* (Paris: A. Delahays, 1858), 263: 'Le simple flâneur est toujours en pleine possession de son individualité. Celle du badaud disparaît, au contraire, absorbée par le monde extérieur qui le frappe jusqu'à l'enivrement de l'extase. Le badaud, sous l'influence du spectacle, devient un être impersonnel: ce n'est plus un homme: il est public, il est foule.' Shaya provides a fascinating and densely referenced account of the appropriation of both street phenotypes by later writers, including Walter Benjamin, in his 'The *Flâneur*, the *Badaud*, and the Making of a Mass Public in France, circa 1860–1910'.

An indiscriminate being who absorbs and projects himself into the spectacles around him, the *badaud* became emblematic of modern urban experience, an experience that was not only visual but auditory. The listener-cum-gawker was subsumed into this same emerging mass culture, a perceptual complex that signalled stupor, intoxication, bewilderment, sensory overload, astonishment, shock and collective anonymity.

V (Conclusion)

So to return to my leading question: what do we learn of listening from looking at Loie Fuller? The answer, or rather one answer, is that we learn how easy it is to overturn a tradition of critical engagement, as well as an assumed auditory correlate, if we move out from the shadows, the topos of depth or hiddenness, and loosen our grip on a culture of originals that, in the words of art critic Rosalind Krauss, 'has no place among the reproductive mediums'.[65] Of course, there are a few obvious concerns: first, the legitimacy of sweeping statements about audience engagement based on the views of a handful of critics and artists; second, the transparency of connection (could it be another form of indexicality?) between multi-sensorial modes of attention, particularly cognitive perception and physical behaviour, whether that behaviour exhibits in the stalls or on stage. Then there is the business of 'surface reading' with which I began, itself a form of critical engagement that deserves a more careful scrutiny than I have offered here – not least when 'surface' becomes an aesthetic orientation (some might say the primary characteristic of modernist art) as well as a possible mode of scholarly enquiry.[66] Nonetheless, despite this and other loose threads, the ideas presented in this chapter might be salutary, if only because they point to two perceptual extremes. On the one hand, there is a history of critical thinking and hermeneutical extravagance that characterizes the writing of the majority

---

[65] Rosalind Krauss, 'The Originality of the Avant-Garde: A Postmodernist Repetition', *October* 18 (1981), 47–66, at 52.

[66] On the category of surface and its centrality to twentieth-century modernist aesthetics, see Richard Shusterman, *Surface and Depth: Dialectics of Criticism and Culture* (Ithaca, NY: Cornell University Press, 2002); and Cheng, *Second Skin*. There are of course ongoing debates within the interconnected spheres of visual culture and art history about the salience of surface, its relation to the materiality and dimensionality of the picture plane, the business of representation and the mechanics of sensory perception: seminal texts are reprinted in *Art in Modern Culture: An Anthology of Critical Texts*, ed. Francis Frascina and Jonathan Harris (London: Phaidon, 1992); and *Art in Theory, 1900–2000: An Anthology of Changing Ideas*, ed. Charles Harrison and Paul Wood (London: Wiley, 2003).

of Fuller's critics, at the *fin de siècle* and across the last century, as well as the words of Fuller herself: I have labelled this *flânerie*, assuming a mode of aural attention that posits music as fictive, boundless and bounteous in its interpretive potential. On the other hand, there is an almost entirely inverted paradigm of attention, one that emerges from a smattering of press sources and visual evidence of the practical realities of Fuller's danced theatre and its ensuing commercialization. This, I suggest, can be correlated to *badauderie*, a form of involuntary gawking and sensationalist indulgence that renders music indifferent – akin to the visual indifference that exudes from one of Duchamp's Readymades.

But my aim in this chapter is not to divide or reduce music listening to two mutually exclusive ideals. While, in principle, we can easily distinguish between the two, they are only to be found in de facto mixtures. In other words, it is not a question of one or the other, *flânerie* or *badauderie*, but of how both, sharing a predicament of embodiment, can help us map out a space of possibility – what the theoretically inclined, leaning on Deleuze and Guattari, might call a 'zone of indiscernibility', of constant mutation and divergence.[67] Future research might pursue this idea, speculating on the 'archaeologies of interactivity', to quote film expert Thomas Elsaesser, between those in the audience and those on stage during a historical ballet performance; for example, the unforeseen oddity that was the November 1907 *répétition générale* of Fuller's *Salomé*.[68] In this case, too, we would need to broaden our own perception: as well as exploring spectators' perceptual habits, their relation to theatrical technologies, monetized exhibitionary spaces and the supposed 'specularization' of modern everyday life, we might consider how live musical performance can help determine and sustain different attentive economies.

Of course, conceptualizing ballet music as some sort of discursive construct – not only subject to changing modes of audience attention but among the various media forms that might inspire and support them – is no easy task: despite recent innovations in opera and film studies (theories of 'optical' and 'haptic' perception, 'smooth' and 'striated' space), musicological literature on ballet is scarce, and what there is tends towards the methodologically conservative. But the topic of attention, in relation to danced music theatre, is surely ripe for further questioning. If, functioning as Fuller's accompaniment, Wagner's 'Ride of the Valkyries' could simulate

---

[67] Gilles Deleuze and Félix Guattari, *A Thousand Plateaus: Capitalism and Schizophrenia* (Minneapolis: University of Minnesota Press, 2004).

[68] Thomas Elsaesser, *Film History as Media Archaeology: Tracking Digital Cinema* (Amsterdam: Amsterdam University Press, 2016).

illusionistic depth, hidden mysteries and expressive 'wholeness', it could also remind audiences of music's rootlessness and repeatability, in the process serving to deaden (or at least to overwhelm) that audience's auditory imagination. There is, I think, an important history bubbling at the surface here, a history of modernist art and capitalist modernity, signifying regimes and psychic address, besides an in-built concept of the spectator, his/her sensory perceptions and psycho-physiological orientation vis-à-vis a newly nebulous representational idiom and a newly sensualized urban spectacle. I hope here to have sketched some of the contours this history might follow.

PART II

Case Histories

5 | The 'Splendid and Shameful Art': Dancing in and around the Wagnerian *Gesamtkunstwerk*

THOMAS GREY

In his late collection of anti-Wagnerian aphorisms, *Nietzsche contra Wagner*, Nietzsche diagnoses one of the principal 'dangers' of Wagner's style for the development of modern music in terms that should hardly surprise anyone familiar with *Parsifal* (for instance):

> The aim pursued by recent music under the pointed yet indeterminate rubric of 'endless melody' can be clearly represented by imagining that you are walking into the ocean, gradually losing any secure footing on the ground, until you finally surrender yourself entirely to the mercy of the liquid element: you have to *swim*. It was different with earlier music, when in delicate, solemn, or fiery movements this way and that, faster or slower, one was doing something else altogether, namely *dancing* ... Richard Wagner sought a different kind of movement – and so he overturned the physiological basis of all previous music. Swimming, floating – no longer walking, dancing.[1]

Nietzsche's characterization of this broad departure from regularity of rhythmic syntax and metrical order in Wagner's music is apt at many levels, of course. Although he does not mention it here, Nietzsche could have been thinking of the very opening of *The Ring of the Nibelung* cycle. The first thing we see when the curtain rises on *Das Rheingold* are the three Rhine Maidens, trying their best to swim or float, rather than walk or dance. Other moments of a characteristically Wagnerian 'transcendental' choreography include the flying Valkyries of the famous 'Ride' and Parsifal's metaphysical journey from the outer Grail realm to the inner sanctum of the temple ('I scarcely walk', he exclaims, 'and yet seem to have

---

[1] 'Die Absicht, welche die neuere Musik in dem verfolgt, was jetzt, sehr stark, aber undeutlich, "unendliche Melodie" genannt wird, kann man sich dadurch klar machen, daß man ins Meer geht, allmählich den sicheren Schritt auf dem Grunde verliert und sich endlich dem Elemente auf Gnade und Ungnade übergibt: man soll schwimmen. In der älteren Musik mußte man, im zierlichen oder feierlichen oder feurigen Hin und Wieder, Schneller und Langsamer, etwas ganz anderes, nämlich tanzen ... Richard Wagner wollte eine andre Art Bewegung – er warf die physiologische Voraussetzung der bisherigen Musik um. Schwimmen, Schweben – nicht mehr Gehn, Tanzen.' Friedrich Nietzsche, *Nietzsche contra Wagner* (1889), cited from *Der Fall Wagner: Schriften – Aufzeichnungen – Briefe*, ed. Dieter Borchmeyer (Frankfurt: Insel, 1983), 133–4. (Translations my own unless otherwise noted.)

gone far').² 'Endless melody', Nietzsche continues, '*wants* to break down all regularity of time and motion' (*alle Zeit- und Kraft-Ebenmäßigkeit*). 'The emulation, the sovereignty of such taste poses a danger for music that can scarcely be overestimated – the complete degeneration of all rhythmic sense, *chaos* in place of rhythm.' Such music allies itself to a naturalistic conception of acting and gesture: '*Espressivo* at all costs and music in the service of, indeed enslaved to, "attitude" – *that is the end*.'³ It is easy to dismiss Nietzsche's Erda-like warning as mere anti-Wagnerian histrionics, but at some level he had a point. The pronounced failure of much of the musical avant-garde (broadly construed) of the long twentieth century to sustain an audience surely has as much to do with such an erasure of readily perceptible rhythmic and metrical frameworks as it does with the emancipation of dissonance or the dissolution of generic and formal conventions. Leaving aside the actual future of music after Wagner, though, what are the implications of this critique for understanding dance in relation to Wagner's own so-called 'music of the future'? If the Wagnerian 'total artwork' was meant to be a new, more perfect synthesis of the traditional performing arts, what becomes of dance there, if Nietzsche was right that its 'endless melody' leaves no solid purchase for the dancing human body?

Richard Wagner's fundamental opposition to the conventional ballet of his own time, whether as an autonomous genre or as a requisite component of Parisian-style grand opera, is also no surprise. It is well known, above all, from the episode of the revised Paris *Tannhäuser* of 1861, when he notoriously refused to supply the expected mid-opera divertissement, substituting for this an orgiastic bacchanal in his latest style at the very beginning of the opera. Yet theoretically, of course, dance should be a fully equal partner to music, singing and dramatic poetry in that synthesis of the arts or 'total artwork' (*Gesamtkunstwerk*) that distinguished his idea of 'musical drama' from existing approaches to opera. Wagner makes this very clear in his own attempt to draft a theory of that in the essay *The Artwork of the Future* (1849), one of the three major prose essays produced while he was gearing up for his magnum opus, *The Ring of the Nibelung*. He invokes here the idea

---

² 'Ich schreite kaum, / doch wähn' ich mich schon weit' (*Parsifal*, Act 1).
³ 'Die "unendliche Melodie" will eben alle Zeit- und Ebenmäßigkeit brechen ... Aus einer Nachahmung, aus einer Herrschaft eines solchen Geschmacks entstünde eine Gefahr für die Musik, wie sie größer gar nicht gedacht werden kann – die vollkommene Entartung des rhythmischen Gefühls, das Chaos an Stelle des Rhythmus ... Die Gefahr kommt auf die Spitze, wenn sich eine solche Musik immer enger an eine ganz naturalistische, durch kein Gesetz der Plastik beherrschte Schauspiel und Gebärdenkunst anlehnt, die Wirkung will, nichts mehr ... Das espressivo um jeden Preis und die Musik im Dienerschaft, in der Sklaverei der Attitüde – das ist das Ende.' Nietzsche, *Nietzsche contra Wagner*, 134.

of 'three sister arts' – dance, music and poetry – who together form the basis of drama, or specifically, ancient Greek tragedy. Wagner depicts them in an allegorical embrace, engaged in a harmonious round-dance that evokes classical representations of the 'three graces': 'each one lovingly entwined with the other, arm in arm up to the back of their neck'.[4] The muse- or grace-like personifications of these arts tentatively back away from time to time 'so as to display to the others their fair form', but never quite letting go of each other. Each one ultimately returns to the original eroticized, unifying embrace ('finally reuniting into a single ecstatically vital form, breast to breast, limb to limb in the most ardently loving kiss').[5] This harmonious allegory of an original, classical artistic unity contains within it the seed of Wagner's polemic against the professionalized autonomy of the arts down to the present day: 'any one of them, once removed from this dance, can only sustain an artificial, borrowed existence devoid of life and motion, no longer setting down beneficent laws to its sisters, but instead receiving prescriptive rules for its own mechanical movements'.[6] The polemic against the autonomous or 'absolute' art forms is familiar as a cornerstone of the whole theory of a Wagnerian 'total dramatic artwork of the future'. The familiar polemic, however, begs a central question: what became of dance's supposedly equal partnership in this once and future union of the classical 'sister arts'? In practice, certainly, Wagner's music drama seems to neglect rather sorely this one of the sisters in favour of poetry and music, who also dominate the theory.

In the following survey of these constituent art forms in *The Artwork of the Future* (part 2, sections 3–5), dance is initially singled out as the primary, essential one that 'encompasses in itself the conditions for the manifestation of all other art forms'. All forms of artistic expression, it is suggested here, and certainly all the performing arts begin with the human body: 'The singing and speaking man is necessarily a corporeal being; only through his outer figure, through the motions of his limbs, can the inner,

---

[4] 'Eine mit der anderen liebevoll Arm in Arm bis an den Nacken verschlungen' Richard Wagner, *Das Kunstwerk der Zukunft*, in *Gesammelte Schriften und Dichtungen*, vol. 3 (Leipzig: Breitkopf & Härtel, 1911), 67. (Hereafter cited as GSD.)

[5] 'dann bald diese bald jene einzelne, wie um den anderen ihre schöne Gestalt in voller Selbstständigkeit zu zeigen, sich aus der Verschlingung lösend ... um endlich alle, festumschlungen, Brust an Brust, Glied an Glied in brünstigem Liebeskusse zu einer einzigen, wonniglebendigen Gestalt zu verwachsen'. Wagner, *Das Kunstwerk der Zukunft*, 67–8.

[6] 'daß jede einzelne, aus dem Reigen losgelöst, leben- und bewegungslos nur ein künstlich angehauchtes, erborgtes Leben noch fortführen kann, nicht, wie im Dreiverein, selige Gesetze gebend, sondern zwangvolle Regeln für mechanische Bewegung empfangend'. Wagner, *Das Kunstwerk der Zukunft*, 67.

singing and speaking man become manifest; music and poetry become intelligible to the perfected, artistically receptive man, hearing but also seeing, only in dance (or mime).[7] At this abstract theoretical level, dance is fundamental to Wagner's notions of a collaborative synthesis of the arts. It is obviously the most directly 'embodied' form of human artistic expression, and more specifically, it serves to embody the principle of rhythm in visible form. At the same time, dance, as gesture, can give visible, corporeal expression to both the semantic and the affective dimensions of artistic speech (poetry). Not surprisingly, the gestural-mimetic capacity is privileged by Wagner as the more important contribution to the end goal of drama, but in theory he allows that both abstract, formal dance and mimetic gesture are viable so long as they remain in the service of drama.[8] As autonomous practices in contemporary culture, however, both formal ballet choreography (the various extended *pas* and *divertissements*) and balletic pantomime are strenuously resisted by Wagner. Formal dance choreography of the contemporary ballet is suspected of amounting to little more than a publicly sanctioned prostitution of the female body: false, obsequious, simpering smiles above, and mere acrobatics of the legs and feet below – 'the sum of all the arts of the courtesan' (*Buhlerkünste*).[9] Balletic pantomime is denounced for presuming to abrogate the role of dramatic poetry unto itself, rather than properly collaborating with it.[10] The prominence of 'characteristic' national dance styles in contemporary ballet culture meets with similar ambivalence. This practice suggests the possibility of grounding artistic dance in the all-important soil of the *Volk*, but at present it remains superficial and opportunistic, because isolated from any genuine collaboration with the higher powers of music and poetry, that is, from a genuine dramatic matrix. Having first acknowledged the ontological primacy of dance in a theoretical understanding of his desired synthesis of the arts, and having recognized but then largely rejected the potential of modern European ballet, Wagner concludes his discussion of the medium of dance with a vigorous denunciation. The ultimate deficiency of dance as an autonomous art form, in the narrative ballet-pantomime, is revealed by its reliance on a printed explanatory

---

[7] 'Thus dance achieves its highest and fullest potential as part of the drama, delightful where it directs [the scene], and moving where it submits [to the scene]' ('So erreicht im Drama die Tanzkunst ihre höchste Höhe und ihre vollste Fülle, entzückend, wo sie anordnet, ergreifend, wo sie sich unterordnet'). Wagner, *Das Kunstwerk der Zukunft*, 76.
[8] Wagner, *Das Kunstwerk der Zukunft*, 78.
[9] '[pantomime dance] wants to write poetry, without allying itself to poetry itself' ('Sie will dichten, ohne der Dichtkunst sich zuzugesellen'). Wagner, *Das Kunstwerk der Zukunft*, 80.
[10] See Wagner, *Das Kunstwerk der Zukunft*, 78–9.

programme. It aspires to the condition of drama, and it hopes to remove itself from the 'lascivious gaze of frivolity' by grasping at this 'artificial veil' (i.e., the explanatory programme) 'in order to cover up its shameful nakedness'. Yet this figurative 'veil' merely exposes the very dependency on its sister arts that dance, as ballet, tries vainly to resist:

With what wretched distortion must she [the dance] pay the price of its idle longing for an unnatural independence! She, without whose highest, most particular collaboration the highest, most noble artwork can never be realized, she must at present – cut off from communion with her sisters – fly from prostitution to absurdity, and from absurdity back to prostitution!! – Oh splendid art of dance! Oh shameful art of dance![11]

This conflicted outcry that concludes the disquisition on *Tanzkunst* in *The Artwork of the Future* sums up the problem that the remainder of this chapter seeks to illuminate, from the perspectives of Wagnerian theory, Wagnerian practice, and some of the post-Wagnerian manifestations of the 'total art work' idea in the era of early European modernism. As a first step, I consider Wagner's relatively few attempts to include some kind of formally choreographed episodes within his own works: the extended grand operatic ballet sequence of *Rienzi* (1842) and the tentative experiment of the Venusberg Bacchanal in *Tannhäuser* (1845, rev. 1861). After that, dance episodes become modest in scope (the folk-style *Walzer* in the festival meadow scene of *Die Meistersinger*, Act 3), or mere suggestion (the chorus of Flower Maidens in *Parsifal*, Act 2 (allowing, but not demanding, a choreographic reading)). In either case, a separate, professionally trained dance personnel is no longer presupposed. Returning to the case of the Venusberg Bacchanal in *Tannhäuser*, specifically the radical re-conception of this in 1861, I suggest how Wagner, possibly influenced by the example of Heinrich Heine, pioneered a loosely defined modernist genre of 'dance poem', an extended single-movement choreographic work in which pantomime and proto-'free' dance elements are set to (and motivated by) a lushly orchestrated, tonally 'progressive', formally and syntactically free musical score. A logical, if indirect, outcome of this experiment, suggested in a post-Wagnerian epilogue, are the revolutionary

---

[11] 'Mit welch jämmerlicher Entstellung muß sie das eitle Verlangen nach unnatürlicher Selbstständigkeit büßen. Sie, ohne deren höchste, eigentümlichste Mitwirkung das höchste, edelste Kunstwerk nicht zur Erscheinung gelangen kann, muß – aus dem Vereine ihrer Schwestern geschieden – von Prostitution zur Lächerlichkeit, von Lächerlichkeit zur Prostitution sich flüchten! – O herrliche Tanzkunst! O schmähliche Tanzkunst!' Wagner, *Das Kunstwerk der Zukunft*, 81.

products of Diaghilev's Ballets Russes (above all Stravinsky's famous ballets), but many of the broadly experimental practices of modern dance in the early twentieth century generally. These modernist dance-based versions of the *Gesamtkunstwerk* honour the importance of ambitious, original musical scores as a motivating force in the synthesis of art forms, but they also critique the defining role of word, voice and dramatic narrative in the Wagnerian model.

Ballet, Pantomime and Dance in the Wagner Canon: An Overview

On 7 February 1876 Cosima Wagner reports in her diary a dream of her husband's from the previous night. Richard was conducting from backstage a production of *Der fliegende Holländer* (somehow in tandem with *Tannhäuser*), when 'suddenly he notices *Ocean Waves* (*Die Meereswellen*) is being performed, a ballet (so his singers tell him) by Servais which had been inserted in *Holländer*'. His reaction, naturally, is one of alarm and indignation; he runs on stage to chastise the performers for this unauthorized insertion.[12] It is hardly surprising that the threatened incursion of conventional ballet into his own oeuvre would be a matter of anxiety to Wagner. It is also telling that the dream scenario should involve both *Holländer* and *Tannhäuser*, works that deliberately charted a path away from the operatic conventions of the early nineteenth century, but whose histories were bound up with the Paris Opéra and its institutional obligations to the ballet. The *Holländer* project was originated as a proposal to the Opéra for a one-act work suitable for paring with a two-act ballet-pantomime, in accordance with programming practices of the house (after Wagner had withdrawn his bid to have the full-length grand opera *Rienzi* produced). *Tannhäuser*, of course, became the vehicle of Wagner's signal challenge to the balletic routine of the Opéra when it *was* taken up there in 1861, a definitive trauma of his career whose implications for the potential of dance in the reformed 'total artwork' we will return to below. Before turning to that unique effort to 'revolutionize' dance in the spirit of

---

[12] Cosima Wagner, *Diaries*, vol. 1, ed. Martin Gregor-Dellin and Dietrich Mack, trans. Geoffrey Skelton (New York: Harcourt Brace Jovanovich, 1977), 891; cf. 1033. Wagner seems to refer to François Matthieu Servais, the (possibly adopted) son of Adrien-François Servais (1807–66), a Belgian-born cello virtuoso and father of a small musical dynasty; François Matthieu was also rumoured to be the illegitimate son of Liszt and Princess Carolyn Wittgenstein. He conducted *Der fliegende Holländer* in Brussels in 1872.

the Wagnerian artwork of the future, let us consider the outlines of his engagement with more conventionally choreographed dance in his stage works. These outlines are simple enough, and reflect (again, not surprisingly) a diminishing perspective, from the all-out effort in Act 2 of *Rienzi* to the minimal, qualified dance episodes of *Die Meistersinger* and *Parsifal*. The explicit absence of anything like choreographed dance in the *Ring* cycle and *Tristan und Isolde* points to a separate question: whether the interaction of 'orchestral melody' and the bodily gesture of performers theorized in *Opera and Drama* constitutes an alternative conception of choreography appropriate to the reform agenda of the Wagnerian music drama.[13]

In his first three operas, prior to *Der fliegende Holländer*, Wagner was writing very much for the present, not the subsequently theorized 'future'. The lack of any ballet sequences in *Die Feen* (1833–4) and *Das Liebesverbot* (1834–6) reflects the practice of their generic models: the German Romantic opera of Weber and Marschner, in the first case, and the *opéra comique* of Auber (augmented by some ingredients of his grand opera, *La muette de Portici*), in the second. In turning to the full-blown genre of grand opera in *Rienzi* (1837–40), Wagner had no compunction about incorporating ballet on a lavish scale. As he reflected in the early artistic autobiography *A Communication to my Friends* (1851): '"Grand opera", with all its scenic and musical splendor, its effect-laden and grandly scaled musical passion stood before me as a model; my artistic ambition was not merely to emulate this, however, but to outdo all previous examples in reckless extravagance of means'.[14] This was by no means a cynical exercise, as he also stresses in the *Communication*. He was perfectly intent on showing what an ambitious German composer might achieve in the genre, following what Meyerbeer had done with *Robert le diable* and *Les Huguenots*. The more immediate model for the ballet sequence in *Rienzi* is probably Halévy's *La juive* (1835), an opera particularly admired by Wagner at the time, and whose setting against the Council of Constance in 1414 was not far removed from the medieval Rome of Bulwer-Lytton's heroic tribune. The chivalric ballet-divertissement celebrating Prince Léopold's victory over the Hussites in Act 3 is preceded by a pantomime

---

[13] Insofar as the gestural dimension of Wagner's music dramas remains either an imaginative projection of the orchestral score or is restricted to what can be accomplished through the stage direction of the singers, its claim to embodying the 'dance' component of a theoretical synthesis of art forms is limited. For that reason, this idea of a gestural alternative to choreographed dance is not developed in the present chapter. For some critical perspectives on that topic, see Mary Ann Smart, *Mimomania: Music and Gesture in Nineteenth-Century Opera* (Berkeley and Los Angeles: University of California Press, 2004), 163–204.

[14] Wagner, *Eine Mitteilung an meine Freunde*, GSD vol. 4, 258.

combat between a Saracen warrior and Christian knights, issuing in the release of captive maidens from an 'enchanted castle'. In the Act 2 finale of *Rienzi*, as Wagner originally conceived it, the public celebrations of Rienzi's victory over the renegade Roman nobles begin with an extensive pantomime representing the founding myth of the Roman republic: the rape of Lucretia by Sextus Tarquinius and the ensuing overthrow of the Roman 'tyrants' led by the virtuous Romans Brutus and Collatinus. In both finales the pantomime and ballet are the centre of a grand public spectacle upended by the critical dramatic turn of the plot: Léopold is exposed as the secret suitor of the Jewess Rachel and condemned with her and her father to prison and/or death; Rienzi is set upon by the conspiring *nobili*, survives the attack and decrees their capital punishment.

Characteristic here are both the expanded dimensions and the attempt to increase dramatic relevance. The pantomime in *Rienzi*, which also includes an extended decorative dance for Lucretia's handmaidens, takes up no less than twenty-five pages in the Breitkopf & Härtel piano-vocal score, followed by a full thirty pages of mostly martial-style ballet music. (A complete performance of both would take at least forty minutes.) At the conclusion of the pantomime, Brutus spares the life of Tarquinius, in an example of noble anti-tyrannical clemency, while he warns the Romans to remain armed against future threats to the Republic. The relevance to Rienzi's own vulnerable position vis-à-vis the disgruntled patricians is clear enough. The thematically integrated entertainment suggests how the charismatic populist leader is a canny curator of his own image within the carefully stage-managed 'total artwork' of his political career.[15] But the assassination plot of the *nobili* against the tribune framing the ballet gives the Lucretia pantomime an additional significance: Rienzi's own fatal cycle of clemency and betrayal has already begun. And at this early point in his career, Wagner believed in the dramatic potential of the grand operatic formula. The greater the balletic pomp and circumstance, the more thrilling the subsequent reversal.

Wagner was never to see the totality of his choreographic inspiration for *Rienzi* on stage. And while the Dresden premiere of the opera was his first great success as a composer, the ballet component became a focus of disillusionment with this work and with the conventions of opera, opera houses and their audiences generally. The entire pantomime had to be cut

---

[15] The alleged inspiration *Rienzi* offered to a young Adolf Hitler is of course related to this element of the character and the work. See, e.g., David Huckvale, 'Rienzi's Reich', *Wagner* 19, no. 3 (1998), 103–16.

from the production even before the premiere, which, even so, ran far longer than anticipated. Although Wagner put much more stock in the dramatic pantomime of Lucretia and Tarquinius than in the formal dances (loosely conceived as a series of military and gladiatorial displays contrasting ancient and medieval Roman power), there was no question of preserving the former in preference to the latter. A formally choreographed sequence of dances, he understood, would have to remain the centre of gravity for an operatic ballet. And 'gravity' is all too apt a term for music that did remain. The energetic military dances of *Rienzi* aim for something of the sprightly, buoyant character of the ballet numbers in *La juive*, but the result sounds as if performed under a heavy suit of armour. (Indeed, the centrepiece of the sequence is a so-called *Waffentanz* or dance of arms.)[16] The movements are more numerous, much longer (though equally regular), and more heavily scored. The special favour shown to the ballet sequence by the Prussian King Wilhelm I only further discredited it in the composer's eyes, as did other signs of philistine approval for this music that had been 'tossed off ... in Riga in a matter of a few days, contemptuously and in intentional haste, such was my lack of interest in it'.[17] The disillusionment goes back to the conditions of the original Dresden production, too. The element of 'shame' Wagner was to attach to the ballet in *The Artwork of the Future* here applies in a personal artistic sense, exacerbated by an insufficiency of personnel. Whereas the Berlin choreography admired by the Prussian king had at least benefited from a robust and disciplined execution, the Dresden production is recalled wryly in the composer's memoirs both for its insufficiency and, notwithstanding that, its popular appeal:

I had to reconcile myself shamefully to two little *danseuses* executing some silly steps, until at last a company of soldiers marched in, their shields held above their heads forming a roof of sorts to remind the audience of an ancient Roman 'testudo', only to have the ballet master and his assistant, dressed in flesh-colored tights, leap

---

[16] The *Waffentanz* appears to have been a genre of male ensemble dance in operatic ballet of the early nineteenth century, to judge from a comment in Eduard Hanslick's review-essay on 'the present and future of the ballet' apropos an 1855 work entitled *Carita*. Hanslick criticizes the role of male dancing in contemporary ballet generally, but regrets the diminishing presence of the *Waffentanz*, 'this powerfully attractive, stately, but unfortunately now scarce type of production whose value is felt twice as keenly against the general feebleness [*Weichlichkeit*] of most modern dancing'. Eduard Hanslick, 'Musikalische Briefe' (7 August 1855), in *Sämtliche Schriften: Historisch-kritische Ausgabe*, vol. 3, ed. Dietmar Strauß (Vienna, Cologne, Weimar: Böhlau Verlag, 1995), 112.

[17] Richard Wagner, *My Life*, trans. Andrew Gray (Cambridge: Cambridge University Press, 1983), 244.

onto the shields and turn somersaults, a proceeding which they considered redolent of gladiatorial combat. This was the instant when the house invariably exploded in applause, and I had to regard [it] ... as the pinnacle of my success.[18]

The cynicism of this reminiscence is no doubt influenced by the artistic distance the composer had travelled between the time of *Rienzi* and the late 1860s, when he dictated his autobiography to Cosima. Even at the otherwise encouraging moment of the opera's Dresden success, though, he was clearly frustrated by the necessary suppression of his ambitious 'tragic pantomime' of the Lucretia story in favour of the crowd-pleasing acrobatics of the conventional ballet numbers that remained.[19]

When Wagner arrived in Paris in autumn 1839, the era of the French ballet-pantomime genre was in full swing. While there is evidence that he later paid close attention to ballet performances at the Opéra while he was rehearsing the revised *Tannhäuser* for production there in 1860–1, we know little about his experience of ballet during the 1839–41 sojourn (apparently he did attend a performance of *Giselle* during its first run in the early summer of 1841).[20] Since the full score of *Rienzi*'s Act 2 seems to have been completed shortly before Wagner got to Paris, the music of the pantomime must predate any experience of the latest French ballets. To judge from the style of both the score and the scenario, it seems to draw on operatic and melodramatic practices of the preceding decades. Despite Wagner's increasing resistance to most aspects of musical culture in the French capital during his first extended stay there, some ideas about the potential for theatrical dance may have been planted by his exposure, however limited, to grand opera and ballet performances during this moment when both genres were being intensively cultivated.

The opening Venusberg scene of *Tannhäuser* (1843–5) certainly suggests an idea of merging iconographic topoi of the classical bacchanal with the kinds of stage technologies Wagner might have encountered in Parisian operatic or balletic *féeries* of the time to create a new kind of choreographed spectacle. This first version of the Venusberg Bacchanal, before its radical amplification for Paris in 1861, also presents an attempt to merge the dramatic gesture of pantomime with more formally choreographed dance. In this regard, as

---

[18] Wagner, *My Life*, 244.
[19] The music of that pantomime scene remains one of the more obscure corners of the Wagner canon: no full score of the music even exists today. The complete autograph score was lost at the end of World War II, as was a manuscript copy in the Dresden opera library. The pantomime was not included in the first or any subsequent printings of the full score.
[20] Marian Smith, *Ballet and Opera in the Age of 'Giselle'* (Princeton: Princeton University Press, 2000), 14.

well as in the extravagant multi-media conception of the staging, the Bacchanal represents the composer's most conscious effort to 'reform' operatic ballet in terms of an emergent ideal of integrated musical-dramatic totality, tentatively in 1845, and more extravagantly in 1861.[21]

The music of the first version consists essentially of a reprise and rearrangement of the 'leaping' main theme (Example 5.1a) and passionately insistent chromatic transitional materials (Example 5.1b) of the overture, in the same key (E major). Stage scenery and choreography materialize for the audience what the central portion of the overture was to have suggested to its aural imagination. Venus and Tannhäuser lie passively in the foreground of the fantastical grotto, in the background a blue lake with bathing naiads, with a rosy pink light illuminating the whole scene. The dance element consists of a group of nymphs cavorting to the leaping gestures of the overture's main Allegro theme, joined variously by pairs of reclining lovers who stand in, as it were, for the main (non-dancing) dramatic couple. Subsequently a train of bacchantes enters from the rear of the stage, 'tumbling forth in a wild dance', urging the nymphs and amorous couples to greater abandon, which climaxes in a brief 6/8 Presto transformation of the leaping main theme (see Example 5.2).

This fairly simple arc of orgiastic intensification is momentarily inflected near the end by the acousmatic effect of off-stage 'sirens' beckoning, in a series of a cappella harmonic suspensions, what would seem to be hypothetical subjects behind or outside the scene ('Naht euch dem Strande! / Naht euch dem Lande, / wo in den Armen / glühender Liebe / selig Erwarmen still' euren Triebe!').[22] Following the climactic I^{6-4} arrival, a chromatically descending dominant prolongation intimates a post-coital relaxation, to be much expanded (along with the whole of this trajectory) in the Paris revision.[23] Wagner indicates a visual dissolve of bodies and atmospheric effects to parallel the aural dissolve in the score, concluding

---

[21] Gundula Kreuzer interprets the Venusberg Bacchanal as emblematic of the *Gesamtkunstwerk* idea itself, as an immersive, multi-media performance event, drawing an analogy between Venus, as author-director of this phantasmagoric spectacle aimed at overwhelming and thus subduing Tannhäuser, and Wagner's similar aims regarding his audience. Moreover, as Kreuzer points out, this unusual beginning 'prefigures a basic premise of Wagner's early conception of the *Gesamtkunstwerk*: it enacts the birth of music drama out of dance', which *The Artwork of the Future* 'placed at the helm of his three "purely human" (*reinmenschliche*) arts of dance, poetry, and music'. See Gundula Kreuzer, *Curtain, Gong, Steam: Wagnerian Technologies of Nineteenth-Century Opera* (Berkeley and Los Angeles: University of California Press, 2018), 33.

[22] 'Approach these shores, approach the land where the blessed warmth of love's glowing embrace will satisfy your desires.' *Tannhäuser*, Act 1, scene 1.

[23] As the stage directions put it: 'At the moment of the most inebriated Bacchic fury a process of quiescence and self-containment is suddenly initiated' ('Mit dem Momente der trunkensten

Example 5.1 Main 'Allegro theme' (a) and chromaticized transition theme (b) from overture to *Tannhäuser* (1845 Dresden version)

with an effect that mixes scenic-musical resolution and transition to the first dramatic scene to follow (see Example 5.3).

Although we have no record of precisely how this Bacchanal was carried out under Wagner's original direction in 1845, his remarks in the production notes he drew up in 1852, when some German theatres were showing

bacchantischen Wut tritt eine schnell um sich greifende Erschlaffung ein'). *Tannhäuser*, Act 1, scene 1.

Example 5.2 Presto 6/8 variant of 'Allegro theme' from Venusberg Bacchanal, *Tannhäuser*, Act 1, scene 1 (1845 Dresden version)

an interest in producing the opera, are telling with regard to the possibilities of dramatically integrated choreography. The Bacchanal ('the dance, if I may call it so', as Wagner writes) is described in terms of a synthesis of formal, abstract ballet and gestural pantomime, challenging the limits of both:

I hardly need to indicate that this is far from the manner of dance to which we are accustomed in our operas and ballets today; were we to assign the job of choreographing this music to a regular ballet master, we would quickly be set straight on

Example 5.3 'Aural dissolve' and transition from conclusion of Venusberg Bacchanal, *Tannhäuser*, Act 1, scene 1 (1845 Dresden version)

its unsuitability for the purpose. What I have in mind here, on the contrary, is a synthesis of everything that the arts of dance and pantomime have so far been able to accomplish [separately]: a seductively wild, gripping chaos of groupings and movement, ranging from the most placid contentment, feelings of languishing and yearning, all the way up to the most intoxicated state of revelry and abandon. Certainly this is no simple task, and it would require the most painstaking attention to details of artistic arrangement in order to create successfully the desired effect of chaotic frenzy. The essential traits of this wild scenic trajectory are indicated distinctly enough in the score.[24]

[24] 'Daß es sich hier nicht um einen Tanz, wie er in unseren Opern und Balletten üblich ist, handelt, brauche ich wohl nicht erst zu bedeuten: der Ballettmeister, dem man die Zumutung stellte, zu dieser Musik eine solche Tanzszene zu arrangieren, würde uns bald einen anderen belehren, und die Musik für durchaus untauglich erklären. Was ich dagegen im Sinne habe, ist ein Zusammenfassen alles dessen, was irgend Tanz- und Pantomimenkunst zu leisten vermag: ein verführerisch wildes und hinreißendes Chaos von Gruppierungen und Bewegungen, vom weichsten Behagen, Schmachten und Sehnen, bis zum trunkensten Ungestüm jauchzender Ausgelassenheit. Gewiß ist die Aufgabe nicht leicht zu lösen, und die gewünschte chaotische Wirkung hervorzubringen bedarf es ohne Zweifel der sorgfältigsten künstlerischen Anordnung des feinsten Details. In der Partitur ist der Verlauf dieser wilden szenischen Situation nach den

The licensed freedom of choreographic invention suggested here must, Wagner insists, not lose sight of the basic outline he describes. Beyond that, the best advice he can give with regard to realizing the scene is to let the imagination be guided by 'repeated listening to this music, performed by the orchestra'. Because the scenic trope of 'bacchanal', with its cavorting ensemble of satyrs, fauns, nymphs and naiads, is such a standard element of classicizing European visual culture from the Renaissance to the nineteenth century, it is easy to overlook the radical implications of even Wagner's initial version of the Venusberg ballet scene, which is in a way far closer to the world of Mallarmé's or Debussy's (or Nijinsky's) *L'après-midi d'un faune* (in conception, if not in tone) than to the courtly entertainments that had generated much of this iconography.[25]

Aside from the ambitious revision of the Venusberg Bacchanal in 1861 (further discussed in the next section), Wagner's subsequent efforts to integrate dance in his later music dramas were few, tentative and largely peripheral. The only explicitly composed dance music in the post-*Tannhäuser* works is the pseudo-rustic German *Walzer* episode that follows the pageant-like procession of the guilds at the opening of the Festival Meadow scene in Act 3 of *Die Meistersinger*. This is a modest affair of only 128 bars, broken off by the arrival of the masters to initiate the song contest. The scene in which the Flower Maidens teasingly welcome Parsifal to Klingsor's magic garden in Act 2 of *Parsifal* is arguably choreographic in conception, too, though essentially a choral ensemble scene, without any extended instrumental dance score as such. (The Rhine Maidens' appearance to Siegfried in Act 3, scene 1 of *Götterdämmerung* partakes of the siren-like character of the Flower Maidens in terms of situation and musical gesture; but as with their first appearance in *Das Rheingold*, their supposed aquatic environment poses a constraint on their movements, as do the obligations of their ensemble singing.)

The limited choreographic opportunities presented by any of these scenes underline a basic point. For all the striking, often implausible

---

wesentlichen Zügen mit Bestimmtheit angegeben.' 'Über die Aufführung des *"Tannhäuser"'* (1852), GSD vol. 5, 148.

[25] Among specifically balletic precedents Theresa Cameron mentions, for example, a pantomimic *scène d'action* from the first of Jean-Georges Noverre's *Lettres sur la danse et sur les ballets* (1760) outlining a scenario of nymphs and fauns engaged in a very similar pattern of erotic pursuit, flight and rapprochement. See Theresa Cameron, 'The Third Art of the Gesamtkunstwerk', *Wagner* 12, no. 1 (1991), 3–12, at 9–10. Marian Smith includes 'infernal bacchanals' among the types of scenic display (along with grand processions, prayers, wedding ceremonies, etc.) common to both opera and independent ballet-pantomimes on the Paris stage throughout the July Monarchy and before. Smith, *Ballet and Opera in the Age of 'Giselle'*, 25–8.

ambitions of Wagner's musical-dramatic oeuvre, it was conceived in an institutional context that did not include a professional *corps de ballet*. The frustrations he experienced in his Dresden staging of the conventional (if oversized) ballet sequence in *Rienzi* as well as the anti-conventional Bacchanal in *Tannhäuser* pointed up this lack of resources all too clearly, and probably discouraged further ambitions to serious integration of dance in his works. (Even the signal exception, the revised Bacchanal of the Paris *Tannhäuser*, was to be frustrated by institutional and technical limitations, in the event.) While modern productions might occasionally conscript some added professional dance personnel for the folksy waltzing in *Die Meistersinger* or the seductive gyrations of Klingsor's Flower Maidens in *Parsifal*,[26] neither episode demands it, any more than the thumping dance chorus of the Norwegian sailors that opens Act 3 of *Der fliegende Holländer*. Institutions such as the Berlin or Vienna court theatres were exceptions to this limitation of dance personnel in the German-speaking (and singing) orbit in Wagner's day, but none of his works were directly developed for those stages. So long as the choreographic element of his operas had to rely mainly on the contributions of vocal soloists, chorus and a few supernumeraries, even Wagner was forced to be pragmatic.

With these limitations in mind, we might still ask whether the choreographic episodes in *Meistersinger* or *Parsifal* shed any light on dance as a theoretical component of the 'total artwork' – that first but seemingly least among the three 'sister arts'. One hesitates to place too much emphasis on the short waltz episode in *Die Meistersinger*. Just like the 'maidens from Fürth' whose arrival precipitates it, the dancing seems to be little more than a casual import; in this case, from generic precedents such as Weber's *Freischütz* or Marschner's *Hans Heiling* where folk-style waltzing serves as a similar piece of scenic background to village-festival scenes. That generic filiation of national style is indeed part of the work performed by the dance music here. Similarly, both the Weber and the Marschner operas utilize their folk-style *Walzer* as a foil to dramatic conflict among the main characters. On a broader scale, Wagner's innocuous German dancing contrasts not only with the weighty, self-important entry of the Mastersingers, but also with the

---

[26] Cameron's essay (cited in note 25) originated in her participation in Wolfgang Wagner's 1989 Bayreuth production of *Parsifal*, which included an auxiliary unit of twelve female dancers for the Flower Maidens scene. The limited impact of this addition, as gauged by critical reaction, 'unmistakably illustrates the state of neglect suffered by this (supposedly) contributory art form within the total work of art' (Cameron, 'The Third Art of the *Gesamtkunstwerk*', 3). The first recorded choreographic credit (Maja Lex) for a Bayreuth production of *Parsifal*, she notes, comes from the first post-war season in 1951 (Cameron, 'The Third Art of the *Gesamtkunstwerk*', n. 1).

(likewise more weighty and important) contest between Beckmesser and Walther played out across the end of the act. In all three cases (*Freischütz*, *Heiling* and *Meistersinger*) the short piece of diegetic dancing dissolves, either by means of fade-out or interruption, in order to highlight its role as popular background to more serious dramatic content. In no case, however, can the dancing as such be said to constitute serious dramatic content itself. Dance is integrated, naturally and unassumingly, but not really 'synthesized'.[27]

The choreographic element in the Flower Maidens scene of *Parsifal* is less explicit but, for that very reason perhaps, closer to achieving a synthesis with the other elements of the music drama. Stage directions, libretto and, ultimately, the score divide the florally bedecked women into two groups (each vocally subdivided into tripartite solo and choral groups). The competitive banter exchanged by these groups as they vie for Parsifal's attention generates a simple choreographic dynamic, underscored by gently caressing motions in musical setting, which settles into a gentle waltz-like movement, decorated by small vocal arabesques when the Maidens join in chorus ('Komm! Komm! Holder Knabe, laß mich dir blühen!'; see Example 5.4).

The only direction for movement or gesture is that which prefaces this central, melodic chorus: 'During the following the Maidens turn around Parsifal, as in a pleasant children's game, gently stroking his cheeks and chin.'[28] The staging of this scene allows for either more or less precision and synchronization of gestural detail, but this will be in any case more a matter of choreographed gesture than formally patterned dance. Breaking down that distinction, of course, has much to do with the emergence of 'modern dance' in the decades after Wagner, just as the eroding distinction between recitative and formal lyrical numbers had been a defining feature of his music drama. Wagner himself never theorized this process as part of dance's role in the 'total dramatic artwork of the future', although as we have seen, he registered an interest in the combined contributions of pantomimic gesture and formal dance. Still, one might argue that he *did* contribute to emergent notions of modern dance through his theorizing of the dramatic

---

[27] Wagner's stage directions outline a kind of geometric by-play between the girls, the younger boys and the apprentices (generally not observed in productions), while more central, and more thoroughly scripted (via the sung text), is the stage business between David and the apprentices as they interrupt his dancing with the threat of Magdalena's surveillance.

[28] 'Während des Folgenden drehen sich die Mädchen, wie in anmutigem Kinderspiele, um Parsifal, sanft ihm Wange und Kinn streichelnd.' *Parsifal*, Act 2.

Example 5.4 Flower Maidens scene, main (slow, waltz-like) theme, *Parsifal*, Act 2

Gesamtkunstwerk in general, and through the example of his one advanced exercise in 'dramatic ballet', the revised Venusberg Bacchanal of 1861.

The 1861 Venusberg Bacchanal as 'Anti-Ballet'

Wagner's ill-fated yet culturally productive attempt to stage a revised version of *Tannhäuser* at the Parisian Académie Imperiale de Musique (the 'Opéra') in the early months of 1861 is one of the most familiar episodes of his biography. Let us review the basic outlines of that episode, as a preface to considering the implications of the much-amplified Venusberg Bacchanal of that production for a more complete participation of dance in the *Gesamtkunstwerk*. If that increased participation remained unrealized in Wagner's own subsequent works, there is reason to suppose that Wagner, and the example of his revised Bacchanal, exerted some influence on explicitly dance-oriented versions of a 'total artwork' idea after the turn of the twentieth century.

During the time he was completing *Tristan und Isolde*, Wagner set his sights on Paris as a launching-pad for his re-entry into the public sphere after a decade of political exile from Germany, mostly spent in Switzerland. Between his arrival in September 1859 and the early months of 1860 it was decided that *Tannhäuser* was the best vehicle for presenting himself to the Parisian public (following three concerts of excerpts from his works at the Salle Ventadour, home of the Théâtre-Italien). Once he had secured the services of the Opéra (thanks to the support of Princess Pauline Metternich, wife of the Austrian ambassador, and an imperial order from Napoleon III authorizing the production), Wagner channelled all his energies into translating, revising, rehearsing and producing the French *Tannhäuser* until its famously troubled brief run a year later in March 1861. Central to the process of revision and eventually – at least, allegedly – to the catastrophe of the production was the matter of the 'ballet', that is, the new Bacchanal introducing the scene between Venus and Tannhäuser that opens the opera.

Accounts of the Paris *Tannhäuser* are ample, yet rife with contradictions. The composer himself blows hot and cold over the whole enterprise, now enthusiastic at the chance to update his opera and produce it with hand-picked singers and the world-class resources of the Opéra, now uninterested in any translated production, disillusioned with the tenor Albert Niemann, and convinced of journalistic and political cabal that will ensure its failure. Despite no fewer than 183 rehearsals over many months, the requirement of finally handing over the baton to house conductor Pierre-Louis Dietsch is described as definitively ruinous to the actual performances; yet descriptions of these performances (merely three, before the work was withdrawn at the end of March 1861) focus almost exclusively on the vocal animosity of the Jockey Club, abetted by other hostile contingents, with little reference to the musical performance and almost none to the results of Dietsch's conducting.

One constant through all of this is the 'ballet problem'. The legendary conflicts generated by the problem of a ballet for the Paris *Tannhäuser* might indeed be taken to symbolize, more abstractly, Wagner's conflicted attitude towards the potential of dance in his musical-dramatic synthesis of the arts: the challenge of reconciling 'debased' practices of contemporary ballet with his ambitious, if somewhat inchoate, visions of reform. From the beginning of negotiations with the general director of the Opéra, Alphonse Royer, the need for a 'grand ballet in the second act' was a continual sticking point.[29] The placement of ballet sequences within the four-to-five acts normal for the grand opera repertoire was in fact considerably more variable than Wagner's well-known litany about the 'second-act ballet' requirement has led most writers to assume. But certainly his insistence that an amplified Bacchanal at the very *opening* of the opera should serve the purpose of the obligatory ballet was bound to be a point of contention. Whether the infamous Jockey Club members protesting the eventual performances at the Opéra were principally outraged by the composer's intransigence on this issue or seizing an opportunity for political statement (to protest the influence of Wagner's advocate, Princess Metternich, and issues of France's Austro-German relations in general) is another unresolved point in the story of *Tannhäuser*'s troubles.[30] When Jockey Club members apparently attended the third performance (24 March) from the beginning, waiving their vaunted right of late arrival, no mention is made of protests specifically targeting the non-conventional ballet spectacle that would have greeted them with the rise of the curtain.

What the original audiences actually saw in the opening scene of the production is hard to say (or what they heard: if the reprehensible Dietsch was so ill-equipped to conduct the score as a whole, one can only imagine how he fared with the *Tristan*-esque frenzies of the new Bacchanal music). The ballet master of the Opéra, Lucien Petipa (brother of the subsequently celebrated Marius), could have had almost no time to choreograph and rehearse the scene, whose new score was not even completed until the end of January, some weeks before the intended premiere. Furthermore, Wagner maintains that the unconventional placement of the ballet scene forced him to relinquish access to the regular *corps de ballet* and its soloists,

---

[29] 'At no single interview did the man fail to press upon me the need to insert a ballet into the second act; I may have benumbed him with my eloquent protestations, but I never managed to convince him.' Wagner, *My Life*, 614.

[30] See, e.g., Ernest Newman, *The Life of Richard Wagner*, vol. 3 (1859–66) (Cambridge: Cambridge University Press, 1976), 68–9. The relationship of this aristocratic club to the politics of the imperial court is, however, yet another subject of conflicting reports.

having instead to make do with three 'Hungarian dancers' borrowed from one of the boulevard theatres (Porte St Martin) to play the Three Graces and 'a few skinny youths' (low-paid supernumeraries) for the male dancers.[31] The scenery and décor of the production overall impressed Wagner greatly, befitting the reputation of the institution. The look of the Venusberg dance scene itself, however, as one could infer from the circumstances, left almost everything to be desired. The essay 'On Conducting', written some years after this episode (1869), includes a suggestive reminiscence, intended more generally to illustrate the inhibiting effect of bourgeois decorum on artistic expression in modern culture: 'I pointed out to the ballet master how incongruously the pitiful little hopping steps of his Maenads and Bacchantes contrasted with my [new] music, and how I would rather have him devise for his forces something corresponding to those well-known antique reliefs representing groups of Bacchanalian procession, something wildly bold and sublime.' Petipa, he recalls, merely whistled in dismay: 'I understand you quite well, he replied, but for this we would need to rely entirely on lead dancers; and if I were to communicate this to my personnel and direct them to present the kind of poses you suggest, we'd end up with the "cancan" and that would be the end of us.'[32] The same encounter is alluded to in *My Life*, where Wagner recalls:

I threw myself enthusiastically into the task of setting up the huge and unconventional dance scenes of the first act, for which I now tried to win the sympathy of the ballet-master Petipas [*sic*]; what I demanded was unheard-of and departed radically from traditional choreographic practices; I drew attention to the dances of the Maenads and the Bacchantes, but only astounded Petipas by my assumption that such things, which he well comprehended, could be done by his little dancing pupils.[33]

---

[31] Wagner, *My Life*, 629.
[32] 'Den Ballettmeister wies ich nun darauf an, wie die jämmerlich gehüpften kleinen Pas seiner Mänaden und Bacchantinnen sehr läppisch zu meiner Musik kontrastierten, und wie ich dagegen verlange, daß er hierfür etwas den auf berühmten antiken Reliefs dargestellten Gruppen der Bacchantenzüge Entsprechendes, Kühnes und wild Erhabenes erfinden und von seinem Korps ausführen lassen solle. Da pfiff der Mann durch die Finger und sagte mir: "Ah, ich verstehe Sie sehr wohl, aber dazu bedürfte ich lauter erster Sujets; wenn ich diesen meinen Leuten ein Wort hiervon sagen und ihnen die von Ihnen gemeinte Attitüde angeben wollte, auf der Stelle hätten wir den 'Cancan' und wären verloren."' Wagner, 'Über das Dirigieren', GSD vol. 8, 315.
[33] Wagner, *My Life*, 629. A satirical description of the choreography by the critic Pier Angelo Fiorentino, if not perhaps totally accurate, gives a sense of the fairly ludicrous discrepancy with the music that frustrated the composer. Fiorentino describes symmetrical lines of Bacchantes and Fauns walking in contrary motion with their arms upheld; nymphs, youths and little cupids follow suit. 'Apparently the dance of the future only permits arms in the air. I admit indeed that

'Such things, which he well comprehended', like 'those well-known antique reliefs', seems to refer to some relatively frank representation of sexual relations, as confirmed by Petipa's mention of the 'shameful' cancan (which both Wagner and Heinrich Heine understood to mimic the sexual act in some sense), and on another level by the musical contours of the revised Bacchanal itself, like the elements of the *Tristan* score that inform it.

Whatever happened on the stage of the Paris Opéra when the curtain rose on those three unlucky performances of *Tannhäuser* in March 1861, then, the expanded scenario of the Bacchanal and the expanded musical score for the scene are the best evidence we have of how Wagner, at least in one particular case, imagined a re-integration of dance commensurate with his mature views on musical drama as 'total artwork'. It was the recent experience of writing *Tristan und Isolde* that prompted him to undertake a wholesale revision of Venus's role in the first scene: 'only now that I have written Isolde's final transfiguration have I been able to find the right ending for the *Flying Dutchman* overture, as well as – the horrors of the Venusberg' ('das Grauen dieses Venusberges').[34] This oft-cited remark about the creative epiphany of *Tristan* as a motivation to recompose the domain of Venus in *Tannhäuser* comes from a key document, a long letter to Mathilde Wesendonck of 10 April 1860, just a month after the official order was given for the Paris production. With a vivid notion, clearly, of how the passionate chromatic idiom of *Tristan und Isolde* might inform a newly modern 'Wagnerian' Bacchanal, the composer allowed his imagination to run rampant. The extravagance of this new scenario is inspired by the extravagance of both the inner resources of his current musical imagination and the external resources of the Opéra ballet – at least as he expected them to be. 'This court of Frau Venus was clearly the weak point in my work', he confesses in the letter to Mathilde, with reference to the original Dresden production. Lacking proper ballet personnel then, he was forced to make do with 'a few coarse brush-strokes ... the Venusberg left a very dull and indecisive impression'. The spectacle of this lascivious grotto and the corporeal, if nonetheless allegorically stylized, representation of its sensual enticements presented – so Wagner now thought – a legitimate opportunity for dance to contribute something essential to his work: a compelling embodiment of Tannhäuser's

---

this simultaneous elevation of all those assembled arms gives an impression of mysticism and devotion.' Cited in Ivor Guest, *The Ballet of the Second Empire: 1858–1870* (London: Adam and Charles Black, 1953), 43.

[34] Letter to Mathilde Wesendonck of 10 April 1860, from *Selected Letters of Richard Wagner*, trans. and ed. Stewart Spencer and Barry Millington (New York: W. W. Norton, 1988), 489.

experience of the pleasures of the flesh, for which he will be driven to advocate against the narrow feudal-Christian (or for that matter, modern bourgeois) ideology of the Thuringian court with its pallidly virtuous *Minnesänger*: 'Of course, I shall have to ... prescribe every last nuance to the ballet master: but it is certain that only dance can be effective here and complete the sense: but what a dance! People will be amazed at all that I have hatched here.'[35] This outburst of confident enthusiasm prefaces an improvised draft of the new Bacchanal scenario.

The outlines of the first Bacchanal are retained: Venus and Tannhäuser recline in the foreground, vicariously partaking of the bacchanalian revels behind and around them. The cast of these revels is greatly augmented, however, as is the overall arc of mounting Dionysian frenzy and subsequent relaxation. The mythological Three Graces are now enlisted to chaperone the wild proceedings, as best they can. Also on hand is a band of little cupids armed with quivers of aphrodisiac arrows. The Graces attempt to mediate the games of erotic pursuit and flight performed by the nymphs and fauns, youths and maidens, satyrs and cupids. (These attempts are completely in vain, until the revellers finally wear themselves out through their protracted abandon.) The letter draft further introduces 'all manner of monstrous beasts', a black ram to be sacrificed over a waterfall in the background, 'all the animals sacred to the [pagan] gods', and a Nordic river god, the 'Strömkarl', whose outsized folk fiddle serves as a wilder, earthier counterpart to Orpheus's lyre: 'He now plays to the dance, and you can imagine what I shall have to invent here in order to give this dance its appropriate quality; more and more ... mythological rabble are drawn in.' In a postscript of sorts within the letter draft, Wagner adds: 'I could perhaps replace [the black ram] with something else. Jubilant maenads ought to carry in the murdered *Orpheus*: they would toss his head into the waterfall – and then the Strömkarl would spring up. But this is not so easy to understand without words. What do you think?')[36] Not surprisingly, the version of the scenario printed in the libretto and score omits some of the more fantastical suggestions: the sacrifice of the black ram ('to the accompaniment of hideous gestures'), the menagerie of 'monstrous beasts' and additional 'mythological rabble' (*mythologisches Gesindel*), including some centaurs who were to abduct the Graces towards the end, and – unfortunately, perhaps – the Strömkarl with his neo-Orphic fiddle. The remaining

---

[35] *Selected Letters of Richard Wagner*, 489–90.
[36] *Selected Letters of Richard Wagner*, 490–1. Original text in Richard Wagner, *Sämtliche Briefe*, vol. 12, ed. Martin Dürer (Wiesbaden: Breitkopf & Härtel, 2001), 121–3.

Dionysian 'tumult' (a word that occurs repeatedly in the draft) is still enough to fuel the 339-bar revision of the scene, with its greatly intensified harmonic and timbral resources and the distended phraseology of a *Tristan* style of 'endless melody'.

Comparing Wagner's score for this revised choreographic scene with his account of Dietsch's profound inadequacy as a conductor, Lucien Petipa's incongruously banal, under-rehearsed choreography, and the ultimately inadequate personnel, it is a wonder that the audience of the Paris performances did not break out in full revolt right at the beginning. The conditions on all sides would seem to have anticipated those of the similarly famous debacle of the Stravinsky–Diaghilev–Nijinsky *Rite of Spring* in Paris a little over half a century later. Wagner's own (re-)conception of the scene, together with his staunch refusal to accommodate any alternative ballet sequence later in the production, was itself an act of protest against standard practices of operatic ballet. It might not be far-fetched to imagine the Three Graces here, in their initially thwarted efforts to maintain classical grace and decorum amidst all the frenzied mayhem, as an emblem of that ballet culture he had denounced for its 'shameful', hypocritical capitulation to corrupt bourgeois mores in *The Artwork of the Future*. At any event, the new Bacchanal was intent on tearing away what Wagner had described as ballet's hypocritical veil of decorum in order to get at the physical and psychological truth that animates the opera's hero.

Thinking of the Parisian Venusberg Bacchanal in these terms it becomes a kind of polemic 'anti-ballet'. The institutional context for this reading is clear enough: Wagner's protracted resistance to demands for a mid-opera divertissement-style ballet and his genuine belief that a new and quite different kind of dance, developing his initial conception for the opening scene, could benefit the opera significantly. The draft scenario of the new scene, what Wagner jokingly dubbed his 'ballet-master letter' (the 10 April 1860 letter to Mathilde), also underlines the idea of a broader genre polemic against Parisian ballet. The letter begins with an extended screed against the cultural shortcomings of 'such a talented but at the same time so dissolute nation as the French'.[37] Wagner inveighs against an innate lack of 'poetry' in the French character and language (as opposed to their native values of rhetoric and eloquence), no doubt reflecting his frustrations with the process of translating the *Tannhäuser* libretto; and he suggests that music, namely German music, might help to compensate for

---

[37] 'einer so begabten, aber so unglaublich verwarhlosten Nation, wie der französischen'. Wagner, *Sämtliche Briefe*, vol. 12, 118.

this cultural lack, justifying the effort behind the current production as a contribution to the aesthetic education of this 'talented but dissolute' nation. If *Tannhäuser* as a whole was supposed to provide the French with a Wagnerian lesson in music, drama and German Romantic aesthetics, what might be the lesson of the new Bacchanal itself? Rooted in the composer's own conflicted attitudes towards theatrical dance, it would seem to encourage a frank admission of the dancing body's fundamental affiliation with representations of sexual instincts, desire, courtship ritual and all manner of sensual materiality along with a rejection of the coy, hypocritically decorous facade of ballet as a modern bourgeois cultural institution. In *The Artwork of the Future*, Wagner had associated the fixed, artificially ingratiating smiles of the ballerina with the sterile, morally and aesthetically bankrupt autonomy of modern professional dance. Far from using gesture and movement to give physical presence to poetry (to 'redeem' poetry's longing for corporeal reality), contemporary ballet was accused, we will recall, of sinking to a form of culturally sanctioned prostitution.[38] By contrast, the Dionysian revels of the Venusberg cast off the bourgeois pretenses of classical ballet in order to celebrate the libidinal energy of the dancing body in a pure, extreme form, serving a higher dramatic purpose (*dichterische Absicht*)[39] with regard to the drama of *Tannhäuser*, while ultimately submitting to the moderating influences of 'art' in the form of the Three Graces.

Epilogue: The 'Dance Poem' as Wagnerian Genre and the Elevation of Dance in the Post-Wagnerian *Gesamtkunstwerk*

Wagner's implicit critique of traditional ballet in the revised Venusberg Bacchanal and the suggestion it may have provided for aspects of the 'modern dance' revolution some decades later are closely intertwined with the example of Heinrich Heine, a crucial influence whom Wagner admired and resisted in equal measure through much of his life. It was Heine's justifiable view that Wagner had liberally borrowed from his essay on Germanic folklore and legend, 'Elemental Spirits' ('Elementargeister', 1837), in the libretto of *Tannhäuser*, particularly in the portrayal of Venus

---

[38] Wagner, *Das Kunstwerk der Zukunft*, 77–8.
[39] The 'poetic intent' is a key phrase from *Oper und Drama*, Part 2, section 6: GSD vol. 4, 98–103. See also Frank Glass, *The Fertilizing Seed: Richard Wagner's Concept of the Poetic Intent* (Ann Arbor, MI: UMI Research Press, 1983).

and the Venusberg. Heine returned to that material ten years later when commissioned by the director of Her Majesty's Theater (Covent Garden) in London, Benjamin Lumley, to provide ballet scenarios that would, presumably, emulate the success of *Giselle*. (The scenario of Adolphe Adam and Jules Perrot's ballet was based on material from Heine's 'Elemental Spirits' and 'De l'allemagne'.) Lumley was presumably unaware that, as a critic, Heine was fundamentally antagonistic to the contemporary ballet, even if he could admire some of its celebrated stars, such as Carlotta Grisi. Some years earlier he had criticized the whole agenda of French classical ballet since the era of Louis XIV in domesticating the art of dance to a courtly etiquette wholly at odds with what he argued were its sensual, pagan roots. Heine's description of a hypocritical veneer of chastity and virtue belying the baser instincts to which modern ballet truly appeals distinctly anticipates the rhetoric of Wagner's critique in *Artwork of the Future*: 'Indeed, the form and essence of the French ballet is chaste, yet all the while the eyes of the dancers are making a scandalous commentary to those decorous steps, and their lascivious smiles form a running contradiction to their feet.'[40] The two scenarios Heine provided to Lumley, both based on motifs of Germanic legend and folklore, were entitled *Die Göttin Diana* (1846) and *Der Doktor Faust* (1847). Both are defiantly wild, impractical, grotesque and essentially parodistic in conception – in effect, 'anti-ballets' exhibiting unmistakable commonalities with Wagner's revised Venusberg Bacchanal for Paris, as Dieter Borchmeyer has pointed out.[41]

Die Göttin Diana involves the death and resurrection of a Tannhäuser-like knight who captures the erotic fancy of the eponymous goddess in her medieval Germanic exile, similar to Wagner's Venus. It is in fact a Dionysian crew assembled in that same grotto who manage the knight's resurrection, for which thanks are paid to Venus and Tannhäuser, as hosts, and which is celebrated in a concluding bacchanalian *danse générale* in the

---

[40] 'In der That, die Form und das Wesen des französischen Ballets ist keusch, aber die Augen der Tänzerinnen machen zu den sittsamsten Pas einen sehr lafterhaften Kommentar, und ihr liederliches Lächeln ist in beständigem Widerspruch zu ihren Füßen.' Heinrich Heine, *Gesammelte Werke*, ed. Gustav Karpeles, vol. 7 (Berlin: G. Grote'sche Verlagsbuchhandlung, 1887), 191. The original article of 7 February 1842 was taken up in vol. 2 of Heine's *Lutetia*.

[41] Dieter Borchmeyer, 'The "Dance of the Future": Heine's and Wagner's Venusberg Ballets', *Drama and the World of Richard Wagner*, trans. Daphne Ellis (Princeton: Princeton University Press, 2003), 133–43, at 134–7. Heine's *Faust* ballet scenario and its deferred twentieth-century settings by Frantisek Skvor, Henry Krips and Werner Egk are discussed by David Conway, 'Heinrich Heine's *Faust* Ballet Scenario, 1846-1948', in *The Oxford Hanbook of* Faust *in Music*, ed. Lorna Fitzsimmons and Charles McKnight (New York: Oxford University Press, 2019), 483–504.

form of quadrilles. The satirical note suggested by the light, sociable genre of the quadrille here is intensified in *Der Doktor Faust*, where the Devil's emissary takes the form of a modern ballerina dubbed 'Mephistophela' who instructs her charge in the steps of both social dance and decorative balletic routines. What emerges here is a spectacular, satirical *ballet fantastique* on mythological-literary motifs that aims to critique the conventions of classical-Romantic ballet from within the medium itself while gesturing, so it seems, at some higher, more literary, more 'totalizing' conception of dance as an art form.

Something of that gesture is captured in Heine's novel and self-conscious designation of his *Faust* ballet scenario as a 'dance poem' (*Tanzpoem*). In a subsequent preface, Heine complained that the ballet master of Her Majesty's Theatre (alluding either to Paul Taglioni or, most likely, Jules Perrot) 'considered it a dangerous innovation' to have commissioned a dance libretto from a real poet, 'since up to now these have always been the products of some dancing ape of his own type'. Addressing his publisher Campe, he asserted that the text is 'a poem, which merely takes the form of a ballet, yet is in fact one of my greatest and most completely poetic works'.[42] Whether or not we take Heine at his word here, the quasi-Wagnerian aim to elevate and redeem the debased, commodified genre of modern ballet by an appeal to the 'poetic' imagination seems genuine. Wagner's Venusberg Bacchanal, especially in its radically expanded (and elaborately scripted) Paris revision, could also be considered a *Tanzpoem* in the spirit of Heine. And where Heine's scenarios still involve an operatic sequence of full tableaux or acts, Wagner's Bacchanal presents a single, free-form 'movement' (as continuation of or appendix to the overture) whose non-conventional syntax, emphasis on expressive motive and gesture, and progressive uses of timbre, dynamics and texture (etc.) seem to encourage a radical re-thinking of dance movement such as would preoccupy pioneers of 'new ballet' and modern dance such as Isadora Duncan, Michel Fokine or Vaslav Nijinsky after the turn of the century. Most of the works associated with those figures and others in their wake could be said to cultivate such a 'dance poem' genre, based on shorter single-movement compositions whose innovative musical language or sonic traits are in dialogue with analogous innovations in the style or language of dance. As creative outsiders to the world of professional ballet, Heine and Wagner seem to have contributed obliquely, and in intersecting ways, to a subsequent 'revolution in dance'.

---

[42] 'Ein Gedicht, welches vom Ballett nur die Form hat, sonst aber eine meiner größten und hochpoetischsten Produktionen ist.' Heine, *Gesammelte Werke*, vol. 5, xxii.

The catchphrase 'revolution in dance', associated above all with the highly publicized performances of (largely) solo female dancers in the wake of Isadora Duncan (including Loïe Fuller, Maude Allan, Ruth St Denis, Adorée Villany, Tórtola Valencia and Grete Wiesenthal) in the first decades of the twentieth century, deliberately echoed a broader revolution in social mores and cultural practices associated with such performances.[43] The publicity attending Duncan and her followers was fuelled, no less than that of Sergei Diaghilev's collective enterprise of the Ballets Russes, by the 'scandal' of modernism, for which Wagner's Paris *Tannhäuser* serves as a prototype of sorts. At play here, too, was that dialectic of debauchery and decorum that fascinated both Wagner and Heine in the culture of modern ballet and the whole history of dance, as they perceived it. That dialectic is neatly summed up by the crass and brassy stripper of Stephen Sondheim and Jule Styne's 1959 musical *Gypsy* in describing the 'gimmick' she has chosen to sell her routine: 'Once I was a schlepper [-ah], / Now I'm Miss Mazeppa, / With my Revolution in Dance.'[44] Where Duncan's primly chaste and classical persona recalls that veil of decorum that provoked Wagner's scepticism, the overtly erotic and 'Oriental' overtones of Maude Allan's famous Salome dances, or much of the Ballets Russes repertoire, point out clearly enough the path to burlesque. One way or another, though, some such 'revolution in dance' seems to have been required to gain full entry for this first-but-least of Wagner's three sister arts into his own ideal of a modern-day total artwork.

And indeed, the leading exponents of this modernist revolution invoked Wagner's name and ideas directly, above all Isadora Duncan herself and the principal theorist of Diaghilev's project, Russian painter and writer Alexandre Benois. For Duncan, a reform-minded appeal to Hellenistic notions of beauty, purity, unity and so on was easily merged with a now familiar, even ubiquitous, Wagnerian discourse of aesthetic-cultural reform, as Mary Simonson has demonstrated.[45] Benois, together with painter and

---

[43] For a nuanced, partially sceptical look at the cultural dynamic behind the alleged 'revolution in dance' of this period, see Davinia Caddy, *The Ballets Russes and Beyond: Music and Dance in Belle-Époque Paris* (Cambridge: Cambridge University Press, 2012). On the social contexts and the major female exponents of the 'revolution', see Edward Ross Dickinson, *Dancing in the Blood: Modern Dance and European Culture on the Eve of the First World War* (Cambridge: Cambridge University Press, 2017), chapter 1.

[44] Stephen Sondheim, *Finishing the Hat: Collected Lyrics (1954–1981)* (New York: Alfred A. Knopf, 2010), 71.

[45] Mary Simonson, 'Dancing the Future, Performing the Past: Isadora Duncan and Wagnerism in the American Imagination', *Journal of the American Musicological Society* 65, no. 2 (Summer 2012), 511–55.

scene designer Léon Bakst, sought to elevate the contribution of visual art as well as dance to a new, post-Wagnerian synthesis in which the human body would be restored to its rightful centrality, in the terms of Wagner's original theory. David Roberts cites Benois's reflection that 'It was us, the painters (not the professionals of theatre design, but "true" painters [...]), who helped to order the main lines of dance and the whole *mise-en-scène*.'[46] The Ballets Russes enterprise also highlights the logical, practical importance of a professional impresario role (Diaghilev) in negotiating a more complete integration of media than Wagner had achieved, something that Wagner's idealistic theorizing and his antagonism to a commodified culture 'market' would not have countenanced. Thus Igor Stravinsky's epochal ballet scores, revolutionary masterpieces in their own right, had genuinely collaborative roots in the contributions of choreographers Fokine and Nijinsky, designer-scenographers Benois, Bakst and Nicholas Roerich, and Diaghilev himself as commissioner, advisor, producer and overall moderator. The first of these collaborations, *The Firebird* (1910), originated when circumstances forced Diaghilev to shift his activities from opera to ballet, and Richard Taruskin comments on the extent to which the score, in its leitmotivic and dramaturgical conception, 'conspicuously emulates Wagnerian music drama'.[47] At the time, as Taruskin notes, that legacy was seen as 'an earnest of the new seriousness with which Diaghilev's company addressed ballet' and which was 'perhaps his greatest bequest to the esthetics of the twentieth century'.[48]

Inevitably, though, nearly all the exponents of a modern, dance-centred artistic 'totality' resisted the paramount role accorded to drama in the Wagnerian conception of the total artwork. Isadora Duncan had bluntly asserted to Cosima Wagner, who had invited her to choreograph the Venusberg Bacchanal in *Tannhäuser* for the 1904 Bayreuth Festival: '*Musik-Drama kann nie sein*' ('Music drama can never be'). Rational speech, emotional song and the 'Dionysian ecstasy' of dance are ultimately incompatible, she explained; in her view, Wagner's tendency to let the music 'absorb everything' worked against his stated goal of re-uniting dance, music and poetry in a newly integrated form.[49] Duncan's choreographies, in the spirit of most subsequent modern dance, were abstractly

---

[46] David Roberts, *The Total Work of Art in European Modernism* (Ithaca, NY: Cornell University Press, 2011), 151.
[47] Richard Taruskin, 'Diaghilev without Stravinsky? Stravinsky without Diaghilev?' in *Russian Music at Home and Abroad: New Essays* (Berkeley and Los Angeles: University of California Press, 2016), 392.
[48] Taruskin, 'Diaghilev without Stravinsky?', 392.
[49] Simonson, 'Dancing the Future, Performing the Past', 539. The remark to Cosima Wagner is from Duncan's memoir, *My Life* (New York: Boni and Liveright, 1927), 152, a text prone to

expressive and non-narrative, even those set to Wagner's own music. All her performances aspired to something we could call a 'dance poem', to invoke Heine's term (and the resonance of that for Wagner's Venusberg Bacchanal), but one whose poet is the dancer, not a librettist or a composer. For Alexandre Benois, and by extension his collaborators, 'ballet was the final step in music theatre's liberation from the tyranny of spoken drama'.[50] And as suggested earlier, many of the Ballets Russes productions could also be linked to that notional genre of the dance poem by way of Wagner's Venusberg. The scenarios tend towards the modes of lyric, ritual, folkloric, symbolic or anecdotal; mythic characters and atmosphere predominate over functional narrative. (Nijinsky's *L'après-midi d'un faune*, after Mallarmé and Debussy, is just such a dance poem, divested of its already non-narrative text. Similarly, Ravel's score for *Daphnis et Chloë* approaches the mythic-pastoral tropes of its scenario through the language of the atmospheric tone-poem or tone-picture, along with character or genre dances.) Taruskin notes how Benois's advocacy of ballet as high art is allied to his rejection of the 'utilitarian' and hence aesthetically limiting nature of language, invoking the Kantian postulate of aesthetic disinterest in the era of 'art for art's sake'. 'A baby crying for its milk is utilitarian and boring', he asserted. 'But a smiling baby – that one is holy, surrounded by a divine aureole.'[51] In elevating dance to a newly central role in the *Gesamtkunstwerk*, Benois also happens to re-value those 'smiles' that both Wagner and Heine had associated with the dubiously commodified, sub-aesthetic body of the ballerina, as they viewed it. 'In ballet, the chief meaning is the smile' he contends. 'That is the reason for its existence.' Artistic dance is nothing but 'a full-length smile', in which the whole body participates. This is quite far removed from the aesthetic of *Tristan und Isolde* or *Parsifal*, certainly (and it may not sound much like *The Rite of Spring*, for that matter). But, as an aesthetic objective, 'a smile in which the whole body participates' seems quite as worthy of the combined efforts of any or all art forms as anything else in the totalizing discourse of the Wagnerian *Gesamtkunstwerk*.

---

some degree of self-dramatization. Duncan also danced the role of the first of the Three Graces in the *Tannhäuser* Bacchanal.

[50] Richard Taruskin, *Oxford History of Western Music*, vol. 2 (Oxford and New York: Oxford University Press, 2005), 151.

[51] Benois, 'Colloquy on Ballet' (1908), cited in Taruskin, *Oxford History*, vol. 4, 150.

6 | Hymnody, Dance and the Sacred in the Illustrated Song

MARIAN WILSON KIMBER

In 2009 and again in 2012, the Mull Singing Convention, a long-running television programme from Knoxville, Tennessee, replayed a video of two older women pantomiming to Perry Como's recording of 'Silent Night'.[1] Twins Ella and Stella Brown were the sisters of one of the Southern gospel music programme's original announcers, Elizabeth Mull, and the show's current host, Mull's daughter Charlotte, introduced the segment by describing her aunts as 'singing their song'.[2] Dressed in choir robes and standing in front of Grecian pillars, the two women's performance consists of poses for each line of the Christmas carol. Standing largely stationary, the twins maintain expressionless faces and do not look directly into the camera. Their feet only sometimes move, and they gesture primarily with their upper bodies: their arms open into a cross for 'Son of God', their hands are clasped in front of their bodies for the 'tender and mild' infant, and they cross their arms on their chests for 'Sleep in heavenly peace'. The women make no sounds, raising the question of how their pantomimed gestures could be considered 'singing'. When the choir that accompanies Como sings an interlude between verses two and three of 'Silent Night', the sisters stand motionless throughout, waiting for the identifiable 'song', such as would be sung by a church congregation. Although the carol clearly shapes their motions, it is nonetheless difficult to determine how some of their poses relate to its text, such as two arms extended in front of the body, palms down, for the words 'holy night' in all three verses. Perhaps because of these passages, the few commentators among the approximately hundred and three thousand viewers of the performance's two YouTube postings frequently express confusion over the meaning of the twins' movements. One sarcastically identifies their purpose of expressing the

---

[1] *Stella and Ella*, www.youtube.com/watch?v=nloojCEjXOY, uploaded 24 December 2009, and *The Brown Twin Sisters (Ella & Stella) Pantomime to Perry Como's Silent Night*, broadcast 25 December 2012, uploaded 15 August 2013, www.youtube.com/watch?v=WuNZOdffFR8. This performance may have been similar to that mentioned in 'South Side News', *Arizona Republican*, 23 December 1913: a 'duet to pantomime' of *Silent Night* by Hattie Martin and Marion Cook of Tempe Union High School.

[2] One of the twins was already deceased by the earlier airing of the clip.

text of the hymn but denies that they were successful: 'You turn off the sound and you can guess every word of the song because their pantomime is so impressively descriptive', adding, 'I could not write that while keeping a straight face!'[3]

Although it appears singularly odd to modern viewers, this combination of religious music and physical movement dates from over a century ago; it was typical of women's Delsarte performances in the long nineteenth century. For example, the recital by the dramatic reader Erma May Bashford, at the Christian Church in Mason City, Iowa, in September 1904 concluded with her pantomime of 'Nearer, My God, to Thee'. Bashford's programme was reported in the *Cerro Gordo Republican*, but the paper did not provide any details about her performance. Nonetheless, contemporary guides for posing to the popular hymn suggest that Bashford's movements would have been much like those of the Brown sisters. Her feet would have largely remained in place, and she would have made numerous arm motions, reaching both out to her sides and upward above her head (see Figure 6.1), or clasping her hands together in front of her body; she may have also knelt in prayer.[4]

Just as the twins' gestures reflected the strophic structure of 'Silent Night', published directions indicate that Bashford would also have moved from pose to pose every two lines of the hymn's text, making two or sometimes three poses per verse, as many as twenty in all. Although these choreographed physical motions to music might now be considered 'dance', the word was not used to describe Bashford's performance. To do so would have undoubtedly inspired controversy in Mason City, as the same issue of the newspaper that reported on her recital also recounted a recent sermon by a local Methodist pastor, William Carlton, who asserted the 'plain truths as to the tendencies of the dance', which 'led to immoral thoughts and was the cause of the wrecking of lives'.[5]

Because performances stemming from the Delsarte movement such as Bashford's featured interrelationships between text, music and movement, they were situated between artistic forms; thus, the musical practices that shaped them have been invisible to dance and music historians alike. Many of the poses performed by the Brown Twins and their predecessors from

---

[3] User name 'zzzut', comment in response to *Stella and Ella*, uploaded 24 December 2009.
[4] Grace B. Faxon published instructions in her *Popular Recitations and How to Recite Them* (Danville, NY: F. A. Owen, 1909), 5–8, and *Favorite Pantomimed Songs and Poses* (Danville, NY: F. A. Owen, 1917), 63–9.
[5] 'A Fine Entertainment', and 'Recital Program', *Cerro Gordo Republican* (Mason City, Iowa), 29 September 1904.

Figure 6.1 Pose for 'Still, all my song shall be / Nearer, my God, to Thee', in 'Nearer, My God, to Thee'; Grace B. Faxon, *Favorite Pantomimed Songs and Poses* (Danville, NY: F. A. Owen, 1917), 69

earlier in the century can be identified using Delsarte-era instruction books. Delsarte performances were originally associated with physical depictions of statuary from ancient Greece, but a particular variant, in which a series of poses undertaken to music generate an 'illustrated song', was a prominent artistic offshoot of the movement. Not to be confused with the music designed for audiences to sing to lantern slides projected in movie theatres, the illustrated song consisted of poses to parlour songs, patriotic tunes or, most often, hymns. In this genre, the original goal of Delsarte poses was transformed; instead of the visual reproduction of unmoving sculpture, ongoing motions would interpret a well-known musical work.

Leading dancers such as Isadora Duncan and Ruth St Denis are often credited with bringing spirituality into modern dance, yet professional and, most often, amateur elocutionists performing Delsarte poses to music in the Progressive era also contributed to the shifting cultural understanding of the capacities of the art form. While dance historians have explored the role of the Delsarte movement in helping to legitimize dance in America at the beginning of the twentieth century,[6] they have not considered the role that musical accompaniment played in increasing the understanding that physical movements could evoke the sacred.[7] This chapter explores the ways in which female amateurs adopted hymns to make Delsarte poses socially acceptable for the performance contexts available to them: schools, churches and civic assemblies. It draws on pedagogical materials, press reports of women's performances and contemporary understandings of hymnody to explain how musical accompaniments in the illustrated song helped to mediate its potentially precarious position within American culture, given its deep suspicion of dance.

Delsarte – described as 'physical culture' and consisting of part exercise, part pantomime and part self-improvement – was first taken up by middle- and upper-class women in the 1880s and 1890s, a period of changing gender expectations and the resulting rise of the 'New Woman'. Historians have considered Delsartism to be part of the Progressive-era movement to improve women's health, liberating them from corsets and other dangerously restrictive Victorian attire.[8] The new physical freedoms of the period also resulted in the loosening of codes of behaviour and made social dancing more acceptable, despite continued criticism in religious circles. The many nineteenth-century pastors who authored anti-dancing

---

[6] See Nancy Lee Chalfa Ruyter, *Reformers and Visionaries: The Americanization of the Art of Dance* (New York: Dance Horizons, 1979), 17–30.

[7] Ruth St Denis and Isadora Duncan both studied Delsarte in their youth and portrayed their dancing as having spiritual qualities. Denis saw Genevieve Stebbins perform, and her partner Ted Shawn studied Delsarte and wrote the book *Every Little Movement: A Book about François Delsarte*, 2nd edn (rept edn, Brooklyn: Dance Horizons, 1968).

[8] See Lenox Browne and Emil Behnke, 'Voice, Song, and Speech: Sixth Paper', *Werner's Magazine* 17 (1895), 485–8.

sermons and pamphlets were primarily adversaries of social dance and the resulting sexual temptations faced by couples who whirled in each other's arms. Yet the parents urged by Mason City's Rev. Carlton to 'take a firm stand' against dancing would undoubtedly have found their daughters dancing on a stage for a paying audience even more morally questionable. Delsarte posing might not have been mistaken for the theatrical dance of the period, but it nonetheless took place before audiences who viewed the bodies of their wives and daughters in motion.

Fundamentalists' writings regularly decried social and theatrical entertainments available in increasingly urban environments and emphasized that dancing could seductively lead women into passion and immorality.[9] Stage dancing retained its disrepute, in part due to objections to the mind being abandoned to bodily excesses:[10] Winona, Minnesota, pastor John Morley's 1882 sermon lauded a 'cultured mind' as opposed to 'nimble feet'.[11] Earlier in the century Presbyterian revivalist Lyman Beecher had warned about the dangers to the moral character of women who appeared in public, whether praying at revivals or as actresses: 'There *is* generally and *should* be always, in the female character, a softness and delicacy of feeling which shrinks from the notoriety of public performance.'[12] Theatrical dancing was associated with lower-class women; Michigan Methodist Charles Eastman believed that 'dancing was more common as one moved "downward" to the gin palace, beer garden, theatre, and "house of infamy"'.[13] As in Eastman's commentary, prostitution was an ongoing theme in anti-dance rhetoric. In 1919 the editor of the *Western Recorder* blamed dancing for the thousands of girls 'in houses of ill repute',[14] and evangelist Billy Sunday preached, 'I say to you, young girl ... Don't go to that dance.'[15]

---

[9] Ann Louise Wagner, *Adversaries of Dance: From the Puritans to the Present* (Urbana: University of Illinois Press, 1997), 193–7; Betty A. DeBerg, *Ungodly Women: Gender and the First Wave of American Fundamentalism* (Minneapolis: Fortress Press, 1990), 104.

[10] Wagner, *Adversaries of Dance*, 206.

[11] Nancy Lee Chalfa Ruyter, *The Cultivation of Body and Mind in Nineteenth-Century American Delsartism* (Westport, CT: Greenwood Press, 1999), 207.

[12] Lyman Beecher, letter in the *Christian Observer* (August and September 1828), 473–81, 537–44, quoted in Sandra S. Sizer (Tamar Frankiel), *Gospel Hymns and Social Religion: The Rhetoric of Nineteenth-Century Revivalism* (Philadelphia: Temple University Press, 1978), 62, 190.

[13] Rev. John H. Morley, *The Relative Place of Amusements: A Discourse Preached at the Congregational Church in Winona* ... (Winona, MN: Republication Steam, 1882), 9, quoted in Wagner, *Adversaries of Dance*, 207.

[14] 'School Dancing', *Western Recorder* 94, no. 33 (22 May 1919), 8, quoted in DeBerg, *Ungodly Women*, 105.

[15] Billy Sunday, 'A Plain Talk to Women', in William T. Ellis, *Billy Sunday: The Man and His Message* (Philadelphia: L. T. Myers, 1914), 223.

Delsarte's ability to transcend the perceived depravity of dance was linked to a whole host of cultural factors, not the least of which was a lack of clarity about what exactly constituted Delsarte training. Historical understanding of Delsarte performance most often centres on its avowed relationship to ancient Greek culture and its tableaux arrangements of women wearing white gowns; Genevieve Stebbins and other leading pedagogues promoted posing to evoke mythical or biblical characters and their stories. However, the French actor and singer François Delsarte, who offered training for theatrical professionals and for whom the practices were named, wrote little about his teaching method, allowing it to be reconfigured in a variety of ways in America, where he achieved something of a cult status decades after his death (inspiring the sales of Delsarte soap and corsets).[16] Practitioners argued vociferously in print about what was and was not true Delsarte, jockeying for the position of authentic Delsarte disciple. When Delsarte's daughter Marie visited America in 1892, she expressed surprise that Americans' versions of her father's teachings in no way resembled them.[17] The range of historical activities linked to the term 'Delsarte' is perhaps even broader than those she criticized. In America, Delsarte training frequently consisted of physical exercises that promoted flexibility and relaxation, and expressive poses that were, in fact, related to the gestures traditionally provided for orators, such as those in Gilbert Austin's *Chironomia* (1806);[18] these poses could be applied to speakers' performances of poetic recitations, and American Delsarte was closely associated with elocution and came to permeate the field's textbooks and literature. That physical actions formerly associated with men were now being undertaken by female practitioners demonstrated the new vocal and physical freedoms that had become available to the huge influx of women into elocution.

Movement and pantomime regularly appeared on programmes, dominated by women, that primarily featured poetic recitations by spoken word performers. In addition to serving as the final selection of a mixed musical and literary entertainment, women's systematic physical movements could be accompanied simultaneously by music, poetry or both. Because of Delsarte's late nineteenth-century performance contexts, its wider dissemination retained Grecian influences mainly in its costuming; however,

---

[16] Delsarte lived from 1811 to 1871, dying before the height of American Delsartism.
[17] Ruyter, *Cultivation of Body and Mind*, 12–13.
[18] Rev. Gilbert Austin, *Chironomia; or, A Treatise on Rhetorical Delivery: Comprehending Many Precepts, Both Ancient and Modern, for the Proper Regulation of the Voice, the Countenance, and Gesture* (London: Printed for T. Cadell and W. Davies; by W. Bulmer, 1806), plates.

classical antiquity was replaced with the sorts of texts and music from American popular culture that were typically heard at women's events. Thus, under the umbrella of Delsarte-related performance types can also be included not only the pantomimic poses of the illlustrated song, but also 'drills' for multiple women, related to tableaux but involving considerably more motion. Whether or not some of these activities should be considered 'Delsarte' or largely peripheral to the core of the practice is perhaps an unnecessarily artificial question, given that during the period the term sometimes functioned merely as a 'brand' added to elocution books that were entirely representative of their type, with the minor difference of a few added photos of posing, gowned women.

In general, Delsarte performers were successful in constructing their physical activities as something other than dance; Genevieve Stebbins's performances did include some dancing, though whether or not this constituted 'Delsarte' is unclear. American Delsarte was sometimes cast more as healthy exercise than artistic performance, allowing it to be positioned farther from its original theatrical basis and the potential sexualized implications of stage or social dance. The group drills to music, sometimes with physical props such as scarves, fans, tambourines or brooms, were far more dance-like than statue posing and were common activities for young women and school children.[19] Instructions for 'broom drills', praised as the most 'graceful' exercise for girls and the most 'pleasing to onlookers', appeared in published elocution manuals and in activity guides for educators.[20] Young women marched in formations holding gender-appropriate instruments of domestic life in place of weapons. The *Indiana Democrat* claimed that this sort of drill had been created by young women in Lowell, Massachusetts, who had tied streamers to their brooms, but preferred that women use brooms for their intended purpose: 'after all, perhaps, the best broom drill is the one that takes place in the kitchen, where there is only one broom and no streamers'.[21] The *Daily Miner* of Butte, Montana, recognized that the broom drill was closer to entertainment than athletics, announcing, 'All sport should be amusement, but it does not follow that all amusements can be called sporting

---

[19] Nancy Lee Chalfa Ruyter, 'Antique Longings: Genevieve Stebbins and American Delsartean Performance', in *Corporealities: Dancing, Knowledge, Culture and Power*, ed. Susan Leigh Foster (London: Routledge, 1996), 73–4.

[20] Alfred M. A. Beale, *Calisthenics and Light Gymnastics for Home and School* (New York: Excelsior, 1888), 71.

[21] *The Indiana Democrat* (Indiana, Pennsylvania), 14 April 1881, quoted in 'The Broom Brigade and Broom Drill', *Yesteryear Once More*, https://yesteryearsnews.wordpress.com/2010/page/23/.

events.'²² These activities were nonetheless in keeping with Christian writer Marvin Vincent's preference for exercise over dance: 'Youth must not dance, but they may march to music in company ... it is very hard to see how skipping to music converts the exercise to sin.'²³

Such adaptations and modifications within Delsartism have been overshadowed in the scholarship's concentration on the careers of major practioners and their publications, highlighting the work of a few professionals leading what was primarily an amateur's art form; fewer scholars have concentrated on the contexts for amateur performance or the actual poses and drills undertaken by women that will be considered here. Linda J. Tomko has described Delsarte as fundamentally private entertainment in the home; however, the contemporary press regularly reported that performances took place in more public venues, before women's clubs and at schools and churches, environments that came to shape the content of these events.²⁴ The bulk of the *c.* 125 Delsarte performances reported in Iowa newspapers between 1888 and 1920 were by amateur performers, and a large portion of them were public events presented by a town's female citizens designed to raise funds for the benefit of local hospitals, libraries, churches or other civic institutions. Erma Bashford's Iowa town can serve as a representative example of the ways in which women's Delsarte activites were part of a community.²⁵ In 1894 Mason City had a Delsarte ensemble of twenty-four young women who rehearsed at the Methodist Church, and the town boasted several professional instructors over two decades. Kindergarten teacher Rosalie Willson studied Delsarte in 1898 to enhance her pedagogical offerings for children; her son Meredith Willson grew up to author the 1957 Broadway musical *The Music Man*, which satirized Delsarte in its depiction of the ladies of River City posing as 'Grecian urns', one of the few surviving popular references to a cultural practice that was at one time widespread. Because small-town life was often centred on its religious institutions, approximately 30 per cent of Iowa's Delsarte performances took place in churches, where the notion of women's bodies moving on the platform had the potential to be controversial.

---

[22] *The Daily Miner* (Butte, Montana), 26 May 1882, quoted in 'The Broom Brigade and Broom Drill'.

[23] Marvin Richard Vincent, *Amusement a Force in Christian Training* (Troy, NY: Wm. H. Young, 1867), 21–3, 15, quoted in Wagner, *Adversaries of Dance*, 212.

[24] Linda J. Tomko, *Dancing Class: Gender, Ethnicity, and Social Divides in American Dance, 1890–1920* (Bloomington and Indianapolis: Indiana University Press, 1999), 65.

[25] For more on Delsarte, particularly in Iowa, see Marian Wilson Kimber, *The Elocutionists: Women, Music, and the Spoken Word* (Urbana: University of Illinois Press, 2017), 92–104.

The belief that Delsarte was good for the soul as well as the body came in part from its appearance within the broader context of elocution, the practioners of which already aspired to present great literature as part of the increasing 'sacralization' of the arts in America described by Lawrence Levine and others.[26] Elocutionists' voices were to be the vessels of high culture, and the literature of their discipline regularly called for performers to programme spoken texts that exemplified morality and truth, in order to enoble themselves and their audiences.[27] The proponents of Delsarte claimed that such highbrow ideals could now be embodied in women's bodies as well as their voices. In addition to promising women a new level of physical grace, fitness and beauty, Delsarte exercises could affect their emotional lives.[28] Delsartism was not merely training for performance – it had a strongly mystical tinge and aspired to both a spiritual dimension as well as a physical one; Stebbins, in particular, was drawn to the spirituality of a variety of Eastern religions, not just Christianity.[29] The statue posing that she helped popularise was to be personally transforming as well as performative; in aiming for 'expression' through 'physical culture', a Delsarte student would come to feel the specific emotion expressed.[30] American Delsarte's triparte division drew on long-standing pseudo-scientific ideas about the specific relationship of character and appearance, and was derived from the similar 'mental', 'motive' and 'vital' classifications of physiognomy; instructor Anna Morris's 'Delsarte Thought Lesson' stressed that a 'considerate heart' does not 'dwell in a noisy, slovenly body' because '*the body reveals the mind*'.[31] Thus, training the body would improve a woman's moral character; one Delsarte student wrote, 'It is the soul which has a body, instead of the body which has a soul.'[32] Through portraying Greek statues or female characters from myths,

---

[26] Lawrence Levine, *Highbrow/Lowbrow: The Emergence of Cultural Hierarchy in America* (Cambridge, MA: Harvard University Press, 1988), 155.

[27] See, e.g., William Chamberlain, 'The President's Opening Address', *Proceedings of the National Association of Elocutionists* 5 (1896), 20; 'Should Public Readers Follow or Lead Public Taste in the Choice of Selections?', *Proceedings of the National Association of Elocutionists* 4 (1896), 92; and Eleanor O'Grady, *Elocution Class: A Simplification of the Laws and Principles of Expression* (New York: Benziger Brothers, 1895), 20.

[28] Taylor Susan Lake, 'American Delsartism and the Bodily Discourse of Respectable Womanliness', PhD diss. (University of Iowa, 2002), 98.

[29] Ruyter, *Cultivation of Body and Mind*, 98.   [30] Lake, 'American Delsartism', 108–9.

[31] R. Anna Morris, *A Manual of Physical Training, Plays and Games for the Primary Grades of the Cleveland Public Schools* (Cleveland: Britton, 1901), 29.

[32] Ida Elizabeth Sisson, 'A Chautauqua Journal by Ida Elizabeth Sisson', 5 July 1895, 46, Chautauqua Institution Archives, Chautauqua, NY, quoted in Andrew C. Rieser, *The Chautauqua Movement: Protestants, Progressives, and the Culture of Modern Liberalism* (New York: Columbia University Press, 2003), 232.

women embodied the highest art of Western culture; their pantomimes to hymn tunes would likewise enable them to present religious truths with their bodies.

Beyond the construction of Delsarte as spiritual by Stebbins and other practitioners, the music that accompanied it played a major role in viewers' interpretations of its movements as sacred expression. It is often not possible to determine exactly what music was used to accompany any given performance, though in general accompaniments seem to have been primarily instrumental, not vocal. Delsarte's spiritual aspects were frequently suggested in its musical underpinnings, which functioned to create a mood or filled the time frame created by statue-like stillness. Florence Fowle Adams wrote that music for the 'slow, mystic transition' from one posing group to another should be 'as dreamy and spirituelle as possible',[33] and the piano music provided in Stebbins's *Society Gymnastics and Voice-Culture* (1888) largely consisted of Romantic character pieces with lyrical, slow-tempo melodies over left-hand arpeggiated patterns to accompany 'Swaying for Poise' or 'Arm Movements'.[34] Philadelphia elocutionist Rachel Shoemaker's list of suggested compositions in her book *Delsarte Pantomimes* included piano pieces with religious titles: 'The Two Angels', 'The Monastery Bells' and 'The Hundredth Psalm', a set of variations on Old One Hundredth.[35]

When the poetic texts commonly heard in entertainments were entirely abandoned for posing, music became essential to a performance's expression of meaning. Audiences who were unfamiliar with Grecian art were sometimes unable to discern the emotive content of women's pantomimes. After the Tableaux d'Art Company appeared in Elyria, Ohio, in 1903, the local newspaper reported that, 'had not the story ... been printed on the program no one could have guessed what they attempted to portray'.[36] Music could provide specific meaning through a song text, either sung or implied through an instrumental version. After Miss Thomas performed a series of poses representing particular emotions in 1891, the Estherville,

---

[33] Florence A. Fowle Adams, 'Studies in Posing', *Werner's Magazine* 15 (December 1893), 416–17.

[34] Genevieve Stebbins, *Society Gymnastics and Voice-Culture; Adapted from the Delsarte System*, 6th edn (New York: E. S. Werner, 1888), 97–106.

[35] Mrs J. W. Shoemaker, *Delsartean Pantomines with Recital and Musical Accompaniment* (Philadelphia: Penn Publishing, 1902), 176–9. These works are *Le deux anges*, op. 8, by Jacques Blumental; *Les cloches du Monastere*, op. 54, by Louis Lefébure-Wély, op. 54; and *The Hundredth Psalm* by William V. Wallace. In contrast, accompaniments with strongly emphasized metrical patterns and repeated strains, such as marches and waltzes, were in keeping with the more exercise-oriented Delsarte.

[36] 'Nellie Peck Saunders', *Elyria Reporter* (Ohio), 15 October 1903.

Iowa, paper happily described how the 'Music harmonized every emotion portrayed'.[37] Although the 1890 program of the Charleston, South Carolina, Female Seminary was entitled 'A Dream of Ancient Greece',[38] Margaret Jenkins recalled how her pupils conveyed the 'spirit' of the songs that accompanied them, which included 'Auld Lang Syne', 'My Country 'tis of Thee' and 'Home, Sweet Home'.[39] In spite of their flowing white gowns, many performers completely abandoned evocations of distant antiquity, instead making songs such as 'The Last Rose of Summer' or 'Old Folks at Home' central to their performance. Emma Griffith Lumm's recitation anthologies included photographs of her student with brief musical selections; the young woman poses flirtatiously to 'Comin' Thro' the Rye' to express 'coquette' and kneels to 'Nearer, My God, to Thee' for 'prayer', concluding with a triumphantly patriotic pose to 'The Star Spangled Banner'.[40]

The adaption of such songs into Delsartean performance generated the illustrated song genre, which drew on musical works already well known to potential audiences. Extant instruction materials suggest that the practice lasted somewhat longer than statue posing. Elocution anthologies and periodicals provided performers with song texts, instructions for accompanying motions and sometimes photographs and musical scores; individual illustrated songs were also published in small, inexpensive brochures available for under fifty cents. The simple technical level of any accompaniments that were provided ensured that they were readily accessible to those with little musical training. The bulk of these publications, most of which were by women, post-date press reports of performances and thus may have reflected contemporary practices already underway. It is not clear whether the songs to which performers moved were heard with sung texts or purely as instrumental versions, though it seems that the latter occurred more frequently, as it was assumed that audiences would already know the songs' texts. There is no indication that the performers themselves sang; rather, their physical motions served to represent or to interpret the words. Women continued to wear the pseudo-Greek attire of Delsarte statue posing for entertainments based in popular song, sometimes contributing to historical misunderstanding. When the students of Hollins Institute in Roanoke, Virginia, performed a pantomime of 'Nearer, My God, to Thee' in 1893, the singer who

---

[37] 'Miss Thomas' Reading', *Northern Vindicator* (Estherville, Iowa), 12 March 1891.
[38] Margaret Virginia Jenkins, 'A Study in Attitude', *Werner's Voice Magazine* 12 (December 1890), 297–300.
[39] Jenkins, 'A Study in Attitude', 298.
[40] Emma Griffith Lumm, *The Twentieth Century Speaker* (N.p.: K. T. Boland, 1903), 31, 35–6.

accompanied them, Kate Hopkins, erroneously stated that although 'the hymn was modern, the pantomime was arranged according to the principles as laid down by the ancient Greeks'.[41]

Basing performances entirely on the music and text of a song, most frequently a well-known hymn tune, allowed for a linguistic masking of the emergence of women performers engaged in a new physicality on platforms across America.[42] To call what was primarily a series of bodily motions a 'song' was a means of evading the criticisms of dance by leaders in various American religious groups. The introduction of sacred music as the inspiration for women's dance-like motion lent it a new social respectability and made it appropriate for performances in church settings. The numerous events organized by women's clubs and civic groups during this era provided entertainment for their communities while simultaneously serving to benefit charitable causes, another means by which women could create social acceptance for their entertainments. However, in churches these kinds of extra-religious activities were not unproblematic; though not as adamant in their rejection of entertainments as of dancing, many pastors warned of their possible impropriety. Elocutionists were always careful in how they presented themselves to church groups to avoid any possible association with morally suspect actresses. Rachel and Jacob Shoemaker opened their performances from *c.* 1869 to 1872 with scripture before turning to poetic selections, and decades later, one cautious church committee cut the obviously theatrical word 'dramatic' off the phrase 'dramatic and humorous recitals' from the flier of Canadian elocutionist Jessie Alexander.[43] Even uncostumed spoken-word performances by amateurs in literary entertainments were potentially inappropriate, and many clergymen's critiques centred on women's involvement in such activities. Rev. George Wesley Marvin of Lockport, New York, complained that such events 'defiled' the sanctuary, and he expressed his disapproval of women's activities in a poem:

Fair and Festival, frolics untold,
    Are held in the place of prayer;

---

[41] 'Pupils' Concert at Hollins', *The Roanoke Daily Times*, 23 December 1896.
[42] Hymns published as illustrated songs include 'Abide With Me', 'At the Golden Gate', 'The Holy City', 'Jesus, Lover of My Soul', 'Lead, Kindly Light', 'The Listening Ear of Night', 'My Faith Looks Up to Thee', 'Nearer, My God, to Thee', 'Rock of Ages' and 'Safe in the Arms of Jesus'.
[43] Jacob W. Shoemaker and Rachel H. Shoemaker Ephemeral Papers, 1862–1877, McNairy Library and Learning Forum, Special Collections and Archives, Millersville University, Pennsylvania; Jessie Alexander, *Encore!: New Book of Platform Sketches* (Toronto: McClelland & Stewart, 1922), 129.

And maidens, bewitching as sirens of old,
> With worldly graces rare,
Invent the very cunningest tricks,
> Untrammeled by gospel or laws,
To beguile and amuse, and win from the word
> Some help for the righteous cause.[44]

In his book *What Harm Is There in It?*, Byron Laing warned readers that 'John the Baptist was beheaded through the bewitching appearance of that young lady who thought it was not harmful to spend an hour in frivolity.'[45] Rev. B. Carradine pointed out that men should not prostitute the bodies of their wives and daughters in song or dance in order to raise money: 'What if the church thrusts out its lovely daughters upon stage and platform ... where the bold glance of the worldly man roves unchecked and critically over their forms, all for a few pennies?'[46] Carradine's list of activities 'purely worldly in character' that he found inappropriate included pantomimic posing, a Delsarte parody and dancing, and Rev. Marvin criticized church entertainments as 'feeders of the opera and the theatre, and not counter attractions', amusements that promoted 'carnality and worldliness'.[47]

Nonetheless, as many women did perform Delsarte in school and church settings, motion by the female body had to be mediated through meanings that prevented any possibility of erotic or sexualized interpretations. Hymns were a natural choice to ensure that posing expressed sacred content. Audiences would need to be intimately familiar with a tune and text to understand the pantomimed motions of an illustrated-song version, so not surprisingly, hymns adapted for illustrated songs consisted of the best-known works most often reprinted in the hymnbooks of the era.[48] In

---

[44] Rev. Marvin of Presbyterian Church, Lockport, NY, 'Ecclesiastical Amusements', in Byron Laing, *What Harm Is There in It?*, 2nd edn (Toronto: William Briggs, 1886), 125.

[45] Laing, *What Harm Is There in It?*, 21.

[46] Rev. B. Carradine, *Church Entertainments: Twenty Objections* (Syracuse, NY: A. W. Hall, 1891), 63.

[47] Marvin, 'Ecclesiastical Amusements', 128, 131.

[48] Stephen Marini's database of hymns reveals that 'Jesus, Lover of My Soul', 'Nearer, My God, to Thee', 'Rock of Ages', 'Abide With Me' and 'My Faith Looks Up to Thee' were among the most reprinted hymns, all but one appearing in seventy or more printings. 'From Classical to Modern: Hymnody and the Development of American Evangelicalism, 1737–1970', in *Singing the Lord's Song in a Strange Land: Hymnody in the History of North American Protestantism*, ed. Edith L. Blumhofer and Mark A. Noll (Tuscaloosa: University of Alabama Press, 2004), 11, 18. That the hymns adopted as illustrated songs were widely popular is also suggested by the notebook of poet Lucretia Howe of Rumford, Maine, who in 1891 copied out both 'Jesus, Lover of My Soul' and E. H. Sears's 'The Listening Ear of Night' in her

addition to their role in religious services, the same hymns were occasionally included in elocution books to be performed as recitations without music or spoken to their musical settings;[49] specific hymns also served as musical accompaniments to poetry that mentioned them, such as 'Jesus, Lover of My Soul', regularly heard in performances of Marianne Farningham's poem, 'The Drowning Singer', or 'Rock of Ages', heard in the poem of the same name by Edward H. Rice.[50]

The hymns selected for posing revolved around themes that were socially acceptable for women's performances. Though the musical works commonly included in entertainments were written by both men and women, much evangelical hymnody from between 1870 and 1920 drew on what June Hadden Hobbs has identified as 'the language and epistemology of the private sphere', which helped to create 'a feminized Christianity'[51] that stressed a personal relationship with God. The hymns chosen for illustrated songs are thus characteristic of the work of hymnodists whose texts emphasized 'service rather than conquest'.[52] These hymns stressed the weakness or sin of the singer and the need for sanctuary or purification in Christ, the safe haven. The language of this hymnody sometimes evokes sexual submission as a metaphor for spiritual unity with the divine, such as expressed in 'Safe in the Arms of Jesus' by Fanny Crosby, in which the speaker treats Christ as her lover and lies 'safe on His gentle breast'.[53] The texts of the three hymns most

---

notebook, held in the Jerry Tarver Elocution, Rhetoric and Oratory Collection, Ohio State University Rare Books and Manuscripts Library.

[49] 'Nearer My God to Thee', by Sarah Flower Adams, appeared in James Murdoch's *Analytic Elocution* (Cincinnati and New York: Van Antwerp, Bragg & Co., 1884), 497–8. Charles Wesley's 'Jesus Lover of My Soul' and several other hymns were printed in 1886 in Jacob Shoemaker's *Practical Elocution; for Use in Colleges and Schools and by Private Students* (Philadelphia: National School of Elocution and Oratory, 1886), 295–6, reprinted as late as the 1920s. Rachel Shoemaker published eleven hymns in *Advanced Elocution* (Philadelphia: Penn Publishing, 1896), 390–9, and E. B. Warman's book, *How to Read, Recite and Impersonate* (Chicago: M. A. Donohue & Co., 1889), 16–76, provided instructions for how to recite hymns.

[50] 'The Drowning Singer', sometimes known as 'The Last Hymn', appears in Henry Davenport Northrop, *The Peerless Reciter* (Chicago: E. C. Morse, 1894), 43–5, and elsewhere. 'Rock of Ages' can be found with mention of music in Hallie Quinn Brown, *Bits and Odds: A Choice Selection of Recitations for School, Lyceum and Parlor Entertainments* (Xenia, OH: Chew Press, n.d.); Frank H. Fenno's *The Science and Art of Elocution* (Philadelphia: John H. Potter, 1878), 264, describes how Rice's poem should be performed.

[51] June Hadden Hobbs, *'I Sing for I Cannot Be Silent': The Feminization of American Hymnody, 1870–1920* (Pittsburgh: University of Pittsburgh Press, 1997), 102–3.

[52] Hobbs, *'I Sing for I Cannot Be Silent'*, 102.

[53] C. Michael Hawn and June Hadden Hobbs, '"Thy Love ... Hath Broken Every Barrier Down": The Rhetoric of Intimacy in Nineteenth-Century British and American Women's Hymns', in *Music and Theology in Nineteenth-Century Britain*, ed. Martin V. Clarke (Burlington, VT: Ashgate, 2012), 62–3.

often illustrated with movement – 'Jesus, Lover of My Soul', 'Nearer, My God, to Thee' and 'Rock of Ages' – all share an emphasis on the poet's need to be united with God. In 'Jesus, Lover of My Soul', the singer longs to fly to the bosom of Christ in order to be hidden from life's tempests; likewise, in 'Rock of Ages', she longs to 'Let me hide myself in thee' and be cleansed of sin. The public performances of moving female bodies were thus made possible through depicting the content of hymns that expressed personal weakness and subjugation to God's will.

Although Delsarte's exercises were supposed to provide women with new strength, the texts of the hymns to which they posed stressed physical and emotional weakness, and the wider biographical constructions purporting to document songs' origins sometimes noted that they were created by authors who were themselves struck down by sickness and suffering. Cardinal Newman was reportedly ill for three weeks before producing 'Lead, Kindly Light', and Ray Palmer, lonely and in poor heath, was supposed to have penned the last stanza of 'My Faith Looks Up to Thee' in tears.[54] This sort of emotional 'tenderness' in the face of worldly cares was especially associated with female hymn writers; it served as an autobiographical justification for the creative works they were inspired to produce, works that would, in their entry into the larger world, leave the gender-appropriate domestic sphere behind. J. R. Watson has described how writing about women hymn writers demonstrated 'the way in which the subordinate status of women, their timidity, sadness, pain and sorrow, are transmuted into the appropriate religious posture of humility and dependence'.[55] Thus, the dance-like motions of women engaged in Delsarte posing were made, through their associated musical compositions, feminine, domestic and sacred in ways that did not threaten their condoned social position.

Many of the poses and gestures women performed in illustrated songs permitted a range of motions while at the same time expressing the submissiveness in the hymns' texts. In her pantomime guide, Ethel Eldridge wrote that 'entire forgetfulness of oneself should be the highest goal', and Grace Faxon admonished performers not to let their eyes stray to the audience and instead to watch their own gestures, stressing private devotion over the creation of

---

[54] H. Augustine Smith, *Lyric Religion: The Romance of Immortal Hymns* (New York: Century Co., 1931), 217, 258.

[55] J. R. Watson, *The English Hymn: A Critical and Historical Study* (Oxford: Clarendon Press, 1997), 423.

a public spectacle;[56] in their video, the Brown twins, who do not visually engage with the camera, abide by these guidelines. The stress on submissiveness and the manner in which the religious sentiments dominated period performers' movements through the controlling force of the hymn is in sharp contrast to the attitude of some contemporary dancers, such as Isadora Duncan, who acknowledged her own egotism as central to her art, which she asserted was inextricably bound up with her own life.[57]

The Grecian gowns adopted for posing as statuary, reconceived as biblical costumes or angel's robes, allowed for fluidity of movement, though some women might still have worn corsets, which could account for the dominance of arm motion.[58] The photographed poses for 'At the Golden Gates' devised by Helen Merci Schuster show a corseted woman, and her minimal arm and hand gestures are more similar to those prescribed for orators than to the expansive possibilities of Delsarte. Nonetheless, the directions call for the accompanying poem to be read slowly, 'thus securing unity of movement and avoiding abrupt transitions', suggesting a certain fluidity.[59] Judy Burns, who described her recreation of Delsarte performances in 1992, noted its emphasis on the upper body – 'the head and face, the shoulders, arms and hands, plus the overall dispensation of weight' – as a spiritual means of expression.[60] Given the number of pedagogical guides that show women kneeling (and in one instance, reclining), more motion below the waist may have taken place than is apparent from published sources.[61] In contrast to *tableaux vivants*, or 'living pictures', Delsarte publications described group posing as *tableaux mouvants* (moving) to suggest the degree of motion, rather than stasis, that took place.[62] Extant pictures may now suggest stiff pantomime, but contemporary descriptions of Delsarte performers, such as Stebbins, stressed their

---

[56] Ethel May Eldridge, *Old Home Song Pantomimes* (Franklin, OH: Eldridge Entertainment House, 1910), 4; Faxon, *Popular Recitations and How to Recite Them*, 93. Faxon is referring to 'The Last Rose of Summer', not a hymn, but there are similar comments for hymns.

[57] Peter Kurth, *Isadora Duncan: A Sensational Life* (Boston: Little, Brown, and Co., 2001), 495.

[58] On costuming, see Lisa Suter, 'The Arguments They Wore: The Role of the Neoclassical Toga in American Delsartism', in *Rhetoric, History, and Women's Oratorical Education: American Women Learn to Speak*, ed. David Gold and Catherine L. Hobbs (New York: Routledge, 2013), 134–53.

[59] 'At the Golden Gates', words by Father Ryan, music by Sumner Salter, pantomimed and posed by Helen Merci Schuster (New York: Edgar S. Werner, 1904).

[60] Judy Burns, 'Reconstructions', *Women & Performance* 5, no. 2 (1992), 135–6.

[61] The woman photographed reclines at the final line, 'Wait till the night is o'er', for Fanny Crosby and W. H. Doane, *Safe in the Arms of Jesus: Illustrated Pantomimed Hymn*, poses and directions by Cozette Keller (New York: Edgar S. Werner, 1917), 19. Photographs in Faxon's *Favorite Pantomimed Songs and Poses* show women rising on their toes.

[62] Ruyter, 'Antique Longings', 73.

'slow, rhythmic motion', and 'gracefully' flowing poses.[63] Chautauqua performer Gay MacLaren described her girlhood training as taking place to music and consisting of 'changing slowly from one pose to another with Delsarte movements to the count of ten'.[64] A 1908 book of pantomimes issued by Edgar S. Werner, the leading elocution publisher, provided motions similar to those of hymn pantomimes to accompany a reading of Henry Wadsworth Longfellow's poem about an angel, *Sandalphon*, with instructions that stressed continuous motion: 'All movements of hands and body gradually and continuously blend one into another gracefully without any awkwardness and as if a harmonious whole – a continuous harmonious unfoldment [*sic*] of thought.'[65]

Many of the poses called for in illustrated songs' instructions can be divided into four types. The first, reaching or pointing upward towards the heavens, signified God or the divine. Both hands were raised upward to lines such as 'Rise to all eternity' in 'Jesus, Lover of My Soul', 'I triumph still if Thou abide with me' in 'Abide with Me' and 'O bear me safe above / A ransomed soul' in 'My Faith Looks Up to Thee'. A variant of this pose consisted of only one hand raised, which could express a similar meaning, though it sometimes took on a more specific expression of triumph or the dominance of the divine, such as a pose provided for 'Great God our King', the final line of 'America'.[66] In contrast, texts about grief, defencelessness or need for God required downward motions, drooping heads or kneeling, poses that assured audiences that women's performances did not step outside acceptable social and moral boundaries. For example, in 'My Faith Looks Up to Thee' the motion to accompany the lines, 'While life's dark maze I tread, / And griefs around me spread', is to let clasped hands fall to the low front and to bow the head on the chest. In a commonly used third type, hands are held together, either in prayer or, more often, to represent pleading for God's grace or care, a pose seen in numerous elocution books. A version of 'My Faith Looks Up to Thee' published in 1906 shows hands clasped under a young girl's chin for the entreaty, 'Nor let me ever stray / From Thee aside'.[67]

---

[63] 'Genevieve Stebbins', *Werner's Magazine* 15 (December 1893), 444, quoted in Ruyter, 'Antique Longings', 86.
[64] Gay MacLaren, *Morally We Roll Along* (Boston: Little, Brown, & Company, 1938), 44.
[65] Stanley Schell, ed., *Werner's Book of Pantomimes* (New York: Edgar S. Werner, 1908), 201.
[66] Faxon, *Favorite Pantomimed Songs and Poses*, 46.
[67] Ray Palmer, *My Faith Looks Up to Thee*, pantomine by Augusta Gaywood, directions by Anna Cooper (New York: Edgar S. Werner, 1906), 19.

In a fourth, subtler type of motion, one hand or both hands are placed on the heart or the arms are overlapped across the chest; these actions generally suggest the speaker's inner spiritual life, or more specifically her heart, emotions or soul. Both hands on the heart, fingers slightly intertwined, is shown in the pose for 'The depths of my soul were stirred', in 'At the Golden Gates'.[68] Arms crossed are used to express the speaker's feelings about 'angel faces', 'which I have loved long since and lost awhile', in Faxon's version of 'Abide With Me'.[69] The pose seems also to be linked with the theme of willingness to be one with Christ, common to performers' chosen hymns; the drawings for a Delsarte drill in *Mrs Bosworth's Elocutionary Studies* (1889) identify a version of this pose, with head tilted downwards, as 'submission'.[70] In an arrangement of Crosby's well-known 'Safe in the Arms of Jesus', crossed arms express 'Safe on Jesus's breast'; the posing woman's hands are held together slightly lower for 'Jesus, my heart's dear refuge'.[71] The various motions of the entire upper body could be given an even more religious expression if performed while in a kneeling position. Anna Morris's physical education textbook identified a kneeling figure with arms crossed over her chest as representative of 'faith' (though in Austin's *Chironomia*, the same pose was labelled 'resignation'), and hands clasped on one knee, head bowed, suggested 'religious devotion' (see Figure 6.2).[72]

The most pictoral pose, called for in many of the illustrated hymns, is arms open wide to physically signify a cross. Faxon's instructions for 'Nearer, My God, To Thee' require the performer to 'Throw arms straight out at sides, palms down ... Hold arms perfectly steady, and let eyes look steadily out into audience'. The arranger considered this 'one of the most effective poses of the piece', especially if it could be illluminated with a white light.[73] The small girl photographed for F. E. Weatherly's 'The Holy City' strikes a similar pose for the lines, 'As the shadow of the cross arose / Upon a lonely hill'.[74] The image of a desperate woman clinging to

---

[68] 'At the Golden Gates', posed by Helen Merci Schuster, Picture VI.
[69] Faxon, *Favorite Pantomimed Songs and Poses*, 14.
[70] Bessie Bryant Bosworth, *Mrs. Bosworth's Elocutionary Studies* (Chicago: Bedford, Clark, and Co., 1889), 21.
[71] 'Safe in the Arms of Jesus', poses by Keller, 6, 17.
[72] R. Anna Morris, *Physical Education in the Public Schools: An Eclectic System of Exercises, Including the Delsartean Principles of Execution and Expression* (New York: American Book Company, 1892), 106, 98.
[73] Faxon, *Favorite Pantomimed Songs and Poses*, 74–5.
[74] F. E. Weatherly, *The Holy City: Illustrated Pantomimed Hymn* (New York: Edgar S. Werner, 1904), 8, 13. The instructions read: 'extend arms at sides, palms front, eyes raised'.

Figure 6.2 Pose for 'Religious Devotion', in R. Anna Morris, *Physical Education in the Public Schools: An Eclectic System of Exercises, Including the Delsartean Principles of Execution and Expression* (New York: American Book Company, 1892), 98

a cross, commonly associated with 'Rock of Ages', became part of the illustrated version of the hymn. For the text, 'Simply to the cross I cling', a 1909 guide reads: 'Both hands carried high with arms curved toward each other' in a pose meant to suggest the woman's arms around the cross.[75] A recital by students of Anna Morgan in Chicago featured a chorus singing 'Rock of Ages', during which one girl held her arms out like a cross, while another clung to her.[76] Such performances drew on a longer tradition of

---

[75] Faxon, *Popular Recitations and How to Recite Them*, 138. A photograph of the pose is found in 'Rock of Ages', poses by Agnes Walsh, *Werner's Magazine* 27 (May 1901), 156.

[76] Joyce Chalcraft Sozen, 'Anna Morgan: Reader, Teacher, and Director', PhD diss. (University of Illinois, 1961), 69, n. 13. The event was held at McVicker's Theater.

tableaux vivants, in which a young woman created a 'living picture' by clinging to an actual cross, in imitation of a widely reprinted engraving.[77]

While some of the gestures provided for illustrated song have obvious meanings that would have been readily apparent to audiences, even to those without any previous encounters with Delsartean posing, others are more abstract in nature. For example, in Margaret Wood's arrangement of 'Rock of Ages', the line 'Let the water and the blood' is incongruously accompanied by clasped hands.[78] Some poses that regularly appear in illustrated songs, such as one arm extended in front of the body or both arms lifted, with one slightly higher than the other, lack immediate or consistent extra-musical associations. For these movements, audiences' knowledge of a familiar hymn tune and text would have been the main force influencing their understanding of women's performances as generally religious in meaning. The use of well-known sacred music helped immunise these and other physical motions against any possible notions of impropriety.

The Delsarte movement peaked and declined before World War I. Nonetheless, instructions for illustrated songs and various hymn-related tableaux continued to appear in publications for children and amateur performers into the 1920s. The illustrated song had some influence on the rise of pageantry as a means for communal artistic endeavours, events which took place in churches as well as in civic venues.[79] Though considerably shortened, performers' pseudo-classical gowns were also seen in later dance forms, such as aesthetic dancing and the dances associated with May Day festivals held at American women's colleges. The occasional pastor who advocated rather than opposed dance, such as Joseph B. Gross, a defrocked Lutheran pastor who authored *The Parson on Dancing*, continued to be rare and sometimes polemical.[80] Tisa Wenger has linked Rev. William Guthrie of St Mark's Church in the Bouwerie in New York City and his presentations of white-gowned women dancing and posing in

---

[77] The tableau is described in *Tableaux, Charades, and Pantomimes* (Philadelphia: Penn Pub. Co., 1910), 10–11, and Mathilda Blair, *The Nonpareil Reader and Speaker for Young People* (New York: McLoughlin Bros., 1905), 158. A period engraving of it is reproduced in Robert M. Lewis, 'Tableaux vivants: Parlor Theatricals in Victorian America', *Revue français d'études américaines* 36 (April 1988), 289.

[78] Margaret Wood, *Rock of Ages* (New York: Edgar S. Werner, 1903).

[79] See, e.g., William V. Meredith's discussion of tableaux, pantomime and pageants, in *Pageantry and Dramatics in Religious Education* (New York: Abingdon Press, 1921), 146–9, 154–6.

[80] Rev. J. B. Gross, *The Parson on Dancing as it is Taught in the Bible, and was Practiced Among the Ancient Greeks and Romans* (Philadelphia: J. B. Lippincott, 1879; rept edn, New York: Dance Horizons, 1975). See also Wagner, *Adversaries of Dance*, 213–15.

tableaux in religious services in the 1920s to contemporary pageantry; however, given that at these events Guthrie also sometimes recited poetry, it is possible that their roots were farther back, in elocution and Delsarte.[81] By 1937, *Life* magazine could reprint photos from 'song-pantomimes' as quaint curiosities.[82] However, if the video of the Brown twins in 'Silent Night' is any indication, one should not assume that hymn pantomiming disappeared entirely with the abandonment of elocution and Delsarte in women's entertainments.[83]

Conventional generic divisions between dance, music and literature have limited our historical understanding of the role of religious music in creating the expressive content of American dance, as has the tendency to overlook performances in non-professional settings. Delsarte's strong association with statuary and ancient Greece has overshadowed the ways in which it continued to be manifest after its peak of popularity in the 1890s. In spite of its claims to 'high' art, its classical cultural connections were highlighted less frequently in performances by average American women, who were drawn to songs that were already part of their everyday lives. Adapted to become the illustrated song, hymnody made possible new kinds of movement by women in church and school settings. Through poses to hymns that shaped the rhythm and pacing of their changing motions, the physicality of dance became associated with religious meaning – dance became acceptable in new social contexts through masquerading as 'song'.

---

[81] See William Norman Guthrie, *The Relation of Dance to Religion* (New York: Petrus Stuyvesant Book Guild, 1923), and Tisa Wenger, 'The Practice of Dance for the Future of Christianity: "Eurythmic Worship" in New York's Roaring Twenties', in *Practicing Protestants: Histories of Christian Life in America, 1630–1965*, ed. Laurie F. Maffly-Kipp, Leigh E. Schmidt and Mark Valeri (Baltimore, MD: Johns Hopkins University Press, 2006), 222–49.

[82] 'Speaking of Pictures . . . These are Song-Pantomimes', *Life* (27 September 1937), 18–21.

[83] While the Grecian pillar behind the twins is perhaps coincidental, it nonetheless suggests the Delsartean roots of their performance.

7 | Pavanes and Passepieds in the Age of the Cancan

CARLO CABALLERO

Among the most famous pieces of music from the modern French school are a pair of pavanes by Fauré and Ravel, dating from 1887 and 1899. These two pieces, it turns out, belong to a larger repertory of pavanes composed in France between 1878 and 1910. Indeed, the genre became so popular that, according to Jann Pasler, at least eighty-nine pieces entitled 'pavane' were published in France between 1875 and 1900.[1] My own focus is on a smaller corpus of new pavanes that conform in movement and metre to their distant historical antecedents. Yet the more basic question is: why should late nineteenth-century French composers write pavanes at all? The historical vogue of the pavane, as dance and music, belongs to the 1500s. Musicologists have usually considered that Henry Purcell's pavanes, composed in the late 1600s, gave the final caress to a dying cultural form.

Table 7.1 lists in chronological order a specific subset of 'neo-pavanes', most of which will be discussed in this chapter. It is a curious assembly, joining three or four extremely familiar pieces to some wholly forgotten. Among the old favourites, we find the one by Fauré and two by Ravel. I also include the Passepied from Debussy's *Suite bergamasque*, which still bore the title 'Pavane' in advertisements and its last set of surviving proofs; the composer revised his title at a very late stage in production.[2] (How this interchange of titles could plausibly occur is a question this chapter will sort out.) Debussy's is the only piece that appears in Table 7.2 as well, since it may be treated as either a pavane or a passepied.[3] As for Fauré's seductive

---

[1] Jann Pasler, *Composing the Citizen: Music as Public Utility in Third Republic France* (Berkeley and Los Angeles: University of California Press, 2009), 506 n. 30. Pasler used the corpus of the Bibliothèque nationale de France, and, incredible as it may seem, the number may be even larger. However, some of the pieces Pasler goes on to mention are not pavanes, and others she counted, in contrast to those treated in this chapter, are not modelled on the dance type but merely carry the evocative title.

[2] *Œuvres complètes de Claude Debussy*, series 1, vol. 1, ed. Roy Howat (Paris: Editions Durand, 2000), 145, a facsimile of a flyleaf advertisement from the publisher Fromont (1900–1) listing 'Pavane' as the title of the fourth movement. On page xxiii Howat suggests that Debussy 'probably changed [the title] at the eleventh hour to avoid embarrassing comparisons with Fauré's Pavane in the same key'. Howat also lists the extant sources for the *Suite bergamasque* and notes the persistence of the title 'Pavane', unchanged in the proofs (p. 122).

[3] As explained below, the referent for this kind of dance was the *passepied de Bretagne* or *trihori*.

Table 7.1 The pavane returns, 1878–1910

Year composed	Composer	Work	Medium	Metre	Key	Era of setting	Drone
1878–9	Saint-Saëns	*Etienne Marcel*	Opera: ballet-divertissement; arr. for 2 pianos by Debussy (1890)	2/2	D minor	1400s	
1882	Delibes	*Le roi s'amuse*, No. 2 Pavane	Incidental music	2/2	G minor	Early 1500s	
"	"	*Le roi s'amuse*, No. 3 Scène du bouquet	"	4/4	F# minor	"	
"	"	*Le roi s'amuse*, No. 4 Lesquercarde	"	4/2	G major	"	
"	"	*Le roi s'amuse*, No. 6 Passepied	"	2/2	C# minor	"	occasional
1886	Paladilhe	*Patrie*	Grand opera, No. 12 (soprano and chorus)	2	F# minor	Late 1500s	middle section
1886	Saint-Saëns	*Proserpine*	Drame lyrique, scene 4	2/2	D minor	1500s	
1887	Fauré	*Pavane*, op. 50	Orchestra with mixed chorus	4/4	F# minor	Late 1600s–1700s	middle section
1888	Messager	*Isoline*	Conte des fées, tableau 8 (ballet with chorus)	2/2	E minor	Fairy play	middle section
1890	Debussy	*Suite bergamasque*, No. 4 'Petite pavane'	piano	4/4	F# minor		occasional
1892	Paladilhe		Piano four hands (for children)	4/4	G minor		
1896	Chausson	*Quelques danses*, op. 26, no. 3	piano	4/4	A minor		
1899	Ravel	*Pavane pour une infante défunte*	piano	4/4	E minor / G major		
1910	Ravel	*Ma mère l'Oye*, no. 1	Piano four hands (for children)	4/4	A minor		

Table 7.2 So-called passepieds

TRIHORI (Passepied de Bretagne), duple						
Year composed	Composer	Work	Medium	Metre	Key	Era of Setting
1882	Delibes	*Le roi s'amuse*, No. 6 Passepied	Incidental music	2/2	C♯ minor	Early 1500s
1890	Debussy	*Suite bergamasque*, No. 4 Passepied	piano	4/4	F♯ minor	

BAROQUE MODEL, triple						
Year composed	Composer	Work	Medium	Metre	Key	Era of Setting
1886	Paladilhe	*Patrie*, No. 10 Passepied et scène	Grand opera	9/8	E major	Late 1500s
1888	Messager	Passe-Pied I & II	piano	3/8	B minor and major	
1890	Messager	*Le basoche* (use part of Passe-pied II above)	Opéra comique, No. 13bis (ballet entr'acte)	3/8	B♭ minor	1514

Pavane in F♯ minor, the present author, like most musicologists, was long content to hum the tune and give it no thought.[4] Indeed, Fauré himself gave us leave for such an attitude by calling it, in his own words, 'a work of little importance'.[5] Around 2006 my attitude changed, as I was embarking on studies of ballet and social dance and began to see such 'character pieces' in a different light. But my long-standing inattention to a famous work by a composer to whom I had devoted years of study was really symptomatic of a more general bias in my professional world; that is, the practices of historical musicology. Especially among nineteenth-century specialists, there has long been a certain disdain for dance music, stand-alone short pieces, and the public popularity that brings repeated play to such morsels on radio or underwrites their use as background music in smart boutiques.

---

[4] My work on the present chapter dates back more than a decade: its first version, covering a smaller set of pavanes, was part of 'Ballet and the Secret of Style', given at the University of British Columbia, Department of Music, 21 September 2006. I presented increasingly developed variants of this oral paper at the University of Georgia (2007), the University of Colorado (2007) and the University of Melbourne (2014). I would like to thank Vera Micznik, Richard Zimdars, Elizabeth Kertesz and Michael Christoforidis, all of whom gave impetus to continuing work on this project through their generous invitations.

[5] Gabriel Fauré, *Correspondance*, ed. Jean-Michel Nectoux (Paris: Flammarion, 1980), 131 n. 4.

It is not only musicologists who feel this way: biases against these sort of pieces are shared by many professional musicians, whose connoisseurship rises to exasperation at seeing masters such as Fauré, Debussy and Ravel 'misrepresented' by their entries in a classical hit parade. This impatience or even embarrassment is curiously related to another repertory that many musicologists prefer to ignore: the gigantic load of forgotten nineteenth-century ballet scores. It is no coincidence that these two intellectually discomfiting repertories – late nineteenth-century ballet on the one hand, and short character (or dance) pieces on the other – are intimately related.

I

My interest in pavanes and passepieds grew gradually, as I began to notice more and more *passéiste* (i.e., deliberately old fashioned) compositions of this sort in my studies of theatre music and wondered how they related to more familiar examples in the keyboard, chamber or orchestral repertories – for example, to minuets and pavanes by Debussy, Fauré and Ravel. Delibes's incidental music for the revival of Victor Hugo's *Le roi s'amuse* at the Comédie-Française, which presented a suite of neo-Renaissance dances to audiences in 1882, provided an earlier instance of the same retrospective attitude and prompted me to investigate the web of relationships among other pieces to fill in the gaps. Delibes's remarkable incidental music may be described paradoxically as forward-thinking in its backward gaze, its *passéisme* pointing the way to much later works, such as Stravinsky's *Pulcinella* (1919) and Peter Warlock's *Capriol Suite* (1926). *Le roi s'amuse* also served notice that answers to questions about the revival of the pavane would ultimately not be found in the world of piano music, where the famous pieces by Fauré, Debussy and Ravel ended up making their way in the world, but in the precedent world of theatre music, especially ballet-divertissements and choral numbers in French opera, a vital repertory now largely lost to memory. Thus at the head of Table 7.1 stands Saint-Saëns's Pavane from his opera *Etienne Marcel* (1878), another theatre piece; indeed, the mother of all neo-pavanes.

Before we consider some of these attractive pieces and their interrelationships, this project calls for sharper focus on its historical and historiographic enterprise. In the broad view, it is fair to ask this: why conduct this research on pieces that have elicited more apology than wonder? What can we learn from such an inquiry? And what historical trends does it open to new understanding?

Let us start by laying out some possible historiographic stakes. First, the transfer of music written for ballets and operas into other musical media has been greatly underestimated by scholars who work primarily on instrumental music. The neo-pavane, moving from the public stage to the domestic piano, exemplifies this process heuristically. Even in an era when composers sought liberation from theatrophilia[6] (one way to characterize a vital stream of French song and instrumental music after the Franco-Prussian War), they all nevertheless aspired to compose for the theatre. Opera and ballet remained centrally prestigious stations of musical life, and Wagner's influence in France was about to reach its crest towards 1895. In short, even after 1870, we must study theatre music to understand instrumental music in France. Second, our sense of the unimportance of the short pieces in Tables 7.1 and 7.2 (and all sorts of artfully refashioned bygone dances) is unjustified. Their continuing popularity in the public sphere and strong lines of influence in their own time challenge modern scholarly indifference. Third, this pride of pavanes runs up against presumptions about innovation as an aesthetic priority in nineteenth-century music, and in this quality they are like almost all nineteenth-century music for the theatre, whether we are talking about a pavane written for the stage or not. These pieces provide examples of the creation of successful music through adherence to the generic contracts between composer and consumer. This way of working encouraged modelling and observation of conventions, an eye on historical continuity but also cultivation of finishing touches that would make the composition individual and memorable. In other words, these pieces show composers in the 1880s operating largely like composers in the 1780s. The possibility of such a traditional attitude not only in Saint-Saëns but also in Fauré and Ravel is inherently intriguing. Finally, these pavanes are part of the more general cults of nineteenth-century historicism and exoticism: the potentially re-creative awareness of ever more distant times and places. The European revival of interest in old dance forms of course began as early as the 1840s and ranged across many lands, from France to Russia.[7] Yet the French revival was historically

---

[6] Henri Duparc articulated this position bluntly: 'In France we cherish dramatic music too much. Dramatic music is an exterior and inferior type. It does not allow the artist to speak to us directly and freely express the beautiful spirit, the great spirit, that he must be, lest he be nothing at all' (response to survey by Paul Landormy, 'L'état actuel de la musique française', *La revue bleue* (26 March 1904), 397).

[7] Richard Taruskin, in his magisterial *Oxford History of Western Music*, vol. 4 (Oxford: Oxford University Press, 2005), 449–56, offers a parenthetical mini-essay ('Pastiche as Metaphor') that reaches back to revivals of ancient Greek rhythmic principles in the chansons of Claude Le Jeune and then builds a historical bridge to later retrospectivism in Mozart, Ambroise Thomas,

deeper, broader and more *self-possessive* than it was anywhere else. One finds Delibes and Saint-Saëns drawing from late Renaissance musical sources such as Arbeau and Jean d'Estrées to write galliards and pavanes a few years after the end of the Franco-Prussian war. In contrast, in the German-speaking lands one certainly finds minuets and gavottes, that is, revivals of eighteenth-century dances, but not, so far as I know, revivals of Renaissance dances.[8] The reason for the difference, I believe, is that German-speaking composers' interests fell almost entirely on late baroque dance forms rediscovered through contemporary research on J. S. Bach and Handel. Whereas German nation-building in the 1870s focused on the contributions of individual (German) geniuses such as Bach and Handel, the continuous political history of France as a single kingdom made it possible to embrace the whole legacy of French early music in a wider-ranging way, under the broad rubric of the *ancien régime*. Anything that came between Charlemagne and the Revolution was fair game: from plainchant to passepieds.

Historiography is best savoured with an equal dish of history (if indeed the two can be separated), and the study of dance pieces such as the neo-pavanes opens up a surprising number of new historical perspectives and details. At the most basic level, historical enquiry unearths forgotten traces of the past: in order to assert the likeness between Paladilhe's Pavane (Example 7.1) and Fauré's Pavane (Example 7.2), as I do below, I first had to find a reason to obtain a score of Paladilhe's utterly forgotten opera *Patrie* (1886). Then I had to play the score at the piano, as no recording exists. The only way one can hear Émile Paladilhe's Pavane in F♯ minor

---

Lachner, Anton Rubinstein and Tchaikovsky in order to prepare the reader for his presentation of Stravinskian Neoclassicism. This parenthetical section has points of resonance with my own account, but is understandably driven by an underlying Stravinskian narrative. Perhaps for this reason, Taruskin, to my way of thinking, leans too heavily on the 'culinary' or lollipop nature of revived dance types and also correspondingly renders this wide sprawl of music more homogeneous than it really is. For instance, I cannot agree that '*in all cases,* it was the pretext for modern harmonic, melodic, and (in the case of orchestral music) timbral invention that justified pastiche and cinched its popularity with audiences' (454, emphasis mine). As for revivals in the German-speaking lands, scholars have not surprisingly gravitated to Brahms: Robert Pascall, 'Unknown Gavottes by Brahms', *Music & Letters* 57, no. 4 (October 1976), 404–11; William Horne, 'Through the Aperture: Brahms's Gigues, WoO 4', *Musical Quarterly* 86, no. 3 (Fall 2002), 530–81.

[8] A telling (because Gallic) exception is Joachim Raff's late Suite, op. 210, for violin and piano (1879), whose second movement is a pavane (in 2/4, and not very true to type). Significantly, the titles of the five movements, unlike Raff's other suites, openly claim their alliance with French models: Prélude, Pavane, Chanson de Louis XIII varié, Gavotte et musette, and Tambourin – a touching example of German Francophilia in 1879, although the music sounds much more like Brahms than Saint-Saëns.

178　　CARLO CABALLERO

Example 7.1 Paladilhe, Pavane from *Patrie*, bars 1–9

a)

b)

Example 7.2 Fauré, Pavane in F♯ minor, op. 50, bars 27–30

today is to locate a score and to play or sing it. Beyond the rediscovery of forgotten music, which has always been a central task of historical musicology, this project seeks historical evidence in two domains. First, we learn more about the social context of this music by asking *why* anyone would want to revive pavanes in the late nineteenth century in the first place. Jann Pasler has dealt with many of the general questions around the revival of early music in this period, including pavanes, in her book *Composing the Citizen*,[9] and Katharine Ellis and Catrina Flint de Médicis have written even more closely focused monographs on the revival.[10] I seek to carry this work further and to link it more deliberately with the world of dance. Second, the resemblances among these pavanes allow us to see how composers worked on a technical or creative level in the wake of particular modes of training at French conservatories.

We turn first to the socio-political matter – the question of *why* antique dances such as pavanes and passepieds were revived. It is significant that the revival took off just at the point (1877) when France resolved its two

---

[9] See Pasler, *Composing the Citizen*, 501–7 and 629–41, for a somewhat different view of the correspondences between the revival of old dance forms and contemporary political events. My interest here is less in unfurling the explosion of a corpus than in focusing on a smaller group of pieces whose interrelationships might give us a deeper understanding of style.

[10] Katharine Ellis's *Interpreting the Musical Past: Early Music in Nineteenth-Century France* (Oxford: Oxford University Press, 2005) focuses on choral music but ranges widely (a reference to the pavane 'Belle qui tiens ma vie' appears on pp. 33–4, where we learn that Adolphe Adam, Delibes's composition teacher, praised its beauty). On the influential activity of the Schola Cantorum and Chanteurs de Saint-Gervais, see Catrina M. Flint, 'The Schola Cantorum, Early Music and French Political Culture, from 1894 to 1914', PhD diss. (McGill University, 2006). Chapter 1 of Scott Messing's *Neoclassicism in Music: From the Genesis of the Concept through the Schoenberg-Stravinsky Polemic* (Rochester: University of Rochester Press, rept 1996) remains a seminal survey with many original insights.

competing fates as a polity: whether to become a republic with a king, or a republic without a king. After the municipal elections of January 1878, 'with republicans sweeping to power in thousands of communes', Maréchal MacMahon resigned as president, and the 'Republic of Dukes' with its royalist aspirations came to an end.[11] It was a period when the French nobility still retained great influence but felt the grounds of power shifting beneath it. I contend that one of the reasons for the revival of antique aristocratic dances after 1871 was symbolically political. With the establishment of durable Republican institutions in France, the courtly distinctions of the *ancien régime* were gradually being replaced by other distinctions. But the titled classes' leadership of taste in arts and fashion continued apace. They were not unaware of their advantages in this domain, and in the effort to be cultural leaders and to set themselves apart in new ways, the aristocracy pursued whatever was most rare and esoteric in art.[12] This pursuit took two seemingly opposite forms: on the one hand, to revive the forgotten, the passé, the out of date; on the other, to promote modern outsiders and the avant-garde. Nobles embraced this double perspective shrewdly: they had already been the primary supporters of the early music revival since the July Monarchy, and now they also underwrote some of the most challenging new music – composers such as Wagner, Fauré, Ravel and Stravinsky. Beyond all this, the French nobility had always been one of the primary supporters of ballet, an alliance which was as predictable as it was ancient, since ballet's forms and styles were first codified by the Bourbon court as an aristocratic practice and entertainment in the seventeenth century. Ballet was a noble art par excellence. To use the medium of the ballet-divertissement as a greenhouse for antique dances elegantly dovetailed the nobility's double investments in ballet and early music. The piquancy and opulence of pavanes, minuets, passepieds and other dances recalling the French royal court served as an effective symbol of that inegalitarian 'différence' French aristocrats wished to express in public life in order to stand apart from the commoner. Because they continued to provide patronage both to individual composers and to major institutions and musical societies, aristocrats were already in an excellent position to

---

[11] Robert Gildea, *France 1870–1914*, 2nd edn (London and NY: Longman, 1996), 9.
[12] I owe the origins of this hypothesis to a more general argument made by David Higgs, *Nobles in Nineteenth-Century France: The Practice of Inegalitarianism* (Baltimore: Johns Hopkins University Press, 1987). Higgs contends that because they 'wished to stand apart from their fellow Frenchmen', 'families of *noblesse, titrés,* and aristocrats, defined in turn by origin and wealth, valued otherness' (xvi).

shape the tastes of directors of state-sponsored theatres and the creative artists who worked for them.

This aristocratic taste-making might not have worked so well as to spawn so many *danses dans le style ancien*, unless other factors, more widely shared across social strata, had not also been in play. As I have already noted, the revival of old dances answered a nineteenth-century fascination with all forms of historicism and exoticism. That fascination was not restricted to the upper classes. It is no less important to note that state and public support for the art of ballet was strong in the Third Republic and gave dances such as our pavanes venues for frequent public exhibition and enjoyment, whether at national theatres, at independent houses in Paris, or in the numerous provincial theatres. That operas produced at the Académie Nationale de Musique (known informally as the Opéra) always included an obligatory, embedded ballet-divertissement (usually at the beginning of Act 3) is a familiar historical fact. That independent ballets in several acts, produced in the same house, were just as popular with the public as the operas which gave the theatre its nickname is more often forgotten. The high repute of the Parisian ballet reached far and wide; its audiences were international. A guide published in Chicago for Americans planning to visit the World's Fair in Paris in 1900 reminds us that our received historiography of a decline in the quality of ballet productions in Paris at the end of the nineteenth-century needs to be re-examined. The authors of this guide caution that the singing side of the opera is in decline, but they praise the ballet as having retained its pre-eminence: 'The performers at the Opéra are now no longer the very best in the world, but you are sure of a smooth performance and of at least one ballet that cannot be surpassed.'[13] Ballet was never out of sight when French directors planned their seasons – for reasons of public appeal as much as for answering state regulations.

The late 1890s saw increasing public interest in ballet, especially in mixed spectacles. We may cite two examples that show the persistence and growth of this appeal. The popularity of ballet ramped up to the point where the Opéra-Comique formed its own permanent *corps de ballet*, led by Madame Mariquita, in its first attempt to compete on this ground with the Opéra. With this innovation, Albert Carré, director of the Opéra-Comique, who was no longer bound by the earlier regimes of theatrical exclusion, boldly staked

---

[13] Barrett Eastman and Frédéric Mayer, *Paris, 1900: The American Guide to the City and Exposition* (Chicago: Northern Trust Company Bank, 1899), 143.

a challenge to the formerly exclusive dance prerogatives of the Opéra.[14] In another example, when the management of the Opéra itself (Eugène Bertrand and Pierre Gailhard) decided to take a risk on a Sunday concert series in 1895 (the Concerts de l'Opéra) with the aim of giving exposure to modern young French composers, the one element common to every single concert in the first season was not new music at all, but choreographic and nostalgic. A medley of 'Dances anciennes', choreographed in historical dress by ballet-master Joseph Hansen and performed by the *premiers sujets* of the Opéra, was considered the highlight of the afternoon by members of the public (as critics somewhat grudgingly admitted[15]), and this union of 'dances of yesteryear' to early music bespoke the house's unapologetic traditionalism and deep balletic heartbeat, overpowering its gingerly embrace of new music.[16] The orchestral music for these quaint dances was by Rameau, Gluck, Handel, Lacoste, Lully, Handel, J. S. Bach, Destouches and Lambert, plus the much older sixteenth-century pavane 'Belle qui tiens ma vie', which Delibes had already borrowed in his incidental music for *Le roi s'amuse*. The presence of that old pavane would seem difficult to explain if it were not for the management's clever insertion of some related modern music into the scheme. The reader will already have guessed: into these suites of *ancien régime* dances, Hansen knowingly slid two neo-pavanes, those by Paladilhe and Fauré.[17] All the initiatives described in this paragraph, regardless of

---

[14] See Carlo Caballero, 'Dance and Lyric Reunited: Fauré's *Pénélope* and the Changing Role of Ballet in French Opera', in *Bild und Bewegung im Musiktheater / Image and Movement in Music Theatre*, ed. Roman Brotbeck, Laura Moeckli, Anette Schaffer and Stephanie Schroedter (Schliengen, Germany: Argus Editions, 2018), 55–6.

[15] H. Fierens-Gevaert called them 'the real attraction' of the series and, despite his own reservations about the attention they took away from major works by living composers, he had to admit, 'the historical dances still remain the major success of the Concerts de l'Opéra' (*Le Guide musical* 41, no. 50 (15 December 1895), 963).

[16] Elinor Olin, 'The Concerts de l'Opéra, 1895–97', *19th-Century Music* 16, no. 3 (Spring 1993), 253–66. Olin excludes the 'danses anciennes' from discussion, not seeing them as significant (see p. 256), but her catalogue of the programmes of the concerts (pp. 265–66) is invaluable.

[17] Hansen was ballet-master at the Opéra from 1887 to 1907. One should like to know just how he choreographed either the old or new pavanes – to what extent he worked from *fantaisie* or from historical dance patterns, or to what extent 'Belle qui tiens ma vie' looked similar to or different from the modern pavanes by Fauré and Paladilhe. These are matters I seek to answer in another stage of research. Although there is little hope of recovering exact details about Hansen's choreography, contemporary accounts suggest that he had historicist pretentions. The critic Fierens-Gevaert enthused, 'Elegant French choreography ... was reborn before our eyes, light, witty, here piquant and saucy, there somewhat grave and ceremonious ... And what pretty Louis XVI costumes were on view! Imagine paintings by Latour, Rigault, and Nattier leaving their frames, making long honors [*révérences*] and recovering, for our pleasure, the aristocratic pattern of the courtly dances of old' (*Le Guide musical* 41, no. 47 (24 November 1895), 893).

their resonances with artistocratic taste, operated under state subsidies from the Third Republic.

Now let us move to the second area of historical inquiry: to questions of technique and composition. Several of these neo-pavanes vividly demonstrate how the extremely traditional and rigorous training that composers received at the Paris Conservatoire and the École Niedermeyer allowed them to toy cleverly with one another's pieces and earlier models to produce something similar yet new. Central to this inventive process was the French tradition of teaching composition through *chants donnés* and *basses données* (pre-composed treble lines and bass lines assigned to the student for polyphonic realization), which stems from the old partimento tradition recently given fresh attention by Robert Gjerdingen, Giorgio Sanguinetti and other scholars.[18] These pavanes prove to be case studies in the professional French composer's skills in 'invention through convention' and the close observation of existing pieces. Such observations were not limited to works by a composer's teacher, as we see with the case of Fauré, Saint-Saëns's favourite pupil. Fauré did not model his pavane directly on either of the two by Saint-Saëns shown in Table 7.1. The closest relation to Fauré's pavane (very close indeed) is the pavane from the grand opera *Patrie* by Émile Paladilhe. Paladilhe's Pavane (Example 7.1) was published just one year before Fauré's (Example 7.2). Fauré's direct emulation of Paladilhe's composition has escaped previous observation by modern writers, though audiences in the 1890s and 1900s who sometimes heard both works at the same concert must surely have noticed a similarity. Indeed, when I discovered it, it came as a surprise, as Fauré had no personal connection to Paladilhe, and I would never have looked at the score of *Patrie* if it had not been that the two pavanes were repeatedly programmed in parallel at the Concerts de l'Opéra.[19]

Ravel's early 'Pavane pour une infante défunte' (Example 7.3) takes a key detail from the Pavane by his teacher, Fauré, as we shall see when we scrutinize his counterpoint in the last section of this chapter. But Ravel's most obvious borrowing comes from one of Chabrier's *Dix pièces pittoresques* for piano (1880), the 'Idylle' (Example 7.4), whose main theme happens to fit the type of the pavane. We can see that Ravel's rhythmic motive in bar 1 is the same as

---

Fourcaud, in *Le Gaulois*, 18 November 1895, likewise referred to the 'delightful choreographic restitutions' inspired by the *danses anciennes*.

[18] Robert O. Gjerdingen, *Music in the Galant Style* (Oxford: Oxford University Press, 2007); and idem, 'The Perfection of Craft Training in the Neapolitan Conservatories', *Rivista di Analisi e Teoria Musicale* 15 (2009), 26–49; Giorgio Sanguinetti, *The Art of Partimento: History, Theory, and Practice* (Oxford: Oxford University Press, 2012).

[19] Olin, 'The Concerts de l'Opéra, 1895–97', 265–6.

Example 7.3 Ravel, 'Pavane pour une infante défunte', bars 1–6

Example 7.4 Chabrier, 'Idylle' from *Dix pièces pittoresques*, bars 1–5

Chabrier's 'Idylle' in bar 1, but even more curiously, one may merge Ravel's melody with Chabrier's 'Idylle' by transposing the last three quavers of Ravel's first bar and all of his second bar up a step and accompanying it with Chabrier's lower two parts just as they are. (To make this duplex piece, begin with Chabrier's A to G♯ and then continue after the tie with Ravel's melody at the transposition B-G♯-F♯ | E F♯-G♯-G♯-F♯ F♯ | C♯.) Ravel also borrowed the stepwise bass progression VI^7–v^6 (bars 1–2) from Chabrier's extraordinary off-tonic opening on ii–iii–IV^7 with its rising stepwise progression.[20] Debussy, too,

---

[20] There is a fundamental ambiguity of key in Ravel's Pavane, between E minor and G major, which is too complex to analyse here. I read the piece in E minor, moving progressively to the final bar on G (open fifth). All the half cadences on B minor underwrite the E minor hearing.

Example 7.5 Debussy, Passepied from *Suite bergamasque*, bars 1–6, with harmonic analysis

honoured the freshness of Chabrier's 'Idylle' some ten years before Ravel to form the opening phrase of *his* Pavane (later retitled Passepied) for the *Suite bergamasque* (Example 7.5). Debussy's Pavane-Passepied begins with the same three bass notes as Chabrier, though harmonized more conventionally because Debussy works them into the tonic and dominant of a key one step higher. It hardly seems coincidental that many of these pieces (Paladilhe, Fauré, Debussy) are in the striking key of F♯ minor. (Even though Chabrier's 'Idylle' is, of course, in E major, part of its magic is that it convinces us that it is F♯ minor for the first four bars.) Ravel's choice of E minor as the key for his Pavane, the last in this series, one step down from the others, may have been a conscious effort at differentiation. Then again, Messager's earlier Pavane from *Isoline* was also in E minor. Minor mode (if not specifically F♯ minor) is a unifying tonal colour for the neo-pavane. A final point: all the composers on our list experimented to different degrees with diatonic modality and alternative tonal syntaxes, usually emphasizing modal degrees of the scale and chains of harmonic sevenths. The imitation of *danses anciennes* harking back to the Renaissance provided an explicit pretext for modal explorations in modern musical composition. For individualistic composers who were nonetheless strongly trained in the craft, such pieces offered a way to transform what might have been an exercise in historicism into modest adventure and, paradoxically, modernity.

Further, if Ravel was imitating Chabrier's off-tonic opening, parsing bars 1–6 as a motion from III to v rather than I to iii makes more sense.

II

It is rare to be able to point to an originating composition in the history of music. But it seems clear that the nineteenth-century revival of the musical pavane began with Camille Saint-Saëns, a composer especially interested in early music. In 1878, he composed a pavane for the ballet-divertissement of his opera *Etienne Marcel*. This opera is set in the fourteenth century, and the fastidious and erudite Saint-Saëns probably knew that the pavane did not go back that far in time. But his was an inspired (faux-)archaic gesture, and it touched off a series of imitations and variations. Saint-Saëns cast the mould: traits of the neo-pavane that would occur again and again include the descending tetrachord from tonic to dominant in natural minor (usually in the bass); a broken-chord accompaniment, often with staccato articulation, and clear two-plus-two-bar phrasing in cut or common time that makes the music danceable as a pavane.[21] (Only that last feature is truly historical, though the descending tetrachord has some roots in the tradition, too.) From Saint-Saëns's first effort, we may follow the sequence of pavanes and passepieds by Delibes, Paladilhe, Fauré, Messager, Debussy and Ravel between 1882 and 1899. The next-to-last of these examples, the Passepied from Debussy's *Suite bergamasque*, neatly links up with our first, for in 1890 Debussy published his arrangement (for two pianos) of none other than the ballet music from Saint-Saëns's *Etienne Marcel*, including the Pavane, and in that same year he also composed the first version of his *Suite bergamasque*. One suspects that he did them in just that order! The generic story of the neo-pavane is, however, slightly complicated by Delibes's incidental music for Victor Hugo's *Le roi s'amuse* (1882) because, four years after Saint-Saëns's initial gambit in *Etienne Marcel*, Delibes unwittingly introduced a sort of confusion between the pavane and the passepied.

In 1882 the Comédie-Française decided to revive Hugo's play on its fiftieth anniversary (the government of Louis-Philippe banned it after a single performance in 1832). The theatre commissioned incidental music from Delibes for this revival, and since *Le roi s'amuse* is set in the time of François I, Delibes turned to the dances and styles of the Renaissance. This historicizing decision was perhaps prompted by the administration of the Comédie-Française itself, as Édouard Dujardin

---

[21] The basic steps of the pavane may be studied in a short video on the Library of Congress website, *An American Ballroom Companion*: www.loc.gov/item/musdivid.039. I encourage readers to apply these steps to the pavanes by Saint-Saëns, Fauré and Paladilhe.

suggests in his review of the production.²² Delibes wrote six orchestral pieces, all for the nocturnal party scene in Act 1 ('une fête de nuit au Louvre'), as well as a song for Triboulet in Act 3. When Delibes brought together the orchestral pieces as a suite subtitled *Airs de danse dans le style ancien (Dance Tunes in Olden Style)*, his title was not an overstatement. Delibes drew melodies from sixteenth-century prints for at least two of the numbers. In 1882, such a return to the sources was remarkable and in contrast to the more conventional approach to incidental music – 'evocative' rather than historical (Delibes followed that more conventional approach in the movements entitled 'Scène du bouquet' and 'Madrigal'). In the end, the six-movement suite from *Le roi s'amuse* offers two pavanes verifiably borrowed from sixteenth-century sources and also a brilliant opening galliard whose melodic and rhythmic character reveals his active study of Renaissance dances. Reviews of Delibes's music by two critics, Louis Gallet and Édouard Dujardin, come to our aid here; both convey information so detailed that they must have had privileged access to the composer or someone close to the production at the time of the premiere. Dujardin cites by title and date five of the Renaissance sources Delibes consulted in the search for 'local colour'; he also mentions the role of the dancer and historian Laure Fonta in the composer's research.²³ Gallet specifies that the first Pavane ('Belle qui tiens ma vie', Example 7.6) is taken from the harmonization published in Arbeau's *Orchésographie* (1588) and the 'Pavane Lesquercarde' (Example 7.7) from the *Danseries* of Jean d'Estrée.²⁴ Gallet is correct on both points. For his part, Dujardin mentions these two borrowings a bit more vaguely, but he helpfully indicates that the opening 'Gaillarde' is 'a pastiche of the galliards of the period; it is entirely M. Delibes's music', and this seems to be true as well.²⁵

---

²² Édouard Dujardin, 'Paris-Musique', *La Renaissance musicale* 2, no. 48 (26 November 1882), 379: 'La couleur locale n'est nulle part plus en honneur qu'à la Comédie-Française; le musicien a dû reproduire des danses du seizième siècle.'
²³ Dujardin, 'Paris-Musique', 379. Dujardin mentions Arbeau's *Orchésographie*, and cites by specific titles musical prints by Gervaise (1554), Attaignant (1530) and Certon (1615). Later in the review he notes that the 'Lesquercarde' came from the fourth book of *Danseries* by Jean d'Estrée (published by Nicolas du Chemin in 1564), an 'extremely rare' volume 'obtained for M. Delibes by Mme Fonta'. Fonta must have pursued her research in the national libraries or private collections and seems, like her younger colleague Jeanne Chasles, to belong to a community of early dance historians – women whose own history has yet to be written.
²⁴ Louis Gallet, 'Revue du théâtre', *La nouvelle revue* 4, no. 19 (November–December 1882), 670.
²⁵ Dujardin, 'Paris-Musique', 379. The failure of diligent searching for the main theme in a sixteenth-century source confirms Dujardin's claim, but Delibes clearly invented a theme based on the study of models in the old prints. Moreover, he definitely took the running melodic figure that opens the middle section (in D major) from the 'Gaillarde La fanfare' which happens

Example 7.6 Delibes, Pavane from *Le roi s'amuse*, arr. piano, bars 1–8

Example 7.7 Delibes, Lesquercarde from *Le roi s'amuse*, arr. piano, bars 1–4

Delibes, a composer famous for his waltzes and mazurkas, managed to write a dance in triple time whose rhythmic character never slips into either of those modern forms and captures the leaping character of the Renaissance dance. I know of no other revival of the galliard before *Le roi s'amuse*. Unlike the pavane, it did not set off a late nineteenth-century vogue, but Delibes's adventure underlines a point made earlier about the wider historical scope of French composers' access to the past.

Delibes had help, and I think we may fairly conclude that it came from the dancer Laure Fonta. As Dujardin noted, it was she who obtained Jean d'Estrée's *Danseries* for the composer, but that is not the only clue. Little in Delibes's previous music or educational background suggests other avenues of exposure to Renaissance dance forms.[26] Delibes had seen Laure Fonta on stage repeatedly; her career as a principal artist (*sujet*, 1863–81) in the company of the Paris Opéra included the entire duration of Delibes's career as a composer of ballets. She played the role of 'L'Aurore' in the

---

to appear in the same print by Phalèse (*Premier livre de danseries*, RISM 1571[14]) that contains another copy of the 'Pavane Lesquercarde'.

[26] However, Delibes's surprising knowledge of early music, already manifested a decade earlier in his use of baroque models in his opera *Le roi l'a dit* (1873), might be connected with the influence of Adolphe Adam, his composition teacher at the Conservatoire. Adam admired Rameau's music and had actively collaborated with the Prince de la Moskova's Société des Concerts de Musique Vocale (1843–6); perhaps Delibes's respect for early choral repertories received some impetus from Adam. (On Adam and Moskova, see Ellis, *Interpreting the Musical Past*, 32–3, 76.) Delibes's much more specific recourse to sixteenth-century dance types, however, seems more likely to have come from Fonta than Adam, who died in 1856.

premiere of his *Coppélia* in 1870.[27] It seems plausible that Delibes knew her personally before working on *Le roi s'amuse*. Fonta, for her part, must have been seriously studying the history of dance even before she left the stage in 1881, for she directed the choreography for a soirée featuring seventeenth- and eighteenth-century dances at the Ministry of Fine Arts on 27 April 1878.[28] Early in Dujardin's review, there is a sentence that allows one to wonder whether Fonta might even have been offered a collaborative role with Delibes in *Le roi s'amuse* at the outset of plans for the production: 'There was even talk of mounting a ballet; the difficulty in procuring the dancers fortunately made [the management] renounce it.'[29] The Comédie-Française was not in the business of competing with the Opéra and music halls: music was a special treat there, and to have both an orchestra and a corps de ballet would have been an innovative and uncustomary expense.

Besides the authentic pavanes 'Belle qui tiens ma vie' and the 'Lesquercarde', two other movements, Delibes's 'Scène de bouquet' and 'Passepied' (in cut time), may also be considered pavanes because of their metrical and phrase structure. Thus we find that four of the six movements of Delibes's suite shake hands with the central genre of this chapter: two are historical pavanes, and two are movements closely related to that type. Delibes shortened the sixteenth-century title 'Pavanne lesquercarde' (used by both Phalèse and d'Estrée) to 'Lesquercarde', probably because the composer did not want to advertise more than one pavane in the same suite.[30] So it seems possible that he chose the title 'passepied' for the last movement of his suite for the same reason: simply to avoid another so-titled pavane in the same work.

---

[27] Ivor Guest, *The Ballet of the Second Empire* (London: Pitman; Middletown, CT: Wesleyan University Press, 1974), 241, 255.

[28] Dujardin, 'Paris-Musique', 379, mentions performance of the pavane 'Belle qui tiens ma vie' at the Ministry, but the source cited immediately below mentions a pavane (1685) by Lully instead, a piece we shall return to later. See *Soirée du 27 avril 1878: Anciens airs de danse, danses des XVIIe et XVIIIe siècles, reconstituées par Melle Fonta ... d'après les documents chorégraphiques du temps et par M. Théodore de Lajarte, d'après les partitions originales* (Paris: D. Jouaust, n.d.).

[29] Dujardin, 'Paris-Musique', 379.

[30] In her detailed introduction to the 1888 edition of *Orchésographie* (1589), Laure Fonta rightly notes that the rhythm of the Pavane Lesquercade [sic] is 'livelier and more brilliant than that of other pavanes' (Jean Tabourot (Thoinot Arbeau), *Orchésographie: Réimpression précédée d'une notice sur les danses du XVIe siècle par Laure Fonta* (Paris, 1888; rept Genève: Slatkine Reprints, 1970), xxiv). Delibes gives his 'Lesquercarde' the faster tempo Allegro, as opposed to the Allegretto of the 'Pavane'. An excellent modern edition, *Trois premiers livres de danseries (1559) ... mis en musique à quatre parties par Jean d'Estrée et Pascale Boquet* (Montaigu: Compagnie Outre Mesure – Label COM, 2012), presents the Pavane Lesquercarde on p. 114.

Example 7.8 Delibes, Passepied from *Le roi s'amuse*, arr. piano, bars 1–5

Here we come to the central confusion or bifurcation in the history of the nineteenth-century neo-pavane. Since the passepied is most often documented as a baroque dance in quick triple time, usually 3/8, the title 'passepied' is otherwise puzzling for a dance in 2/2 (Example 7.8). We might leave the generic adjustment just there, a muddled packaging ploy, as a likely explanation. However, in earlier (oral) versions of the present chapter, I surmised that Delibes might have known about an older kind of passepied, a dance known variously as the *trihori*, *bransle-passepied* or *passepied de Bretagne*. These are quick dances in duple time.[31] The reviews by Gallet and Dujardin, which I discovered in a later phase of my research, bore out this hunch. Dujardin writes as follows concerning the last movement of Delibes's orchestral suite: 'The "Passepied" is a pastiche of a Breton dance of the fifteenth century, which is cited in *Orchésographie* under the list of twenty-five different kinds of branles; it is the "branle" called *triory* de Bretagne.'[32] That seems to put the matter of Delibes's choice of title to rest.

But why did Delibes call it a 'passepied' rather than a 'trihori' or a 'branle' (and why did Dujardin take the term 'passepied' for granted)? Even though scholars today know about the potential equivalence of 'trihori de Bretagne' and 'passepied de Bretagne', the term 'passepied' appears nowhere in Arbeau's *Orchésographie*. Again, the historical traces point to Laure Fonta as the centre of information on this repertoire. She wrote a long introduction to her 1888 edition of *Orchésographie* (the first French re-publication since Arbeau's time) and devotes one section of this introduction to 'Le Triory'. It begins with this sentence: 'Cette danse est le passe-pied Breton.'[33] Fonta goes on to distinguish clearly between the duple-metre passepied (trihory) and the triple-metre passepied later in vogue under Louis XIV and Louis XV.[34] It seems that Delibes must have

---

[31] Thoinot Arbeau, *Orchesography: A Treatise in the Form of a Dialogue*, trans. Cyril W. Beaumont (New York: Dance Horizons, 1925, 1968), 129: 'it will be in a light duple time.'
[32] Dujardin, 'Paris-Musique', 379. Also see Gallet, 'Revue du théâtre', 670.
[33] Arbeau, *Orchésographie* (1888 edn), ed. Laure Fonta, xxix.
[34] Arbeau, *Orchésographie* (1888 edn), xxx.

had access to this historical information through his contact with Fonta in 1882, six years before she published her edition of *Orchésographie*, and Dujardin and Gallet must also have been part of this circle of knowledge.

When Debussy cast about for an alternative title for his own 'Pavane' in the *Suite bergamasque* in 1905 and chose to call it a 'Passepied' instead (perhaps to avoid comparison to the already well-known pavanes by Fauré and Ravel), he probably knew nothing of Fonta's edition of *Orchésographie* or the history I've traced above. But Debussy remembered an alternative label for a duple-metre dance that would lower the stakes of comparison.[35] This, I think, in part explains why Debussy issued the 'stop-press' change of title from 'pavane' to 'passepied' to his publisher Fromont in 1905.[36] At that point in time, Debussy was probably aware of eighteenth-century norms for a passepied (as opposed to the earlier and more obscure trihori), because in the later 1880s his peers Paladilhe and Messager had reminded their fellow composers what a passepied was by default: a light dance in three, something like a fast minuet. Paladilhe included a passepied in 9/8 as No. 10 in his opera *Patrie* (1886), and Messager wrote two passepieds, both in 3/8, for the supplement 'La Danse' in *Le Gaulois* in 1888, the second of which he re-used in his *opéra comique La Basoche* (1890). (It is amusing to consider how modern French composers of the 1880s busied themselves jockeying for the mastery of obsolete dance forms!) In 1905 Debussy was also on the cusp of editorial labours on his assigned volume in the *Œuvres complètes* of Rameau: the opera-ballet *Les fêtes de Polymnie*. This score

---

[35] Although Delibes's suite enjoyed popularity (Messing, *Neoclassicism in Music*, 41, points out that it was performed at the 1889 Exposition Universelle, close to the time of Debussy's composition), by 1905 it was less famous than the pavanes by Fauré and Ravel, and Delibes, dead since 1891, represented less of a threat to Debussy's profound scruples about originality.

[36] See note 2 above for Howat's history of the publication. Messing, *Neoclassicism in Music*, 41, observes the likenesses between the Debussy and Delibes passepieds to make a different point from either Howat's or mine. Curiously, Messing's musical example (p. 42), photoreproduced from an existing edition for piano, shows Delibes's Passepied with a time signature of C rather than ₵. All the scores known to me (the full score and piano reductions published by Heugel) show the cut signature. This detail is of interest because Howat points to Delibes's notation in ₵ as a reason for emending the metre of Debussy's Passepied from C to ₵ in his edition (even though all the sources and editions stemming from Debussy show C). Howat's reference to Delibes's Passepied is found in his Foreword to a separately issued edition of the *Suite bergamasque* (Paris: Durand, 2002), n.p., not in his earlier commentary to the *Œuvres complètes*. I would suggest that the editorial imposition of ₵ exacerbates a recent tendency among pianists to take Debussy's Passepied at faster and faster tempos. The Italian marking 'Allegretto ma non troppo' and the origins of the movement in the neo-pavane tradition might encourage performers to consider a more relaxed pacing. Delibes's own metronome mark in the orchestral score of his Passepied, Allegro, minim = 80, could at least set an upper limit for a piece Debussy chose to notate with all its signs pointing to a less rapid tempo than Delibes's.

contains two passepieds in 3/8. The earliest trace of Debussy's work on the volume seems to date from January 1906,[37] but if he had received the source materials from the publisher Durand a few months earlier and bothered to examine Rameau's music, it would have solidified his knowledge of the baroque passepied. In this light, the choice of the title 'Passepied' for the final duple-metre dance of the *Suite bergamasque* would seem especially deliberate: a knowing evasion of the more usual 'passepied' in three; an evasion of the title 'pavane', made uncomfortably popular since Debussy's initial composition of the movement in 1890; an expression of a tempo faster than most neo-pavanes; and finally an honest tribute to Delibes which (just for once with Debussy) might be a straightforward acknowledgement of stylistic debt, albeit one preferable to comparison with pavanes by his *living* rivals Fauré and Ravel.[38]

Among these various compositions, Fauré's Pavane shows strong (but also wilfully controlled and limited) connections to early music. The phrasing matches the traditional seventeenth-century step of the pavane, making the work danceable, and at the same time Fauré uses (not too obviously) the late Renaissance tradition of the descending tetrachord as a guiding structure for the bass. The famous main tune, of course, is one of Fauré's most ravishing, and for its time, very modern. While its mode is sometimes aeolian, sometimes minor, its style belongs firmly to the late nineteenth century. Though the Pavane is best known as a work for orchestra alone, the original *ad libitum* chorus adds a striking expressive element to the score and has become a more frequent choice for commercial recordings in the past two decades. In 1887, just after receiving Robert de Montesquiou's poetic text for his finished composition, the composer conjured up his ideal image of the work to its dedicatee, the Vicomtesse (soon to become Comtesse) Greffulhe. He envisioned it 'danced and sung at the same time... If the whole wonderful combination of a pretty dance with beautiful costumes, an invisible choir and orchestra, could be realized, what an exquisite dish that would be!'[39] It seems likely that Fauré had the idea of a choral

---

[37] Claude Debussy, *Correspondance, 1872–1918*, ed. François Lesure and Denis Herlin (Paris: Gallimard, 2005), 936 n. 1 (letter to Francisco de Lacerda, 22 January 1906). The edition of *Les fêtes de Polymnie* was published by Durand in 1908 as volume 13 of the complete works.

[38] The likeness of type between Debussy's Passepied and Delibes's is obvious, despite the clearly more developed and detailed structures in the former, but Debussy's movement might be said to resemble the Pavane from Messager's *Isoline* just as much. Debussy also seems to have derived other details in the *Suite bergamasque* from Delibes's Suite. For instance, in the Minuet the distinctive little fanfares at bars 18–21 and 97–101 recall the repeated-note cadence that closes Delibes's Galliard.

[39] Fauré, *Correspondance*, 132.

dance-song in mind from the start: the Pavane was first published as a composition for chorus and piano in a music supplement of *Le Gaulois* (where Messager's passepieds and a rigaudon by Delibes also appeared), and it was also first performed that way and then later orchestrated.

In light of the aristocratic taste-making we have already observed, it is no surprise that Fauré dedicated his Pavane to the Vicomtesse Greffulhe, one of the most powerful cultural arbiters in Parisian high society, or that the author of the text, Robert de Montesquiou, was a count (and her cousin). A decade later, Fauré's pupil Ravel did not fail to observe the social context for such music and dedicated his 'Pavane pour une infante défunte' to the Princesse de Polignac. In this connection, the volume published by *Le Gaulois* where Fauré's Pavane and Messager's Passepieds first appeared merits further comment as a cultural artefact. *Le Gaulois* was a royalist newspaper. *La Danse: Le Gaulois à ses abonnés, 1888* – the musical supplement housing these pieces – was offered as a lavish New Year's Day gift to its subscribers at the end of 1887.[40] The cultural pitch of the 321-page volume would have been readily legible to the predominantly aristocratic readership of the newspaper as a confirmation of their musical tastes and politics; even the choice of blue for the title page and the following lithograph (surrounded by an elaborate vignette in gold) discreetly flew the legitimist flag (blue, white and gold, as opposed to the Republican *tricolore*) from the moment one opened the book. By the very choice of 'Dance' itself as a theme, *Le Gaulois* saluted the role of the nobility as traditional arbiters of taste in that domain, whether social dance or ballet. To the world of the *ancien régime*, aristocratic par excellence, belonged thirteen of the forty dances on offer (about a third of the total – the pieces by Fauré, Messager, Saint-Saëns, Godard, Gounod and Delibes among this third). Every day the newspaper itself richly chronicled the social meaning of such nostalgia on its society page ('Mondanités', always on page two and elaborately subdivided into nine sections). In a typical entry (like a dozen others in any month) we learn that on 7 June 1896 the composer Gaston Lemaire will hold a preview at his home before he departs for London, where 'his gavottes and minuets will be sung and danced in period costume'.[41] In a less quotidian entry, shifted to page one, 'A Literary Feast at Versailles' from 31 May 1894, the author (none other than Marcel Proust) chronicles the details of a garden party given at Versailles by Count Robert de Montesquiou, author of the text

---

[40] The title in English would be *Dance: Le Gaulois to Its Subscribers (1888)*. A rare original copy (oddly misbound) may be consulted at the Bibliothèque nationale de France (Paris BnF Vm^7 4725).

[41] 'Dans le monde', *Le Gaulois*, 7 June 1896.

of Fauré's Pavane. 'For a few hours we believed we were living in the days of Louis XIV!' enthused Proust over the Count's exquisite provisions and choice of literary programme. Mademoiselle Reichenberg read poems including Coppée's 'Menuet', Verlaine's 'Mandoline', and a madrigal by Montesquiou himself. The pianist Léon Delafosse and the singer Maurice Bagès gave a performance of Delafosse's settings of Montesquiou's verse. Mademoiselle Bartet recited Leconte de L'Isle's 'Le parfum impérissable' as well as poems by José de Hérédia and Montesquiou. Sarah Bernhardt, Mlle Reichenberg and Mlle Bartet then joined in a reading of André Chénier's 'Ode à Versailles' (1792), surely eliciting sighs of Bourbon nostalgia.[42] Was the party more about nostalgia for the *ancien régime* or the flamboyant Count himself, given his dominant role in the programme? By holding the party in Versailles, the Count seemed to make that question beside the point.

Le Gaulois reminds us that old forms, and new forms evoking old ones – poetry, dance or music – were not merely cultivated but *performed* in high society. Indeed, Fauré's Pavane, known to most listeners today as a mere piece for orchestra, was in its bones a theatre piece, staged in one way or another repeatedly during Fauré's lifetime. Its origins, first of all, lie in a theatrical tradition whose immediate model, the Pavane from Paladilhe's grand opera *Patrie* (1886), gives us the key to a composition modern listeners might think of purely in terms of instrumental music. The melodies of both Paladilhe's and Fauré's Pavanes (Examples 7.1 and 7.2) rise at once from tonic to mediant in the same key, F♯ minor, then gradually, over the course of eight bars, descend to a half-cadence on the dominant note six scale-steps below. Both are built over a descending tetrachord in the bass. And like Paladilhe, Fauré creates a contrasting middle section in the rustic style – a musette, with long pedal points in the bass. We shall consider some finer technical similarities between these pieces in the last section of the chapter. Here, with an eye to the theatrical inheritance, we must underline the scenic nature of Fauré's own conception of the Pavane, which he described above in his letter to the Vicomtesse Greffulhe as an 'exquisite dish' of a dance-song with visible dancers and an invisible chorus. The Pavane was realized in that theatrical manner (with or without chorus) on at least four separate occasions during his lifetime. In 1891, Fauré succeeded in tempting Elisabeth Greffulhe to serve his 'exquisite dish': with dance and pantomime, it formed

---

[42] 'Tout-Paris' [pseud.], 'Bloc-Notes parisien: Une fête littéraire à Versailles', *Le Gaulois*, 31 May 1894. Translated by Chris Taylor and available in English on his website www.yorktaylors.free-online.co.uk/fete.htm.

part of a nocturnal *fête galante* hosted by her in the Bois de Boulogne.[43] It reached the public stage four years later, in December 1895, where it appeared alongside Paladilhe's Pavane as one of two modern pieces among the sequence of authentically old dances performed on the stage of the Paris Opéra (as part of the Concerts de l'Opéra, discussed above). In 1916, Diaghilev's Ballets Russes turned Fauré's Pavane into a ballet, *Las Meninas*, with choreography by Massine and costumes by José-Maria Sert that were inspired by paintings by Diego Velázquez. Finally, Fauré brought the Pavane back in 1919 for the final number in his last theatre work, the comédie-divertissement *Masques et bergamasques*.[44] For 'a work of little importance', as Fauré called it, the Pavane had a pretty good run.

The choral presentation of the piece, particularly the way the men and women deplore each other's dancing and flirting in a sometimes *parlando* style, resembles its operatic predecessors, both Paladilhe's technique in the Pavane from *Patrie* (the jaded dialogue between La Trémoïlle and Rafaële) as well as the short off-stage Pavane in Saint-Saëns's *Proserpine* (1887, Act 1, scene 4), where Proserpine waves away three suitors. The conceit of a dialogue of 'lovers and others' set against the background of a diegetic dance piece was a standard dramaturgical gambit in French opera. In the case of Fauré's Pavane, I would stress this theatrical effect as a source of the artful sense of detachment between the choir and the orchestra, which is not merely a result of the poem coming to the music late in the process, as critics sometimes assume. Yes, Montesquiou wrote his verse after Fauré had already composed the instrumental framework of the Pavane, but we must remember that it was still Fauré who invented the choral melodies and counterpoints for this verse. Too often the order of events is used as a way to dismiss the integrity of the choral version. Fauré found a way to join, but not marry, the poem to his antique dance, and this sense of independence between music and text is a calculated aesthetic effect to be exploited, not regretted, in performance as an extension of its native theatricality. Fauré's Pavane was composed at the same time as his song 'Clair de lune' (1887), which sets the opening poem from Verlaine's exquisite book *Fêtes galantes* (poetry featured at Montesquiou's garden party, we note). This song provides another key to understanding the Pavane (or vice versa): both pieces create a feeling of injured nostalgia by

---

[43] See Sylvia Kahan, 'Patrons and Society: Gabriel Fauré's "Other" Career in the Paris and London Music Salons', in *Fauré Studies*, ed. Carlo Caballero and Stephen Rumph (Cambridge: Cambridge University Press, forthcoming).

[44] See Jean-Michel Nectoux, *Gabriel Fauré: Les voix du clair-obscur*, 2nd edn (Paris: Fayard, 2008), 129.

detaching a poetic text from an instrumental accompaniment in the form of an antiquated dance. Just as the instrumental music (the pavane) begins and continues independently of the chorus, the piano part of 'Clair de lune' (a minuet) is often out of phase with the solo voice, which never sings the minuet itself but only collects motivic fragments here and there as it goes its own way. A human voice dissociated in the presence of a social dance becomes strongly poetic in Fauré's hands and produces an effect of alienation. Both of these pieces from 1887 capture, better than any other music from the period, a bygone world of courtiers and gallant liaisons, an *ancien régime* almost out of time and mind.

Such nostalgia for vanished worlds captured Sergei Diaghilev's imagination more than once. As part of a wave of backward-looking projects in the early 1920s, he revived *Las Meninas* (set to Fauré's Pavane) and its stylized evocation of the Spanish royal court of Philip IV. During Diaghilev's years in Monte Carlo, as Lynn Garafola observes, 'the past dominated his thought'; he focused especially on the 'courtly origins' of opera and ballet.[45] Many of the company's new ballets of the 1920s bathed in eighteenth-century themes and classical mythology, but of all these nostalgias the one closest to Diaghilev's heart was Tchaikovsky's *Sleeping Beauty*, whose various abbreviated versions produced under the title *Le mariage d'Aurore* (*Aurora's Wedding*) occupied the Ballets Russes for several years despite limited public enthusiasm. Because of Tchaikovsky's music and the French plot and setting, *Aurora's Wedding* was also a 'wedding' of Russian imperial taste to the French *grand siècle*. On 30 June 1923, Diaghilev combined his *passéiste* obsessions in a new way: he surrounded parts of *Aurora's Wedding* with other *entrées*, including *Las Meninas,* and had the whole thing staged in the Hall of Mirrors of the Palace of Versailles under the title 'Une Fête merveilleuse'. Garafola muses that by further 'anachronizing' *Aurora's Wedding* with 'the addition of processionals and vocal interludes', Diaghilev evoked 'the *grandes fêtes* witnessed in that same gallery by *le roi soleil* himself'.[46] A remarkably similar event described earlier in this chapter allows us to deepen this context further. For Diaghilev, probably unknowingly, did nothing less than recapitulate Robert de Montesquiou's nostalgic 'Fête littéraire à Versailles' of 1894. Rather than a literary party, in 1923 it was a balletic and operatic one. Fauré's Pavane, with its text by Montesquiou, would have slid perfectly into

---

[45] Lynn Garafola, *Diaghilev's Ballets Russes* (New York and Oxford: Oxford University Press, 1989), 246.
[46] Garafola, *Diaghilev's Ballets Russes,* 247.

the earlier event. Now, after the war, the Pavane took its proper turn at Versailles – and in the eminently appropriate venue of the Hall of Mirrors, where reflections of the present and the past seem endlessly at play in the slowly melting panes of glass.

III

Earlier, in relation to models, copies and variants, I mentioned the partimento tradition. In his ongoing work concerning nineteenth-century French music and Franco-Italian pedagogical traditions, Robert Gjerdingen shows that French composers were still being trained in eighteenth-century Italian methods well into the twentieth century.[47] The partimento, or a shorthand notation prompting stock contrapuntal solutions, provides a view into how composers in this period emulated and varied musical patterns, a technique that would serve them admirably in reviving and composing new pavanes. As mentioned earlier, many of our neo-pavanes depend on the foundation of a descending phrygian tetrachord, that is, the four descending notes in the upper half of a natural minor scale. The pavanes by Paladilhe, Fauré and Messager use this structure most prominently. But even Ravel's pavane for *Ma mère l'oye* (1910) – which sounds so different in style and was written so much later than the others in Table 7.1 – plainly adopts the descending tetrachord as its first bass progression (Example 7.9). Unlike Ravel's second pavane, with its two-part texture, his predecessors Paladilhe, Fauré and Messager all had to solve the problem of avoiding parallel fifths in harmonizing the descending tetrachord, because they write three- and four-part textures. It was Gjerdingen, in correspondence, who made me fully aware of the techniques and likenesses

Example 7.9 Ravel, 'Pavane de la Belle au bois dormant', no. 1 from *Ma mère l'oye*, bars 1–4

---

[47] Robert Gjerdingen, 'Fauré as Student and Teacher of Harmony', in *Fauré Studies*, ed. Carlo Caballero and Stephen Rumph (Cambridge: Cambridge University Press, forthcoming).

Example 7.10 The descending tetrachord (a) and its contrapuntal realizations by (b) Paladilhe, (c) Fauré and (d) Messager in their pavanes; with thanks to Robert Gjerdingen

that bind these various examples together when I submitted them for his consideration. Each composer applies auxiliary tones to the old Italian model, but each does it differently: a typical example of invention within convention (Example 7.10). Paladilhe solves the problem of parallel motion through passing and changing tones that create clausulae opening from sixths to octaves in the lower voices. Fauré's approach is contrapuntally distinct but 'ends up using the same tones . . . transferred to the bass', and these escape tones in the bass follow a stock pattern known as 'down

Example 7.11 Messager, Pavane from *Isoline*, bars 1–5

a third, up a second'.[48] But, as Gjerdingen observes, Fauré adds a delicate variation to the formula, holding the tenor voice longer to create seventh chords in the second half of each bar. These sevenths in combination with the elegant melody make the music readily identifiable as Fauré's: the master artisan's distinctive finish on an ordinary harmonic routine. Messager's solution, in his Pavane from *Isoline* (the incipit is given in Example 7.11), also operates on the bass but uses rising thirds and falling fourths. The effect is less romantic, more antiquated in sonority, partly because Messager returns to a two-part texture at the cadence and thus to the simple parallel motion of the original Italian model.

Ravel's 'Pavane pour une infante défunte' is an interesting case: its opening bars present feints that conceal an underlying concession to his teacher, Fauré, while more visibly saluting Chabrier, as we noted earlier. Only with the third reprise of the same (main) theme (bars 60–5) can we clearly see Ravel's sweet sacrifice to convention. Ravel's first presentation of the theme (Example 7.12, upper staves) alternates rising fourths and falling fifths for the bass in bars 3–6. These create a series of ninth-to-fifth clausulae between treble and bass on the minim level, a much harsher harmonic framework than the traditional sixth-to-octave clausulae in Paladilhe. While Ravel is a little closer to Fauré's variant of seventh-to-fifth clausulae, his texture sounds less stable. Ravel leaves some of the harmonic background incomplete or ambiguous at the start of the piece, and non-harmonic tones delay the arrival of the upper note of the resolving fifth until the fourth quaver in each bar. One notices, however, a curious homology: the routine of 'down a third, up a second' trails across bars 3–6, but in the treble, where it cannot do the normal structural harmonic service and seems alienated from the bass progessions below. In these three bars, however, we observe a series of three harmonic tenths that predict what will happen in the third reprise of the theme. When we compare bars 62–5

---

[48] Robert Gjerdingen, personal communication, 12 January 2013.

Example 7.12 Ravel, 'Pavane pour une infante défunte' comparing bars 3–6 and bars 62–5

(Example 7.12, top and bottom staves) to bars 3–6, we see that Ravel unfolds these tenths from vertical simultaneities into consecutive bass pitches, and the result is a sequence following the third-down, second-up partimento model, just like his teacher's Pavane.[49] The inherent counterpoint in the opening bars, harmonically frozen into verticality, is finally realized as a more a pleasing bass sequence, and the harmonic functions of bars 4–5 shift from fifths (VII–III–VI–ii) to gentle thirds (v–III–iv–ii). The transformation is subtle and probably only vaguely felt by most listeners as part of the increased opulence of the figuration. But on a technical level, one might see Ravel moving from artful resistance to relaxed acceptance of convention. Finally, we note one last sign of the pupil's debt to the master, going one better than him: Fauré took Paladilhe's clausulae and held the tenor note to create sevenths on every other minim. Ravel carries this process a step further: with treble and bass both moving 'down a third, up a second', *every* minim beat in bars 62–5 forms a harmonic seventh, and so we pass from Fauréan harmony to Ravel's.

Saint-Saëns, who came to this task first of all, took a different path from his younger successors (Example 7.13). Saint-Saëns began with the descending tetrachord, but he combined it with another partimento solution, one that a renaissance or baroque musician would have immediately recognized. Saint-Saëns places the descending minor tetrachord in a middle voice rather than the bass, and he avoids parallel fifths by

---

[49] Gjerdingen, private communication, 25 February 2014. I owe the observation of the bass pattern in bars 62–5 to Gjerdingen's keen ear.

Example 7.13 (a) Saint-Saëns, Pavane from *Etienne Marcel*, arr. piano, bars 1–4 and (b) its contrapuntal modelling, showing the combination of the descending tetrachord (alto) and the minor-mode *romanesca*

embedding this tetrachord in a *romanesca* framework rather than by using auxiliary tones. It is striking that this clever combination of patterns did not prove popular with any of our later composers. Perhaps they found the *romanesca*, paradoxically, too old fashioned, too close to the real thing.

In fact, descending tetrachords are not a particularly regular feature of renaissance or early baroque pavanes. For example, they do not appear in either of Delibes's two borrowings from sixteenth-century sources. One might suppose that here our other French composers embraced a structuring device familiar from baroque music and casually translated it backwards a century or two. There may be another explanation. Composers of neo-pavanes had little access to scores of the historical genre they were supposedly emulating. One of the very few widely accessible examples was Jean-Baptiste Lully's Pavane from his *Pièces de symphonie*, a collection of pieces also called *La Noce de village* (1685, LWV70). This obscure piece was one of the only pavanes to fly out of the archive into print because Théodore de Lajarte included it in his collection *Airs à danser, de Lulli à Méhul* (1876).[50] This handy volume with its easy piano arrangements of fifty-four old dances probably served as a primer for dozens of late

---

[50] Théodore de Lajarte, ed., *Airs à danser de Lulli à Méhul, transcrits d'après les manuscrits originaux de la Bibliothèque de l'Opéra de Paris* (Paris: Durand, Schoenwerk, 1876).

nineteenth-century composers looking to turn out a passable (neo-)forlane, tambourin or bourrée. Indeed, Lajarte's anthology was still being printed and sold as late as 1952. The first bass progression of Lully's Pavane, offered in A minor, is a descending tetrachord. The same bass occurs again two bars later in rhythmic augmentation (bars 4–6). Did Lajarte's quirky choice of a pavane by Lully with descending tetrachord determine the genetic future of the neo-pavane? I speculate, of course, but this one pavane may have a lot of progeny to answer for. We encountered Lajarte before in this chapter: readers may recall that he collaborated with Laure Fonta on the soirée of *anciens airs de danse* at the Ministry of Fine Arts in 1878. As the head librarian of the Opéra, he was one of Fonta's partners in choreographic research. Saint-Saëns was also known to frequent this same library.

A pavane I wish I could say played a role in this history, one of the most beautiful ever composed, is Louis Couperin's Pavane in F♯ minor. There are at least three reasons this pavane should tempt us. First, it is in F♯ minor, a key strangely favoured among our neo-pavanes and an exceedingly rare key in the seventeenth century (Louis Couperin died in 1661). Second, it unfurls no fewer than five descending tetrachords in its first section; they occur with subtle irregularity and travel across its four-part texture (tenor: bars 1–2, bars 2–3, soprano: bars 5–6, bass: bars 9–10, and tenor: bars 14–15). All run diatonically from tonic down to dominant, like our other examples. Third, a sumptuous descending harmonic progression leading from bar 5 to bar 6 sounds (and feels under the hand) like a sixteenth-century cousin of Ravel's parallel-ninth progression in bars 11 and 12 of his 'Pavane pour une infante défunte'. Alas, Couperin's Pavane was revealed to admirers of early music too late for our composers. I could find it in none of the various anthologies of early keyboard music published in the nineteenth and early twentieth centuries. The Bauyn Manuscript still slumbered in obscurity; Henri Quittard would begin studying it in 1901. The return of Louis Couperin's Pavane in F♯ minor to public view would have to wait until 1936, the year of its first publication in a volume edited by Paul Brunold.

In contrast to the evident limitations of style and expression in the repertory of neo-pavanes discussed here, the diversity of functions they served is astonishingly broad: opera, ballet, incidental music, solo piano music, children's pieces (especially piano duets), orchestral music, choral music and uncategorizable choreographic galas and entertainments (like those hosted by the Comtesse Greffulhe or the Ministry of Fine Arts). The story of the neo-pavane provides a knowingly antiquated (*passéiste*) window into some important trends of late nineteenth-century French music.

Aristocratic and grand-bourgeois support for new or deliberately archaic styles filtered down into other social strata, making what was once esoteric into something popular and commercially viable. What began in the theatre, and especially in the ballet, soon landed on pianos, and what was played on pianos led to new instrumental and orchestral arrangements – new compositions seeking the same line of success in the market – and new compositions seeking their own first life on the stage; in other words, more antique dances in ballets and ballets-divertissements. What we are examining here is a fruitful commercial and artistic cycle that touches different social classes and performing spaces. This productive movement from theatre and salon and back again, from aristocracy to middle classes, would continue to hold sway for at least the first three decades of the twentieth century. Indeed, they neatly describe the next major chapter in this story: how after 1907 the Ballets Russes built upon established aristocratic support for such exquisite passé or exotic confections to conquer musical Paris from the top down – for the Comtesse Greffulhe was not only the dedicatee of Fauré's Pavane, but also the patron who launched the first season of Sergei Diaghilev's fabled enterprise.

PART III

Critical Readings

8 | Nijinsky, Modernism, Repression: The Faun Ballet – Once Again – Under Analysis

DAVID J. CODE

> How are we to arrive at a knowledge of the unconscious? It is of course only as something conscious that we know it, after it has undergone transformation or translation into something conscious. Psychoanalytic work shows us every day that translation of this kind is possible. In order that this should come about, the person under analysis must overcome certain resistances – the same resistances that had, earlier, made the material concerned into something repressed by rejecting it from the conscious.[1]
>
> Sigmund Freud, 'The Unconscious' (1915)

What do we expect of modernism, and to what degree do we frame and inflect our experience of modernist art so that it conforms to those expectations? Vaslav Nijinsky's famous ballet *L'après-midi d'un faune* proves a fertile site on which to raise such questions. Choreographed for Sergei Diaghilev's Ballets Russes in 1912, it was set to Claude Debussy's *Prélude* of the same name from 1894, which was inspired, in turn, by the long pastoral poem Stéphane Mallarmé published in 1876. Perhaps this chain of interdisciplinary inspiration has received such copious attention by now that further inspection seems unlikely to deliver much fresh insight for the historiography or criticism of its component art forms. On the other hand, the successive waves of response, washing forward from the earliest reactions into the richest centenary essays and beyond, could well invite a meta-critical 'sounding' of the habits of thought – choices of emphasis as well as attendant repressions – that have underpinned, and indeed constructed, the modernist canon in which Nijinsky, Debussy and Mallarmé all claim a privileged place.[2]

---

[1] Sigmund Freud, 'The Unconscious', in *The Standard Edition of the Complete Psychological Works*, vol. 14, ed. and trans. James Strachey (London: Hogarth Press and the Institute of Psychoanalysis, 1957), 166. (Wie sollen wir zur Kenntnis des Unbewußten kommen? Wir kennen es natürlich nur als Bewußtes, nachdem es eine Umsetzung oder Übersetzung in Bewußtes erfahren hat. Die psychoanalytische Arbeit läßt uns alltäglich die Erfahrung machen, daß solche Übersetzung möglich ist. Es wird hiezu erfordert, daß der Analysierte gewisse Widerstände überwinde, die nämlichen, wlche es seinerzeit durch Abweisung vom Bewußten zu einem Verdrängten gemacht haben. Sigmund Freud, *Gesammelte Werke*, vol. x (Frankfurt: Fischer, 1946), 264.)

[2] For the most substantial recent accounts, see Davinia Caddy, *The Ballets Russes and Beyond: Music and Dance in Belle-Époque Paris* (Cambridge: Cambridge University Press, 2012), 67–114;

As if poetry, music and dance did not already offer enough to sustain such a sounding, the habits in question can be raised into clearest relief by throwing painting, too, into the mix. For after judicious review of the historical development of Nijinsky's choreographic vision, the widespread acceptance of one early, opportunistic claim for Cubist painting as one source of inspiration can only seem symptomatic of unconscious critical reflexes that cry out for Freudian 'transformation or translation'. As is well known, this ostensible parallel was first proposed to Charles Tenroc, editor of the theatrical journal *Comoedia*, in an interview with Diaghilev and Nijinsky a few weeks before the 1912 premiere.[3] In this interview, however, Nijinsky himself says nothing about Cubism or any other style of painting. He only attests that his 'adaptation' met with 'agreement' from Debussy (who had, he says, suggested a 'few little modifications'), and then – ironically – emphasizes how closely (*étroitement*) his 'completely new plastic composition' combines with the music. It is only after Tenroc turns to 'the distinguished M. Diaghilev' that we find the impresario offering the further claim, in the third person: 'it was the Cubist theory that Nijinsky wanted to apply to choreography'.

Maybe the support this claim has received from just about every later commentator is understandable given the 'angular' visual style the ballet shares, superficially, with much Cubist art. On the other hand, we know from the memoirs of Nijinsky's sister Bronislava Nijinska that she began intensive work with him on the *Faune* in late 1910, long before he could have seen the experiments Pablo Picasso and Georges Braque were pursuing at the same time, and long before anything like a 'Cubist theory' had emerged in print.[4] We also know that Nijinsky reported finding inspiration for his new style of movement, at that initial stage, in archaic Greek vase

and Hanna Järvinen, 'Dancing without Space: On Nijinsky's *L'Après-midi d'un faune* (1912)', *Dance Research* 27, no. 1 (2009), 28–64. Previous accounts include Stephanie Jordan, 'Debussy, the Dance, and the *Faune*', in *Debussy in Performance*, ed. James Briscoe (New Haven: Yale University Press, 1999), 119–34; Jean-Michel Nectoux, ed., *Nijinsky: Prélude à l'après-midi d'un faune* (Paris: Éditions Adam Biro, 1989); Lynn Garafola and Nancy van Norman Baer, eds., *The Ballets Russes and Its World* (New Haven and London: Yale University Press, 1999); Lynn Garafola *Diaghilev's Ballets Russes* (1989; repr. New York: Da Capo, 1998); Bronislava Nijinska, *Early Memoirs*, ed. and trans. Irina Nijinska and Jean Rawlinson (London and Boston: Faber & Faber, 1981); Romola Nijinsky, *Nijinsky* (London: Victor Gollancz 1933); Lydia Sokolova, *Dancing for Diaghilev*, ed. Richard Buckle (London: John Murray, 1960).

[3] 'De la peinture à la danse: Nijinski va faire dans l'"Après-midi d'un Faune" des essais de chorégraphie cubiste', *Comoedia*, 18 April, 1912, 4.

[4] From Nijinska's diary, it is clear that the work was almost complete by late 1910. See her *Early Memoirs*, 316. The literature on Cubism is vast: the following paragraphs draw from John Golding, *Cubism: A History and an Analysis: 1907–1914*, 3rd rev. edn (London: Faber & Faber, 1988); T. J. Clark, *Farewell to an Idea: Episodes in a History of Modernism* (New Haven and

paintings. (He also invoked Assyria, but no modern art.)⁵ And finally, we know that Diaghilev, who had grave doubts about his protégé's first ballet from the moment the siblings marked it out for him in early 1911, became so sure of its imminent failure at the 1912 Monte Carlo rehearsals that he threatened to cancel it, exclaiming: 'This is not a ballet, and I cannot give it in Paris.'⁶ (Only the enthusiasm of stage designer Léon Bakst saved the production.) In this light, Diaghilev's canny appropriation of the latest avant-garde '-ism', so soon thereafter, reads like a virtuoso publicist's cynical attempt at an insurance policy against a feared debacle.

Pursuing the point further, consider Nijinska's recollection, from a few months after the *Faune* premiere, of her brother's artistic tastes: 'At that time Vaslav was completely captivated by contemporary French art – Modigliani, Matisse, Cézanne, and particularly Rodin and Gauguin.'⁷ These artists, as it happens, shared a central interest (as the Cubists, in 1910–12, largely did not) in the promises and challenges of modern erotic representation.⁸ Nijinska's further remarks about Vaslav's enthusiasm for Gauguin's 'native women with no hint of European airs and graces' – which extended to exoticist visions of a future wife and children with 'golden bodies' – signal a sensuous visual enthusiasm that would have found little nourishment in arid Cubist experiments with post-perspectival fracturing of the real. The vast Cubist catalogue holds hardly any instances of the imaginary – classical, mythological and erotic – subject-matter of Nijinsky's post-Mallarméan pastoral; in none of the few nudes the Cubists produced do the near-monochromatic shards, in their austere rectilinear grids, retain any sensuous invitation to a desiring gaze.⁹

Still, despite this documented predilection for Gauguin (who died in 1903), neither his paintings nor those of Modigliani, Rodin or Cézanne

---

London: Yale University Press, 1999), 169–224; and Pepe Karmel, *Picasso and the Invention of Cubism* (New Haven and London: Yale University Press, 2003).

⁵ See Nijinska's report of Nijinsky's first ideas in *Early Memoirs*, 315: 'I want to move away from the classical Greece that Fokine wants to use. Instead, I want to use the archaic Greece that is less known and, so far, little used in the theatre … More may even be borrowed from Assyria than Greece.'

⁶ Nijinska, *Early Memoirs*, 328, 429–30, at 430.

⁷ Nijinska, *Early Memoirs*, 442. Nijinska only refers to Picasso in a parenthesis identifying the young dancer Olga Khokhlova as his future wife (333).

⁸ For Cézanne it might be better to talk of 'psychosexually fraught representations of the body' rather than 'erotic representation' in the simpler sense of Modigliani or Rodin. See, e.g., T. J. Clark, *Farewell to an Idea*, 139–68.

⁹ One near-exception is Picasso's *Girl With a Mandolin (Fanny Tellier)*, of late spring 1910, whose *almost* readable body leads some critics to find it a work of exceptional 'lyricism' within a style notable for the opposite. See Karmel, *Picasso and the Invention of Cubism*, 81.

supply compelling reference points for a ballet whose up-to-date visual modernism – notably its disconcerting two-dimensionality or 'flatness' – has struck so many viewers. But the most modern name on Nijinska's list is worth another look. In avant-garde myth-making and popular tales of modern art alike, the painting of Henri Matisse, equally influential in those years, has often been overshadowed by the Cubist accomplishment. Yet in marked contrast to the schematic, monochromatic and anti-expressive trajectory of Picasso and Braque during the period in question, Matisse had been developing, since the 1890s, the richest early twentieth-century synthesis of the colouristic and sensuous lessons of Van Gogh, Gauguin, Cézanne and others. By 1910, Matisse had been engaged for several years in a struggle for artistic supremacy with Picasso. And, most tellingly for the present purposes, he had been pursuing that synthesis and struggle through works whose blend of decorative flatness, colouristic freedom and archaic classical-mythological imagery focused primarily on questions of erotic representation.

One of Picasso's key offerings to this avant-garde exchange – the iconic *Les demoiselles d'Avignon* of 1907 – has featured in a few critical elaborations on Diaghilev's airy gesture towards non-existent 'theory'.[10] But that confrontational, violently fractured image of modern prostitutes (not shown publicly until 1916) seems little more convincing a parallel with Nijinsky's decorously stylized 'archaic classical scenario' than any fully fledged Cubist offshoot. As a more resonant painterly companion, consider instead Matisse's *Le bonheur de vivre*, which inspired Picasso's epochal painterly aggression when he first saw it in Gertrude Stein's Parisian home in 1906.[11]

In Matisse's painting, which resounds to the piping of two cousins of Nijinsky's faun, we see a disconcertingly modern version of the classical pastoral, arrayed beneath a colourful, loosely handled forest canopy akin to Bakst's ballet backdrop. While a ring of dancers whirls in the 'distance' (this flattened illusory space baffled viewers at the 1906 *Salon des Indépendants*), closer individuals and couples offer erotic invitations to the gaze that seem prophetic of Nijinsky's archaic vocabulary. At left, a figure crouches, in homage or abasement, below a standing, preening nude: summary icon for

---

[10] See, e.g., Jordan, 'Debussy, the Dance, and the *Faune*', 130.
[11] This painting, still in copyright, is readily available online. The story about *Les Demoiselles* and the struggle with Matisse has often been told; see, e.g., Anne Baldassari, Elizabeth Cowling, John Elderfield, John Golding, Isabelle Monod-Fontaine and Kirk Varnedoe, *Matisse Picasso*, catalogue of an exhibition held at Tate Modern, London, 11 May–18 August (London: Tate Publishing, 2002).

an immemorial tradition of painted female display. A central figure, catching her ambiguously gendered companion in a hook-armed embrace, flips a fey hand towards some other aspect of the scene – perhaps the two central bodies, or the whirling dance, or the closer, more engulfing embrace at right, whose female partner sprawls in open-legged (but veiled) abandon as her partner, snared by her elbow, hunkers in foetal self-protection.

Matisse's *Le bonheur de vivre* presents a contemporary, erotic pastoral whose play of gazes and bodies within a disorienting two-dimensional field sets up a wholly different order of resonances with Nijinsky's *Faune* than any Cubist image. The sense of family resemblance finds support in the suggestion of one Matisse expert, Jack Flam, that *Le bonheur*'s eclectic sources extended back beyond all recent, post-Impressionist models to the same 'Greek vase painting' that would later inspire the *Faune*.[12] Indeed, Flam offers yet more reinforcement for the idea that Matisse's modern pastoral casts a telling sidelight on Nijinsky's stylized erotic pursuit. With a view to the 'hallucinatory' central pairing of self-concealing 'nymphs' – their thickly brushed outlines a sign of intense visual investment – he proposes that '*Le bonheur de vivre* also seems to be closely related to Stéphane Mallarmé's *Après-midi d'un faune*, which it resembles in imagery, colour, and overall structure.'[13]

Flam may well stretch the circumstantial evidence too far in insisting that 'Matisse used the faun poem as a model for both imagery and the structure of the painting.'[14] But there is no need to argue for a single model in order to recognize a larger point: the eager acceptance of Diaghilev's defensive 'Cubist' ploy has effaced from critical reception of Nijinsky's *Faune* this far more apposite – and more frankly sensuous – contextual tradition of 'symbolist painting in the Arcadian mode' (as Flam describes it). What begins to emerge with this recognition is a much broader point about many constructions of aesthetic modernism, with a near-exclusive emphasis on formalism and objectivity over sensuality and subjectivity, as well as the scientific and schematic over the psychological and erotic. This concept of modernism has also profoundly limited what many have been willing to *hear* in the music Nijinsky claimed to have followed so 'closely' in creating his 'completely new plastic composition'.

In this chapter, I offer a new analysis of the *Faune* ballet that can be considered one small, exemplary step towards a renewed – and

---

[12] Jack Flam, *Matisse: The Man and His Art* (Ithaca: Cornell University Press, 1986), 158.
[13] Flam, *Matisse: The Man and his Art*, 156. Matisse marked a literary turn more explicitly a year earlier in *Luxe, calme et volupté*, titled after Baudelaire.
[14] Flam, *Matisse: The Man and his Art*, 156.

unsettled – modernist historiography. Taking seriously Nijinsky's 1912 claim, I argue that a full appreciation of his close choreographic hearing requires that we attend not only to the objective interplay of visible steps and audible timespans – long central to claims for an archetypically modernist disjunction between music and gesture – but also to a neglected, psychological and sensuous level of dance–music interaction. In what follows, I first present the musical and the choreographic analyses necessary to support this more multi-dimensional appreciation. I then turn back to Matisse, to borrow in closing from a more recent commentary on *Le bonheur de vivre* by art historian Margaret Werth. Werth's reading of this painting within a 2002 study of *fin-de-siècle* 'idyllic' imagery offers suggestive purchase for the contentious idea that the reception of this whole congeries of works has so far been characterized, above all, by pervasive acts of repression – whose unconscious force in the construction of modernism's canons is long overdue for conscious excavation.

Notation and Its Limits

To begin with an obvious problem: nobody can now analyse the sounds Nijinsky heard in 1912 and the gestures they inspired, for both have long been lost to history. But since 1989, thanks to the work undertaken by dance experts Ann Hutchinson Guest and Claudia Jeschke to translate Nijinsky's personal notation of 1915 into the more conventional Labanotation, we have possessed a 'score' of his *Faune* ballet, published bar by bar alongside a piano reduction of Debussy's *Prélude*. We have also been able to scrutinize all its embodied particulars, on video, in the staging Jill Beck directed at Juilliard in 1991 under their guidance.[15]

There has been some predictable disagreement about the accuracy of this recreation, and the translators acknowledge making many small adjustments before ultimately claiming that they have notated something 'extremely close to the original production'.[16] But even if we accept their solutions to a few intriguing local anomalies, a higher-level question remains. It comes most clearly into view in those passages of the editorial

---

[15] See Ann Hutchinson Guest, ed., with Claudia Jeschke, *Nijinsky's 'Faune' Restored* (1991; repr. Binstead, Hampshire: Noverre Press, 2010), and the video published alongside a special issue of the journal *Choreography and Dance* 1, pt. 3 (1991), ed. Jill Beck under the title 'A Revival of Nijinsky's original *L'après-midi d'un faune*' (1991; repr. Basel: Harwood Academic Publishers, 1994).

[16] Hutchinson Guest, *Nijinsky's 'Faune' Restored*, 194; see also 192–3.

commentary – for example, the references to poses of alertness or desirous attention – that touch the limits of *any* attempt to notate a choreographed encounter that depends just as fundamentally on elusive transactions of affect and interiority as it does on specifiable physical gestures.[17] In her contribution to a special issue of the journal *Choreography and Dance* devoted to the reconstruction, Hutchinson Guest writes eloquently about the creative intervention required to fill out this expressive dimension.[18] What has never been adequately acknowledged, however, is the degree to which the very same kind of question impinges on the different, deceptively familiar notation printed alongside the new Labanotation on every page of the published score.

Looking again to those reduced bars of Debussy's *Prélude*, consider the confident parallel with which the choreographers' editorial commentary concludes:

> As with the great classics in music, individual interpretations will vary, but the notes, the work itself will remain, uncorrupted by the vagaries of memory and the temptations of dancers to insert their own material. Nijinsky's *Faune* will endure as he recorded it.[19]

No musicologist can now read that blithe elision – 'the notes, the work itself' – without questioning the implication that the musical qualities of even the most established classic have ever been fully captured in notation.[20] Yet, on the whole, the critical tradition about this ballet has so far proceeded as if the written notes of the *Prélude* have sufficed to hand down an 'uncorrupted' sequence of sounds from 1894 through 1912 to the present day. To put it more bluntly: until recently Debussy's music has entered critical response as if it brought to the choreographed encounter between a faun and seven nymphs little more than a sequence of abstract temporal spans, characterized sonorously (if at all) by the vaguest generalities.[21]

---

[17] See, e.g., the comments on 'Expression', 'Relationship between Faun and Nymphs' and 'Inclining the Head', in Hutchinson Guest, *Nijinsky's 'Faune' Restored*, 19, 21 and 21–2.

[18] See Hutchinson Guest, 'Nijinsky's *Faune*', in Beck, ed. 'A Revival', 26.

[19] Hutchinson Guest, *Nijinsky's 'Faune' Restored*, 194.

[20] See, e.g., Lydia Goehr, *The Imaginary Museum of Musical Works: An Essay in the Philosophy of Music* (Oxford: Clarendon Press, 1992), and any number of contributions to the 'historically informed performance' debate.

[21] There is of course a consideration of disciplinary focus here. But if, for example, the theatre-historical riches of Järvinen's substantial 2009 essay partly make up for its rare and insubstantial references to the *Prélude*, her argument for Nijinsky as a new kind of dance *auteur* still underplays the dependence of that 'authorship' on intimate dialogue with a previous layer of creation. See Järvinen, 'Dancing without Space', 29.

It might seem easy, here, to invoke again the master trope about this work's archetypically modern dissonance between choreography and music. As the composer himself famously complained to a 1914 interviewer:

> Can you imagine the *rapport* between an undulating, rocking music, rich with curved lines, and a scenic action in which the characters move like figures on certain antique Greek or Etruscan vases, without grace or suppleness, as if their schematic gestures were regulated by laws of pure geometry? ... An atrocious 'dissonance', without possible resolution![22]

Perhaps we sense a defensiveness, here, about a work once pivotal to Debussy's own development, or a trace of the frustrations from his more recent experiences with Nijinsky on *Jeux*.[23] But, either way, we have long known that this response was only one extreme on a spectrum that extended all the way to its opposite – for example, in the claim of early critic Louis Schneider that Nijinsky 'has attached a gesture to every syllable of M. Debussy's orchestra'; or in the later paean from dance critic Edwin Denby to the first ballet 'set clearly not to the measures and periods, but to the expressive flow of the music, to its musical sense'.[24]

More recently, we have gained from Davinia Caddy a belated attempt to reassess the case through close analysis of the choreography against the actual sounds of Debussy's *Prélude*. It could be that the judiciously balanced conclusions that emerge from this attentive hearing – the dance's several close congruencies with the music, Caddy shows, occur amidst many passages of much looser fit – have pushed the question about 'consonance' or 'dissonance' as far as it can go.[25] But if some significant implications of Nijinsky's modernism still remain unheard in this most nuanced account, I suggest, it is for the same reason that also applies to all

---

[22] 'Pouvez-vous imaginer le rapport entre une musique ondoyante, berceuse, où abondent les lignes courbes, et une action scénique où les personnages se meuvent, pareils à ceux de certains vases antiques, grecs ou étrusques, sans grâce ni souplesse, comme si leurs gestes schématiques étaient réglés par des lois de géométrie pure? ... Une "dissonance" atroce, sans resolution possible!' François Lesure, 'Une interview romaine de Debussy (1914)', *Cahiers Debussy* nouvelle série 11 (1987), 3–8, at 5.

[23] While Debussy's letters give us a few of his opinions about *Jeux*, the Faun ballet left no trace. Many have noted how starkly his Rome complaint differs from the (possibly ironic) warm words with which he had greeted Nijinsky's 1913 telegram hailing a successful restaging in London. See Claude Debussy, *Correspondance 1872–1918*, ed. François Lesure, Denis Herlin and Georges Liébert (Paris: Gallimard, 2005), 1585 and 1619.

[24] Edwin Denby, *Dance Writings* (London: Dance Books, 1986), 498.

[25] See Caddy, 'Nijinsky's *Faune* Revisited', esp. 74–97. Jordan, noting some broad congruencies and some closer ones ('Debussy, the Dance, and the *Faune*', 126–7), concludes similarly: 'even in the version reconstructed from Nijinsky's notation, it mixes harmonic relationships with disjunction' (127).

vaguer precedents. In a 2001 article, I argued for a new hearing of Debussy's *Prélude*, based in part on an original analysis of Mallarmé's *L'Après-midi d'un faune*, but defined primarily by an audible and dramatic interplay in its orchestration.[26] It is exemplary of my larger concerns to find that Caddy, while acknowledging this study, nonetheless passes over the main sonorous details on which its conclusions rest.[27]

Here we directly confront the question about the multiple sonorous possibilities suggested by the deceptively singular notation of Debussy's *Prélude*. Before turning to consider Nijinsky's choreographic hearing, it will help to elaborate this question briefly through a selective exploration of the recorded tradition. While all readers will no doubt be aware that recordings differ (sometimes radically) in, say, overall pacing and local expressive inflection, it is perhaps less commonly recognized just how much flexibility is available to the performed realization of a notated interplay of orchestral sounds – whose balance, moment by moment, fundamentally determines what can actually be heard.[28] As a preliminary aid to illustrating this range of sonorous possibilities, Example 8.1 presents a much-reduced short score of the *Prélude*, notated to bring clarity to one particularly compelling sequence of sounds – a sequence whose multiple notations of audible importance (reinforced in every musical dimension: orchestration, rhythm, dynamics and motivic progression) have not prevented its pervasive neglect in traditional thematic and harmonic analysis.

No rigorous principles of harmonic prolongation or voice leading inform my stemless reduction in Example 8.1, which aims to give an easily

---

[26] For this previous argument, which includes an extensive bibliography of prior accounts of Debussy's piece, see my 'Hearing Debussy Reading Mallarmé: Music après Wagner in the *Prélude à l'après-midi d'un faune*', *Journal of the American Musicological Society* 54, no. 3 (Fall 2001), 493–554. I further develop my analysis of the poem in 'The Formal Rhythms of Mallarmé's Faun', *Representations* 86 (Spring 2004), 73–119.

[27] See Caddy, 'Nijinsky's *Faune* Revisited', 74, where she accepts the idea that the ballet, like the music, exemplifies a moment that 'hovers between nineteenth- and twentieth-century musical thought'. Her discussion largely leaves the expressive implications of this agonistic 'hovering' behind.

[28] Without wanting to deem the poem an irrelevant subtext (Nijinsky admitted that he had never read it, but it is clear that his chats with Cocteau and Diaghilev had given him a fine sense of many main ideas), I do not think it necessary for the present purposes to revisit the details of the first, literary link in the chain. See the first text in the 'Témoignages' section of Jean-Michel Nectoux, *Nijinsky: L'Après-midi d'un faune* (London: Thames and Hudson, 1990), a little note in which Nijinsky admits: 'I have not read Mallarmé's text *The Afternoon of a Faun*. I do not understand French well enough to read literary texts' ('Je n'ai pas lu le texte de Mallarmé *L'Après-midi d'un faune*. Je ne comprends pas encore assez bien le Français pour lire des textes littéraires' (43)). Nectoux sources the note to Ludwig Kainer, *Ballet russe* (Munich, 1913), and 'Les souvenirs de Nijinsky et Karsavina par eux-mêmes', *Je sais tout*, 15 November 1912.

Example 8.1 Reduced short score of Claude Debussy, Prélude à l'après-midi d'un faune

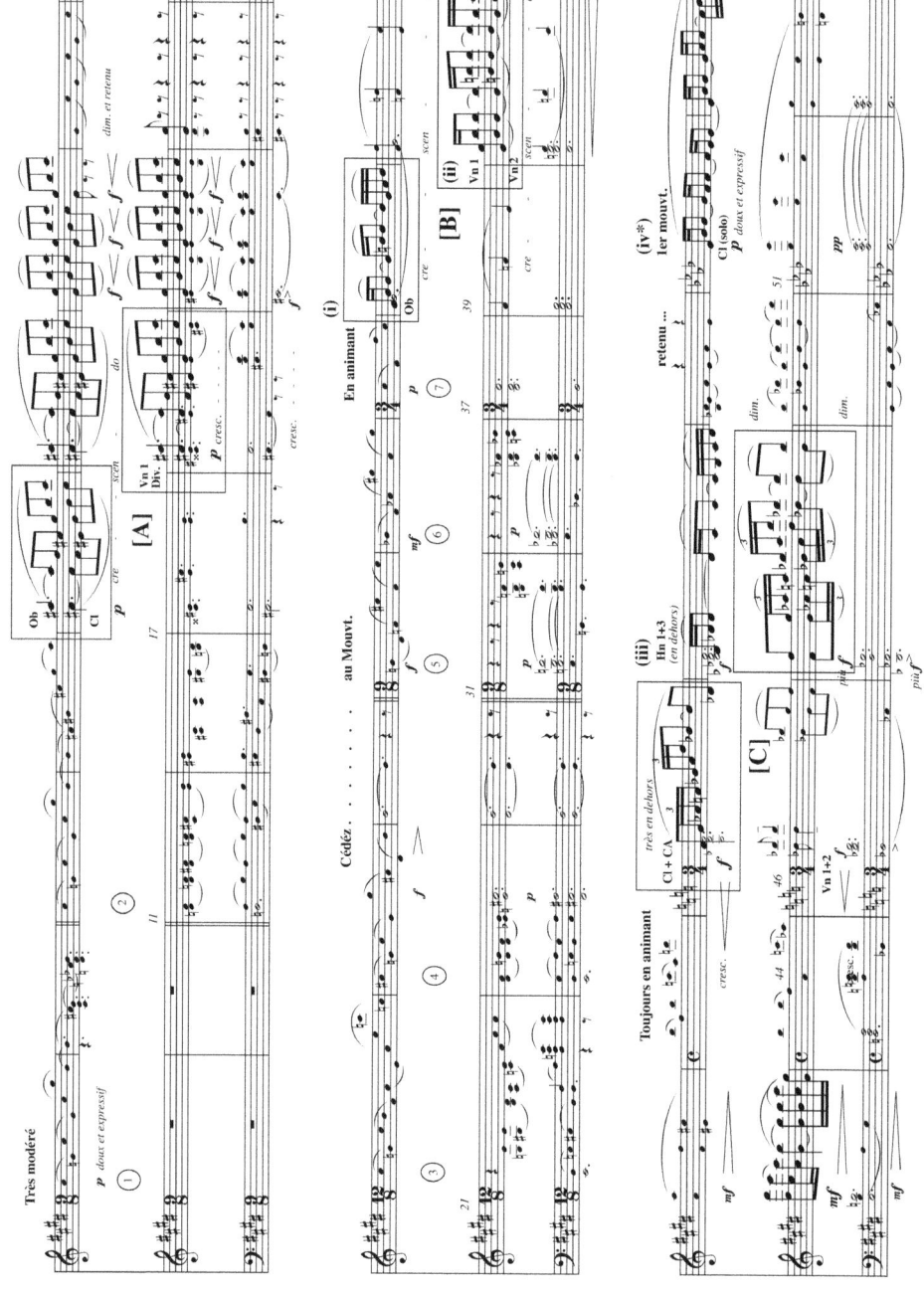

Example 8.1 (cont.)

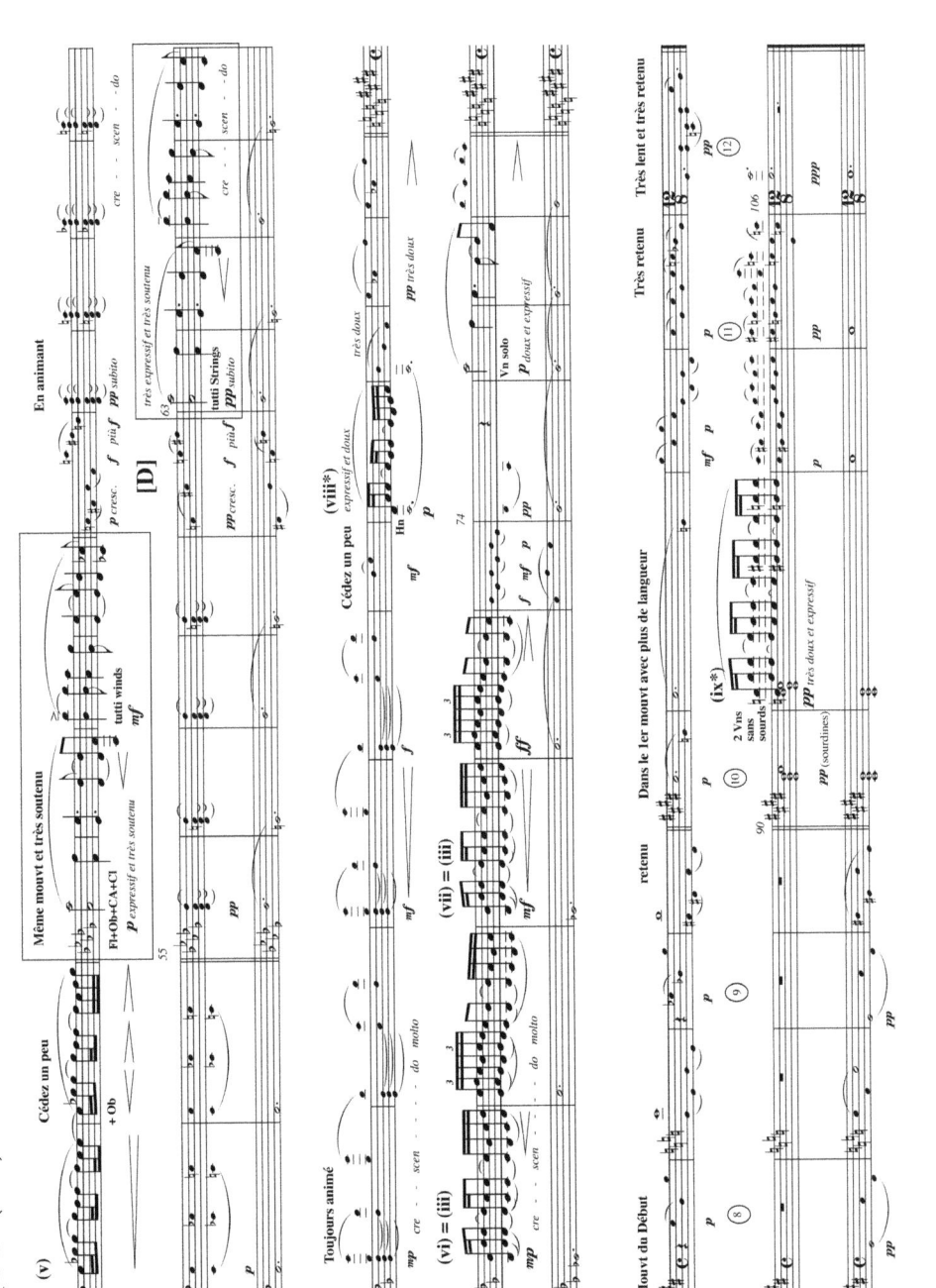

readable summary of the music surrounding the palpably dramatic sonorous events shown, in precise transcription, in larger stemmed notes. Indicating original instruments and dynamics, I also give circled numbers (from 1 to 12) for the several variants of the work's most familiar thematic feature, the flute arabesque.[29] I mark the more dramatically distinctive events with four pairs of boxes labelled [A] to [D]. In three of the four cases (bars 17–18, 39–40 and 46–7), this event consists of a one-bar melodic gesture played by the winds and immediately echoed by high, octave-doubled strings – a sound that first appears at the first gesture, and then disappears again until the second. (The exception to the rule is the expanded exchange of four-bar wind and string phrases shown on page 2, a late addition to the precedent.[30]) Finally, lower-case numerals, from (i) to (ix), indicate a more extended motivic chain that first emerges within these orchestral exchanges but later evolves independently, through the climax, almost to the close.

While there can be no doubting the formal importance of this motivic chain – among other things, it anticipates and delivers the *fortissimo* crux of the work, and follows it with two poignant gestures of recall – the subtlety of its long-range evolution partly explains its neglect by previous analysts.[31] As a pitch idea, it can be traced back (in inchoate form) to the rising minor third G♯–B in the first exchange ([A]). But it is only when the same pitches recur to launch two fully fledged instances at [B] ((i) and (ii), bars 39–40) that the motive gains the undulating, syncopated rhythm (plus semiquaver tail) that fundamentally defines its identity.[32]

---

[29] Some analysts number these variants differently, but the disagreement is irrelevant to this discussion.

[30] It appears that Debussy initially conceived *both* statements of the D♭ tune for strings, and only later changed the first to winds. See the facsimile *particelle* published by the Robert Owen Lehman Foundation (Washington, 1963). The only previous account that implicitly recognizes this long-range timbral evolution is Thomas Munro, '"The Afternoon of a Faun" and the Interrelation of the Arts', *The Journal of Aesthetic and Art Criticism* 10, no. 2 (December 1951), 95–111, where we read of 'vague hints of emotional excitement, which rise in intensity until the contrasting, second part of the composition is reached' (100).

[31] No other account grants any prominence to this motivic thread. The closest exception is the catalogue of loosely interrelated motives presented across three pages in William Austin, *Debussy: Prelude to 'The Afternoon of a Faun'*, a Norton Critical Score (New York: W. W. Norton, 1970), 76–8. Austin identifies the first appearance (bar 39) as the 'syncopated motif' (76) – one of only two such labels he provides. A few (but not all) of the later variants also appear, scattered amidst various other motives.

[32] The term 'undulating' originates in my sense of the relation of this passage to lines 27–9 of Mallarmé's poem: 'sur l'or glauque de lointaines / Verdures, dédiant leur vigne à des fontaines, / Ondoie une blancheur animale au repos' ('on the glaucous gold of the distant / greenery, dedicating their vine to the fountains, / Undulates an animal whiteness at rest'). All caveats

The third instance – a horn call, added to a melodically independent timbral exchange (bar 47) – shows that the evolution of the rhythmic idea will involve some melodic flexibility. In the fourth and fifth instances (the former altered from minor to major third, hence the asterisk), a clarinet muses on a two-bar version (with delayed tail) as a transition to the 'B' section. The motive then reappears twice in its original form – (vi) and (vii), bars 67 and 69 – at the heart of the piece, for full strings, at the same B♭ pitch prefigured by the horn (iii), and sweeps to the work's sole *fortissimo*. In the first of two later recollections (both using the major third) a horn reflects on the D♭ major key of the climax (viii) before a solo violin recalls the central tune. In the second, more distant recall (ix), the undulating shape floats in once more in two high violins, whose (unmuted) recollection of past timbral exchanges – now extending to a tender, rhythmically augmented undulation (quaver and crotchet) in place of the original tail – sounds all the more poignant for its near-independence, melodically, from the (muted) E major harmonic support.[33]

Here is a series of events whose multiply reinforced aural importance identifies it, across the entire piece, as a compelling sonorous 'Other' to the more understated arabesque. Given the clear association of the topical flute idea with the lead character Nijinsky took from Mallarmé's post-Virgilian pastoral, we might already discern – as a new orientation for hearing – an obvious question about the relationship this sensuously 'Othered' string material might bear, in the ballet, to the elusive objects of the faun's desire. But, as an exemplary 'sounding' of the broader question about written notes and their limits, we might first ask how the long-standing analytical neglect of those main sonorous events relates to the fate of the same material within performed and recorded tradition.

I initially recognized the importance of the highlighted progression in a specific recording of the *Prélude* by the New Philharmonia Orchestra with Pierre Boulez in 1966.[34] To listen again to this version is to be struck

---

aside, I find it intriguing how acutely the play with gazes and bodies in Nijinsky's scenario captures (fortuitously or not) a central theme of the 1876 *Églogue*.

[33] Oddly, Austin's chart omits the anticipation at bar 47 and the recollections at bars 74 and 94. My reduction excises a few other motives of audible importance – notably including the descending triplet figure he identifies as the 'flowing motif' (his only other label) when it first appears at bar 28, which conjoins with the 'syncopated motif' at the climax (bars 67–70). It is possible that this idea, too, had some importance in Nijinsky's hearing.

[34] The original LP was sold as *Boulez Conducts Debussy*, CBS Masterworks, 32 11 0056; I refer to the re-mastered CD *Debussy: Orchestral Music*, with Pierre Boulez conducting the New Philharmonia Orchestra, CBS Odyssey MB2K 45620. By contrast, Hutchinson Guest identifies as the recording 'most suitable for rehearsals' Herbert von Karajan's 1965 rendition with the

afresh, first, by the gestural energy of the repeated violin *crescendi* as they emerge forcefully into prominence at [A]; and then, by how in the exchange at [B] – exaggerated by a radical *rallentando* and slight *decrescendo* in bar 39 – the undulating, syncopated high string sound seizes the ear with even more startling vividness. But the same, highly mannered approach has the opposite effect on the more complex event [C], whose timbral clarity is undercut by Boulez's blatant disregard for the *più forte* – which makes the horn–violin collision sound like a premature aftermath of the prior surge to high D♭. Even this preliminary sampling of a single recorded version thus finds a mixture of approximation and realization of expectations fostered by analysis. And one way to underline just how unstable the mixture has always been is to consider, by comparison, the recording Boulez made of the same piece in 1992 with the Cleveland Orchestra. A much sleeker, more normalized experience altogether, with the audible exchanges smoothed of mannerism, this rendition leaves the impression, overall, of a work from which most significant questions for performers or hearers alike have been effaced – or repressed.[35]

With a bit of historical perspective, we might recall that the mannered 1966 version emerged from Boulez's programmatic attempt in those years to appropriate this music to his own high-modernist lineage. Around the same time, he famously stated a desire to 'burn the mist' from Debussy's so-called 'Impressionism'.[36] But, in truth, a quick sampling of prior recordings, extending back to the earliest 78s, finds that the mist had never really been all that pervasive.[37]

Taking Example 8.1 as the guide for a whirlwind précis, note first that amongst the handful of cases that do give an aurally compelling rendition of [A] (including, for one very early example, Sir Landon Ronald and the *Orchestre symphonique* in 1922), there are also many for whom the violin sound remains firmly relegated to an accompanimental colour.[38] (Leopold Stokowski offers a suggestive *mis*reading with the Philadelphia Orchestra

---

    Berlin Philharmonic, whose sonorous conception of the piece – basically, a somewhat eccentric flute concerto – differs radically from the Boulez.

[35] *Debussy: Images, Prélude à l'après-midi d'un faune, Printemps*, The Cleveland Orchestra conducted by Pierre Boulez, Deutsche Grammophon 435 766-2.

[36] William Glock, long-time BBC Controller of Music, reports this intention in his autobiography *Notes in Advance* (Oxford: Oxford University Press, 1991), 192.

[37] For preliminary orientation I am grateful to Margaret G. Cobb, *Discographie de l'œuvre de Claude Debussy* (Geneva: Editions Minkoff, 1975), and the *Catalogue de l'œuvre de Claude Debussy* produced by the publishers Durand (Paris, 1962).

[38] The Ronald 1922 rendition – truncated by the omission of a few short passages, likely reflecting the difficulties of acoustic orchestral recording – is on Gramophone W 317.

in 1928: the irruption of violins speaks clearly even though he reverses the written *crescendi*.[39]) On the other hand, the fact that [B] has always been more consistently projected is easily understandable given both its clearer melodic profile and its first presentation of the undulating rhythmic motive. (Even in this case, however, a few alternative hearings – such as Paul Klenau with the Royal Philharmonic Orchestra in 1926 – choose to emphasize, instead, the contrapuntal crotchet exchange given in smaller stemmed notes.[40]) The much more varied responses to [C], finally, are testimony to the difficulty of this timbral challenge, which calls for the violins to emerge *più forte* even as the motive, sounded by two horns, is to project *en dehors*. Amongst many blatant compromises at this moment we also find a few inventive solutions, notably including (e.g., on a scrappy recording by Debussy's old friend Gabriel Pierné with the *Orchestre des Concerts Colonne* in 1937, and a defter one by Charles Munch with the Boston Symphony Orchestra in 1957) the addition of a *subito piano* in the violins on the downbeat of bar 47 (so that the horns can be clearly heard), followed by an unwritten *crescendo* that gives new dramatic intensity to the string echo of the wind flourish.[41]

Even this radically selective tour should be enough to demonstrate that there has never been a single and stable Debussy *Prélude* against which to read Nijinsky's choreography. Just as a troupe of dancers can only ever provide their own expressive supplements to the gestures encoded abstractly in Labanotation, an orchestra will only ever present one of countless realizations of the notated sounds from which those gestures once took inspiration. But there is one last question to consider before turning to the dance. Given that Nijinsky and his nymphs would have largely worked with a pianist through the countless rehearsals, might it not be absurd to suppose any close 'choreographic hearing' on his part of orchestral details only added later, in the last public rehearsals and performance?[42]

In response, I would say first that the octave-doubled violin material in the *Prélude* often retains an unmistakable dynamic and textural prominence – perhaps even an implicit trace of 'high violin' scoring – in the piano reduction.[43] And although we can never know just how detailed an aural

---

[39] Gramophone D1768.   [40] Columbia L1772.
[41] Pierné/ Colonne is on Odéon 123.689/ SDCR; Munch/ Boston is RCA 630370/ B-339.
[42] Bronislava writes amusingly of her brother's impatience with the pianist Michael Steinman in her *Early Memoirs*, 406. My reference to 'countless' rehearsals here reflects the differing numbers recalled by Nijinsky (60), his sister (90), and his wife (120). See Nectoux, *Nijinsky: L'Après-midi d'un faune*, 40, n. 21.
[43] Compare the much less distinctive reduced wind lines, as in Caddy's interpretive suggestion: 'man's association with the flute, and woman's with reed instruments, goes back at least to the

memory Nijinsky brought to his early read-throughs of the *Prélude* at the piano with Diaghilev, one clue emerges in Bronislava's recollection that 'with his perfect ear for music, Vaslav was able to memorize entire overtures from the operas he heard at the Maryinsky – Tchaikovsky's *Eugene Onegin* and *The Queen of Spades*, Glinka's *Ruslan and Ludmila*, Gounod's *Faust*, Boito's *Mefistofele*'.[44] Reflecting further, we might also look again to the famous 1912 photo of him playing four-hand piano music with Maurice Ravel.[45] The piece they are playing – with Nijinsky seated to Ravel's right, taking the treble (including violin) parts – is always identified as *Daphnis et Chloé*. But might their session have extended to include the four-hand version of the *Prélude* Ravel had prepared for Durand as recently as 1910, letting him bring to their intimate exchanges on the piano bench much expert insight about original scoring?

Ultimately, like all the other questions raised by this ballet, that about the precise hearing that guided its choreography is one to pursue empirically and openly, by looking and listening again with awareness of the multiple, contingent choices behind any particular sonorous and gestural event, and the many other options discarded along the way. I approach the 1991 Juilliard staging of the 1989 transcription in this spirit – perhaps occasionally forcing the question of choreographed response to aural cues, but only in the hope of re-opening (indeed unsettling) our understanding of the modernism this dance has so long been thought to represent.

A Choreographed Realization

My analysis will proceed through close attention to the two video recordings made by the Juilliard team: one in wide view, one in close-up. Clearly, my selective description of several telling moments amounts to another kind of reduction, exemplary at every point of the temporal and cross-disciplinary challenges this artistic interplay raises for verbal translation. The first vision we are given of the faun (soon after the curtain rises) offers a case in point. While exemplary of the 'static' conception that troubled

---

classical tales of Pan, his "syrinx," and the mythological sirens' ('Nijinsky's *Faune* Revisited', 76).

[44] Nijinska, *Early Memoirs*, 122. Later, when recalling the work on *Jeux*, she refers again to his 'unusual talent of being able to hold perfectly in his memory a piece of music he had heard only a few times' – though there she means 'those parts of the music that Debussy had played for him [on the piano]' (444).

[45] The photo is now easily accessible through Google Images. Bronislava often emphasizes Vaslav's skilful practical musicianship in her memoirs.

many early viewers, this opening also brings a suggestive foretaste of the subtle hearing that arguably infuses even relatively uneventful spans.

The faun, reclining on his rock and 'holding the flute at the lips' (in the first of Nijinsky's written instructions) maintains the same pose against Bakst's colourful backdrop, on an otherwise empty stage, through the first two bars. But in the third bar – deepening the illusion that we are hearing him play the visible instrument – he closely matches the more active, arpeggiated half of the solo arabesque with a gently expressive lift of the playing hand. It may be a stretch to see this soloistic gesture – delivered somewhat stiffly in the Juilliard version – as imparting a hint of desirous urgency even to the first thin thread of sound. But such a hearing gains credence when we see how, once he lowers the flute, he proceeds to indicate, with a slow sweep of a rigidly open hand, the emptiness of the landscape now resounding to spacious horn calls. The return of the arabesque at bar 11 finds him back in his indolent pose, giving a more sinuous soloistic flexion before lowering the flute again at a moment that seems (in this version) slightly premature (bar 13, last beat). Maybe this first disjunction reflects an aural sensitivity to a subtlety of scoring lost to the piano reduction: the 'hand-over' of the flute solo to oboe during the final held A♯. And indeed the action that ensues, as the faun leaves his perch to prowl up his rock, seems inspired – indeed, led – by the new reed sound.

Once the oboe line leads to sonorous event [A] in Example 8.1, we reach a first opportunity to weigh what an orchestrally attuned analysis has to offer a musical close reading. At this point, the case seems somewhat mixed. Nijinsky clearly heard the drama of the first *crescendo* to *forte* and the forceful melodic repetition from bars 17–18, for his encounter with two bunches of grapes unfolds as a bar-by-bar alternation of lifts and gazes, first at one then the other. Still, the repetitive nature of this gesture conveys no aural response to the timbral contrast. But in this first instance, exceptionally, the contrast unfolds as an incremental emergence rather than a stark opposition. And the brief play with the grapes – whose symbolic displacement of more satisfying objects comes directly from Mallarmé – spawns a telling continuation, which culminates with a strikingly bestial arch-backed stretch. While the intensifying violin swells are restrained almost to inaudibility by the Juilliard orchestra, a more full-blooded rendition could easily heighten the projection, through this gesture, of urgent, frustrated desire.[46]

---

[46] As I have argued in 'Hearing Debussy Reading Mallarmé', the audible 'intensification' here arises from the notated incremental erosion of the wind textures against the persistent violins, not from an actual string *crescendo*.

After lazily retaking the instrument, the faun reassumes his performer's pose, reversed, for the third variant of the arabesque at bar 21. Remaining still for fully ten bars, he provides an oblivious accompaniment for the successive entry of the seven nymphs from stage left. This most decorously pastoral span of the *Prélude* ultimately delivers all the nymphs to a pose, 'three plus three', on either side of the lead nymph – end of bar 30 – just prior to the next, more dramatic section. The formal conception is acute: it is only after the flute gives way to the first timbral variants of the arabesque (clarinet at 31 and 34; oboe at 37), and the *Prélude* approaches the motivic timbral contrasts [B] and [C], that the faun starts to move towards an interaction with the nymphs. Predictably, however, the evolving pair of relationships – between orchestral timbres and between staged characters – is not straightforward.

A slight puzzle emerges with the energetic first bars of the new section. At bar 31, Nijinsky notes 'Flute at the lips', even as he also instructs the lead nymph to undo, and later drop, the first of the veils she wears over her dress. In the video, after lowering the instrument sooner than the score suggests, the faun turns his attention promptly to this appealing prospect, and is gazing intently by the time she drops the second veil at bar 34. The puzzle may seem trivial. But we have already seen that the gaze, with its inner urges and frustrations, is a crucial aspect of the faun's relationship to his world. And as the music moves on, through the oboe solo, to the ensuing timbral exchanges, it becomes possible to discern, as the main driver of Nijinsky's close hearing, the fine inflections of visual access to the object of desire.

Perhaps the nymph's little dance to the oboe solo at bar 37 seems already to unfold before the faun's eager eyes. But a glance to the wide-angle video shows that his sightlines still remain crowded. Indeed, exactly with the fall of the veils – first at bar 33 (just before the clarinet's sequential repetition), then at bar 36 (just before the oboe solo) – the two groups of nymphs cross swiftly behind, creating a jumbled visual barrier between the disrobing nymph and the watching faun. The sense that these bodies serve as a larger-order veil becomes yet clearer at the second timbral exchange [B]. After starting in a close, centrally paired array as the oboe launches the undulating motive, the two groups separate outwards through bar 39 – leaving the lead nymph exposed to the staring faun precisely as the violin sound washes in (bar 40). As before, this timbre marks more than external gesture: it is as if we share the quickening of his blood as the desired object becomes fully exposed.

After he descends to approach her, the tangled timbres of event [C] prove harder to link with gazes and bodies. The descent lasts through bars

42 and 43; the lead nymph then takes another little dance while her companions gather the veils. By bar 46 the faun has passed behind the leftmost trio and the central nymph, and the wind flourish (almost inaudible here) finds him focusing on the 'fourth nymph' rather than the one just exposed. The echoing violin flourish with horn overlay – also very difficult to hear – brings no corrective to this misplaced attention, for he remains intent, through bar 47, on the other nymph. But a brief confrontation with him, scaring her away, sets up a belated choreographic acknowledgement of the undulating motive. Just as the clarinet begins its expanded variant at bar 51 the faun turns back to gaze at the lead nymph. As if welcoming his attention, she unclasps her dress, holds it before her, and then (to the clarinet up the octave) lets it fall. The other nymphs scatter, as the stage is set for the central encounter.

In fact, this famously odd *pas de deux* only begins after a last hesitation, for no sooner does the lead nymph find herself alone than she crouches, picks up the dress and makes to leave. But the faun strides across to block her escape, and as the winds launch the central D♭ tune their climactic confrontation begins. No doubt the static opening spans of their encounter proved particularly irritating to critics already impatient with the ballet's paucity of 'dancing'. Yet even in the schematic figural reversal by which Nijinsky marks this passage of exceptionally regular phraseology, there is clear evidence of sensitive timbral hearing.

After the initial stand-off, the four-bar wind phrase does not accompany pure stasis: at the high B♭ (the mid-point), the nymph begins lowering into a crouch that leaves her abased before him, with lowered head, by the phrase's end. Rising again through the darker-hued phrase at 59–62, briefly meeting his eyes and arching backwards, she inspires a burst of energy: he paws the ground and (in a small taste of 'dancing') scampers away for a coltish leap. After he turns to find that she has followed, they begin their reversed stand-off to the string-scored D♭ tune. The exact pitch repetition is far from the whole story here, for the new timbre brings a markedly changed interaction. Instead of crouching she now stands tall, holds his eyes and (in this version) coquettishly moves her head, as if riding the sensuous string music right into his answering gaze.

The climactic action that follows further illustrates refined choreographic hearing. This more dynamic phase of intimacy closely tracks the phrasal foreshortenings that carry the music's climax over into fading aftermath before it has attained anything like a satisfying arrival. Following on from the four-bar phrases, the couple marks the climactic reappearance of the undulating motive with two two-bar shuffles (he with reaching arms, her in stiff-armed rejection), first from left to right, then from right to left. As the brief *ff* flowering starts to fade, a further compression – to single bars, right to left, then left to right – shows him in a gentler, bent-elbowed invitation, before which she clutches her dress to her body. One last refinement ensues, as the climactic melody droops to its *pianissimo* close. Turning as if for yet another side-shuffle, the two stop, raise their arms, and at the midpoint of bar 73 (the off-beat of beat 2), sink into the elbow lock that will be their one brief moment of contact. Marking the endpoint of a telescoping phraseology extending all the way from 4+4 bars through 2+2 and 1+1 to ½ + ½, the gesture is timed to culminate all the motivic syncopations that have gone before – and which here return, retrospectively, as a horn recalls the undulating motive to accompany the farewell salute.

Stepping away, the faun holds his salute through the closing bars of the B section as the nymph pauses, turns and casually lets her dress fall before striding off. The end of the ballet, from the return of the flute arabesque (in a new transposition) to the end of the *Prélude*, now focuses on his developing relationship to this symbolic remainder. After fending off the nymphs' attempt to reclaim the dress, he kneels before it as the oboe takes over the arabesque. The connection between this pose and the long-prior prowl towards the grapes seems all the stronger given that he now raises up the dress to the same reedy sound that accompanied those first symbolic objects. But the fact that he already possesses this new object in bar 89 potentially undercuts any clear visual correlate to the last recall of the undulating motive.

Here, again, it is important to consider that sound, in this ballet, does not just mark visible gesture, but also infuses seen relationships with invisible affective energies. Indeed, after the first possession of the scarf inspires scampering laughter, the more formally weighty return of the flute solo on the original tritone, doubled and richly accompanied (bar 94), marks a more intimate phase in the faun's attention. Given that his gaze at the cradled garment has already gained more tenderness here, the high violin entry (bar 95) might seem to pass without clear response. But as that thin, retrospective sound settles into the plangent, augmented form of the undulating motive (bar 96), he lifts the dress closer, and then (to the repetition at bar 97) dips his face to inhale its scent.

If we first heard that timbre as the audible projection of desires thwarted by substitute objects of the gaze, it has now gained an association with a more animal – olfactory – sensuality. And the closing passages of the ballet, after the faun carries his symbolic prey back up to his rock, bring yet more bestial attainments. In the first, as the last oboe solo (bar 103) ties off a long thread of sensuous interplay, he mouths the garment as if to taste the flesh it once covered. In the second – the cause of much controversy at the premiere – he mounts it (bar 108, as the antique cymbal chimes) like a true sexual substitute for the body so recently pursued.

Critical Choices, Meta-Critical Reflections

To accept even my strongest proposals of congruency – for example, the parting 'veil of bodies' for the first undulating motive at bar 37 and the string-scored mutual gaze at bars 63–4 – requires a choice, of hearing and recognition, by other listeners and viewers. Some moments (such as the desirous flexion at bars 16–17) seem less cohesive at first hearing, but may invite us to imagine other realizations of the ballet and its music than this one. Others (the misplaced gaze at bar 47, and the loose interplay of sounds and sensuous acts from bar 94) will likely remain more problematic. Yet here, again, we can choose to consider such slippages between sound and visible gesture as signs of a deeper, more fluid interplay at a partly invisible layer of experience – an interplay whose recognition requires us to follow not only the often disjunctive relation between footsteps and rhythms, but also the shifting dynamic of feeling that embraces these bodies as they move within (and respond to) the flexibly affective sounds of Debussy's *Prélude*.

To confront the conscious choice needed to rehear the music as a richly affective, embracing and penetrating medium, rather than a near-abstract sonorous backdrop, can set up useful meta-critical reflections. Recall first Debussy's 1914 complaint about characters moving 'as if their schematic gestures were regulated by laws of pure geometry'. When looking back through the video, I note now how many of the faun's most 'schematic' gestures – from the open-handed indication of an empty landscape through the stiff- and bent-armed desirous imprecations to the hooked elbows and valedictory salute – are essentially communicative in nature, expressive of powerful urges for interaction with desirable 'Others' in this mythical world. Debussy, with defensive ears for his tone poem, had eyes only for the angular stylization, and not for the expressive intent. More bluntly: he saw only form, not content. And he thus distantly foreshadowed the very similar bias that was to relegate the poetic and sensuous interplay of timbres in his *Prélude* to a distinctly secondary (if not wholly inaudible) place across decades of formalist, pitch-based music analysis.

We might recall, here, Rose Rosengard Subotnik's challenge to the music-theoretical emphasis on 'structure' that has led to such pervasive and long-standing neglect of the more contingent and communicative aspects of music as sounding 'medium'.[47] But all musicological variants and heirs of that particular critique aside, in order to shift onto the interpretive terrain that seems most insistently summoned by Nijinsky's actual – physical, erotic and symbolic – 'medium', I will turn back in conclusion to the modern pastoral painting I introduced earlier, along with Flam's Mallarméan reading. In her more recent study of Matisse's *Le bonheur de vivre*, Werth, who follows Flam so far as to quote repeatedly from *L'après-midi d'un faune*, takes Mallarmé as but one central figure in what she calls the 'dialogic situation (cultural and social) that shaped the painting's production and reception'.[48] Her consideration of many other similarly themed 'Golden Age' paintings brings to light much imagery that could also be drawn into an iconographic background for the *Faune*. But the critical implications of her reading of *Le bonheur*, in particular, extend far beyond issues of iconography alone.

Consider, for example, her sense of the questions raised by the foreground piper whose recumbent pose so closely recalls the faun on his rock:

Is the indeterminateness of this figure meant to suggest Mallarmé's faun – by turns infantile and godlike? Is this a figure for the bisexuality common to erotic themes in classical literary pastoral? Or is it a fantasy of the erasure of sexual difference? Is he/she the origin of the apparent heterogeneity, the multiplication of figures of desire in the painting?[49]

Maybe the heterosexual pursuit that gives Nijinsky his rudimentary plot places his ballet at some remove from such sexual ambiguity. But as is well known, early response to his choreography was complicated by the *frissons* of real-life sexual ambivalence the famous author–dancer (and consort of Diaghilev) brought to the stage. We might thus follow Werth even further:

'His' sexual ambivalence, status as artist-musician, concentrated facial expression, and central position in the composition – lounging just below the outrageously and unmistakably gendered nymphs – make 'him' a cipher or blank space for the viewer's projection into the painting. But this very openness is unsettling.[50]

---

[47] See Ruth Rosengard Subotnik, 'Toward a Deconstruction of Structural Listening: A Critique of Schoenberg, Adorno, and Stravinsky', in her *Deconstructive Variations: Music and Reason in Western Society* (Minneapolis: University of Minnesota Press, 1996), 148–76.

[48] Margaret Werth, *The Joy of Life: The Idyllic in French Art, circa 1900* (Berkeley and Los Angeles: University of California Press, 2002), 150.

[49] Werth, *The Joy of Life*, 176.   [50] Werth, *The Joy of Life*, 176.

Reading these words after many attempts to capture the new kind of 'voyeurism' invited by this ballet, along with the alternative or parallel literature that has traced Nijinsky's historical status as homosexual icon, suggests new hermeneutic perspective on the oddly repetitive, repressive aspects of this ballet's ongoing critical reception.[51] No doubt the unsettling undercurrent of sexual ambivalence has shaped successive viewers' varying degrees of openness to self-projection into the sights and sounds of the *Faune*. Arguably, it has even triggered an interrelated set of defensive reactions: the excision from hearing of Debussy's most seductive sounds; the deflection of *all* hearing into musings on transcendent canonicity; the uncritical acceptance of Diaghilev's desperate reach for Cubism as a safely asexual realm of visual comparison.

The point can be pressed further with the help of Werth's comments on an even more unsettling episode in Matisse's pastoral. Turning to the embracing couple at right, she writes:

Matisse's lovers condense fantasies of intrauterine experience, maternal seduction, castration, and primal scene. All the primal fantasies of the origins of the body, sexuality, sexual difference, and subjectivity are brought together in one stunning pictorial incident.[52]

Here, as in her subsequent elaborations on the work's 'catalogue of infantile fantasies' and the like, Werth's reading moves decisively onto Freudian terrain. Perhaps Nijinsky's ballet, more visually decorous than Matisse's erotic pastoral, includes no single incident so powerfully redolent of 'primal fantasies' as this couple (though it is tempting to highlight the coincidental, sexualized role of a garment or veil in both). But given the *Faune's* patent play with gazes and desires, bodies and symbolic substitutions, it seems reasonable to wonder why the same hermeneutic realm has left so little mark on its scholarly reception.

While it is impractical, at this late stage, to pursue the question in any detail, it may suffice for now to let Freud guide one last meta-critical twist. Diaghilev's 'Cubist' gambit – an opportunistic defence against his own fears for the work – profited from a fortuitously exact coincidence of dates. Just as opportunistically, perhaps, I find my own analyses of *Prélude* and

---

[51] For the idea that the ballet's oblique treatment of sexuality turns its audience into 'voyeurs' of a new kind, see Jill Beck, 'Recalled to Life: Techniques and Perspectives on Reviving Nijinsky's Faune', in her edited special issue, 46–77, esp. 72–3. For a glimpse into the 'queer' reception (and its repression), which includes much useful bibliography, see Penny Farfan, 'Man as Beast: Nijinsky's Faun', *South Central Review* 25, no. 1 (2008), 74–92.

[52] Werth, *The Joy of Life*, 177.

ballet bring to mind a different historical coincidence. In 1912, the year Nijinsky's *Faune* came to the stage, Freud gave the short lecture 'A Note on the Unconscious in Psychoanalysis' to the Society for Psychical Research in London. When later revised for publication in 1915, the essay (now more simply titled 'The Unconscious') was to succinctly characterize the acts of 'repression' Freud had found fundamental to the forming of the unconscious realm, and thus central to the promise of nascent psychoanalysis:

> We know, too, that to suppress the development of affect is the true aim of repression and that its work is incomplete if this aim is not achieved. In every instance where repression has succeeded in inhibiting the development of affects, we term those affects (which we restore when we undo the work of repression) 'unconscious'.[53]

Might this other coincidence, from within the same, febrile pre-war context, lead us to ask afresh, from a proto- or quasi-psychoanalytical perspective, *why* it is that so many stories about the 'modernism' of Nijinsky's *Faune*, with their determined emphases on 'Cubist' schematicism and the like, repeatedly excise (or suppress) precisely the realm of affect, along with all of its ramifications for sexuality and subjectivity? Further, noting the importance of Freud's 1912 lecture not just to his theory of the unconscious but also his developing tripartite model of 'id', 'ego' and 'superego', might we look again at the modern methods of music theory also emerging during those same years – whose obsessive investment in normative pitch structures was effectively to guarantee later analytical repression of the more unruly timbral, rhythmic, motivic and affective flexions I have traced from Debussy's music into Nijinsky's gestures and gazes of desire?[54]

Here, finally, is a worthy goal for the most daring audiovisual analysis of dance, with eyes and ears as closely attuned to invisible or unconscious undercurrents as to overt and conscious gesture. While granting choreography its full power to help us *hear* familiar music afresh, such analysis can also serve to remind us, again and again: when we construct our versions of modernism, we are also constructing ourselves.

---

[53] Freud, 'The Unconscious', 178. (Wir wissen auch, daß die Unterdrückung der Affektenwicklung das eigentliche Ziel der Verdrängung ist, und daß deren Arbeit unabgeschlossen bleibt, wenn das Ziel nicht erreicht wird. In allen Fällen, wo der Verdrängung die Hemmung der Affektenwicklung gelingt, heißen wir dei Affekte, die wir im Redressement der Verdrängungsarbeit wieder einsetzen, 'unbewußte'. Sigmund Freud, *Gesammelte Werke*, vol. 10 (Frankfurt: Fischer, 1946), 277.)

[54] See the 'Editor's Note' to the 1912 lecture in Freud, *Complete Psychological Works*, ed. and trans. Strachey, vol. 12, 257–9; esp. 259. At risk of overdoing the opportunistic coincidences, I note that 1912 also saw the first publication of Heinrich Schenker's analysis of Beethoven's Ninth Symphony – a key early milestone in the development of his theoretical method.

9 | Choreographing Mahler Songs at the Centenary

WAYNE HEISLER JR

Beginning around 1960, choreographers of various stripes increasingly turned their attention to *Lieder* (songs for voice and piano or orchestra), a phenomenon that remains in the margins of both dance and music histories and gave rise to a genre that I term 'song-ballets'. Examples of three choreographers attest to the stylistic, geographical and musical heterogeneity of dances set to songs in the latter half of the twentieth century: Frederick Ashton, *Illuminations* (1950), to Benjamin Britten's cycle for either soprano or tenor with string orchestra; Rudi van Dantzig, *Vergezicht* (1960), to Robert Schumann's *Frauenliebe und Leben*, his *Vier letzte Lieder* (1970), to Richard Strauss's late orchestral songs,[1] and his *Antwoord gevend* (Giving Answer, 1980), to *Lieder*, instrumental and choral works by Anton Webern; and Robert Joffrey, *Remembrances* (1973), to Richard Wagner's *Wesendonck-Lieder*. Of course, diverse examples of dancing to texted (or text-associated) music predate twentieth-century ballet and modern dance, ranging from ancient and classical Greek drama through French baroque *opéra-ballet* and its progeny, from the *air parlant* of Romantic ballet to American Delsartism.[2] Clearly, choreographers' attraction to *Lieder* conforms to the larger twentieth-century drift towards setting music not originally intended for dance, widely cited as having been originated by American

---

I presented earlier versions of this chapter at the 18th Biennial Conference on Nineteenth-Century Music, University of Toronto, June 2014, and at the Annual Meeting of the American Musicological Society, Louisville, KY, November 2015. I am grateful to Carolyn Abbate, Davinia Caddy, Daniel Callahan, Maribeth Clark, Susan Cook, Matilda Butkas Ertz, Peter Franklin, Jeremy Frusco, Sarah Gutsche-Miller, Heather Hadlock, Marian Wilson Kimber, Nicole Koepke, Ryan Minor, Marian Smith and Laura Tunbridge for feedback and encouragement. Research and writing were made possible by Faculty Professional Development Funding and a Support of Scholarly Activities grant from the College of New Jersey between 2013 and 2015.

[1] Strauss's *Vier letzte Lieder* is the work most often set for song-ballets; see Wayne Heisler Jr, 'Reconciling the "Three Graceful Hellenic Sisters": Wagner, Dance, and "Song-Ballets" Set to Richard Strauss's *Vier letzte Lieder* (Four Last Songs)', in *The Total Work of Art: Foundations, Articulations, Inspirations*, ed. David Imhoof, Margaret Menninger and Anthony Steinhoff (New York: Berghahn Books, 2016), 133–56.

[2] The Ballets Russes reinterpreted *opéra-ballet* through a modernist lens in vocal-choreographic hybrids such as Igor Stravinsky and Leonide Massine's *Pulcinella*, and Stravinsky and Bronislava Nijinska's *Les noces*. For a discussion of American Delsartism, see Marian Wilson Kimber, this volume.

dancer and choreographer Isadora Duncan. In terms of the cohabitation of dance and sung music, the vogue for dancing to non-dance scores seems to have begun with Duncan, whose trailblazing concerts of barefoot dancing to Wagner's 'Liebestod' from *Tristan und Isolde* (1911) and the *Wesendonck-Lieder* (1922) for soprano and orchestra were forerunners of song-ballets in my account of the genre.[3]

As I have argued elsewhere, the British-American choreographer Antony Tudor established the immediate precedent for twentieth-century song-ballets. Tudor was pioneering in his setting of Romantic and early modern scores that had gone out of fashion with musical modernism in and around the World War II era. His choreography of vocal music by Mahler includes *Kindertotenlieder* for the ritualistic and mournful ballet *Dark Elegies* (1937), which was staged often in England and the United States in the late 1930s through the 1940s, and is still occasionally revived by American Ballet Theatre. Although it disappeared after its premiere, Tudor's choreography of Mahler's *Das Lied von der Erde* for the extravagant Eastern-tinged ballet *Shadow of the Wind* (1948) has lingered in dance history as something of an intrepid failure.[4] Subsequently, the twentieth-century trend of choreographing songs that is my focus here extended to numerous composers and choreographers. Supplementing those I surveyed at the outset, there is Maurice Béjart's setting of Wagner's *Wesendonck-Lieder* for the dance work *Mathilde* (1963), which was preceded by a companion romantic novel penned by the choreographer, as well as *Amor di Poeta* (1978) to Schumann's *Dichterliebe* cycle. Songs by Richard Strauss found particular favour with dancers internationally: in addition to the popularity of the *Vier letzte Lieder*, noted above, Eliot Feld choreographed a selection of fourteen Strauss *Lieder*, drawn freely from the composer's opuses 10, 17, 19, 21, 27, 29, 37 and 69 for the ballet *Early Songs* (1970), particularly noteworthy for its *pas de deux* experimentation in a neo-Romantic setting. One premise of the present chapter, however, is that Mahler emerged as the most prominent composer for song-ballets. Mahler's songs were set by an array of choreographers, including Kenneth MacMillan's mammoth *Song of the Earth* (1965), Feld's pained *At Midnight* (1967) to the *Rückert-Lieder*, and Béjart's intimate, searching *Le Chant du compagnon errant* (1971),

---

[3] On Duncan's dances to Wagner, see Mary Simonson, *Body Knowledge: Performance, Intermediality, and American Entertainment at the Turn of the Twentieth Century* (Oxford: Oxford University Press, 2013), esp. 95 and 101–3.

[4] On Tudor's Mahler song-ballets, see Judith Chazin-Bennahum, *The Ballets of Antony Tudor: Studies in Psyche and Satire* (Oxford: Oxford University Press, 1994); Elizabeth Sawyer, 'Antony Tudor's Lost Ballets', *Dance Chronicle* 31 (2008), 6–53; and Wayne Heisler Jr, 'Antony Tudor's *Dark Elegies* and the Affirmation of Mahler's Body, 1937–1947', *Dance Chronicle* 36 (2013), 172–95.

as well as Pina Bausch's early experimental *Fritz* (1974) to a compilation score that includes Mahler songs, and her *Adagio–Five Songs by Gustav Mahler* (1974) to both the fourth movement of Symphony No. 5 and the *Kindertotenlieder*. Mahler's feted anniversaries around 1960 – his birth centenary, as well as his 1961 death semicentennial – were by my reckoning a catalyst for the proliferation of Mahler song-ballets and, furthermore, for the late twentieth and early twenty-first century normalization of song choreography.

Choreographies of songs solicit practical and aesthetic concerns common to musicology and dance studies: about reception, involving the repurposing of musical 'works' in unconventional, discursively rich and uniquely embodied contexts; and, relatedly, about performance practice, including piano arrangements of orchestral songs, live versus canned accompaniment, and the placement of instrumentalists and singers – in the pit or onstage, and thus in non-diegetic or diegetic spheres. From the musicological side of the house, song-ballets are sometimes triggers for *Werktreue*-steeped reactions of the 'What would Mahler say?'-variety that dance and performance studies have been wise to obviate: although obviously not conceived for choreography, Mahler's scores have been danced, passionately and often – and that matters. Another interest shared by musicology and dance studies is canonicity, a concept that is complicated when, for instance, Mahler's relatively canonical *Das Lied von der Erde* is set for Tudor's *Shadow of the Wind*, a sub-canonical ballet at best. And one last, but certainly not least, preoccupation of dance and music scholars alike is interrelationships between the arts. Which component(s) of the music–dance–poetry nexus holds sway? Can they, should they, be integrated? There is an antipathy to representation, and by extension language, in mid-twentieth-century dance that overlaps with high modern aesthetics in music and visual art during the period that I am tracing, in which choreographies of texted music emerged against the grain.

A bookend selection from dance criticism serves to illustrate the last point. Reviewing an evening of 'Ballet Ballads' – a dance-play, really – by New York's Experimental Theater in January 1949, Walter Terry made a case for the potential of 'relating dance to text and music alike' in relation to this production of theatrical scenes with lyrics by John LaTouche (adapting the biblical 'Susanna and the Elders', the folk tune 'Willie the Weeper' and 'The Eccentricities of Davey Crockett'), music by Jerome Moross and choreography by Hanya Holm, Katherine Litz and Paul Godkin. Terry was on the defensive in his consideration of the 'Ballet Ballads' as a 'synthesis of music, dance [and] dramatic text', and as 'an engrossing experiment in the application of three different but not inimical artistic truths' given contemporary sensitivity to the 'uneasy relationships among dance, text and music'.[5] Fast forward a generation to summer 1975. Rose Anne Thom praised an Alvin Ailey City Center Dance Theater performance of Donald McKayle's *Rainbow 'Round My Shoulder* (1959), about a prison's chain gang workers in the American South, set to traditional music arranged from the John and Alan Lomax collection. According to Thom, *Rainbow* offered integration of music, lyrics and dance, albeit with 'dancing [at] the center ... the songs serv[ing] the dance, combining them to enhance it', in what was an appropriation of the Wagnerian *Gesamtkunstwerk*, albeit with dance reclaiming the spotlight it was denied by Wagner (see Thomas Grey in this volume). For in the Ailey repertory, Thom reflected, choreography too often 'depend[s] on the lyrics and melody of the accompanying songs for ... power and motivation ... The dance becomes the accompaniment' as opposed to 'solidly constructed abstract modern dance work'.[6] Such suspicion towards mimesis, and pantomime particularly, had been and remained the central pitfall of aligning dance with language, from the Symbolists (for whom dance 'said' more than language ever could) through the high modernists.[7] Here, however, I want to think more positively in the margins, to consider how the potential snare of words, and also the allure of the voices that sing them, tendered productive challenges.

In addition to the tensions sparked by the partnering of dance and language, choreographies of Mahler songs confronted stakes related to the composer's legacy specifically. Mahler once proclaimed that 'vom Tanz geht alle Musik aus' (all music proceeds from dance).[8] Still, as will become clear over the course of this chapter, his was an uphill battle to the ballet just as it had been to the concert hall. The reception of Mahler's music from the late nineteenth through twentieth centuries is obviously complicated. In his own lifetime (1860–1911), Mahler was recognized far more as a conductor-composer than a composer who also conducted, such as his contemporary Richard Strauss. Following Mahler's premature death in 1911, there was a burst of commemorations, including performances of Mahler symphonic cycles globally.[9] These, however, petered out by the 1920s, when composer-Mahler became widely clichéd

---

[5] Walter Terry, '"Ballet Ballads" Is a Synthesis of Music, Dance, and Dramatic Text', *New York Herald Tribune*, 9 January 1949.

[6] Rose Anne Thom, 'Accompanying the Song', *Dance Magazine*, November 1975, 30–1, 71–2, at 30 and 71.

[7] See, e.g., Joan Acocella, *Mark Morris* (New York: Farrar, Strauss and Giroux, 1993), 156–8.

[8] Quoted by Natalie Bauer-Lechner, *Recollections of Gustav Mahler*, trans. Dika Newlin, ed. Peter Franklin (London: Faber Music, 1980), 158.

[9] This period of Mahler reception is surveyed in Heisler, 'Antony Tudor's *Dark Elegies*', among other places.

as a bloated, unfashionable Romantic vis-à-vis Schoenbergian dodecaphony on the one hand, and Stravinskian Neoclassicism on the other.[10] Given that Mahler was Jewish, his obscurity was systematized by the Third Reich. Thereafter, artists and intellectuals, especially of the Jewish diaspora, championed composer-Mahler and his music in the wake of World War II, in what emerged as two strands of Mahler reception. As historian Adam J. Sacks summarizes, the contrast is between Mahler's 'modernist and mediated reading of the classical music tradition' (à la philosopher Theodor W. Adorno) versus the 'Zen-like suffering, spiritually transcendent, purely subjective, consoling, and therapeutic' composer (composer-conductor Leonard Bernstein's Mahler, most prominently).[11]

Returning to song-ballets: what accounts for the exceptions to dance's disquiet in the face of lexicality – for the choreographers, dancers, critics and audiences who believed that music, language and movement might result in a persuasive fusion and/or attractive counterpoint? And why was Mahler's music so often chosen as ideal? For some choreographers, one point of attraction to Mahler's music was its pervasive 'songfulness' in compositions with or without words, as explored across his oeuvre by musicologist Julian Johnson.[12] In the context of Mahler's centenary-era resurrection(s), 'songfulness' (as opposed to naïve programmatic Romanticism) was part and parcel of a bittersweet and thus healthy, modern posture that fell in line with Adorno's assessment of the composer.[13] Moreover, from the vantage point of dancers, the fact that Mahler's music carried with it bodily associations – positive in terms of his above-quoted declaration that 'all music proceeds from dance', but often negative in terms of aesthetics and cultural politics – was cause for special choreographic meditation. Nineteenth-century theories about music, gesture and the body have long affected understandings of Mahler; this legacy is reflected in the affirmative ways that gesture has been used more recently as an analytical and interpretive avenue to investigate Mahler's supposed intentions and their consequences for musical

---

[10] Theodor W. Adorno first painted this context and argued for Mahler as an unrecognized exponent of modernism in 'Mahler Today', included in Adorno, *Essays on Music*, ed. Richard Leppert, trans. Susan H. Gillespie (Berkeley and Los Angeles: University of California Press, 2002), 603–11.

[11] Adam J. Sacks, 'Toward an Expansion of the Critique of the Mahler Revival', *New German Critique* 119 (2013), 113–36, at 113 and 119.

[12] Julian Johnson, *Mahler's Voices: Expression and Irony in the Songs and Symphonies* (Oxford: Oxford University Press, 2009).

[13] Adorno's study *Mahler: Eine musikalische Physiognomik* (Frankfurt am Main: Suhrkamp, 1960) is contemporary with centenary-era Mahler song-ballets, although there is no evidence that Adorno had a direct effect on the choreographers and dancers discussed here.

meaning.[14] From the late nineteenth to mid-twentieth centuries, however, the fascination with gesture in Mahler's music was decisively negative, including well-known debates concerning Mahler and the 'bodily' in nationalist-racialized tracts. Gesticulating, jumping, convulsive, theatrical: musicologist Karen Painter traced such body-related terms to demonstrate how critics and audiences from the *fin de siècle* and beyond explained (away) the timbral and formal behaviours of Mahler's music.[15] These physical analogies drew on anti-Semitic discourses, in which, as cultural historian Sander Gilman and musicologist K. M. Knittel documented, physicality was an important superficial marker of differences in 'body, mind, and essence'.[16] Mahler song-ballets, then, place the composer front and centre again in fixations on the body and its relationship to music and speech/language, but now in a post–World War II aesthetic-political environment that revalued the historical debasement of Mahler's bodily affinities. Put another way: through song-ballets, dance and music were finally assimilated *to* Mahler's body.

In the remainder of this chapter, I investigate the ways in which choreographers and dancers participated in Mahler's centenary renaissance. In terms of dance-musicology, song-ballets enrich the experience of today's well-known music through less familiar dance performances – some aesthetically successful and some not entirely so, but all nevertheless diversifying the centenary Romantic-Modern Mahler binary. Although much attention has been paid to the deluge of Mahler performances and recordings, as well as heightened scholarly and critical consideration in the 1960s and 1970s, dance remains a wallflower in Mahler studies, and vice versa. Relying primarily on film and video footage as well as dance criticism, I explore the aforementioned Mahler song-ballets by Feld, Béjart and MacMillan, all conceived in the latter half of the centenary decade, followed by a final, brief pass through Bausch. Bausch's early choreographies of Mahler simultaneously mark the end of centenary fever and the beginning of a contemporary dance era in which embodied music was not shamed, and in which the distinction between instrumental and vocal music became moot – as it had been for Mahler all along.

---

[14] The literature on Mahler and gesture is extensive; one recent starting point is Seth Monahan, *Mahler's Symphonic Sonatas* (Oxford: Oxford University Press, 2015), 78–80.

[15] Karen Painter, 'The Sensuality of Timbre: Responses to Mahler and Modernity at the "Fin de siècle"', *19th-Century Music* 18 (1995), 236–56; Karen Painter, *Symphonic Aspirations: German Music and Politics, 1900–1945* (Cambridge, MA: Harvard University Press, 2007), esp. 33–43.

[16] K. M. Knittel, *Seeing Mahler: Music and the Language of Antisemitism in Fin-de-Siècle Vienna* (Burlington, VT: Ashgate, 2010), 14. See also K. M. Knittel, '"Ein hypermoderner Dirigent": Mahler and Anti-Semitism in *Fin-de-Siècle* Vienna', *19th-Century Music* 18 (1995), 257–76, and Sander Gilman, *The Jew's Body* (New York: Routledge, 1991).

'I live alone in my own heaven / In my love, in my song!' (Friedrich Rückert)

Eliot Feld's *At Midnight* was premiered by American Ballet Theatre at the New York State Theatre on 1 December 1967 with baritone William Metcalf singing in the pit and a live orchestra under conductor Kenneth Schermerhorn. Feld set *At Midnight* to an idiosyncratic ordering of four of Mahler's *Rückert-Lieder*: 'Um Mitternacht' ('At Midnight'), 'Ich atmet' einen linden Duft' ('I Breathed a Gentle Fragrance'), 'Blicke mir nicht in die Lieder' ('Do Not Look at Me through My Songs') and 'Ich bin der Welt abhanden gekommen' ('I've Gotten Lost to the World'), followed by a reprised 'Ich atmet' einen linden Duft'. (This order is idiosyncratic to the extent that Mahler's non-cycle is ever ordered conventionally, as I will discuss below.) Technically and thematically, *At Midnight* engages late twentieth-century Mahler paragons. Feld's choreographic style is rooted in ballet classicism, but developed in reference to the vocabulary of modern dance,[17] which is analogous to perceptions of Mahler's scores as alluding to classical genres, forms and gestures through a modern lens. And while *At Midnight* does not have a linear plot, it is also not conceived as abstract dance: it is a thematic ballet showcasing a central male, shown downstage centre in Figure 9.1 as danced by Lawrence Rhodes. He is 'a lonely boy', in the words of critic Robb Baker, 'yearning for ... softness and roundness and warmth'.[18] Could this boy be a stand-in for Mahler? He certainly corresponds to one clichéd view of the composer as an alienated sufferer, a martyr even – a romantic aura that continued to gain traction in his centenary period. Indeed, several commentators interpreted Feld's lonely boy specifically as 'Christ-like',[19] a semblance that is suggested several times in the ballet when the group of dancers (behind the boy in Figure 9.1) lifts him to a crucifixion pose, and that Ken Russell would soon exploit ironically in his biopic *Mahler* (1974). Even closer to home, Feld's boy suggested to some a struggling artist. For instance, Doris Hering articulated the central theme of Feld's *At Midnight* as 'the hope that the solitude of the artist and the fulfillment of love can exist side by side'.[20]

---

[17] Marcia B. Siegel, *The Shapes of Change: Images of American Dance* (Boston: Houghton Mifflin, 1979), 343–4.
[18] Robb Baker, 'Spotlight on Daniel Levins', *Dance Magazine*, October 1973, 59–62, at 60.
[19] Clive Barnes, 'Twentieth Century Accent', *Dance and Dancers*, April 1968, 23–7, at 24; Baker, 'Spotlight on Daniel Levins', 60.
[20] Doris Hering, '"Pulse of Anguish ... Loving Hand": Eliot Feld's "At Midnight" Was Premiered in Triumph During American Ballet Theatre's Fall Season', *Dance Magazine*, January 1968, 52–3, at 52.

Figure 9.1 Lawrence Rhodes as the 'lonely boy' in Eliot Feld's *At Midnight*; photo by Martha Swope

The musical introduction to said solitude is Mahler's song 'Um Mitternacht', with which Feld's ballet begins.[21] Laying atop a mass of

---

[21] My discussion of choreo-musical details in Feld's *At Midnight* relies heavily on a dress rehearsal filmed in both wide shot and close up on 4 July 1974 at New York's Newman Theater. New York Public Library for the Performing Arts (call number MGZIDF 5871). A Benesh score of *At Midnight* is housed at the Royal Opera House in Stockholm; this and further references to Benesh scores can be found in Irmgard E. Berry, comp. and ed., *Benesh Movement Notation Score Catalogue: An International Listing to Benesh Movement Notation Scores of Professional Dance Works Recorded 1955–1985* (London: Benesh Institute of Choreology, 1986).

four male dancers, the lonely boy stretches as if awakening, whether from sleep or, metaphorically, to a realization, and tumbles to the floor. The choreography seems inspired not only by the text's beginning – 'Um Mitternacht / Hab' ich gewacht / Und aufgeblickt zum Himmel' ('At midnight / I woke / and looked up to heaven') – but also by the vocal line, which opens up to just shy of an octave range and then closes over the course of the first stanza. In other words, the choreography might be taking textual or musical cues, or both. By the stanza's end, the lonely boy masks his face with his hands before collapsing into the group. Throughout 'Um Mitternacht', he has a conflicted relationship with those around him: he articulates his individuality with an occasional jumping jack-like movement, corresponding to recurring statements of the song's head clarinet motive, but intermittently partners with a porter (à la a prima ballerina), retreats to, is lifted or masked by the group's mass of hands. Then he breaks away yet again. After being raised momentarily as if in crucifixion (again, 'Christ-like'), the boy is alone on the stage for the first time – 'Um Mitternacht / Hab' ich die Macht / In deine Hand gegeben! / Herr!' ('At midnight / I gave the power / Into your Hand! / Lord!') – only to be carried off stage as he curls back into sleep to the song's apotheosis.

Feld's choice to begin *At Midnight* with this titular song is remarkable. For in as many variations in song order that occur in publications, live performances and recordings of the *Rückert-Lieder*, it is rare to encounter 'Um Mitternacht' opening the set. This includes the five songs now commonly grouped as the *Rückert-Lieder*, as well as the collection of seven songs that includes *Des Knaben Wunderhorn* texts 'Revelge' ('Reveille') and 'Der Tamboursg'sell' ('The Drummer Boy'), originally published in 1910 as *Sieben Lieder aus letzter Zeit*.[22] Rearrangement on some level, including song re-ordering, is sometimes deemed necessary in song-ballets, in which the chosen songs are melded to the choreographic, narrative and/or thematic vision; that is, dance logic might take priority over compositional genesis, authorial intention, musical structure, original publication and/or performance conventions. Attributing manipulations of instrumentation or song order to ambivalence to musical works and their creators is misleading, though, since all the choreographers under consideration here seem to have cared deeply about the music they chose, and especially

---

[22] A survey of recordings on WorldCat shows that if any of Mahler's Rückert songs can claim priority in performance order, it is 'Ich atmet' einen linden Duft', the second he composed though it appeared first in the *Sieben Lieder aus letzter Zeit*. Feld jettisoned Mahler's song 'Liebst du um Schönheit' ('If You Love For Beauty'), which, as is well known, was something of an outsider to the *Rückert-Lieder* having been composed last and orchestrated by Max Puttmann.

about Mahler. In these cases, tinkering is indicative of a thoughtful musical investment, albeit on bodily terms.

Indeed, Feld's ordering of the *Rückert-Lieder* inflects meaning within and between songs, forging a cyclical logic that intimates the choreographer's empathy with the composer – Feld's identification with centenary-era Mahler ideals. Following 'Um Mitternacht' comes 'Ich atmet' einen linden Duft', Feld's most romantically optimistic tableau in *At Midnight*, a tender and flirtatious *pas de deux* between two in love, shown in Figure 9.2 as danced by Christine Sarry and John Sowinski. Feld mines the style and vocabulary of a Romantic *pas de deux* to exhibit its markers of the intimacy that eludes the lonely boy and haunts him at night. The man in 'Ich atmet' einen linden Duft' is a faithful porter who supports his partner en pointe and in lifts. He is also a co-dancer, and the ballerina is relatively independent; they are equals, if different, and their *pas de deux* is characteristic of a late twentieth-century gender sensibility. Feld's choreography of 'Ich atmet' einen linden Duft' is thus sympathetic to an Adornian hearing of Mahler's music as refracting the past (here a Romantic *pas de deux*) through the present (modern gender parity). The couple gaze into each other's eyes, culminating in a lift that ends in a profound moment of stasis before he carries her off stage.

This *pas de deux* sets the scene for 'Blicke mir nicht in die Lieder', an exploration through solos and groups of the relationship between the lonely boy and those around him, including the idealized *pas de deux* couple whose bond is beyond his reach. Like the inaugural 'Um Mitternacht', Feld's 'Blicke mir nicht in die Lieder' begins with the spotlight on the lonely boy, who is physically separated from the duos and trios as they enter, exit and overlap with increased frequency. Again, Feld's *At Midnight* is not a straightforward narrative ballet starring an individual who is unlucky in love. He is, rather, a symbol of one's inability to forge authentic, fulfilling relationships on both personal and societal levels, of being uncomfortable in one's skin and somewhat out of place and time – not unlike the widespread perception of Mahler in the centenary imagination.

What one might therefore characterize as the boy's 'Mahlerian condition' is further foregrounded by his counterpart, the lone woman introduced in 'Ich bin der Welt abhanden gekommen', the song that conventionally ends performances of Mahler's *Rückert-Lieder*.[23] Again, Feld tampered with song order, although not at the expense of Mahler's

---

[23] This conclusion is supported by a survey of recordings on WorldCat. See n. 22.

Figure 9.2 Christine Sarry and John Sowinski's *pas de deux* in Feld's *At Midnight*; photo by Martha Swope

spirit. While 'Ich bin der Welt abhanden gekommen' is not the ultimate conclusion of *At Midnight*, it accompanies the ballet's symbolic climax. In addition to the lone woman, Feld's choreography of this song features the female–male *pas de deux* couple introduced in 'Ich atmet' einen linden Duft'. However, 'Ich bin der Welt abhanden gekommen' is not a *pas de trois*, but rather a simultaneous yet detached female solo and female–male *pas de deux*, respectively: two *pas* in the same visual and musical frame. At the beginning the couple is placed downstage right, variably standing, sitting, facing each other, clasping hands, looking upwards, downwards, at and through each other. The lone woman starts upstage right, as forlorn as the solo English horn that issues the opening melody. She commences dancing before the entrance of the voice, but when the singer enters, her isolated body and the lyric are appropriately aligned: 'I am lost to the world.' The couple's *pas de deux* is barely even a *pas*, in that they move in fits and starts, often glacially with almost imperceptible movements. In contrast, the solo woman, as described by critic Marcia Siegel, 'prob[es] [space] . . . scooping up and spilling out great armfuls of it, wrenching into the air behind her with her elbows . . . It's not the pain on her face, but her restlessness and inability to hold onto anything solid that makes her a sympathetic figure against the calm fixity of the couple.'[24] The lone woman and the couple co-exist in a fallaciously fantastic mirror relationship to one another: the couple reflects the woman as she aches to be, or perhaps once was. More cynically, the lone woman might be viewed as an augury of what the couple will inevitably become.

One compelling aspect of Feld's 'Ich bin der Welt abhanden gekommen' is the ostensible mismatch in biological sex between the solo woman and the singer: again, in Feld's *At Midnight*, the *Rückert-Lieder* are performed by a baritone. The gender disparity in dances such as 'Ich bin der Welt abhanden gekommen' with its prominent solo female in 'duet' with a male voice points to the ventriloquist quality that musicologist Jelena Novak highlights in 'postopera', and which is applicable to moments across the song-ballet repertory. Sometimes the sex (or perceived sex) of the voice is in apparent accord with the body. At other times, the (apparent) mismatches serve to draw attention away from the mimetic body to the vocalic body – the voice–body exchange, the ways in which the body and voice (not linguistic content) perform each other, foregrounding their deep relationships through gender play.[25] In the context of a centenary-era portrait of Mahler as heroically alienated (for adherents to an Adorno as well as to a Bernstein), this lone woman might seem to be unfashionably maudlin. Beyond surfaces, though, the intense expressiveness of Feld's choreography

---

[24] Marcia Siegel, 'Feld Re-fielded', *Dance Magazine*, March 1974, 63. Via YouTube, readers can access an excerpt of 'Ich bin der Welt abhanden gekommen' with Elizabeth Lee dancing the lone woman and glimpses of the *pas de deux* couple, from a documentary about Feld's American Ballet Company at the 1968 Spoleto Festival, where they performed *At Midnight*: www.youtube.com/watch?v=NBAI1ZskER0. (The excerpt runs from 10:08 to 11:57 in the documentary.) Silent 8 mm film footage of moments from Elizabeth Lee rehearsing the same dance, with the couple in occasional view, survives from a 1969 shoot at Bavarian Film Studios; it can also be accessed via YouTube: www.youtube.com/watch?v=2ZhErdoj658.

[25] See Jelena Novak, *Postopera: Reinventing the Voice-Body* (Burlington, VT: Ashgate, 2015).

and the dancing digs down to Mahler's conflicted Romantic roots: neither Mahler, nor Feld, nor the lonely boy, nor the lone woman, nor the couple is inclined to represent mere love or even unrequited love, but rather the struggle to find a love so impassioned that it never could be requited.

Digging is a job for hands, *At Midnight*'s focal symbol for dynamic corporeality. As illustrated by Figure 9.1 above, hands stretch, clutch, release, search, beg, haunt. Even the couple in 'Ich bin der Welt abhanden gekommen', moving in slow motion, magnifies physicality rather than negates it. 'The man lifts the woman into the air and she stays there', reflected Siegel, 'kneeling motionless in the crook of his arms, while the solitary woman dances an eternity of questions'.[26] They are not answerable in any single way, but the act of questioning colours *At Midnight*'s ultimate section, set to 'Ich atmet' einen linden Duft'. This musical reprise is structured around duo after duo entering, mixing, accumulating and exiting with each line of poetry, and supports dance and theatre critic Clive Barnes's portrayal of Feld's *At Midnight* as 'headily [and] youthfully romantic'. 'There was a sort of tear-stained quality', Barnes continued, 'that, in its exaggerated nostalgia, precisely matched the Mahler'.[27] It is illuminating to compare Barnes's romantic reading of *At Midnight* – and Mahler – in 1968 with his interpretation of Feld's *Early Songs* two years later (again, set to a selection of Richard Strauss *Lieder*). In relation to the latter ballet, Barnes, not generally a sentimentalist, proclaimed that, 'Yes, Romanticism is back', describing *Early Songs* as 'a most beautiful piece ... [with] tearful elegance'. Barnes focused on this ballet's succession of *pas de deux* as 'an attempt to extend the range of partnering ... [which is] perhaps one of the attractions that Romantic piano music and *Lieder* – their very intimacy and intonations of rapture – hold out to the modern choreographer ... Nostalgia is never far from Mr. Feld's purpose, but his first interest is in a kind of rapturous carelessness.'[28] Returning to *At Midnight*, as long as the gentle fragrance lingers, faith in the possibility of love can endure, too. At the ballet's end, the lonely boy and lone woman are positioned diagonally at opposite corners of the stage (he downstage left, she upstage right) to the final strains of 'Ich atmet' einen linden Duft'. The requited *Lindenduft* couple poses between them, centre stage, occupying the borderland between past and future, love and loss, reality and dream. This is the same margin that Mahler has often been imagined to inhabit, and which aroused that lonely boy's centenary resurrection.

---

[26] Siegel, *The Shapes of Change*, 347.   [27] Barnes, 'Twentieth Century Accent', 23–4.
[28] Clive Barnes, 'Dance: Feld's New Work', *New York Times*, 4 April 1970.

'My companions are love and sorrow!' (Gustav Mahler)

While *At Midnight* hints that Feld felt a kinship with Mahler, Maurice Béjart was an overt Mahlerian. Béjart gravitated to Mahler at several points in his choreographic career: *Le Chant du compagnon errant* (*Song of a Wayfarer*, 1971), set to Mahler's *Lieder eines fahrenden Gesellen*; *Ce que l'amour me dit* (*What Love Tells Me*, 1974), set to movements four to six of Mahler's Symphony No. 3;[29] and the pointedly titled *Mahler* (1978), set to another compilation of the *Rückert-Lieder*. Of Béjart's various Mahler choreographies, my focus here is on *Le Chant du compagnon errant* because of its proximity to the centenary decade and to Mahler song-ballets by Feld and MacMillan.

Over the course of *Le Chant*'s performance history, the orchestra and singer (variably live or canned) that have accompanied Béjart's choreography have changed. One iteration of *Le Chant*'s music is a 1971 EMI LP release of Mahler's *Gesellen* songs featuring Dietrich Fischer-Dieskau with the Philharmonia Orchestra under Furtwängler (originally recorded in 1952) and billed as 'Musique originale du Ballet de Maurice Béjart' in the wake of *Le Chant*'s continental popularity.[30] Unlike Feld's re-ordered *At Midnight* or Béjart's choreography of part of Mahler's Symphony No. 3 for *Ce que l'amour me dit*, Béjart did not tamper with Mahler's *Gesellen* cycle for *Le Chant*; and, unlike the *Rückert-Lieder*, Mahler had conceived *Lieder eines fahrenden Gesellen* as a cycle. In *Le Chant*, Béjart exhibits a reverence for Mahler that befits the centenary period, handling the *Gesellen* score and poems with kid gloves, including song order. As I will show, while Béjart responds to the song texts and musico-poetic nexus that is traditionally the focus of Lieder analyses, he also draws movement symbolically from the poems and score, as well as, more tellingly, the ebb and flow of 'voice', both vocal and instrumental.

Dance critic John Percival reported that at the 1971 premiere of *Le Chant* by Béjart's Ballet of the Twentieth Century at Brussels' Forest National Arena, 'three huge banners [hang] with giant portraits of the

---

[29] Béjart's *Ce que l'amour me dit* barely preceded John Neumeier's *Third Symphony of Gustav Mahler* (1975), which is set to the entire score, as were Neumeier's subsequent choreographies of Mahler symphonies 4 (1977), 1 (1980), 6 (1984), 5 (1989), 9 (1994) and 10 (2011), as well as the *Rückert-Lieder* (1976) and *Des Knaben Wunderhorn* (1989). Neumeier's most recent Mahler project is *Das Lied von der Erde* (2015).

[30] The LP's cover image can be found at Discogs (www.discogs.com/Gustav-Mahler-Richard-Strauss-Elisabeth-SchwarzkopfPhilharmonia-Orchestra-Wilhelm-Furtwaengler-Otto-/release/2439072). Side two of the album features Strauss's *Vier letzte Lieder*, which Béjart set for his *Serait-ce la mort?* (1970).

evening's composers: Bach, Mahler and Stravinsky. These accentuate the feeling that the occasion has an atmosphere ... like the stirring shared purpose of a political rally'.[31] (The other works were *Choreographic Offering* set to J. S. Bach's *Musical Offering* and Béjart's popular *Rite of Spring*.) Feld's use of Mahler for *At Midnight* can be interpreted as implicitly political in light of the choreographer's self-fashioning as a maverick: 'You felt the great force of his will on the work', as Siegel explained, 'more than you felt his dedication to a tradition.'[32] Siegel's characterization resonates with Feld's then-still-novel (1967) choice of choreographing Mahler songs, and also aligns the choreographer with the centenary Mahler, who was championed by all camps as a composer who was ahead of his time. In contrast, Béjart's choreographic and theatrical work was almost always explicitly political on topical and socio-cultural levels, including the sexual revolution of the 1960s and 1970s. His Mahler ballets were no exception.

Simultaneously responding to and participating in the contemporary Mahlerian countercultural vibe, Béjart set *Le Chant* for two male dancers as an extended *pas de deux*. Shown on the aforementioned 'Musique originale du Ballet de Maurice Béjart' LP cover, for instance, are the youthful and infamously liberated celebrity-dancer Rudolph Nureyev along with Paolo Bortoluzzi, on whom Béjart choreographed *Le Chant*'s roles. Superficially, *Le Chant* appeared to be a same-sex construal of Mahler's lovelorn poems, an interpretation broached by numerous critics. For his part, dance critic Jack Anderson queried rhetorically, 'What is a homosexual ballet?' in defence of Béjart's *Le Chant*.[33] Anderson continued: 'While its two men could conceivably be lovers, its situations may also be interpreted as a man's struggle with a spirit or guardian angel, as an artist's or philosopher's grappling with a new concept' – as we have seen, the figure of an artist was also intuited from Feld's *At Midnight* – 'or even ... as a coming to terms with the inevitably with death. This multiplicity of connotations implies that the ballet is to be interpreted in symbolic, rather than literal, terms.'[34] In addition to advocating for more universal implications of Béjart's choreography (and, by association, Mahler's songs), Anderson's challenge to fellow critics witnesses the anxiety surrounding literalism that

---

[31] John Percival, 'Nureyev – Rites for the Traveller', *Dance and Dancers*, May 1971, 28–31, at 28.
[32] Siegel, 'Feld Re-fielded', 63.
[33] Jack Anderson, 'Rudolf and Laura', *Dance Magazine*, June 1977, 33, 35, 70 and 72, at 35. See also Percival, 'Nureyev – Rites for the Traveller', 30.
[34] Anderson, 'Rudolf and Laura', 70. See also Helmut Scheier, 'Von einem Rest Mysterium Gefangen (Béjart-Abend)', *Das Tanzarchiv*, April 1979, 194–7, esp. 194.

has often been triggered by choreographies of texted and sung music, as well as, ironically, the knee-jerk gravitation towards despised literalism.

In the opening song, 'Wenn mein Schatz Hochzeit macht' ('When My Sweetheart is Married'), the first man commences dancing with the entry of the singing voice, stretching and spreading, reaching up and out, lowering, tracing the phrasing, durations, dynamics and attack of the voice as if his body were a seismograph for vocality.[35] This reveals another, albeit varied, instance of choreographed songs as a kind of ventriloquism: Béjart's male–male *pas de deux* was set to Mahler's *Gesellen-Lieder* as performed by a baritone, as is most common for the cycle, and thus is distinct from the gender juxtaposition between male singer and female dancer in Feld's *At Midnight*. The ventriloquism here is concentrated generally on voice–body transference more so than on what the voice is singing, thus showing again that the feared lexicality of language in relationship to movement can be a red herring. Movement motives occasionally repeat in coordination with repeated text ('Hochzeit macht' in stanza one, from first position *port de bras* to high sideways *tendu* to a second position *grand-plié*); but the choreography also coordinates with strophic melody (the first two lines of stanzas one and three). All the while, the second man remains still, standing centre stage facing the audience. He is, though, being *moved upon*: eyes open, but not watching the dance, he is a bodily-being-through-listening, to the voices that are visibly and kinesthetically manifested through dancing. Only to punctuate the cadence at the end of the first stanza does the second man move, in two shifts in unison with the first man that reposition them with their backs to the audience. While the first man re-enters the dance, the second remains facing away and still for the entire second stanza of 'Wenn mein Schatz Hochzeit macht', turning to face the audience once more only upon the stanza's half-cadence.

Hardly an independent being, the second man is inseparable from the first.[36] As articulated by various commentators, he is the 'inner self',[37] 'the

---

[35] My discussion of choreo-musical details in Béjart's *Le Chant* relies on a video recording probably made during the Wiener Ballettwochen in March 1980, with Nureyev and Michael Birkmeyer dancing the two roles. This VHS recording is housed at the New York Public Library for the Performing Arts (call number MGZIA 4-4232). I also relied on a 1988 staging of Béjart's *Le Chant* by the Australian Ballet featuring dancers Steven Heathcote and Adam Marchant. While this video is no longer available, excerpts from various stagings can be found by searching YouTube. A Benesh score of *Le Chant* is housed at the Royal Opera House in Stockholm.

[36] Hartmut Regitz, 'Premieren und Ballettwoche in Stuttgart', *Das Tanzarchiv*, June 1976, 206–9, esp. 208.

[37] Noel Gillespie, 'Perspectives: Washington, D.C.', *Dance Magazine*, November 1975, 78–80, at 79.

embodiment of ... hopes and fears',[38] perhaps even this individual's 'destiny'.[39] Put another way, the second man is a double, and together, the two men form a whole. In the third stanza of Béjart's 'Wenn mein Schatz Hochzeit macht', this 'inner self' takes on a more discomfiting *Doppelgänger* quality as he dances out, engaging with the first man's presence. The double's movements are repetitions and developments of the first man's from the song's inaugural line ('Hochzeit macht', described above). Even when not repeating each other verbatim, the two bodies respond to each other, an example being the declaration 'Alles Singen ist nun aus!' ('All singing is done!'). The first man covers his mouth as to suffocate song and stands in weighty stasis. With his *Doppelgänger* pointing at him, also frozen, it feels as if inertia might set in. In fact, this song-less moment only lasts a few seconds, but it powerfully highlights the voice–body exchange (no singing = no movement) as well as the dissonance within the man, and between him and the world. Mahler and his music became late twentieth-century symbols for all the above. The two dancers almost touch hands, and then the second man nearly consecrates the first man's shoulders before walking away. Unity is deferred.

Béjart's choice to choreograph the intimate *Gesellen* songs for two dancers could be viewed as irreverent to Mahler, but the choreographer's conception of the cycle as a tale of doubles was arguably cued by the composer's score and poetry. Melodically and instrumentally, Mahler drew on Czech folk music for 'Wenn mein Schatz Hochzeit macht'. Mahler scholar John Williamson points to the 'sharp differentiation between the lively [Czech folk] dance music of the woodwind and the lament of the voice and strings' giving 'the sensation of two intersecting planes of musical events',[40] an aural atmosphere that corresponds to Béjart's choreographic doubling. Dance and music are mutually complementary. In the next song, 'Gieng heut' Morgens über's Feld' ('I Walked Across the Fields This Morning'), the discord between the enchanted natural landscape (dewy grasses, birds conversing in song, bluebells ringing, glittering sunshine) and the journeyman's melancholy suggests that nature is something of a *Doppelgänger* from which he is alienated, and with sinister implications. Or, as musicologist Peter Revers put it, in this song as well as others by Mahler, 'nature seems to represent the individual's alter

---

[38] Percival, 'Nureyev – Rites for the Traveller', 30.
[39] Mary Clarke, 'The Gala and the Concert', *Dancing Times*, April 1975, 358–60, at 359.
[40] John Williamson, 'The Earliest Completed Works: A Voyage Towards the First Symphony', in *The Mahler Companion*, ed. Donald Mitchell and Andrew Nicholson (Oxford: Oxford University Press, 1999), 39–61, at 55.

ego'.[41] Revers continues: 'It [nature] is the dreamlike vision of a joyous life set in sharp contrast to the individual's real feelings.' In other words, nature embodies another part of the man that he recognizes and without which he is incomplete.

Indeed, there is at times a hauntingly mocking quality to the second man in Béjart's choreography of 'Gieng heut' Morgens über's Feld'. At the beginning, the second man rests on one knee downstage left while the first dances exuberantly in the centre, all leaps, arabesques and turns. The two reverse positions, with the first now resting downstage on one knee while the second performs a similarly spirited dance for the second stanza. Then, punctuating the bluebells' ringing question 'ist's nicht eine schöne Welt?' ('isn't it a beautiful world?'), the first man spins into the second man's dance, and with hands on each other's shoulders they run upstage in an enraptured, mirror-image duet that continues into the third stanza. Their dance changes, though: with the realization that happiness is an illusion, they almost touch hands again, as at the end of 'Wenn mein Schatz Hochzeit macht'. They proceed to dance in alternation with one another, including the first position *port de bras–tendu–grand-plié* phrase from the ballet's opening, which functions as a musico-choreographic refrain in *Le Chant*. At the end of 'Gieng heut' Morgens über's Feld', the men face and place hands on each other's shoulders in a pre-embrace. Still, they are unable to come together for a genuine, lasting reunion: the second man thrusts his arms up in the air, shattering their physical connection.

It is significant that both men dance throughout the third *Gesellen* song, 'Ich hab' ein glühend Messer' ('I Have a Gleaming Knife'). This metaphorical weapon makes contact with and pierces the man's body; it is a 'böser Gast' (evil guest) and is no less excruciating than a blade of steel. The two men have an analogous rapport. While they dance simultaneously, there is an unwelcome, pained relationship between them, like a dance-off, a choreographic fracas. With the cry 'O weh!' ('Oh, woe!') at the end of the first stanza, the second man somersaults into an embrace with the first man, but it is not the consummation of the earlier, abortive embraces: he wraps his arms around the other's knees, with a flourish that is tender but also brutal in that it restrains the first man so that he can only move his upper body. Acting out the poetic text, the second man then briefly lies flat on his back looking up at the first, who dances over him: 'Wenn ich den

---

[41] Peter Revers, '"... the heart-wrenching sound of farewell": Mahler, Rückert, and the Kindertotenlieder', in *Mahler and His World*, ed. Karen Painter, trans. Irene Zedlacher (Princeton and Oxford: Princeton University Press, 2002), 173–83, at 177.

Himmel seh', / Seh' ich zwei blaue Augen stehn!' ('When I gaze up into the sky, / I see two blue eyes there!'). They dance together, or at least simultaneously, for the rest of stanza two and the beginning of stanza three, but in another attempt at the pre-embrace at the end of the previous song, it is now the first man who thrusts his arms upwards and breaks with the second. At the song's dynamic and dramatic climax, the first man takes his turn on his back – 'Ich wollt', ich läg auf der / Schwarzen Bahr' ('I wish I was lying down / on my black bier!') – and is picked up, consoled and embraced by the second. Predictably, their embrace is abruptly broken again and they part ways, circling around to their own corners upstage and united in their separation once more. Mahler's score foreshadows (echoes?) their renewed estrangement. In the song's accompanying postlude, Mahler specified that, 'Die Figuren der Holzbläser und später der Geiger immer gleichschnell ohne Rücksicht auf das langsame Tempo der Steile.' That is, the winds, marked *a tempo*, enter with short semiquaver runs that are juxtaposed with three slower drone chomps from the string bass, harp and timpani, giving the effect of a split in the music, of two parts that are out of synch. Subsequently, the *a tempo* violin (Mahler specified 'nicht schleppen' ('not dragging')) seems out of time above the growling horns and percussion. These are musical gestures issuing from a fractured orchestral being that dances with a fractured choreographic being.

It is only in the final song, 'Die zwei blauen Augen von meinem Schatz' ('My Beloved's Blue Eyes') that the two parts of the character come into an integrated *pas de deux* as they are united with the music and with each other. The first stanza is marked by a unison melody between the singer and, alternately, the first flute (lines one, two and four) or first violin (lines three and five). The two men move in unison in the first stanza, too, or at least in close counterpoint. Their movements often have a weighty, academic character, in consonance with Mahler's score note: 'Mit geheimnissvoll schwermüthigem Ausdruck. Ohne Sentimentalität' ('With mysterious, melancholic expression. Without sentimentality'). In the second stanza, the vocal line is not mirrored by other instruments. Analogously, the two men traverse the stage as one, propelled by the singing voice, although the second man seems to be trying to lead the first away, somewhere else. Their dance finally transforms into a true *pas de deux* beginning with the sweetly pastoral F major third stanza – 'Auf der Straße steht ein Lindenbaum' ('On the road stands a linden tree'), an image that, we will recall, also beckoned Feld to a *pas de deux* – with more unison movement and portering by the *Doppelgänger*, who now supports the first and drives the dance. Facing the audience, the first man reaches out into space, searching, but the second grabs hold to stop him, and to lead him upstage. Upon grasping hands, the first man's body wilts and he is escorted to the dark vanishing point while still reaching out in vain in the direction of the audience.

'A man and a woman; death takes the man; they both return to her at the end of the ballet, we find that in death there is the promise of renewal'[42] (Sir Kenneth MacMillan)

The ending of Béjart's *Le Chant* intimates that on some level this ballet concerns death, an experience one hopefully undergoes with a unified sense of self, if not complete surrender. Mahler was fixated on death, which is inexorable in *Das Lied von der Erde*. While not a story ballet, MacMillan's *Song of the Earth*, then, is correspondingly concerned with lovers who confront death's inevitability, as expressed in the choreographer's succinct summary quoted above.

The genesis of MacMillan's ballet was coloured by changing centenary attitudes towards Mahler (again, the symphonies were still in the process of becoming canonic at mid-century), and, more generally, mixed feelings towards late Romantic and early modern music.[43] Tudor's *Dark Elegies*, an important progenitor of song-ballets, was criticized for its setting of the *Kindertotenlieder*, which were regarded as too erratic and expressionist for dance in the 1930s and 1940s; that is, Mahler's score obviously was not conceived to be choreographed – though, of course, many twentieth-century choreographies were not set to dance scores – and the music seemed to be dominated by the poetic content vis-à-vis the familiar song-ballet 'problem' regarding mimesis.[44] MacMillan's first, rejected proposal to the Royal Ballet to set Mahler's *Das Lied von der Erde* dates to 1959, just a decade after Tudor's orientalist *Shadow of the Wind* (1948), set to the same score, failed miserably at American Ballet Theatre. According to the official Kenneth MacMillan website, in 1963, 'When he tried again [to pitch *Das Lied von der Erde*], after the huge success of *Romeo and Juliet* [his first three-act ballet], he was told that Mahler was a composer whose music was unsuitable for ballet.'[45] Expanding on the earlier criticisms directed towards

---

[42] Among other places, this quotation can be found at: www.kennethmacmillan.com/new-page-28.

[43] For an overview of the genesis of Macmillan's *Song of the Earth*, see Jann Parry, *Different Drummer: The Life of Kenneth MacMillan* (London: Faber & Faber, 2009), 217–19 and 297–306.

[44] See Heisler, 'Antony Tudor's *Dark Elegies*', esp. 177–9.

[45] www.kennethmacmillan.com/new-page-28.

Tudor's setting of Mahler, we should ask: 'unsuitable' in what sense(s)? The Royal Ballet had established a reputation for pristine classicism, and while choreographer Frederic Ashton introduced twists to classical technique, his works for this company ultimately maximized the tradition. Conversely, with *Song of the Earth* MacMillan envisioned a relatively daring experiment: while grounded in classical technique, this choreography is heavier, with movements that weigh down into the floor, and is occasionally decorated with orientalisms that were undoubtedly stimulated by the poetry and musical atmosphere of Mahler's *Das Lied von der Erde*.[46] And in terms of score choice, MacMillan's musical vision was still unconventional in the context of the Royal Ballet. Discussing the company's second, 1963 rejection of MacMillan's *Song of the Earth*, dancer and choreographer Monica Mason, who would eventually dance in this ballet in the UK, reflected that, 'there hadn't been a Mahler ballet before [at the Royal Ballet]', and captured evolving centenary sentiments about Mahler's music when she speculated that, 'maybe people felt that it was a little *sacred* in a way'.[47] That is, in contrast to the criticism of Tudor's use of dance-deficient Mahler, MacMillan's concept of choreographing *Das Lied von der Erde* was viewed as blasphemous given the emerging view of the composer's transcendent universality. (Later, in the Mahler-adoring twenty-first century, dancer and ballet master Donald McLeary confidently modulated the situation as, 'the board considered it not good to write a ballet to such a wonderful, special piece'.[48])

In any case, while *Song of the Earth* was rejected twice by the Royal Ballet, MacMillan's close colleague John Cranko, who was the director of the Stuttgart Ballet, 'had extended an open invitation for [MacMillan] to choreograph whatever he wanted'.[49] That Stuttgart was a friendlier birthing place for MacMillan's *Song of the Earth* owed in part to the influence of Expressionism and the concomitant extension of classical technique in German ballet and modern dance, and to the fact that Mahler's music had found a place quicker in German-speaking lands. MacMillan's Mahler song-ballet premiered in Stuttgart in 1965 with a live orchestra, mezzo-soprano Margarethe Bence and tenor James Harper; it was part of a triple

---

[46] See the interview with Monica Mason included in 'Monica Mason, Barry Wordsworth and Grant Coyle on *Song of the Earth* (The Royal Ballet)'; the video is available through the Royal Opera House website: roh.org.uk/news/watch-song-of-the-earth-discussed-the-unique-quality-of-the-choreography-and-wonderful-score-make-it-a-masterpiece.

[47] Quoted from 'Monica Mason, Barry Wordsworth and Grant Coyle on Song of the Earth (The Royal Ballet)', emphasis mine.

[48] Quoted from an interview included as part of 'Ballet. TV STEPS & TIMES', available at: www.staatsoper.de/en/productioninfo/steps-times/2012-01-04-19-30.html.

[49] www.kennethmacmillan.com/new-page-28.

bill with MacMillan's *Danses Concertantes* (1955, to Stravinsky) and Cranko's *Opus 1* (1965, to Anton Webern's Passacaglia). Based on its overwhelming success, MacMillan's *Song of the Earth* was subsequently accepted and staged in 1966 by the Royal Ballet, which still has this ballet in its repertory.

The three main figures in MacMillan's *Song of the Earth* are the central woman, the leading man whom she loves and The Eternal One (*Der Ewige*).[50] Corresponding to Mahler's existential drinking song, MacMillan's 'Trinklied vom Jammer der Erde' ('Song of the Sorrow of the Earth') is an all-male bacchanal that includes the lead male lover among the corps de ballet. They are a party of 'young people who are blissfully unaware of their own mortality'.[51] Their innocence stands in contrast to The Eternal One, who intrudes the carousal in tandem with the song's eerie vision of a ghostly ape: 'Im Mondschein auf den Gräbern / Hockt eine wildgespenstische Gestalt— / Ein Aff ists! Hört ihr, wie sein Heulen / Hinausgestellt in den süssen Duft des Lebens!' ('In the moonlight, on the graves / a wild ghostly figure— / It's an ape! Listen to how his howl / goes out in life's sweet fragrance!'). Aligned with the poetry, The Eternal One emerges as a figure of death, or at least as a negation of earthly life. We are reminded time and time again in Mahler's oeuvre that death is a fact of life, and that a revitalized life can result from the acceptance of death. Again, as a Mahler sympathizer like MacMillan put it, 'in death there is the promise of renewal', a rebirth akin to that which Mahler found in the decade that song-ballets to his music bloomed. His face half-covered with a mask, The Eternal One is sometimes interpreted as an evil force, yet he is rather more an imposing figure of experience, other-worldly wisdom and transcendence, characteristics attributable to the Eastern influences on Mahler (and by extension MacMillan) rather than to the Western, Judeo-Christian association of death with atonement. The Eternal One wears a black leotard and tights, while the central man is dressed in grey; the male dancers of the corps de ballet wear black leotards and grey tights, resulting in a symmetrical visual field. And although the man and The Eternal One initially tussle, they and the corps end up partying and dancing

---

[50] MacMillan's choreography is preserved in a Benesh score housed at the Royal Opera House at Covent Garden. Although never released on a commercial video, a DVD of a BBC broadcast of the Royal Ballet's 2007 performance for 'Darcey Bussell's grand finale' is housed in the library of London Metropolitan University. There are also numerous excerpts available online, some of which I cite below. For an image of the Woman and Der Ewige, see www.kennethmacmillan.com/the-ballets-1960-#1960-1966.

[51] www.kennethmacmillan.com/new-page-28.

together. During the final utterance of the refrain 'Dunkel ist das Leben, ist der Tod!' ('Dark is life, dark is death!'), The Eternal One is the apparent leader as he dances downstage centre, his movements mirrored by the corps around and behind him. On the word 'Tod', The Eternal One drops back to centre stage while the lead man alone moves downstage left, arms extended in veneration rather than out of fear of The Eternal One. The corps lifts The Eternal One as in offering before dropping him to a cradled position on the final chord.[52]

In 'Der Einsame im Herbst' ('The Solitary One in Autumn'), the central woman is introduced. Although she participates in the partner dances (four men and four women, including her), she is an outsider, relatable to the lonely male and female personages in Feld's *At Midnight*, and, by the centenary logic on both sides of the aisle, to Mahler himself. She yearns for love. The men exit and The Eternal One appears, first standing to the side of the all-female *pas de quatre*, unnoticed as if invisible. Like in the previous song, The Eternal One interlopes, plucking the central woman from the dance and portering her in a *pas de deux* that is uncanny for its premonition of death rather than affirmation of love: 'Ja, gib mir Ruh', ich hab' Erquickung not!' ('Yes, give me rest, I have need of refreshment!'). He puts her over his knee and flexes with fists down, lays her on the floor and picks her up again. But at the end of 'Der Einsame in Herbst', it is the lead man, the woman's longed-for love, who is lured away by The Eternal One, thus leaving her alone once more.

Mahler's third and fourth songs, 'Von der Jugend' ('Of Youth') and 'Von der Schönheit' ('Of Beauty'), are the most pictorial, and hence decorative movements of *Das Lied von der Erde*. MacMillan clearly responded to the cues in the poetry and score.[53] For example, in the penultimate stanza of 'Von der Jugend', four women are lined up on their knees upstage while men carry another woman upside down, that is, 'Alles auf dem Kopfe stehend' ('Everyone stands on their head'). The men then cradle and swing the woman in an arch towards the audience, before passing her off in cartwheels, like a pinwheel: 'Wie ein Halbmond steht die Brücke, /

---

[52] Excerpts from the 2012 staging of *Song of the Earth* at the Bayerische Staatsoper, Munich are included in 'Ballet. TV STEPS & TIMES'.

[53] Commentaries that address the (too mimetic) relationships between poetry and movement include Noel Goodwin and Hörst Koegler, 'To Earth and Other Places: Two Views of the MacMillan/Cranko Programme in Stuttgart', *Dance and Dancers*, January 1966, 20–7, 49, esp. 22, 27 and 49. In MacMillan's original conception, 'Von der Jugend' and 'Von der Schönheit' functioned as intermezzi given the absence of the central woman and man as well as The Eternal One. By the 1990s, MacMillan revised the choreography and The Eternal One appears, however briefly, in every song.

Umgekehrt der Bogen' ('The bridge is like a half-moon / with its arch upturned'). And in 'Von der Schönheit', seven women demurely cup their mouths and cover their faces with their hands, waving their arms left and right and gesturing as if picking fruit from trees. The poetic suggestiveness of such *port de bras* is strengthened by correspondence with the song's text: 'Junge Mädchen pflücken Blumen, / Pflücken Lotusblumen an dem Uferrande' ('Young girls are picking flowers / picking lotus flowers on the riverbank'). Yet without slavish reference to the poem, such mimetic movements seem to be more a matter of general style than of pantomime, akin to Mahler's vaguely orientalist-atmospheric harmonies and orchestral colouration. Donald McLeary maintains that MacMillan 'never actually explained how he was inspired by the poems, he just showed us the movement ... And you can see it especially in the fourth song ["Von der Schönheit"]. It's very Chinese, the hands are never classical, and the movement is very Oriental.'[54] Movement, like music, can rarely speak precisely, although the galloping entry of the male corps in the third stanza is also fairly unambiguous: 'O sieh, was tummeln sich für schöne Knaben / Dort an dem Uferrand auf mut'gen Rossen?' ('Oh see, why are the beautiful boys romping about / there on the riverbank on gamely horses?').

Widely deemed a masterpiece following its Stuttgart premiere (and thus propelling it to the Royal Ballet that had initially rejected it), MacMillan's *Song of the Earth* was still not spared the scrutiny that attends to dances set to texted music, not to mention choreographers who take on Mahler at such a reverential moment. Again, while not a narrative ballet, *Song of the Earth* slips intermittently into a representational mode; for example, the simultaneous appearance of The Eternal One with the ape in 'Das Trinklied vom Jammer der Erde'. (I say 'slip', although this assumes that narrative and mimesis are necessarily damning vices.) Regarding the choreographer's occasional literalism, dance critic Hörst Koegler reported that 'there were some people who considered [MacMillan's *Song of the Earth*] pure kitsch', and asserted that the choreographer 'tried very hard to treat ... illustrations in a freer vein, but he could not ... avoid taking some concrete hints from the poems – and wherever he did, he borders on the ridiculous'.[55] Koegler's complaint broaches once again the resilient song-ballet problem (the fear of words scripting movement) as well as growing pains surrounding Mahler's renaissance. Registering both the word-movement concern and the Mahler centenary context, dance and music critic Noel Goodwin expressed apprehension that 'Mahler's long

---

[54] 'Ballet. TV STEPS & TIMES'.   [55] Goodwin and Koegler, 'To Earth and Other Places', 27.

song-[symphony] is so intensely subjective in emotion, so self-contained in the expression of reflective thoughts and feelings, that to render them visually would seem to threaten all manner of pitfalls.'[56] Koegler drove the point harder, giving voice to post-modern, historicist values. Reducing MacMillan's ballet to 'neo-*art nouveau*'[57] (a stylistic classification stirred by Nicholas Georgiadis's original Stuttgart costumes and colour shades, which were altered to the aforementioned blacks and greys in subsequent productions[58]), the critic queried, 'how on earth could a choreographer today, in his middle thirties, want to convert a typical Viennese *fin-de-siècle* farewell to life into a ballet?' Unintentionally voicing irony in that Mahler's now celebrated, resurrected music would seem to rise above such a specific place and time, Koegler went on to distinguish between the continental and English perceptions of Mahler: the composer was allegedly 'more suspect' to the European 'middle generation'. 'Nor is it a ballet for music critics, at least not for German ones ... (how will the Viennese music critics react to it ... ?)',[59] pondered Koegler rhetorically. In addition to being an issue of representation (music and words by dance, the past by the present), the quandary is Mahler – he's 'suspect' – although it is not entirely clear why: was it Mahler's momentous Romanticism (channelled by Bernstein, for example), or his nascent but unrecognized modernism (Adorno's line)? Or was Koegler himself also reverting to the *fin de siècle*, with suspicion being triggered all over again by the bearing of the body against/in Mahler's music, and apparent concern for Mahler's reputation only caving to the celebratory moment?

Returning to MacMillan's choreography: 'Von der Jugend' and 'Von der Schönheit' constitute a paired centrepiece in *Song of the Earth*, while his 'Der Trunkene im Frühling' ('The Drunkard in Spring') connects to and forms a frame with the bacchanal in 'Das Trinklied vom Jammer der Erde'. The Eternal One plays a pivotal role once more, instigating the male quartet in which he takes part to binge drink; their movements mutate from revelry to stumbling. At the end, The Eternal One takes the man away, ostensibly in death, once and for all.

Bound to The Eternal One, the man – now also half-masked – returns in 'Der Abschied' ('The Farewell') for last dances with his beloved, who reconciles herself to fate. Towards the end of the long instrumental interlude that precedes the final stanza – 'Er stieg vom Pferd und reichte ihm

---

[56] Goodwin and Koegler, 'To Earth and Other Places', 20.
[57] Goodwin and Koegler, 'To Earth and Other Places', 24.
[58] See www.kennethmacmillan.com/new-page-28.
[59] Goodwin and Koegler, 'To Earth and Other Places', 26.

den Trunk / Des Abschieds dar' ('He dismounted from his horse and handed him the farewell drink')[60] – the leading man approaches the woman, who is lying face-down on the floor. The Eternal One comes in from behind and grabs the man's arm to stop him. Leaping in a circle around the stage, the man seems to flee, but The Eternal One shadows him, replicating his every move. Two have become one, and reminiscent of Béjart's *Le Chant* they dance a *pas de deux* of sorts – perhaps more akin to stylized wrestling. The woman, having risen, wedges herself between them, and the dance seamlessly transforms into a *pas de trois* with the co-porters turning, spinning and dragging her. As the man and The Eternal One watch her closely, the woman takes a resigned solo – 'Ich geh', ich wand're in die Berge' ('I go, I wander in the mountains') – culminating with a fast run and leap into her porters' arms: 'Ich suche Ruhe für mein einsam Herz' ('I seek peace for my lonely heart'). The woman is left alone momentarily, but in the final section, 'Ich wandle nach der Heimat' ('I wander homeward'), the entire corps re-enters and forms a backdrop of a multitude of couple dances.[61] The woman weaves between them with a determined walk. As the corps slowly departs stage left she walks backwards, in the opposite direction, and positions herself for her final moment.

Mahler's *Das Lied von der Erde* is built to deliver a tremendous impact – poetically, symphonically and, above all, vocally – which MacMillan matches, perhaps even intensifies, through dance. 'Although ... I filled five pages with notes', reported Richard Buckle, 'I rather funk writing about [MacMillan's *Song of the Earth*] until I have seen it again'.[62] Indeed, it is difficult to capture in words the effect when Mahler's music reaches its apotheosis, or embarks, with the increasingly hesitant scalar climb that transforms from G Dorian to G (almost-) Phrygian to a G♭ whole-tone scale (ten bars before rehearsal 58), and the contralto rhapsodizes about 'Die liebe Erde' (The lovely earth). What else could this now-resolved soul do than what she does? With protracted rise to point, the woman's dance trades in the grey area between Romantic ballet's conventional symbolism – gravity-defiance as meta-physicality – and determined physicality. As she criss-crosses the stage, every contact of her foot and muscle flex counts and it is all gravity, forcing her to fall into the arms of the man on the first of

---

[60] Rehearsal footage of this stanza can be viewed at 'Song of the Earth in rehearsal (The Royal Ballet)', available through the Royal Opera House website: roh.org.uk/productions/song-of-the-earth-by-kenneth-macmillan/news.

[61] Film footage from the culmination of *Song of the Earth* can be viewed via the official Kenneth MacMillan website: www.kennethmacmillan.com/new-page-28.

[62] Richard Buckle, 'Exit Kenneth, Grinning', *Sunday Times*, 2 May 1966.

many repetitions of *ewig*, the word-sound that cues The Eternal One. He and the couple join arms and proceed upstage, forming an opiated walking chain towards the audience that, like Mahler's C^{6-9} suspension, seems to be without beginning or end.

'EMBODY: to give a body to (a spirit); to cause to become a body or part of a body'[63] (Merriam-Webster)

Feld's *At Midnight*, Béjart's *Le Chant du compagnon errant* and MacMillan's *Song of the Earth*: each of these ballets is distinguished by their choreographers' individual styles, and each sets different scores. What links Feld, Béjart and MacMillan, though, is their embodied responses to song, bringing music, words and dance in contact, and into conversation. Related to their shared themes of lonely searching and the hope for new beginnings, the thread that connects their respective song-ballets is Mahler, who regarded dance as the origin of music, and for whom all music was imagined as embodied song. By participating in Mahler's centenary moment, choreographers venerated Mahler in their own unique ways by reminding audiences of the bodies that preceded and populate his song-music.

Moreover, these choreographers, among others, helped to establish Mahler's scores and song generally as dance music for the next generation of contemporary dancers. Pina Bausch, for example, first set Mahler in her early dance works *Fritz* and *Adagio*; that was 1974, by which time Mahler's music had comfortably reached its own *Heimat* and *Stätte*, in concert halls, on turntables and on dance stages. (By 1985, critic Jack Anderson could report that 'the music that dance companies dance to these days is surprisingly often music by Mahler'.[64]) Bausch's *Fritz* and *Adagio* are remarkable in that they forge dance music out of multiple Mahler scores (again, a collection of Mahler songs in the former, movement four of Symphony No. 5 and the *Kindertotenlieder* in the latter), and in *Fritz* Bausch placed Mahler's song-music side by side with multifarious dance musics. One need only think a few years ahead to Mark Morris, whose prolific choreography of song (although not Mahler) from the 1980s forward rendered

---

[63] merriam-webster.com/dictionary/embody.
[64] Jack Anderson, 'Mahler Works in Vogue among Choreographers', *New York Times*, 12 March 1985.

obsolete the distinction between vocal and instrumental music, and between 'high' and 'low' once and for all.[65]

In a commemoration of Bausch, dance historian Norbert Servos celebrates how she 'made a universal need the key subject of her work... Hers is a world theater which does not seek to teach, does not claim to know better, instead generating experiences ... exploring the precise state of human feelings while never giving up hope that the longing for love can one day be met.'[66] Servos's précis (and Bausch's, too) bridges the romanticist/modernist agendas that divided Mahlerites and captures the empathy of an entire generation for him, an important, if as-yet undocumented bond between Feld, Béjart, MacMillan and Bausch, among many other dancers, audiences and musicians. Indeed, conductors, whose participation in and experiences of Mahler's centenary renaissance are already well documented, relay encounters that are complementary to song-ballets set to his music. Mariss Jansons declared that one had to give 'absolutely everything' in a Mahler performance, implying that a disembodied approach would not do. Sir Simon Rattle recounted how, as a student, he and his peers 'were going in and hearing [Mahler's] pieces for the first time and being simply swept off our feet', meaningfully evoking a metaphor of bodily engagement with Mahler. Or, rather, bodily surrender: Franz Welser-Möst told how his encounter with Symphony No. 5 under Sir Georg Solti, 'was like an earthquake for me'.[67] The enthralling corporeal kinship between Mahler's music and late twentieth- and early twenty-first-century bodies speaks to the value of writing song-ballets into the composer's history, and, more generally, of practising a dance-attentive musicology, one that derives from dance studies nuanced ways of knowing our musical performances as well as our 'music itself' as embodied phenomena.

---

[65] Acocella, *Mark Morris*, esp. 138–42; and Stephanie Jordan, *Mark Morris: Musician-Choreographer* (London: Dance Books, 2015).

[66] Norbert Servos, 'Tanztheater Wuppertal', in Program Notes in *BAMbill*, trans. Steph Morris, October 2012.

[67] Wolfgang Schaufler, ed., *Gustav Mahler: The Conductors' Interviews* (Vienna: Universal, 2013), 130, 203 and 229, respectively.

10 | Embodied Heritage: English Country Dance in Austen Screen Adaptations

MARIBETH CLARK

Jane Austen's love of dance animates her novels, providing a socially and emotionally charged context for important moments in her plots: the balls at Netherfield in *Pride and Prejudice* and at the Crown Inn in *Emma* provide two of the most scenically and dramatically evocative examples. Such circumstances contribute to the important role given to dance in screen adaptations.[1] These choreographic performances hold considerable ideological significance and symbolic power for the novels and their cinematic transformations, representing in microcosm what Austen's prose achieves over hundreds of pages. As her characters move through figures of English country dances on screen, these scenes condense her lengthy narratives into rich minutes of gaze and gesture, movement and sound that can stand in for the whole. Yet at the same time that performances of country dance reduce the plot to an intense and brief performance, they also confuse the historical moment. Open to interpretation as both historically informed and simultaneously timeless or transcendent, the dances found in Austen films from the 1970s to the early 2000s suggest the impossible: that the repertory of English country dances with which Austen was familiar spanned from the early years of John Playford's *Dancing Master* to the present, a phenomenon that points to the importance of the twentieth-century English country dance revival to the reception of Austen on screen.

Using examples from adaptations of *Pride and Prejudice* and *Emma*, this chapter illustrates how these films support the continued development of

---

[1] Although scholars have examined music in Austen screen adaptations from a variety of angles, none has yet to include the choreographic experience. Robynn Stillwell and Marian Wilson Kimber discuss the non-diegetic film score, and invoke sonata form in their analyses of *Sense and Sensibility* (1995) and *Pride and Prejudice* (1995) respectively. See Robynn Stillwell, '*Sense and Sensibility*: Form, Genre and Function in the Film Score', *Acta Musicologica* 72, no. 2 (2000), 219–40; and Marian Wilson Kimber, 'Musical Topics, Historical Styles, and Narrative in Carl Davis's Score for *Pride and Prejudice* (1995)', *Journal of Adaptation in Film and Performance* 6, no.2 (2013), 121–35. See also Annette Davison, 'High Fidelity? Music in Screen Adaptations', in *The Cambridge Companion to Literature on Screen*, ed. Deborah Cartmell and Imelda Whelehan (Cambridge: Cambridge University Press, 2007), 212–25; and Kim Rooney, 'Parlor Music in Film Adaptations of Jane Austen's Novels', *Music Research Forum* 20 (2005), 39–54.

this folk revival that began early in the twentieth century. In this process, the choreography and its musical accompaniment marry an idealized early twentieth-century view of Englishness to an impossible past, reinforcing conservative structures related to English identity while constructing a seductive and sensuous fiction associated with embodied and material concepts of heritage.

Dance in Austen Novels as Sites of Conflict

In Austen novels, readers encounter the idea of dance as an important site of conflict that drives the narrative. *Pride and Prejudice* and *Emma* in particular feature conversations as well as activities associated with balls or assemblies to support tension-filled exchanges between characters.[2] The events involving dance highlight social struggles, such as how dancers pair reluctantly or readily into couples or refuse one another. Consider Harriet Smith's movement from misery to happiness when shunned by Mr Elton and then asked to dance by Mr Knightley at the Crown ball in *Emma*, or Elizabeth Bennet's distress at the request of socially awkward Mr Collins that she reserve the first two dances for him at the Netherfield ball in *Pride*

---

[2] Literary scholars have published a number of analyses of how dance works as an element of plot in Austen's novels. In *Literature and Dance in Nineteenth-Century Britain: Jane Austen to the New Woman* (Cambridge: Cambridge University Press, 2009), Cheryl Wilson explores country dance as a site of conflict and courtship, and as a well-understood skill among readers of Austen's novels during the early nineteenth century. See also Cheryl Wilson, 'Dance, Physicality, and Social Mobility in Jane Austen's *Persuasion*', *Persuasions* 25 (2003), 55–75. See also Nancy M. Lee-Riffe, 'The Role of Country Dance in the Fiction of Jane Austen', *Women's Writing* 5, no. 1 (1998), 103–12. Alison Sulloway discusses dance's inevitable relationship to courtship in 'Dancing and Marriage: The Province of the Ballroom', in *Jane Austen and the Province of Womanhood* (Philadelphia: University of Pennsylvania Press, 1989), 138–59. For discussion of women as musicians in Austen's novels, sometimes accompanying dancers at the keyboard, see Juliette Wells, '"In music she had always used to feel alone in the world": Jane Austen, Solitude, and the Artistic Woman', *Persuasions* 26 (2004), 98–110 and 'A Harpist Arrives at Mansfield Park: Music and the Moral Ambiguity of Mary Crawford', *Persuasions* 28 (2006), 101–14. In particular, Wells describes the self-effacing Mrs Weston in *Emma*, who calls little attention to herself while accompanying dance. Musicologist Kathryn L. Shanks Libin makes a similar argument in 'Music, Character, and Social Standing in Jane Austen's *Emma*', *Persuasions* 22 (2000), 15–30. Timothy Dow Adams sees country dance as a potential model for Austen's plots in 'To Know the Dancers from the Dance: Dance as a Metaphor of Marriage in Four Novels of Jane Austen', *Studies in the Novel* 14, no. 1 (1982), 55–65. As literary critic Kathryn Sutherland discusses, for the contemporary reader/viewer of Austen novels/screen adaptations, the experiences of watching and reading are unpredictably entangled. See Kathryn Sutherland, 'Jane Austen on Screen', in *The Cambridge Companion to Jane Austen*, ed. Edward Copeland and Juliet McMaster (Cambridge: Cambridge University Press, 2011), 215.

and Prejudice.³ Disappointment and frustration colour the experience of social dance, as much as pleasure.

Conversations about dance in the novels reveal the conflict associated with dance and the emotions it inspires. Well known is the infamous exchange between Darcy and Elizabeth while they dance together at Netherfield. Elizabeth's queries explore Darcy's cruel treatment of Wickham; Darcy's responses reveal him to be, in her estimation, superior and unkind.⁴ The scene also reveals Darcy's distrust of dance as an expression of elevated taste. In an inactive moment of the dance, one presumes, Sir William Lucas approaches Elizabeth and Darcy and describes dance as 'one of the first refinements of polished societies'. Darcy responds, 'Certainly, sir; and it has the advantage also of being in vogue amongst the less polished societies of the world; every savage can dance.'⁵

Tension between 'high' and 'low' also colours a less-examined but equally contentious moment about dance in *Pride and Prejudice* when Darcy questions Elizabeth about a reel heard as part of an informal entertainment. After Miss Bingley and her sister perform 'a lively Scotch air' at the keyboard, Darcy asks, 'Do not you feel a great inclination, Miss Bennet, to seize such an opportunity of dancing a reel?' She responds with a smile and silence, which leads Darcy to repeat the question, which she interprets as aimed at uncovering some low aspect of her character, which her eventual reply reveals:

'Oh', said she, 'I heard you before; but I could not immediately determine what to say in reply. You wanted me, I know, to say "Yes", that you might have the pleasure of despising my taste; but I always delight in overthrowing those kind of schemes, and cheating a person of their premeditated contempt. I have therefore made up my mind to tell you, that I do not want to dance a reel at all – and now despise me if you dare.'⁶

Austen here constructs the reel as a complex subject for small talk. Elizabeth's guarded response may arise in part from the fashion for dancing the reel in the first decades of the nineteenth century, and its lively character associated with the unsophisticated folk of the Scottish Highlands. While the reel as performed at the keyboard may have demonstrated a woman's skill and provided entertainment, admitting a desire to

---

³ Jane Austen, *Emma*, ed. Richard Cronin and Dorothy McMillan (Cambridge: Cambridge University Press, 2005), 354–5; and *Pride and Prejudice: An Authoritative Text, Backgrounds and Sources, Criticism*, ed. Donald Gray, 3rd edn (New York and London: W. W. Norton, 2001), 60.
⁴ Austen, *Pride and Prejudice*, 62–4.   ⁵ Austen, *Pride and Prejudice*, 18.
⁶ Austen, *Pride and Prejudice*, 35.

dance suggested to Elizabeth contemptible taste. Her body does not respond mindlessly to music. The reel only moves her to think.[7]

These two exchanges, both involving Darcy, recognize a double-sidedness to dance. It can be elevated and refined or savage and out of control. Brief quotations from just one character in the novels can misrepresent the complexity of dancing as an experience, as in the case of the famous statement from Henry Tilney in *Northanger Abbey* that 'I consider a country-dance as an emblem of marriage.' Catherine Morland's response to Tilney, who is her partner in dance at that moment, contests this pronouncement: 'But they are such very different things!' Such exchanges reveal a broad terrain between romantic fantasy and the reality of limited possibilities that dance charts in the novels and leaves open for adaptations to explore further.

The Sensuous Fiction of English Country Dance

Literary critic Kathryn Sutherland has recognized Austen adaptations as part of a process of rebranding the author as 'the godmother of twenty-first-century romances. This Jane Austen is not what she once was: a writer of impeccable Johnsonian credentials, barbed wit and complex morality; now she is savvy, sexy, and very modern.'[8] Written works construct gaps – absences – in regard to physical bodies, gesture and sound that adaptations fill. Creating ball scenes for Austen screen adaptations revises Austen's prose by making it concrete and embodied. This process both expands and limits the narrative through the imposition of image and sound, with actors moving through sets in a time-based genre. Literary and film critic Erica Sheen explores Roland Barthes's concept of *Tmesis* to describe the sensuality of Austen's narratives as they relocate to the screen.[9] Sheen (*pace* Barthes)

---

[7] Rosemary Coupe discusses the early nineteenth-century popularity of the reel in 'The Evolution of the "Eightsome Reel"', *Folk Music Journal* 10, no. 5 (2010), 696. For a discussion of Scottish folk song and conflict around the concepts of Scot and Scottish music, see Karen E. McAulay, 'From "Anti-Scot" to "Anti-Scottish" Sentiment: Cultural Nationalism and Scottish Song in the Late Eighteenth to Nineteenth Centuries', *Library and Information History* 26, no. 4 (2010), 272–88. Austen's *Nachlass* suggests that she was familiar with Scottish folk music. Two collections of 'Scots Songs' for voice and harpsichord can be found among the manuscripts and printed editions held by the Jane Austen Memorial Trust at Chawton. See Ian Gammie and Derek McCulloch, *Jane Austen's Music* (St Albans: Corda Music Publications, 1996), 30–1.

[8] Sutherland, 'Jane Austen on Screen', 219–20.

[9] Erica Sheen, '"Where the garment gapes": Faithfulness and Promiscuity in the 1995 BBC *Pride and Prejudice*', in *The Classic Novel from Page to Screen*, ed. Robert Giddings and Erica Sheen (Manchester: Manchester University Press, 2000), 14–30.

understands *Tmesis* as the introduction of the concrete and visual aspect into the film where it had been absent in the novel. Such insertions reveal gaps in the fabric of the novelist's language. This gap-filling allows 'an intrusion that upset some viewers, in particular those who are loyal readers of the texts, because of how it reveals the falseness of the adaptation'.[10] Dance scenes are extreme examples of *Tmesis* because scenes of dance on screen overdetermine actions where words alone had once served the reader, literally fleshing out gesture and gaze that are choreographed to musical accompaniment.

Tmesis also points to a conundrum in regard to the use of historical sources in processes of adaptation. In a work of literature there is no such thing as a historical source. No sounds were heard; no bodies moved. Jane Austen was not Elizabeth Bennet despite what biopics and adaptations of *Pride and Prejudice* suggest. Performance in film is shared among observers in the here and now. In contrast, the historical object, as musicologist Richard Taruskin has written, is an unachievable utopic goal. Although 'high fidelity' has been attributed to the use of historical musical sources in the context of Austen adaptations, such an achievement is impossible.[11] The use of English country dance, rather than providing moments of lived historical reconstruction within the film, extends and deepens contemporary folk practices based on mythical relationships to the past. The use of English country dance in Austen can be seen as both an extension of English folk traditions established during the twentieth century and a continued process of obscuring practices of the past.

The Heyday and Decline of the Flexible Country Dance

Curiously, the English country dance was known for its instability and flexibility from its origins in the seventeenth century to its decline during Austen's own lifetime. In the two centuries before Austen's novels were published, it was associated with what historian Christopher Marsh describes as a tendency towards 'crossover and fusion'.[12] He illustrates how exemplars of the genre circulated in print and were performed as songs, on theatrical stages and in ballrooms, showing how country dances performed in rural locales could differ markedly from those performed in

---

[10] Sheen, 'Where the garment gapes', 15.
[11] Davison, 'High Fidelity? Music in Screen Adaptations', 212.
[12] Christopher Marsh, *Music and Society in Early Modern England* (Cambridge: Cambridge University Press, 2010), 390.

urban and courtly settings. They reinforced the separation of villagers from city dwellers and members of courtly society, and suggested important connections. Musicologist Wye J. Allanbrook, who reflected on country dance as a genre to explain aspects of Mozart's operatic style, draws a similar conclusion. She claims that this type of dance suggested the general unravelling of social order during the second half of the eighteenth century. Its flexibility and irregularity as a genre, in particular its ability to absorb all metres, kept it from fitting into a metrical spectrum of affects. Its 'careless freedom ... swallows up all social and affective distinctions'.[13] Neither wholly aristocratic nor merely bourgeois, it allowed for the mingling of the classes in its longways lines, functioning as a 'plebian counterpart' to the noble dances, and allowing dancing bodies to take on 'bad habits' at odds with the elegant comportment derived from performing the minuet. Because the country dance and its music were popular in two ways (both 'of the people' and circulating in a market for entertainment), they were ephemeral, responding to changes in taste, uses of leisure time and the desire of publishers and dancing masters to make a living, resulting in the publication of hundreds if not thousands of named dances associated with specific tunes over nearly two centuries.[14]

Country dances and their tunes continued to circulate in an unstable and effervescent set of publications and related practices during Austen's lifetime. Although the popularity of the country dance as a part of English theatre productions had waned, publications of affordable collections of dances suggest the genre's social role remained important.[15] New collections of dances accompanied by new tunes were printed each year for an audience eager for the latest entertainment, emphasizing innovation as well as tradition. Publishers such as Charles and Samuel Thompson, John Johnson, Bland and Weller, and William Randall distributed collections

---

[13] Wye J. Allanbrook, *Rhythmic Gesture in Mozart: 'Le nozze di Figaro' and 'Don Giovanni'* (Chicago: University of Chicago Press, 1983), 60–3.

[14] Claude Simpson, *The British Broadside Ballad and Its Music* (New Brunswick: Rutgers University Press, 1966) documents the peregrinations of many seventeenth- and early eighteenth-century tunes that served as accompaniment for country dances. See also Richard Semmens, '"La Furstenberg" and "St Martin's Lane": Purcell's French Odyssey', *Music & Letters* 78, no. 3 (1997), 337–49; and 'Branles, Gavottes and Contredanses in the Late Seventeenth and Early Eighteenth Centuries', *Dance Research* 15, no. 2 (1997), 35–62.
A number of scholars focus on the *Dancing Master* and its numerous editions between 1651 and 1728. See, e.g., Margaret Dean-Smith, ed., *Playford's English Dancing Master 1651* (London: Schott & Co., 1957) and William A. MacPherson, 'The Music of the English Country Dance 1651–1728', PhD diss. (Harvard University, 1984).

[15] Carol Marsh describes the country dance in 'French Court Dances in England, 1706–1740: A Study of the Sources (Dance Music, Notation, Dancing Masters)', PhD diss. (City University of New York, 1985), 70–2.

of twenty-four country dance tunes complete with figures representing activities in London, at court, Bath and 'all assemblies'.[16]

By the beginning of the nineteenth century, the country dance was coming to the end of its popularity and, according to dancing masters such as Thomas Wilson, dancers performed it with little precision and greater flexibility than is represented in Playford's editions of the *Dancing Master*. This flexibility may have ultimately led to its undoing. By the second decade of the nineteenth century, Wilson addressed the country dance's decline in treatises aimed at ameliorating it.[17] He described how performances frequently fell apart because of the lack of skill of the participants in both leading and learning the dance. Despite Wilson's efforts to rejuvenate the practice, cotillions and quadrilles usurped the country dance as dominant figure dances early in the nineteenth century, providing square and circular frames, as opposed to longways lines, for couples' interactions in the ballroom.[18]

Alongside this decay of the quality of the dance as a social experience developed an understanding of the dance as an artefact of folk culture. Encyclopedist Nicolas Étienne Framery characterized country dance as literally of the country, where dancers are shaped by their regular, physical labour. According to him, these country folk experience joy in the dance that increases with the number of dancers involved, featuring no gentry or the mixing of the classes, but an imagined community of agrarian labourers:

En effet, c'est au village sur-tout que l'on aime à se réunir et que l'on préfère les plaisirs partagés. Le grave menuet, qui n'emploie que deux personnes, et qui ne

---

[16] A number of collections of twenty-four country dances produced by a variety of publishers are available through the International Music Score Library Project (imslp.org). The titles often list a number of locations where the dances took place – court, Bath Tunbridge and all 'publick assemblys' [sic]. See, e.g., *Twenty Four Country Dances for the Year 1766 with Proper Tunes and Directions to Each Dance as They are Performed at Court, Bath, Tunbridge & All Publick Assemblys* (London: John Johnson, 1766).

[17] See Thomas Wilson, *An Analysis of Country Dancing [. . .]. Illustrated with Engravings on Wood by J. Berryman*, 3rd edn (London: J. S. Dickson, 1811); and *The Treasures of Terpsichore; or, A Companion for the Ball-room. Being a Collection of All the Most Popular English Country Dances, Arranged Alphabetically, with Proper Figures to Each Dance*, 2nd edn (London: Sherwood, Neely and Jones, 1816); as well as *The Complete System of English Country Dancing, Containing All the Figures Ever Used in English Country Dancing, with a Variety of New Figures, and New Reels* (London: Sherwood, Neely and Jones, c. 1815). These manuals and many others are digitally available through 'An American Ballroom Companion: Dance Instruction Manuals ca. 1490–1920', American Memory, Music Division, Library of Congress, http://memory.loc.gov/ammem/dihtml/dihome.html.

[18] Although over its long existence the country dance took numerous forms, including square four-couple formations called *contredanse française*, and three-couple and four-couple longways sets, the country dance that Wilson describes at the beginning of the nineteenth century is in a longways line for as many couples as the space can accommodate.

laisse aux spectateurs d'autre occupation que celle d'admirer, n'a pu prendre naissance que dans les villes où l'on dansé par amour-propre. Au village, on danse pour le seul Plaisir de danser, pour agiter les membres accoutumé à un violent exercice; on danse pour exhale un sentiment de joie qui s'accroit toujours en raison du nombre, et qui n'as pas besoin de spectateurs.

(Indeed it is in the village above all that people love to gather, and prefer shared pleasures. The slow minuet, which employs only two people and does not allow the spectators any occupation except admiring the dancers, could only be born in the cities, where people dance for the sake of *amour-propre*. In the village people dance for the sole pleasure of dancing, to move limbs accustomed to violent exercise; they dance to breathe out a feeling of joy which grows constantly in proportion to the number of dancers, and has no need for spectators.)[19]

Despite Framery's idealistic understanding expressed in the *Encyclopédie*, ambivalence surrounded country dance during Austen's lifetime. James Edward Austen-Leigh, Austin's nephew, reflected on its waning popularity in his description of the 'interminable country dance, in which all could join'. As he wrote,

This dance presented a great show of enjoyment, but it was not without its peculiar troubles. The ladies and gentlemen were ranged apart from each other in opposite rows, so that the facilities for flirtation, or interesting intercourse, were not so great as might have been desired by both parties. Much heart-burning and discontent sometimes arose as to *who* should stand above *whom*, and especially as to who was entitled to have the high privilege of calling and leading off the first dance: and no little indignation was felt at the lower end of the room when any of the leading couples retired prematurely from their duties, and did not condescend to dance up and down the whole set.[20]

For Austen-Leigh, the structure of the dance, which separates same-sex lines into opposing rows, represented an obstacle to the type of social engagement that the dancers desired, contributing to the conflict around courtship and status so central to Austen's plots. The longways lines, rather than serving as vehicles of romantic transport, separated partners for most of the dance and obstructed communication. This frustration of romantic aspirations points to its usefulness as a complicating factor in the plots of novels that aimed to unite lovers happily at the end of a complex narrative.

---

[19] Nicolas-Étienne Framery, *Encyclopédie méthodique: Musique* (Paris: Chez Panckoucke, 1791), 316. Trans. Allanbrook, *Rhythmic Gesture*, 62.

[20] James Edward Austen-Leigh, *Memoir of Jane Austen* (London: Richard Bentley and Son, 1871), 34. Austen herself shares no distaste for country dance in her letters.

Folk Revivals and Heritage

Fast forward 100 years to the early twentieth century and, although Austen's novels still enjoy a popular currency, the English country dance as a ballroom practice has been all but forgotten, allowing the folk revivalist to step into the frame. A view resembling Framery's vision of country dance as provincial folk practice wins pride of place.

The early practices of folk revivalists erased many nuances of the historical record in the service of conservative ideology. The controversial folk song and dance collector Cecil Sharp conducted his influential activities with the goals of constructing a middle-class art form at odds with modernist and commercial urbanism, fostering what Simon Featherstone has termed a 'new Englishness'. As Featherstone described Sharp, '[he] was oppressed by a sense of national decline, physical degeneracy and urban corruption ... He sought to revive a national body-culture by an appeal to primitive values developed through sophisticated modern systems of organization and publicity.'[21] The folk organizations that Sharp founded were filled with educated middle-class participants who took a detail-oriented approach to participation, and who continued the development of the processes he began, supporting such organizations as the English Folk Dance and Song Society.[22]

This interest in preserving folk culture among twentieth-century country dance practitioners connects with ideas associated with heritage developed in recent decades. As a term, 'heritage' raises ideological issues in regard to individual identity and relationships to the past. It became an important political concept during the 1980s for the Thatcher government, referring to the best of England's past and strategies for preserving that past.[23] Film critic Andrew Higson employed the term to distinguish a genre

---

[21] Simon Featherstone, *Englishness: Twentieth-Century Popular Culture and the Forming of English Identity* (Edinburgh: University of Edinburgh Press, 2008), 28, 36. His discussion of Cecil Sharp's folk dance revival spans 36–46. Richard Snape constructs a narrative similar to Featherstone's, focusing on the shifts in English country dance in response to World War I, the rise of jazz in the 1920s, and the opportunities for an alternative to 'modern commercialized dance and dance venues' in 'Continuity, Change and Performativity in Leisure: English Folk Dance and Modernity 1900–1939', *Leisure Studies* 28, no. 3 (2009), 308.

[22] For a history of English country dance in the United States, see Daniel J. Walkowitz, *City Folk: English Country Dance and the Politics of the Folk in Modern America* (New York: New York University Press, 2010). Douglas Kennedy discusses the role of English country dance in primary schools in *English Folk Dancing: Today and Yesterday* (London: G. Bell and Sons, 1964), 22–5.

[23] Greg M. Colón Semenza and Bob Hasenfratz, *The History of British Literature on Film 1895–2015* (London and New York: Bloomsbury, 2015), 343–4.

of film that transforms images of an imperialist, pastoral, upper-class English legacy into commodities for consumption, in the process establishing a dialogue between an imagined past and an uncertain global, multicultural, capitalist present.[24] The Thatcherite motivation to preserve the best of the past supports the process of reception that Higson attributes to costume dramas filmed on grand estates.[25]

This grand aesthetic of heritage films infiltrates Austen adaptations beginning in the 1990s. *Emma* and *Pride and Prejudice* in particular have plots in which interactions at balls are central to development of the story, and that lend themselves to scenes with high production values. Adaptations of both *Emma* (dir. Lawrence, ITV, 1996; dir. McGrath, 1996) and *Pride and Prejudice* (dir. Langton, BBC 1, 1995; dir. Wright, 2005) have dance scenes that put the *mise en scène* of the heritage films in motion, emphasizing somatic experience as part of the visual spectacle, deepening the viewer's engagement with scenic imagery through dance rhythms and musical phrases that animate bodies. For those who have ever participated in English country dance, the performance allows for a visceral experience of familiar choreography, with movement and sound calling attention to sensory experiences beyond the visual. The encouragement of a physical, embodied engagement aids in the construction of what Higson calls 'pastness', an important element of heritage.

The concept of heritage overlaps with that of folk. As Higson writes, 'the image of the past in the heritage films has become so naturalized that, paradoxically, it stands removed from history: the evocation of pastness is accomplished by a look, a style, the loving recreation of period details – not by any critical historical perspective'.[26] Such lack of critical historical perspective characterizes Cecil Sharp's approach to constructing the English folk during the early twentieth century. The songs, tunes and dances he collected suggest the existence of an unchanging, uncreative body of people who spontaneously sang and danced, expressing the values of a non-commercial past, an attitude that ultimately has come, according to Georgina Boyes, to 'sell Englishness'. As she writes in *The Imagined Village*, 'the broad attractions of their Arcadian connotations have assured

---

[24] Andrew Higson, 'Re-Presenting the National Past: Nostalgia and Pastiche in the Heritage Film', in *Fires Were Started: British Cinema and Thatcherism*, ed. Lester D. Friedman (New York: Wallflower Press, 2006), 91–109.

[25] Higson discusses film's role in the construction of heritage in *English Heritage, English Cinema. Costume Drama since 1980* (Oxford: Oxford University Press, 2003). See also Claire Monk, 'The British Heritage Film Debate Revisited', in *British Historical Cinema*, ed. Claire Monk and Amy Sargeant (London: Routledge, 2001), 176–98.

[26] Higson, *English Heritage*, 25.

the Revival's signifiers a place in high and mass culture'.[27] In the act of representing balls, assemblies and informal entertainments from the Regency period, adaptors of Austen's novels for film and television have resorted to English country dances more resonant with the twentieth-century folk revival than with the conditions found in the early nineteenth century articulated by dancing masters such as Wilson.

Austen Adaptations as Frames for English Country Dance Revival

Although country dance has played a part in BBC screen adaptations of Austen since the 1970s, such performances became a focus of more detail-oriented historical and artistic attention with *Pride and Prejudice* (dir. Langton, BBC 1, 1995) and *Emma* (dir. Lawrence, ITV, 1996). Choreographer Jane Gibson realized the dance for both these series relying on two sets of sources: *The Apted Book of Country Dances* (Apted 1931) and editions of *Dancing Master* published between 1651 and 1728, as shown in Tables 10.1 and 10.2.[28]

Apted and the numerous editions of *Dancing Master* reflect the aesthetic of country dance established by Cecil Sharp and his followers in the twentieth century, and support the activities of contemporary English country dancers, a group constituted, according to historian Daniel Walkowitz, of 'middle-class folk whose social composition does not differ (and never has) appreciably from that of the collectors/revivalists'.[29] Perhaps tongue-in-cheek, the editors of *Apted* propose that its dances, which originated during the early years of Austen's life, could have been experienced by her fictional characters. As they wrote, 'perhaps it was in

---

[27] Georgina Boyes, *The Imagined Village* (Manchester: Manchester University Press, 1993), 3.

[28] W. S. Porter, Marjorie Heffer and Arthur Heffer, *The Apted Book of Country Dances: Twenty-four Country Dances from the Last Years of the Eighteenth Century with Tunes and Instructions* (Cambridge: W. Heffer and Sons, 1931). The two dances not from Apted were taken from John Playford's *Dancing Master*: 'Grimstock' (1651), a set dance for three couples, also danced at Mrs Philips home, and 'Mr Beveridge's Maggot' (1695), which framed the complex conversation as Elizabeth and Darcy dance together at Netherfield. Dances from Playford have been collected in numerous modern editions, from the work of Cecil Sharp himself in 1912 to that of Jeremy Barstow in 1985. See Jeremy Barstow, *The Complete Country Dance Tunes from Playford's Dancing Master, 1651–ca. 1728, Showing Variants, Misprints between the 18 Original Editions* (London: Faber Music, 1985). Daniel Walkowitz provides a postmodern definition of folk as 'continually constructed groups presented everywhere in time and space' in 'Patrolling the Boundaries', *Radical History Review* 84 (2002), 122.

[29] Walkowitz, *City Folk*, 242–4.

Table 10.1 English country dances performed in *Pride and Prejudice* (dir. Langton, BBC 1, 1995)

Name of Dance	Modern Source (Original Pub.)	Occurrence in Film
The Touchstone	*Apted* 18 (Thompson 1773)	Meryton Assembly, heard from the street (Episode 1)
Trip to Highgate	*Apted* 10 (Thompson 1777)	Meryton Assembly
Mutual Love (tune: The Flight)	*Apted* 4 (Thompson 1777)	Meryton Assembly
Comical Fellow, 6/8 D major	*Apted* 5 (Thompson 1776)	Meryton Assembly
The Happy Captive (tune: Dusky Night)	*Apted* 22 (Thompson 1777)	Meryton Assembly
The Barley Mow (tune: Linnen Hall)	*Apted* 12 (Thompson 1779)	Mrs Philips' home (Episode 2)
Shrewsbury Lasses	*Apted* 24 (Thompson 1765)	Netherfield Ball (Episode 2)
Pleasures of the Town (to Maid of the Inn)	*Apted* 21 (Thompson 1777)	Netherfield Ball
Mr Beveridge's Maggot	*Dancing Master* (1695)	Netherfield Ball
Grimstock	*Dancing Master* (1651)	Mrs Philips' home (Episode 3)
The Corporation (to Fête Champêtre)	*Apted* 23 (Thompson 1777)	Mrs Philips' home

Table 10.2 English country dances performed in *Emma* (dir. Lawrence, ITV, 1996)

Name of Dance	Source	Occurrence in Film
Jack's Maggot	*Dancing Master* (1702)	Randalls
Purcell, Hole in the Wall	*Dancing Master* (1698)	Crown Inn
Purcell, Juice of Barley	*Dancing Master* (1689)	Crown Inn
Kelsterne Gardens	*Dancing Master* (1728)	Crown Inn
Mr Isaac's Maggot	*Dancing Master* (1695)	Harvest Celebration

one of them that Harriet [of *Emma*] "bounded higher than ever, flew further down the middle, and was in a continual course of smiles"; or after another that Mr. Tilney [of *Northanger Abbey*] made his famous comparison between country-dancing and matrimony'.[30] The editors imagine these dances inserted within the stories in a way that resembles their use within adaptations. Such imagining also explains why

---

[30] Apted, *Book of Country Dances*, vii.

a choreographer would find *Apted*'s dances appropriate to Austen adaptations.

At a certain level, however, *Apted*'s editors demonstrate a rejection of values associated with a late eighteenth-century experience of dance. They chose content for the volume from a collection of over 100 dances found in an old cupboard purchased for a shilling by the father of Mrs Apted, who gave her name to the collection. Finding these dances 'mostly poor', the editors selected the twenty-four best dances and tunes, and revised them to make them attractive to their communities of folk dancers in the 1930s.[31] In general they increased the activity within the dance by transforming them from triple minor dances, a form that left two of every three couples inactive, to duple minor dances in which couples engage more equally in the figures. Changing these dances from triple to duple minor progressions diminished opportunities for conversation between couples.[32] The result is a dance characterized by more constant activity than in the past, when participants waited for the privilege to begin to move and appreciated the opportunities to converse with a partner that inactivity provided. Contemporary folk interpretations of English country dance shun inactivity in favour of continuous motion and flow, which makes conversation in the course of dancing more difficult.

This great value placed on both activity and dance as divertissement combined can be seen in the movie version of *Emma* (dir. McGrath, 1996), an example that shows a mainstream Hollywood adaptation of 'Mr Beveridge's Maggot', from the *Dancing Master* (1695).

Performed by Gwyneth Paltrow as Emma and Jeremy Northam as Mr Knightley, along with four other couples, the dance represents the community as integrated and in synchrony, with Emma and Knightley losing their individuality in the utopic performance. Activity, artistry, grace and equality are emphasized over conversation or furthering the plot. The camera remains stationary at one end of the room, making no attempt to follow

---

[31] Jane Gibson discusses her use of *Apted* in Sue Birtwhistle and Susie Conklin, *The Making of 'Pride and Prejudice'* (London: Penguin Books, 1995).

[32] For most English country dancers during Austen's time the experience would be a gradual activation of the dancers by the head or leading couple, situated at the top of the double line. Each couple below the first moves to action through the progression of the first couple down the line away from the music towards the bottom of the room. In other words, the head couple's set, whether consisting of four (duple minor) or six (triple minor) dancers, provided the example for those below them in the line of the dance. As historical social dance practitioner Christine Rogers describes the process, 'the figures were danced by the top minor set and everyone else waited until the leading couple reached them, when they joined in as second (or third if a triple minor) couples and continued until all were dancing'. See Christine Rogers, 'Dances for Jane Austen', *English Dance and Song* 69, no. 3 (2007), 20–1.

Figure 10.1 'Mr Beveridge's Maggot' from *The Dancing Master* (1695)

the progress of Emma and Mr Knightley down the line of five couples, nor do any participants speak, whether dancing or observing from the sides of the room. The moment is pure divertissement. Although at the beginning of the performance the dancers take a few seconds to find their place on the dancefloor, they fall into a performance of unusual flow and evenness of technique. A string quartet of refined modern instruments provides the accompaniment, the first violin carrying the melody.

The smooth continuity of 'Mr Beveridge's Maggot' in *Emma* (dir. McGrath, 1996), choreographed by Sue Lefton, represents twentieth-century values of the folk community fused with the filmed musical, in which dances provide visual entertainment, and can represent moments of idyllic interaction between members of the stage world. Heritage dance here is fantastic and other-worldly, creating a hybrid between dance as spectacle and social dance as participatory act. In most ways the performance realizes the dance as represented in the eighth edition of Playford's *Dancing Master* (1695), as seen in Figure 10.1. Certain details of the tradition of English country dance, however, are disregarded, such as the movement of the dancers from the top of the room, where the musicians are traditionally situated, to the bottom, the end opposite the musicians. In this performance the progress of the line is reversed, with Emma and Mr Knightley, leaders of the community, rightly placed as the top couple of the set, progressing towards the music from the bottom of the room to the top because such motion serves the camera's gaze. To end the performance, the couples cast off to the outside of the lines of the dance, then file through the space they had occupied in two lines with a flourish reminiscent of Busby Berkeley. The scene then fades to black.

Despite the attractiveness of constant movement for contemporary dancers and those that watch them, activity presents a challenge when dialogue is necessary, as in the most famous of Austen's danced encounters, that of Darcy and Elizabeth at the Netherfield ball. When in *Pride and Prejudice* (dir. Langton, 1995), Elizabeth (Jennifer Ehle) and Darcy (Colin Firth) dance this same dance, 'Mr Beveridge's Maggot', it lacks the cheerful and upbeat character generally associated with the dance. The tempo of the triple-time melody is plodding, and the dancers respond to it with a sharp stiffness and military precision as they begin with no conversation, accompanied by a mixed group of period instruments, including gut strings, a serpent and basso continuo. The serpent's baritone timbre in particular lends martial strangeness to the scene through its quirky, unstable intonation and the punchy bass line. The ensemble emphasizes the music's status as source material, music heard as historical artefact.

Elizabeth and Darcy's dance in *Pride and Prejudice* (dir. Langton, 1995) requires the careful unfolding of exchanges, a merging of dialogue with the figure dance and its musical accompaniment. In order to realize this integration, the dancer's script is carefully fitted to the figures of the dance. After one complete time through the figures, allowing the couples to progress, Elizabeth speaks to the accompaniment of the second repetition. Darcy responds at the beginning of the third time, as he and Elizabeth progress again. The scene also takes advantage of the inactivity of Elizabeth and Darcy at the end of the line. As they wait to re-enter the dance (an appropriate moment for conversation historically and pragmatically), observer Sir William Lucas (Christopher Benjamin) addresses Darcy on his good luck at dancing with Elizabeth, and comments on the relationship developing between Bingley and Jane, the couple dancing next to Elizabeth and Darcy. These details map precisely onto the dialogue as presented in the novel, and foreshadow complications that must be resolved: Darcy's negative perception of Bingley's relationship with Jane, and the increasing feelings between Darcy and Elizabeth.

And yet this choreographic moment reflects a combination of times and places. The tune and figures for 'Mr Beveridge's Maggot' date from over 100 years before Austen published *Pride and Prejudice*. The historical source provides a sensual frame for the dialogue of the characters, which distorts not only the late seventeenth-century practice represented by the dance notation, but also misrepresents late eighteenth-century practice in its lack of teaching and calling, and the continuous dancing of the dancers aside from the moment out at the end. Rather than thinking of this performance as some sort of historical re-enactment, it is more easily understood as the product of a continuing folk tradition allied with nostalgia for a past Englishness. The Austen adaptation makes the nostalgia come alive anew.

Purcell's Music as Art and Folk

Contemporary dancers of English country dance hold the various tunes that accompany associated dances in high esteem, often attributing a greatness, timelessness and 'classical' quality to the music accompanying the dance. Walkowitz, in his study of modern English country dance and dancers, asserts that compositions by Arcangelo Corelli, Henry Purcell, George Friedrich Handel, or 'in the style of these and other classical and Baroque composers' function as a signifier of the activity's 'distinctiveness' and high status. Quoting English country dancer Thom Yarnall, Walkowitz writes that the dance and its music 'has nothing to do with the twentieth century. It takes you to a different place and it takes you mentally and physically.'[33]

Tunes by Purcell take pride of place as accompaniment to English country dances performed in *Pride and Prejudice* (2005), probably because of the composer's status as the English composer par excellance, an importance articulated in 1995 by a collection of his dance tunes prepared for contemporary English country dance.[34] This idea of transport to a 'different place' through dance informs the examination of Purcell's dances and tunes as presented in *Pride and Prejudice* (2005) (Table 10.3).

The music for dance scenes contrasts with music for the soundtrack composed by Dario Marianelli, which consists of piano sometimes accompanied by the English Chamber Orchestra, in a dreamy, contemporary, mostly diatonic musical language.[35] And yet the distance between music as

---

[33] Walkowitz, *City Folk*, 238.

[34] Christine Helwig and Marshall Barron, eds., *Purcell, Playford, and the English Country Dance. Vol. I: The Dances* (New Haven, CT: Playford Consort Publications, 1995).

[35] Sheet music for excerpts from *Pride and Prejudice* (2005) for violin solo and piano solo contain two pieces by Henry Purcell. 'Meryton Hall' is attributed to Purcell, adapted and arranged by Dario Marianelli in collaboration with William Lyons. 'Another Dance' also comes from Purcell's works, and 'The Kit Kat Club' was published posthumously in 1728 by Playford in *Dancing Master*. The arrangement of the Rondeau from the incidental music for *Abdelazar*,

Table 10.3 English country dances in *Pride and Prejudice* (dir. Wright, 2005)

Name of Dance	Source	Occurrence in Film
Dutch Dollars (Tune: Purcell, Tythe Pig)	Helwig, Christine and Marshall Barron, eds., *Purcell, Playford, and the English Country Dance. Vol. I: The Dances*. New Haven, CT: Playford Consort Publications, 1995. p. 33 (PPECD); *Dancing Master* (DM) (1695).	Meryton Assembly
Black Bess	PPECD 2 (*DM* 1696).	Meryton Assembly
The Young Widow	Retreads no. 53, Charles Bolton (Griffiths 1788)	Meryton Assembly
Wakefield Hunt	(Thompson 1779)	Meryton Assembly
Duke of Gloucester's March	PPECD 6–7. (*Indian Queen*, 1695. Not published as a dance in Playford.)	Netherfield Ball (heard as entering Netherfield)
The Bishop	*Apted* 16 (Thompson, 1778)	Netherfield Ball
Philippe Callens, comp., Moneike's Maggot; Purcell, Rondeau from *Abdelazar*	Purcell, Rondeau from *Abdelazar*, 1695. Not published as a dance in Playford, or in the PPECD collection.	Netherfield Ball

soundtrack and music as part of the filmed world collapses in the context of the dance between Darcy and Elizabeth at the Netherfield ball. The power of this moment arises in part from the juxtaposition of a folk sound in the Meryton Assembly with the more polished performance of high culture at the Netherfield ball.[36] These styles, presented as if they are two sides of the same coin, stand in opposition to a more diegetic absorption of the music for the Netherfield ball into the soundtrack. This collapse demonstrates a new recognition that both concepts blend in the understanding of Austen as sexy, savvy and modern, to use Sutherland's words.

The soundscape as heard in the first minutes of the film begins to shape the viewer's understanding of the Bennets and those who attend the Meryton Assembly as folk, identified with a timeless sense of English

---

'Postcard to Henry Purcell', is not provided as sheet music, although it is one of the discrete downloadable pieces from the soundtrack, and suggests through the title an homage to the composer.

[36] According to his website, Lyons served as composer, arranger and historical consultant for the film. See www.william-lyons.com.

character. In the process, the viewer is introduced to how sound will be used in the film: as soundscape, as film score featuring piano and orchestral accompaniment, as music within the world of the film's characters, and as dialogue. While the natural sounds and the dialogue remain diegetic, the music as heard in the world of the film bleeds into the soundtrack and back again, with pianists playing versions of what we hear as accompaniment to action, and, in the case of the dance between Darcy and Elizabeth at the Netherfield ball, the melody of that tune becoming absorbed into the soundtrack.

Sound in the first minutes of the film demonstrates the porousness between the world of the film and the soundtrack. As the sun rises over a pasture, the melodic and variable song of the blackbird (associated with Elizabeth according to Joe Wright's director's commentary) is heard to the accompaniment of a babbling brook. The palate of the natural expands as Lizzy (Keira Knightley) walks towards her house, book in hand. The noisy barnyard animals – lowing cows, quacking and splashing ducks, and clucking hens – join the dawn chorus just before the first piece from the soundtrack begins. 'Dawn', as it is named, performed by the unseen, modern pianist Jean-Yves Thibaudet, begins with a subtle repeated pitch. Seconds later the camera pans through a doorway where the audience views the back of Elizabeth's contrary sister, Mary, as she sits with her hands moving at the piano. The viewer thinks, perhaps, she is the pianist. As the camera approaches Mary at the keyboard, however, fantasy is dispelled – Mary produces a tinny C major scale, not the romantic, yearning rubato of Thibaudet's modern piano. Although it creates no discord against Marianelli's composition, the scale's disciplinary rigour contrasts with the first images of the Bennet's disorderly domestic world, and hints at Mary's contrary position within it. If the soundtrack represents interiority, the scale represents Mary's exterior sonic presentation of self, which concludes as the voices of the Bennet parents emerge with exciting news for parents of five girls of marriageable age: the property at Netherfield is now occupied by a wealthy and eligible bachelor, Mr Bingley.[37] Despite their having servants, land and a sizeable house, the Bennets live among their animals, with chickens, ducks and geese in their yard and the pig occasionally traipsing into the house. Far from being peasants, their existence is still bucolic.

---

[37] The movie is saturated with meaningful sounds. In addition to dialogue and the usual noises made by human bodies in motion (footsteps, claps, the swishing of clothing), the viewer hears the spray of fountains, drips of rain and thunder claps. Clocks mark time in the aristocratic settings, while the rolling wheels of carriages and the gallops of horses accompany travel.

A playful, overtone-rich performance on the fiddle constructs the sonic resonance with folk style at the Meryton Assembly, which follows the scene that introduces the Bennets. Fiddler Aidan Broadbridge's performance showcases a rawness of expression, the melody providing the grain against which the bass and the countermelodies are realized. Media critic Catherine Stewart-Beer has commented on the refreshing 'lowness' of the dance that the fiddle accompanies:

> The assembly at Meryton is recreated here as a true rustic hoe-down, a riot of swirling movement and sweaty bodies, wigs askew, accompanied by jaunty, folksy music – seemingly most un-Austenlike, or so we have been led to believe by the rather strait-laced tradition of BBC costume drama. There is altogether something quite refreshing and remarkably unstuffy in this particular take on Austen's society.

The lively dance provides a context for seeing the difference of the urban (but not urbane) Mr Bingley, his sister Caroline and Mr Darcy. The dancers of Meryton know each other, connect with each other, dance effortlessly with each other without instruction. To further emphasize their rustic qualities, the townspeople wear natural-hued rough fabrics – browns and greens – that stand out against Caroline's gleaming cream Empire-cut gown, and Darcy's and Bingley's formality of appearance. Indeed, Darcy's resistance to participation in the Meryton Assembly might be read as a very modern moment. Darcy reveals discomfort as a member of the unwashed masses. The aristocratic man steps away from the dance. Unlike Bingley, who enters into the dance freely, Darcy does not descend to the role of common man, even in the potentially carnivalesque moment of a community entertainment, where, aside from the interlopers from Netherfield, everyone involved appears to be of equal status.

In contrast to the Meryton Assembly, the music and dance for the Netherfield ball provides a classical and refined sound, exploiting the timbres of modern instruments and maintaining the comportment and physical discipline of a courtly entertainment. Elizabeth and Darcy dance 'Moneike's Maggot', a late twentieth-century example of choreography written to be danced to the tune of Purcell's Rondeau from *Abdelazar* (1695).[38] The strangeness of this dance between Elizabeth and Darcy has

---

[38] Philippe Callens, a well-known English country dance instructor from Belgium, composed 'Moneike's Maggot' to Purcell's Rondeau from stage music for *Abdelazar* (1695). Oddly enough, Andrew Lloyd Weber arranged and orchestrated a version of the Rondeau's primary theme for the Conservative Party to support John Major's candidacy for prime minister of Great Britain in 1992. According to David Haigron, the music contributed to the attempt to construct Major as connecting with Margaret Thatcher's legacy while at the same time moving

attracted critical attention. Literary and film scholar Jessica Durgan observed how the cinematography 'crosses the line', a technique that repositions the camera so that Darcy and Elizabeth reverse positions from right to left in the frame, an action usually avoided because it confuses the audience. Her analysis suggests that this confusion is purposeful as it pushes the audience to engage with the dance as an important moment of development in the relationship between the two characters.[39]

Another strange aspect of the dance is the disappearance of all the dancers but Darcy and Elizabeth during the last figures, which they complete alone on the dance floor. The other dancers reappear for the final cadence of the music, and the couple is presumably reintegrated with the social whole. Critics express mixed views of this moment. As philosopher Hugh Bredin wrote in a review for the Belfast-based magazine *Fortnight*,

In the worst scene, Darcy and Lizzy are tripping the light fantastic when, in an instant, everyone else in the ballroom disappears. Not a bit nonplussed the dancing duo continues mingling hands and distrustful glances until, as the last bar of music sounds, the absent revelers reappear as mysteriously and swiftly as they had vanished. All films are products of a committee, but one would love to know who persuaded them to go for this unusually asinine visual trick.[40]

In a more sympathetic response to the disappearance, Rachel Gollay attributes a 'telling' quality to Darcy and Elizabeth's dance at the Netherfield ball. As she writes,

While their conversation shuns the usual politeness and pleasantries, the way in which they dance suggests a mutual gravitation toward one another (especially evident when the rest of the dancers vanish from the shot, leaving only Elizabeth and Darcy coupled).[41]

For Gollay, this moment presents the dance as an idealized frame for the couple, the camera's trick constructing a transcendent moment of togetherness, an idealized moment of union between Elizabeth and Darcy long before the denouement, absorbing Elizabeth smoothly – if but for seconds – into Darcy's privileged world.

---

towards a 'One-Nation Toryism' of the past. See '"Caring" John Major: Portrait of a Thatcherite as a One-Nation Tory', *Observatoire de la société* 7 (2009), paragraph 26.

[39] Jessica Durgan, 'Framing Heritage: The Role of Cinematography in *Pride and Prejudice*', *Persuasions On-Line* 27, no. 2 (2007).

[40] Hugh Bredin, 'More than a pair of marble buttocks . . .' *Fortnight* no. 438, October 2005, 25.

[41] Rachel Gollay, '"The Most Determined Flirt": The Dynamics of Romantic Uncertainty in Joe Wright's *Pride and Prejudice*', *Persuasions On-Line* 27, no. 2 (2007).

If, however, the dance is considered as an interpretation of Austen as modern and sensual, the dancers around Darcy and Elizabeth disappear to highlight the emotion between the couple that defies clear expression or categorization. This overload of feeling appears to be deposited in the melody accompanying the dance, Purcell's well-known rondeau, which moves from its diegetic position as accompaniment for the dance to a space in the soundtrack unheard by the characters, yet seemingly expressive of their unspoken thoughts. As Darcy and Bingley leave Netherfield and depart the territories inhabited by their love interests, the rondeau accompanies the clatter of the carriage. Purcell is appropriated to serve contemporary goals. His tune sonically marks the oldness and the Englishness of the moment, the dance as lost opportunity, the relationships as unlikely. This complex of dance and sound suggests the use of English country dance and music associated with it to support a movement to make Austen more modern through calculated gestures towards the past.

Adopting dances and tunes from the past is not a neutral process, but ideologically loaded. Through screen adaptations (film and television), a relatively small group of English country dances and the tunes accompanying them have become understood as dating from Austen's lifetime. These attractive and engaging performances reflect more about an imagined past Englishness than dance as Austen may have experienced it, serving as powerful exemplars of a generalized English heritage. The act of dancing in Austen adaptations, when taken as a whole, constructs a sense of the past that collapses over two centuries of practice into an ambiguous, imprecise, yet powerful set of gestures. As a genre imbedded in these screen adaptations, this heritage/folk version of English country dance serves as an example of *mise en abyme* within Austen adaptations for film and television.[42] Performances construct revelry that distills the fantasy of the Austen film – community and romance – into a few minutes, constructing in the process an embodied and timeless experience of nostalgia.

---

[42] Carolyn Abbate introduces Lucien Dällenbach's understanding of *mise en abyme* to musicological literature in *Unsung Voices: Opera and Musical Narrative in the Nineteenth Century* (Princeton: Princeton University Press, 1991), 67.

Select Bibliography

Abbate, Carolyn. *Unsung Voices: Opera and Musical Narrative in the Nineteenth Century*. Princeton: Princeton University Press, 1991.
  In Search of Opera. Princeton: Princeton University Press, 2001.
  'Overlooking the Ephemeral'. *New Literary History* 48, no. 1 (2017), 75–102.
Acocella, Joan. *Mark Morris*. New York: Farrar, Strauss and Giroux, 1993.
Adams, Timothy Dow. 'To Know the Dancers from the Dance: Dance as a Metaphor of Marriage in Four Novels of Jane Austen'. *Studies in the Novel* 14, no. 1 (1982), 55–65.
Adorno, Theodor W. *Mahler: Eine musikalische Physiognomic*. Frankfurt am Main: Suhrkamp, 1960.
  'Mahler Today (1930)'. In *Essays on Music*. Edited by Richard Leppert, translated by Susan H. Gillespie, 603–11. Berkeley and Los Angeles: University of California Press, 2002.
Agawu, Kofi. *Playing with Signs: A Semiotic Interpretation of Classical Music*. Princeton: Princeton University Press, 1991.
Aldrich, Elizabeth. 'Social Dancing in Schubert's World'. In *Schubert's Vienna*. Edited by Raymond Erickson, 119–40. New Haven and London: Yale University Press, 1997.
Alexander, Jessie. *Encore! New Book of Platform Sketches*. Toronto: McClelland & Stewart, 1922.
Allanbrook, Wye J. *Rhythmic Gesture in Mozart: The Marriage of Figaro and Don Giovanni*. Chicago: University of Chicago Press, 1983; 2nd edn 2016.
Arbeau, Thoinot. *Orchésographie* (1588). Translated by Mary Stewart Evans, *Orchesography*. New York: Dover, 1967.
  Orchesography: A Treatise in the Form of a Dialogue. Translated by Cyril W. Beaumont. New York: Dance Horizons, 1925; 2nd edn 1968.
Arcangeli, Alessandro. 'Dance under Trial: The Moral Debate, 1200-1600'. *Dance Research* 12, no. 2 (1994), 127–55.
Arkin, Lisa. 'The Context of Exoticism in Fanny Elssler's *Cachucha*'. *Dance Chronicle* 17, no. 3 (1994), 303–25.
Arkin, Lisa C. and Marian Smith. 'National Dance in the Romantic Ballet'. In *Rethinking the Sylph: New Perspectives on the Romantic Ballet*. Edited by Lynn Garafola, 11–68. Hanover, NH: Wesleyan University Press, 1997.

Austen, Jane. *Pride and Prejudice: An Authoritative Text, Backgrounds and Sources, Criticism*. Edited by Donald Gray, 3rd edn. New York and London: W. W. Norton, 2001.

Emma. Edited by Richard Cronin and Dorothy McMillan. Cambridge: Cambridge University Press, 2005.

Austen-Leigh, James Edward. *Memoir of Jane Austen*. London: Richard Bentley and Son, 1871.

Austin, Rev. Gilbert. *Chironomia; or, A Treatise on Rhetorical Delivery: Comprehending Many Precepts, Both Ancient and Modern, for the Proper Regulation of the Voice, the Countenance, and Gesture*. London: Printed for T. Cadell and W. Davies; by W. Bulmer, 1806.

Bakhtin, Mikhail. *Rabelais and His World*. Translated by Helene Iswolsky. Bloomington and Indianapolis: University of Indiana Press, 1984.

Baldwin, John W. *Masters, Princes, and Merchants: The Social Views of Peter the Chanter and His Circle*. 2 vols. Princeton: Princeton University Press, 1970.

Banes, Sally. *Writing Dancing in the Age of Postmodernism*. Hanover, NH: Wesleyan University Press, 1994.

Bargiel, Réjane and Ségolène le Men, eds. *Catalogue: La Belle Époque de Jules Chéret de l'affiche au décor*. Paris: Bibliothèque nationale de France, 2010.

Barker, Andrew. *Greek Musical Writings. Volume 1: The Musician and His Art*. Cambridge: Cambridge University Press, 1984.

Barrell, John. *The Dark Side of the Landscape: The Rural Poor in English Painting, 1730–1840*. Cambridge: Cambridge University Press, 1980.

Barrows, Susanna. *Distorting Mirrors: Visions of the Crowd in Late Nineteenth-Century France*. New Haven and London: Yale University Press, 1981.

Barstow, Jeremy. *The Complete Country Dance Tunes from Playford's Dancing Master, 1651–ca. 1728, Showing Variants, Misprints between the 18 Original Editions*. London: Faber Music, 1985.

Barthes, Roland. 'The Death of the Author'. In *Image–Music–Text*. Translated by Stephen Heath, 142–8. New York: Hill and Wang, 1977.

Bauer-Lechner, Natalie. *Recollections of Gustav Mahler*. Translated by Dika Newlin. Edited by Peter Franklin. London: Faber Music, 1980.

Beale, Alfred M. A. *Calisthenics and Light Gymnastics for Home and School*. New York: Excelsior, 1888.

Belting, Hans. *Looking through Duchamp's Door: Art and Perspective in the Work of Duchamp, Sugimoto, Jeff Wall*. Cologne: W. König, 2009.

Berry, Irmgard E. *Benesh Movement Notation Score Catalogue: An International Listing to Benesh Movement Notation Scores of Professional Dance Works Recorded 1955–1985*. London: Benesh Institute of Choreology, 1986.

Birtwhistle, Sue and Susie Conklin. *The Making of Pride and Prejudice*. London: Penguin Books, 1995.

Blair, Fredrika. *Isadora: Portrait of the Artist as a Woman*. New York: McGraw-Hill, 1986.

Blair, Mathilda. *The Nonpareil Reader and Speaker for Young People*. New York: McLoughlin Bros, 1905.

Böhme, Franz Magnus. *Geschichte des Tanzes in Deutschland*. Wiesbaden: Breitkopf und Härtel, 1967.

Bonds, Mark Evan. *Music as Thought: Listening to the Symphony in the Age of Beethoven*. Princeton: Princeton University Press, 2006.

Borchmeyer, Dieter. 'The "Dance of the Future": Heine's and Wagner's Venusberg Ballets'. In *Drama and the World of Richard Wagner*. Translated by Daphne Ellis, 133–43. Princeton: Princeton University Press, 2003.

Borio, Gianmario. *Musical Listening in the Age of Technological Reproduction*. Aldershot: Ashgate, 2015.

Bosworth, Bessie Bryant. *Mrs. Bosworth's Elocutionary Studies*. Chicago: Bedford, Clark, and Co, 1889.

Boyd, Malcolm. *Bach: The Brandenburg Concertos*. Cambridge: Cambridge University Press, 1993.

Boyes, Georgina. *The Imagined Village*. Manchester: Manchester University Press, 1993.

Brainard, Ingrid. *The Art of Courtly Dancing in the Early Renaissance. Part II: The Practice of Courtly Dances*. West Newton, MA: n.p., 1981.

Brion, Katherine. 'The *Fin-de-siècle* Poster: A Healthy Modern Stimulus in the French Interior'. In *Designing the French Interior: The Modern Home and Mass Media*. Edited by Anca I. Lasc, Georgina Downey and Mark Taylor, 107–18. London: Bloomsbury, 2015.

Brooks, Lynne Matluck. *Women's Work: Making Dance in Europe before 1800*. Madison: University of Wisconsin Press, 2007.

Brown, Hallie Quinn. *Bits and Odds: A Choice Selection of Recitations for School, Lyceum and Parlor Entertainments*. Xenia, OH: Chew Press, n.d.

Buck-Morss, Susan. 'The Flâneur, the Sandwichman and the Whore: The Politics of Loitering'. *New German Critique* 39 (1986), 99–140.

The Dialectics of Seeing: Walter Benjamin and the Arcades Project. Cambridge, MA: MIT Press, 1989.

Burden, Michael and Jennifer Thorpe. *Ballet de la Nuit: Rothschild B1/16/6*. Hillsdale, NY: Pendragon Press, 2009.

Burnham, Scott. *Beethoven Hero*. Princeton: Princeton University Press, 1995.

Burns, Judy. 'Reconstructions'. *Women & Performance* 5, no. 2 (1992), 112–47.

Buskirk, Martha and Mignon Nixon, eds. *The Duchamp Effect*. Cambridge, MA: MIT Press, 1996.

Caballero, Carlo. 'Dance and Lyric Reunited: Fauré's *Pénélope* and the Changing Role of Ballet in French Opera'. In *Bild und Bewegung im Musiktheater / Image and Movement in Music Theatre*. Edited by Roman Brotbeck, Laura Moeckli, Anette Schaffer and Stephanie Schroedter, 51–64. Schliengen, Germany: Argus Editions, 2018.

Caddy, Davinia. 'Representational Conundrums: Music and Early Modern Dance'. In *Western Music and Representation*. Edited by Joshua Walden, 144–64. Cambridge: Cambridge University Press, 2013.

Callahan, Daniel. 'The Gay Divorce of Music and Dance: Choreomusicality and the Early Works of Cage-Cunningham'. *Journal of the American Musicological Society* 71, no. 2 (2018), 439–525.

Cameron, Theresa. 'The Third Art of the Gesamtkunstwerk'. *Wagner* 12, no. 1 (1991), 3–12.

Campana, Alessandra. *Opera and Modern Spectatorship in Late Nineteenth-Century Italy*. Cambridge: Cambridge University Press, 2015.

Caplin, William. *Classical Form: A Theory of Formal Functions for the Instrumental Music of Haydn, Mozart, and Beethoven*. New York: Oxford University Press, 1998.

Carter, Alexandra. 'Locating Dance in History and Society'. In *The Routledge Dance Studies Reader*. Edited by Alexandra Carter, 193–5. London and New York: Routledge, 1998.

Carter, Curtis. 'Intelligence and Sensibility in the Dance'. *Arts in Society: Growth of Dance in America* 13, no. 2 (1976), 210–21.

Carter, Karen L. 'The Spectatorship of the *Affiche Illustrée* and the Modern City of Paris, 1880–1900'. *Journal of Design History* 25 (2012), 11–31.

Cavicchi, Daniel. *Listening and Longing: Music Lovers in the Age of Barnum*. Middletown, CT: Wesleyan University Press, 2011.

Chamberlain, William. 'The President's Opening Address'. *Proceedings of the National Association of Elocutionists* 5 (1896), 20.

  'Should Public Readers Follow or Lead Public Taste in the Choice of Selections?' *Proceedings of the National Association of Elocutionists* 4 (1896), 92.

Chazin-Bennahum, Judith. *The Ballets of Antony Tudor: Studies in Psyche and Satire*. Oxford: Oxford University Press, 1994.

Cheng, Anne Anlin. *Second Skin: Josephine Baker and the Modern Surface*. Oxford: Oxford University Press, 2010.

  'Skins, Tattoos, and Susceptibility'. *Representations* 108, no. 1 (2009), 98–119.

Cimini, Amy. 'Vibrating Colors and Silent Bodies. Music, Sound and Silence in Maurice Merleau-Ponty's *Critique of Dualism*'. *Contemporary Music Review* 31, nos. 5–6 (2012), 353–70.

Clark, Maribeth. 'Bodies at the Opéra: The Hermaphrodite in the Dance Criticism of Théophile Gautier'. In *Reading Critics Reading: Opera and Ballet Criticism in France from the Revolution to 1848*. Edited by Roger Parker and Mary Ann Smart, 237–53. Oxford: Oxford University Press, 2001.

  'The Quadrille as Embodied Musical Experience in 19th-Century Paris'. *Journal of Musicology* 19 (2002), 503–26.

  'Review of *Ballet and Opera in the Age of 'Giselle'*, by Marian Smith. Princeton: Princeton University Press, 2000'. *Cambridge Opera Journal* 13, no. 2 (2002), 191–6.

Cole, Jonathan and Barbara Montero. 'Affective Proprioception'. *Janus Head* 9, no. 2 (2007), 299–317.

Colón Semenza, Greg M. and Bob Hasenfratz. *The History of British Literature on Film 1895–2015*. London and New York: Bloomsbury, 2015.

Cornazano, Antonio. *The Book on the Art of Dancing* (1455). Translated by Madeleine Inglehearn and Peggy Forsyth. London: Dance Books, 1981.

Coupe, Rosemary. 'The Evolution of the "Eightsome Reel"'. *Folk Music Journal* 9, no. 5 (2010), 693–722.

Cox, Arnie. 'Embodying Music: Principles of the Mimetic Hypothesis'. *MTO: A Journal of the Society for Music Theory* 17, no. 2 (2011), www.mtosmt.org/issues/mto.11.17.2/mto.11.17.2.cox.php.

Crary, Jonathan. *Techniques of the Observer: On Vision and Modernity in the Nineteenth Century*. Cambridge, MA: MIT Press, 1990.

Crosby, Fanny and W. H. Doane. *Safe in the Arms of Jesus: Illustrated Pantomimed Hymn*. Poses and directions by Cozette Keller. New York: Edgar S. Werner, 1917.

Cruz, Maria Teresa, ed. *Media Theory and Cultural Technologies: In Memoriam Friedrich Kittler*. Newcastle upon Tyne: Cambridge Scholars Publishing, 2017.

Cusick, Suzanne. 'Feminist Theory, Music Theory, and the Mind/Body Problem'. *Perspectives of New Music* 32, no. 1 (1994), 8–27.

Dahlhaus, Carl. *Foundations of Music History*. Cambridge: Cambridge University Press, 1983.

David, Hans T. and Arthur Mendel, eds. *The New Bach Reader: A Life of Johann Sebastian Bach in Letters and Documents*. Revised edition by Christoph Wolff. New York and London: W. W. Norton, 1999.

Davison, Annette. 'High Fidelity? Music in Screen Adaptations'. In *The Cambridge Companion to Literature on Screen*. Edited by Deborah Cartmell and Imelda Whelehan, 12–25. Cambridge: Cambridge University Press, 2007.

Dean-Smith, Margaret, ed. *Playford's English Dancing Master 1651*. London: Schott & Co. LTD., 1957.

DeBerg, Betty A. *Ungodly Women: Gender and the First Wave of American Fundamentalism*. Minneapolis: Fortress Press, 1990.

Debussy, Claude. *Correspondance, 1872–1918*. Edited by François Lesure and Denis Herlin. Paris: Gallimard, 2005.

Deleuze, Gilles and Félix Guattari. *A Thousand Plateaus: Capitalism and Schizophrenia*. Minneapolis: University of Minnesota Press, 2004.

Dolan, Emily I. 'Musicology in the Garden'. *Representations* 132 (2015), 88–94.

Dreyfus, Laurence. *Bach and the Patterns of Invention*. Cambridge, MA: Harvard University Press, 1996.

Ducrey, Guy. 'La Danseuse et *Le Figaro*'. *Littérature et nation* 2, no. 14 (1995), 161–72.

'La Danseuse Loïe Fuller et L'Art nouveau'. *Mélange* 1 (2000), 119–31.

Durgan, Jessica. 'Framing Heritage: The Role of Cinematography in *Pride and Prejudice*'. *Persuasions On-Line* 27, no. 2 (2007), www.jasna.org/persuasions/on-line/vol27no2/durgan.htm?.

Dürr, Alfred. *The Cantatas of J. S. Bach*. Translated and edited by Richard Jones. Oxford: Oxford University Press, 2005.

Eastman, Barrett and Frédéric Mayer. *Paris, 1900: The American Guide to the City and Exposition*. Chicago: Northern Trust Company Bank, 1899.

Eldridge, Ethel May. *Old Home Song Pantomimes*. Franklin, OH: Eldridge Entertainment House, 1910.

Ellis, Katharine. *Interpreting the Musical Past: Early Music in Nineteenth-Century France*. Oxford: Oxford University Press, 2005.

'Paris, 1866: In Search of French Music'. *Music & Letters* 91, no. 4 (2010), 536–54.

'Opera Criticism and the Paris Periodical Press'. *Revue belge de Musicologie* 66 (2012), 127–31.

Elsaesser, Thomas. *Film History as Media Archaeology: Tracking Digital Cinema*. Amsterdam: Amsterdam University Press, 2016.

Faxon, Grace B. *Favorite Pantomimed Songs and Poses*. Danville, NY: F. A. Owen, 1917.

Popular Recitations and How to Recite Them. Danville, NY: F. A. Owen, 1909.

Featherstone, Simon. *Englishness: Twentieth-Century Popular Culture and the Forming of English Identity*. Edinburgh: University of Edinburgh Press, 2008.

Feder, Stuart. *Gustav Mahler: A Life in Crisis*. New Haven and London: Yale University Press, 2004.

Feldtenstein, Carl Joseph von. *Erweiterung der Kunst nach der Chorographie zu tanzen: Tänzen zu erfinden, und aufzusetzen; wie auch Anweisung zu verschiedenen National- Taenzen, als zu Englischen, Deutschen, Schwaebischen, Pohlnischen, Hannak- Masur- Kosak- und Hungarischen; nebst einer Anzahl englischer Tänze*. Braunschweig, 1772.

Fenno, Frank H. *The Science and Art of Elocution*. Philadelphia: John H. Potter, 1878.

Ferguson, Priscilla Parkhurst. *Paris as Revolution: Writing the Nineteenth-Century City*. Berkeley and Los Angeles: University of California Press, 1994.

Finke-Hecklinger, Doris. *Tanzcharaktere in Johann Sebastian Bachs Vokalmusik*. Trossingen: Hohner-Verlag, 1970.

Finnegan, Ruth. 'Music, Experience, and the Anthropology of Emotion'. In *The Cultural Study of Music*. Edited by Martin Clayton, Trevor Herbert and Richard Middleton, 353–63. New York and London: Routledge, 2003.

Fleischer, Mary. *Embodied Texts: Symbolist Playwright-Dancer Collaborations*. London and New York: Rodopi, 2007.

Flint, Catrina M. 'The Schola Cantorum, Early Music and French Political Culture, from 1894 to 1914'. PhD diss., McGill University, 2006.

Forkel, Johann Nikolaus. *Ueber Johann Sebastian Bachs Leben, Kunst und Kunstwerke*. Leipzig: Hoffmeister und Kühnel, 1802. Edited by Axel Fischer; reprint Kassel: Bärenreiter, 1999.

Fort, Joseph. 'Incorporating Haydn's Minuets: Towards a Somatic Theory of Music'. PhD diss., Harvard University, 2015.

Foster, Susan Leigh. 'The Ballerina's Phallic Pointe'. In *Corporealities*. Edited by Susan Leigh Foster, 1–24. New York: Routledge, 1996.

   'Choreographing Empathy'. *Topoi* 24, no. 1 (2005), 81–91.

Fournel, Victor. *Ce qu'on voit dans les rues de Paris*. Paris: A. Delahays, 1858.

Fraleigh, Sondra. *Dance and the Lived Body: A Descriptive Aesthetics*. Pittsburgh: University of Pittsburgh Press, 1987.

   Dancing Identity: Metaphysics in Motion. Pittsburgh: University of Pittsburgh Press, 2004.

Framery, Nicolas-Étienne and Pierre Louis Ginguené, eds. *Encyclopédie méthodique: Musique*. Paris: Chez Panckoucke, 1791.

François, Anne-Lise. *Open Secrets: The Literature of Uncounted Experience*. Stanford: Stanford University Press, 2007.

Frascina, Francis and Jonathan Harris, eds. *Art in Modern Culture: An Anthology of Critical Texts*. London: Phaidon, 1992.

Friedel, Johann. *Galanterien Wiens: Auf einer Reise gesammelt, und in Briefen geschildert* (1784).

Frizot, Michel, ed. *A New History of Photography*. Cologne: Könemann, 1998.

Gamboni, Dario. *Potential Images: Ambiguity and Indeterminacy in Modern Art*. London: Reaktion, 2002.

Gammie, Ian and Derek McCulloch. *Jane Austen's Music*. St Albans: Corda Music, 1996.

Garafola, Lynn. *Diaghilev's Ballets Russes*. New York and Oxford: Oxford University Press, 1989.

Garelick, Rhonda. *Electric Salome: Loie Fuller's Performance of Modernism*. Princeton: Princeton University Press, 2007.

Garratt, Peter, ed. *The Cognitive Humanities: Embodied Music in Literature and Culture*. London: Palgrave Macmillan, 2016.

Gelbart, Matthew. *The Invention of 'Folk Music' and 'Art Music': Emerging Categories from Ossian to Wagner*. Cambridge: Cambridge University Press, 2007.

Gilbert, Jeremy and Ewan Pearson. *Discographies: Dance Music, Culture and the Politics of Sound*. London: Routledge, 1999.

Gildea, Robert. *France 1870–1914*. 2nd edn. London and New York: Longman, 1996.

Gilman, Sander. *The Jew's Body*. New York: Routledge, 1991.

Ginot, Isabelle. 'From Shusterman's Somaesthetics to a Radical Epistemology of Somatics'. *Dance Research Journal* 42, no. 1 (2010), 12–29.

Gjerdingen, Robert. *Music in the Galant Style*. Oxford: Oxford University Press, 2007.

   'The Perfection of Craft Training in the Neapolitan Conservatories'. *Rivista di Analisi e Teoria Musicale* 15 (2009), 26–49.

'Fauré as Student and Teacher of Harmony'. In *Fauré Studies*. Edited by Carlo Caballero and Stephen Rumph. Cambridge: Cambridge University Press, forthcoming.

Glass, Frank. *The Fertilizing Seed: Richard Wagner's Concept of the Poetic Intent*. Ann Arbor, MI: UMI Research Press, 1983.

Gluck, Mary. 'The Flâneur and the Aesthetic: Appropriation of Urban Culture in Mid-Nineteenth-Century Paris'. *Theatre, Culture and Society* 20, no. 5 (2003), 53–80.

Popular Bohemia. Cambridge, MA: Harvard University Press, 2005.

Gollay, Rachel. '"The Most Determined Flirt": The Dynamics of Romantic Uncertainty in Joe Wright's *Pride and Prejudice*'. *Persuasions On-Line* 27, no. 2 (2007), www.jasna.org/persuasions/on-line/vol27no2/gollay.htm?

Goodall, Jane. 'Transferred Agencies: Performance and the Fear of Automatism'. *Theatre Journal* 49, no. 4 (1997), 441–53.

Gramit, David. 'Between *Täuschung* and *Seligkeit*: Situating Schubert's Dances'. *Musical Quarterly* 84 (2000), 221–37.

Grau, Andrée. 'Myths of Origin'. In *The Routledge Dance Studies Reader*. Edited by Alexandra Carter, 197–202. London and New York: Routledge, 1998.

Gross, Rev. J. B. *The Parson on Dancing as it is Taught in the Bible, and was Practiced Among the Ancient Greeks and Romans*. Philadelphia: J. B. Lippincott, 1879; reprint edn, New York: Dance Horizons, 1975.

Grover-Friedlander, Michal. '"The Phantom of the Opera": The Lost Voice of Opera in Silent Film'. *Cambridge Opera Journal* 11, no. 2 (2008), 179–92.

Guest, Ivor. *The Ballet of the Second Empire: 1858–1870*. London: Adam and Charles Black, 1953.

The Ballet of the Second Empire. London: Pitman; Middletown, CT: Wesleyan University Press, 1974.

Gunning, Tom. 'Loïe Fuller and the Art of Motion: Body, Light, Electricity, and the Origins of Cinema'. In *Camera Obscura, Camera Lucida: Essays in Honor of Annette Michelson*. Edited by Richard Allen and Malcolm Turvey, 75–89. Amsterdam: Amsterdam University Press, 1995.

Guthrie, William Norman. *The Relation of Dance to Religion*. New York: Petrus Stuyvesant Book Guild, 1923.

Gutsche-Miller, Sarah. *Parisian Music-Hall Ballet, 1871–1913*, Eastman Series in Music. Rochester, NY: University of Rochester Press, 2015.

Hadlock, Heather. *Mad Loves: Women and Music in Offenbach's 'Les Contes d'Hoffmann'*. Princeton: Princeton University Press, 2000.

Hahn, H. Hazel. *Scenes of Parisian Modernity: Culture and Consumption in the Nineteenth Century*. London and New York: Palgrave Macmillan, 2009.

Hall, Joshua M. 'Core Aspects of Dance: Condillac and Mead on Gesture'. *Dance Chronicle* 36, no. 3 (2013), 352–71.

Hanna, Judith Lynne. *Dance, Sex and Gender*. Chicago: University of Chicago Press, 1988.

Hanslick, Eduard. 'Musikalische Briefe' (7 August 1855). In *Sämtliche Schriften: Historisch-kritische Ausgabe*, vol. 3. Edited by Dietmar Strauß. Vienna, Cologne, Weimar: Böhlau Verlag, 1995.

Harrison, Charles and Paul Wood, eds. *Art in Theory, 1900–2000: An Anthology of Changing Ideas*. London: Wiley, 2003.

Harriss, Ernest C. *Johann Mattheson's Der vollkommene Capellmeister: A Revised Translation with Critical Commentary*. Ann Arbor: UMI Research Press, 1981.

Harris-Warrick, Rebecca and Bruce Alan Brown, eds. *The Grotesque Dancer on the Eighteenth-Century Stage: Gennaro Magri and His World*. Madison: University of Wisconsin Press, 2005.

Hasty, Christopher. *Meter as Rhythm*. New York: Oxford University Press, 1997.

Hawn, C. Michael and June Hadden Hobbs, '"Thy Love ... Hath Broken Every Barrier Down": The Rhetoric of Intimacy in Nineteenth-Century British and American Women's Hymns'. In *Music and Theology in Nineteenth-Century Britain*. Edited by Martin V. Clarke, 61–78. Burlington, VT: Ashgate, 2012.

Heisler Jr., Wayne. 'Antony Tudor's *Dark Elegies* and the Affirmation of Mahler's Body, 1937–1947'. *Dance Chronicle* 36 (2013), 172–95.

  'Reconciling the "Three Graceful Hellenic Sisters": Wagner, Dance, and "Song-Ballets" Set to Richard Strauss's *Vier letzte Lieder* (Four Last Songs)'. In *The Total Work of Art: Foundations, Articulations, Inspirations*. Edited by David Imhoof, Margaret Menninger and Anthony Steinhoff, 133–56. New York: Berghahn Books, 2016.

Heller, Wendy. 'Dancing Desire on the Venetian Stage'. *Cambridge Opera Journal* 15 (2003), 281–95.

Helwig, Christine and Marshall Barron, eds. *Purcell, Playford, and the English Country Dance. Vol. I: The Dances*. New Haven, CT: Playford Consort, 1995.

Henisch, Heinz K. and Bridget A. Henisch. *The Photographic Experience, 1839–1914: Images and Attitudes*. University Park, PA: Pennsylvania State University Press, 1994.

Hibberd, Sarah. *French Grand Opera and the Historical Imagination*. Cambridge: Cambridge University Press, 2009.

  'Cherubini and the Revolutionary Sublime'. *Cambridge Opera Journal* 24, no. 3 (2012), 293–318.

Hibberd, Sarah and Richard Wrigley, eds. *Art, Theatre, and Opera in Paris, 1750–1850: Exchanges and Tensions*. Aldershot: Ashgate, 2014.

Higgs, David. *Nobles in Nineteenth-Century France: The Practice of Inegalitarianism*. Baltimore: Johns Hopkins University Press, 1987.

Higson, Andrew. *English Heritage, English Cinema. Costume Drama since 1980*. Oxford: Oxford University Press, 2003.

'Re-Presenting the National Past: Nostalgia and Pastiche in the Heritage Film'. In *Fires were Started: British Cinema and Thatcherism*. Edited by Lester D. Friedman, 91–109. New York: Wallflower Press, 2006.

Historisches Museum der Stadt, Wien. *Fasching in Wien: der Wiener Walzer 1750–1850*. Vienna: Historischen Museum der Stadt Wien, 1979.

Hobbs, June Hadden. *'I Sing for I Cannot Be Silent': The Feminization of American Hymnody, 1870–1920*. Pittsburgh: University of Pittsburgh Press, 1997.

Hobsbawm, Eric. 'Introduction: Inventing Traditions'. In *The Invention of Tradition*. Edited by Eric Hobsbawm and Terence Ranger, 1–14. Cambridge: Cambridge University Press, 1983.

Hogwood, Christopher. 'In Defence of the Minuet and Trio'. *Early Music* 30 (2002), 236–51.

Holloway, Robin. '*Salome*: Art or Kitsch?' In *On Music: Essays and Diversions 1963–2003*, 107–121. Cambridge: Cambridge University Press, 2003.

Holman, Peter. *Dowland: 'Lachrimae' (1604)*. Cambridge: Cambridge University Press, 1999.

Holub, Robert. *Reception Theory: A Critical Introduction*. London: Methuen, 1984.

Horne, William. 'Through the Aperture: Brahms's Gigues, WoO 4'. *Musical Quarterly* 86, no. 3 (Fall 2002), 530–81.

Howard, Skiles. *The Politics of Courtly Dancing in Early Modern England*. Amherst: University of Massachusetts Press, 1998.

Howat, Roy, ed. *Œuvres complètes de Claude Debussy*, series 1, vol. 1. Paris: Editions Durand, 2000.

Huckvale, David. 'Rienzi's Reich'. *Wagner* 19, no. 3 (1998), 103–16.

Hutcheon, Linda and Michael Hutcheon. 'Staging the Female Body'. In *Siren Songs*. Edited by Mary Ann Smart, 201–21. Princeton: Princeton University Press, 2000.

Huyssen, Andreas. 'Mass Culture as Woman'. In *After the Great Divide: Modernism, Mass Culture, Postmodernism*, 44–62. Basingstoke: MacMillan, 1986.

Irwin, Joyce. 'Bach in the Midst of Religious Transition'. In *Bach's Changing World: Voices in the Community*. Edited by Carol K. Baron, 108–26. Rochester, NY: University of Rochester Press, 2006.

Isaacson, Joel. 'Review of *Impressionism: Art, Leisure, and Parisian Society* by Robert L. Herbert'. *Art Journal* 49, no. 1 (1990), 63–8.

Iskin, Ruth E. *The Poster: Art, Advertising, Design, and Collecting, 1860s–1900s*. Hanover, NH: Dartmouth College Press, 2014.

Jauss, Hans Robert. *Toward an Aesthetic of Reception*. Translated by Timothy Bahti. Brighton: Harvester, 1982.

Johnson, Julian. *Mahler's Voices: Expression and Irony in the Songs and Symphonies*. Oxford: Oxford University Press, 2009.

Jones, David Wyn and Otto Biba. *Haydn*. Oxford: Oxford University Press, 2002.

Jordan, Stephanie. 'Choreomusical Conversations: Facing a Double Challenge'. *Dance Research Journal* 43, no. 1 (2011), 43–64.

Mark Morris: Musician–Choreographer. London: Dance Books, 2015.

Judovitz, Dalia. *Drawing on Art: Duchamp and Company*. Minneapolis: University of Minnesota Press, 2010.

Unpacking Duchamp: Art in Transit. Berkeley and Los Angeles: University of California Press, 1998.

Jürgensen, Knud Arne. *The Verdi Ballets*. Parma: Istituto Nazionale di Studi Verdiani, 1995.

Kahan, Sylvia. 'Patrons and Society: Gabriel Fauré's "Other" Career in the Paris and London Music Salons'. In *Fauré Studies*. Edited by Carlo Caballero and Stephen Rumph. Cambridge: Cambridge University Press, forthcoming.

Kamien-Kazhdan, Adina. *Remaking the Readymade: Duchamp, Man Ray and the Conundrum of the Replica*. London and New York: Routledge, 2018.

Karnes, Kevin. *Music Criticism and the Challenge of History: Shaping Modern Musical Thought in Late Nineteenth-Century Vienna*. Oxford: Oxford University Press, 2008.

Kelly, Michael and Roger Fiske. *Reminiscences*. Oxford: Oxford University Press, 1975.

Kendall, G. Yvonne. *The Music of Arbeau's 'Orchesographie'*, The Wendy Hilton Dance and Music Series, no. 17. New York: Pendragon Press, 2013.

Kennedy, Douglas. *English Folk Dancing: Today and Yesterday*. London: G. Bell and Sons, 1964.

Kermode, Frank. 'Poet and Dancer before Diaghilev'. In *Puzzles and Epiphanies: Essays and Reviews 1958–1961*, 1–28. New York: Chillmark Press, 1962.

Kittler, Friedrich A. *Discourse Networks: 1800/1900*. Stanford: Stanford University Press, 1990.

Gramophone, Film, Typewriter. Stanford: Stanford University Press, 1999.

Knittel, K. M. '"Ein hypermoderner Dirigent": Mahler and Anti-Semitism in Fin-de-Siècle Vienna'. *19th-Century Music* 18 (1995), 257–76.

Seeing Mahler: Music and the Language of Antisemitism in Fin-de-Siècle Vienna. Burlington, VT: Ashgate, 2010.

Korhonen, Joonas. 'Urban Social Space and the Development of Public Dance Hall Culture in Vienna, 1780–1814'. *Urban History* 40, no. 4 (2013), 606–24.

Kramer, Lawrence. 'Tropes and Windows: An Outline of Musical Hermeneutics'. In *Music as Cultural Practice, 1800–1900*, 1–20. Berkeley and Los Angeles: University of California Press, 1990.

The Thought of Music. Berkeley and Los Angeles: University of California Press, 2016.

Krauss, Rosalind. 'The Originality of the Avant-Garde: A Postmodernist Repetition'. *October* 18 (1981), 47–66.

Kraut, Anthea. *Choreographing Copyright: Race, Gender, and Intellectual Property Rights in American Dance*. New York and Oxford: Oxford University Press, 2015.

Kreuzer, Gundula. *Curtain, Gong, Steam: Wagnerian Technologies of Nineteenth-Century Opera*. Berkeley and Los Angeles: University of California Press, 2018.

Kurth, Peter. *Isadora Duncan: A Sensational Life*. Boston: Little, Brown, and Co., 2001.

Lajarte, Théodore de, ed. *Airs à danser de Lulli à Méhul, transcrits d'après les manuscrits originaux de la Bibliothèque de l'Opéra de Paris*. Paris: Durand, Schoenwerk [1876].

Lake, Taylor Susan. 'American Delsartism and the Bodily Discourse of Respectable Womanliness'. PhD diss., University of Iowa, 2002.

Lange, Johann Christian. *Vernunfft-mässiges Bescheidenes und Unparteyisches Bedencken Uber die Durch macherley öffentliche Schrifften und anderwertig zum öfftern angeregte Streitigkeit vom Tantzen*. Frankfurt and Leipzig, 1704.

Lanza, Joseph. *Elevator Music: A Surreal History of Muzak, Easy-Listening and Other Moodsong*. Ann Arbor: University of Michigan Press, 2004.

Le Guin, Elisabeth. *Boccherini's Body: An Essay in Carnal Musicology*. Berkeley and Los Angeles: University of California Press, 2005.

Lee-Riffe, Nancy M. 'The Role of Country Dance in the Fiction of Jane Austen'. *Women's Writing* 5, no. 1 (1998), 103–12.

Lepecki, André. *Exhausting Dance: Performance and the Politics of Movement*. London and New York: Routledge, 2006.

Leppert, Richard and Susan McClary, eds. *Music and Society: The Politics of Composition, Performance and Reception*. Cambridge: Cambridge University Press, 1987.

Levine, Lawrence. *Highbrow/Lowbrow: The Emergence of Cultural Hierarchy in America*. Cambridge, MA: Harvard University Press, 1988.

Lewis, Robert M. '*Tableaux vivants:* Parlor Theatricals in Victorian America'. *Revue français d'études américaines* 36 (April 1988), 280–91.

Libin, Kathryn L. Shanks. 'Music, Character, and Social Standing in Jane Austen's *Emma*'. *Persuasions* 22 (2000), 15–30.

Lidov, David. 'Mind and Body in Music'. *Semiotica* 66, nos. 1–3 (1987), 69–97.

Lista, Giovanni. *Loïe Fuller: Danseuse de la Belle Époque*. Paris: Stock, 1994.

Little, Meredith. 'Courtly, Social and Theatrical Dance'. In *The Worlds of Johann Sebastian Bach*. Edited by Raymond Erickson, 207–28. New York: Amadeus Press, 2009.

Little, Meredith and Natalie Jenne. *Dance and the Music of J. S. Bach*. Bloomington and Indianapolis: Indiana University Press, 1991; expanded edition 2009.

Locke, Ralph. 'Constructing the Oriental "Other": Saint-Saëns's *Samson et Dalila*'. *Cambridge Opera Journal* 3 (1991), 261–302.

'Beyond the Exotic: How "Eastern" Is *Aida*?' *Cambridge Opera Journal* 17 (2005), 105–39.

Lotringer, Sylvère, ed. *Foucault Live: Interviews, 1961–84*. Translated by John Johnston. New York: Semiotext(e), 1989.

Lowe, Melanie. 'Falling from Grace: Irony and Expressive Enrichment in Haydn's Symphonic Minuets'. *Journal of Musicology* 19, no. 2 (2002), 171–221.

Pleasure and Meaning in the Classical Symphony. Bloomington and Indianapolis: Indiana University Press, 2007.

MacLaren, Gay. *Morally We Roll Along*. Boston: Little, Brown, & Company, 1938.

MacPherson, William A. 'The Music of the English Country Dance 1651–1728'. PhD diss., Harvard University, 1984.

Magdanz, Teresa. 'The Waltz: Technology's Muse'. *Journal of Popular Music Studies* 18, no. 3 (2006), 251–81.

Mallarmé, Stéphane. *Œuvres complètes*. Edited by Georges Jean-Aubry and Henri Mondor. Paris: Gallimard, 1945.

Marini, Stephen. 'From Classical to Modern: Hymnody and the Development of American Evangelicalism, 1737–1970'. In *Singing the Lord's Song in a Strange Land: Hymnody in the History of North American Protestantism*. Edited by Edith L. Blumhofer and Mark A. Noll, 1–38. Tuscaloosa: University of Alabama Press, 2004.

Marks, Laura U. *The Skin of the Film: Intercultural Cinema, Embodiment and the Senses*. Durham, NC: Duke University Press, 2000.

Marsh, Carol. 'French Court Dances in England, 1706–1740: A Study of the Sources (Dance Music, Notation, Dancing Masters)'. PhD diss., City University of New York, 1985.

Marsh, Christopher. *Music and Society in Early Modern England*. Cambridge: Cambridge University Press, 2010.

Mattheson, Johann. *Der vollkommene Kapellmeister*. Hamburg: Herold, 1739.

McAulay, Karen E. 'From "Anti-Scot" to "Anti-Scottish" Sentiment: Cultural Nationalism and Scottish Song in the Late Eighteenth to Nineteenth Centuries'. *Library and Information History* 26, no. 4 (2010), 272–88.

McClary, Susan. *Georges Bizet: 'Carmen'*. Cambridge: Cambridge University Press, 1992.

'Music, the Pythagoreans, and the Body'. In *Choreographing History*. Edited by Susan Leigh Foster, 82–104. Bloomington and Indianapolis: Indiana University Press, 1995.

McGee, Timothy J. *The Sound of Medieval Song: Ornamentation and Vocal Style According to the Treatises*. Oxford: Clarendon Press, 1998.

ed. *Instruments and their Music in the Middle Ages*. Aldershot: Ashgate, 2009.

McKee, Eric. 'Influences of the Early Eighteenth-Century Social Minuet on the Minuets from J. S. Bach's French Suites, BWV812–17'. *Music Analysis* 18 (1999), 235–60.

'Mozart in the Ballroom: Minuet-trio Contrast and the Aristocracy in Self-portrait'. *Music Analysis* 24 (2005), 383–434.

Decorum of the Minuet, Delirium of the Waltz. Bloomington and Indianapolis: Indiana University Press, 2012.

McKinnon, James. 'The Meaning of the Patristic Polemic against Musical Instruments'. *Current Musicology* 1 (1965), 69–82.

Mellers, Wilfrid. *Bach and the Dance of God*. London: Faber, 1980.

Meredith, William V. *Pageantry and Dramatics in Religious Education*. New York: Abingdon Press, 1921.

Merleau-Ponty, Maurice. *Phenomenology of Perception*. Paris: Gallimard, 1945; translated by Colin Smith, London and New York: Routledge, 2002.

Messing, Scott. *Neoclassicism in Music: From the Genesis of the Concept through the Schoenberg-Stravinsky Polemic*. Rochester, NY: University of Rochester Press, 1988, reprint 1996.

Mester, Terri A. *Movement and Modernism: Yeats, Elliot, Lawrence, Williams and Early Twentieth-Century Dance*. Fayetteville: University of Arkansas Press, 1997.

Miller Frank, Felicia. *The Mechanical Song: Women, Voice, and the Artificial in Nineteenth-Century French Narrative*. Stanford: Stanford University Press, 1995.

Mirka, Danuta. *Metric Manipulations in Haydn and Mozart: Chamber Music for Strings, 1787–1791*. Oxford: Oxford University Press, 2009.

Moffitt, John. *Alchemist of the Avant-Garde: The Case of Marcel Duchamp*. New York: State University of New York Press, 2012.

Molderings, Herbert. *Duchamp and the Aesthetics of Chance: Art as Experiment*. New York: Columbia University Press, 2010.

Monahan, Seth. *Mahler's Symphonic Sonatas*. Oxford: Oxford University Press, 2015.

Monk, Claire. 'The British Heritage Film Debate Revisited'. In *British Historical Cinema*. Edited by Claire Monk and Amy Sargeant, 176–98. London: Routledge, 2001.

Morley, Thomas. *A Plaine and Easie Introduction to Practicall Musike* (1597). Westmead, Farnborough, Hants, UK: Gregg International, 1971.

Morris, R. Anna. *Physical Education in the Public Schools: An Eclectic System of Exercises, Including the Delsartean Principles of Execution and Expression*. New York: American Book Company, 1892.

A Manual of Physical Training, Plays and Games for the Primary Grades of the Cleveland Public Schools. Cleveland: Britton, 1901.

Moscovici, Serge. *L'Âge des foules: Un traité historique de psychologie des masses*. Paris, 1981.

Mulvey, Laura. 'Visual Pleasure and Narrative Cinema'. In *Visual and Other Pleasures: Language, Discourse, Society*, 14–26. London: Palgrave Macmillan, 1989.

Murdoch, James. *Analytic Elocution*. Cincinnati and New York: Van Antwerp, Bragg & Co., 1884.

Nectoux, Jean-Michel. *Nijinsky: L'Après-midi d'un faune*. London: Thames and Hudson, 1990.

Gabriel Fauré: Les voix du clair-obscur, 2nd edn. Paris: Fayard, 2008.

Neumeyer, David. 'The Contredanse, Classical Finales, and Caplin's Formal Functions'. *Music Theory Online* 12, no. 4 (2006), www.mtosmt.org/classic/mto.06.12.4/mto.06.12.4.neumeyer.html.

Nevile, Jennifer. *The Eloquent Body: Dance and Humanist Culture in Fifteenth-Century Italy*. Bloomington and Indianapolis: Indiana University Press, 2004.

Newman, Ernest. *The Life of Richard Wagner*, vol. 3 (1859–66). Cambridge: Cambridge University Press, 1976.

Nietzsche, Friedrich. *Nietzsche contra Wagner* (1889). In *Der Fall Wagner: Schriften – Aufzeichnungen – Briefe*. Edited by Dieter Borchmeyer. Frankfurt: Insel, 1983.

Noland, Carrie. *Agency and Embodiment: Performing Gestures/Producing Culture*. Cambridge, MA: Harvard University Press, 2009.

Northrop, Henry Davenport. *The Peerless Reciter*. Chicago: E. C. Morse, 1894.

Novak, Jelena. *Postopera: Reinventing the Voice-Body*. Burlington, VT: Ashgate, 2015.

Nye, Robert A. *The Origins of Crowd Psychology: Gustave LeBon and the Crisis of Mass Democracy in the Third Republic*. London: Sage, 1975.

O'Grady, Eleanor. *Elocution Class: A Simplification of the Laws and Principles of Expression*. New York: Benziger Brothers, 1895.

Olin, Elinor. 'The Concerts de l'Opéra, 1895–97'. *19th-Century Music* 16, no. 3 (1993), 253–66.

Ortner, Sherry B. *Making Gender: The Politics and Erotics of Culture*. Boston: Beacon Press, 1996.

Page, Christopher. 'German Musicians and their Instruments: A 14th-Century Account by Konrad of Megenberg'. *Early Music* 10 (1982), 192–200.

Painter, Karen. 'The Sensuality of Timbre: Responses to Mahler and Modernity at the "Fin de siècle"'. *19th-Century Music* 18 (1995), 236–56.

  Symphonic Aspirations: German Music and Politics, 1900–1945. Cambridge, MA: Harvard University Press, 2007.

Parakilas, James. 'How Spain Got a Soul'. In *The Exotic in Western Music*. Edited by Jonathan Bellman, 137–93. Boston: Northeastern University Press, 1997.

Parry, Jann. *Different Drummer: The Life of Kenneth MacMillan*. London: Faber & Faber, 2009.

Pascall, Robert. 'Unknown Gavottes by Brahms'. *Music & Letters* 57, no. 4 (October 1976), 404–11.

Pasch, Johann. *Beschreibung wahrer Tanz-Kunst*. Frankfurt, 1707.

Pasler, Jann. *Composing the Citizen: Music as Public Utility in Third Republic France*. Berkeley and Los Angeles: University of California Press, 2009.

Polk, Keith. 'Instrumentalists and Performance Practices in Dance Music, *c.* 1500'. In *Improvisation in the Arts of the Middle Ages and Renaissance*. Edited by Timothy McGee, 98–114. Kalamazoo, MI: Medieval Institute Publications, Western Michigan University, 2003.

Porter, W. S., Marjorie Heffer and Arthur Heffer, eds. *The Apted Book of Country Dances: Twenty-four Country Dances from the Last Years of the Eighteenth Century with Tunes and Instructions*. Cambridge: W. Heffer and Sons, 1931.

Proksch, Bryan. 'Vincent d'Indy as Harbinger of the Haydn Revival'. *Journal of Musicological Research* 28 (2009), 162–88.

Prynne, William. *Histrio-mastix*. London: E. A. and W. I. for Michael Sparke, 1633.

Puchner, Martin. *Stage Fright: Modernism, Anti-Theatricality, and Drama*. Baltimore and London: Johns Hopkins University Press, 2002.

Puffett, Derrick. *Richard Strauss: 'Elektra'*. Cambridge: Cambridge University Press, 1989.

Rancière, Jacques. *Aisthesis: Scenes from the Aesthetic Regime of Arts*. Translated by Zakir Paul. London: Verso, 2013.

Ratner, Leonard. *Classic Music: Expression, Form and Style*. New York: Simon & Schuster, 1980.

Revers, Peter. '". . . the heart-wrenching sound of farewell": Mahler, Rückert, and the Kindertotenlieder'. In *Mahler and His World*. Edited by Karen Painter, translated by Irene Zedlacher, 173–83. Princeton and Oxford: Princeton University Press, 2002.

Rieser, Andrew C. *The Chautauqua Movement: Protestants, Progressives, and the Culture of Modern Liberalism*. New York: Columbia University Press, 2003.

Riley, Matthew. *Musical Listening in the German Enlightenment: Attention, Wonder and Astonishment*. Aldershot: Ashgate, 2004.

Robinson, Paul. 'Is *Aida* an Orientalist Opera?' *Cambridge Opera Journal* 5 (1993), 133–40.

Rodin, Auguste. *L'Art: entretiens réunis par Paul Gsell*. Paris: Bernard Grasset, 1911.

Rogers, Christine. 'Dances for Jane Austen'. *English Dance and Song* 69, no. 3 (2007), 20–1.

Rooney, Kim. 'Parlor Music in Film Adaptations of Jane Austen's Novels'. *Music Research Forum* 20 (2005), 39–54.

Rosemont, Franklin, ed. *Isadora Speaks*. San Francisco: City Lights Books, 1981.

Rüetz, Caspar. *Widerlegte Vorurtheile von der Beschaffenheit des heutigen Kirchenmusic und von der Lebens-Art einiger Musicorum*. Lübeck, 1752.

Russell, Tilden. *Theory and Practice in Eighteenth-Century Dance: The German-French Connection*. London: Rowman & Littlefield, 2018.

Ruyter, Nancy Lee Chalfa. *Reformers and Visionaries: The Americanization of the Art of Dance*. New York: Dance Horizons, 1979.

The Cultivation of Body and Mind in Nineteenth-Century American Delsartism. Westport, CT: Greenwood Press, 1999.

'Antique Longings: Genevieve Stebbins and American Delsartean Performance'. In *Corporealities: Dancing, Knowledge, Culture and Power*. Edited by Susan Leigh Foster, 72–91. London: Routledge, 1996.

Sacks, Adam J. 'Toward an Expansion of the Critique of the Mahler Revival'. *New German Critique* 119 (2013), 113–36.

Sale, Stephen and Laura Salisbury, eds. *Kittler Now: Current Perspectives in Kittler Studies*. Cambridge: Polity, 2015.

Samuels, Robert. *Mahler's Sixth Symphony: A Study in Semiotics*. Cambridge: Cambridge University Press, 1995.

Sanguinetti, Giorgio. *The Art of Partimento: History, Theory, and Practice*. Oxford: Oxford University Press, 2012.

Sawyer, Elizabeth. 'Antony Tudor's Lost Ballets'. *Dance Chronicle* 31 (2008), 6–53.

Sayer, Karen. *Women of the Fields: Representations of Rural Women in the Nineteenth Century*. Manchester: Manchester University Press, 1995.

Schaufler, Wolfgang, ed. *Gustav Mahler: The Conductors' Interviews*. Vienna: Universal, 2013.

Schell, Stanley, ed. *Werner's Book of Pantomimes*. New York: Edgar S. Werner, 1908.

Schwartz, Vanessa. *Spectacular Realities: Early Mass Culture in fin-de-siècle Paris*. Berkeley and Los Angeles: University of California Press, 1998.

Scott, Derek. 'Orientalism and Musical Style'. *Musical Quarterly* 82, no. 2 (1998), 309–35.

Sedgwick, Eve Kosofsky. *Touching Feeling: Affect, Pedagogy and Performativity*. Durham, NC: Duke University Press, 2002.

Semmens, Richard. 'Branles, Gavottes and Contredanses in the Late Seventeenth and Early Eighteenth Centuries'. *Dance Research* 15, no. 2 (1997), 35–62.

'"La Furstenberg" and "St Martin's Lane": Purcell's French Odyssey'. *Music & Letters* 78, no. 3 (1997), 337–49.

Shawn, Ted. *Every Little Movement: A Book about François Delsarte*. 2nd edn. Reprint edn, Brooklyn: Dance Horizons, 1968.

Shaya, Gregory. 'The *Flâneur*, the *Badaud*, and the Making of a Mass Public in France, circa 1860–1910'. *The American Historical Review* 109, no. 1 (2004), 41–77.

Sheen, Erica. '"Where the Garment Gapes": Faithfulness and Promiscuity in the 1995 BBC *Pride and Prejudice*'. In *The Classic Novel from Page to Screen*. Edited by Robert Giddings and Erica Sheen, 14–30. Manchester: Manchester University Press, 2000.

Shoemaker, Jacob. *Practical Elocution; for Use in Colleges and Schools and by Private Students*. Philadelphia: National School of Elocution and Oratory, 1886.

Shoemaker, Mrs J. W. *Delsartean Pantomines with Recital and Musical Accompaniment*. Philadelphia: Penn, 1902.

Shusterman, Richard. *Surface and Depth: Dialectics of Criticism and Culture*. Ithaca, NY: Cornell University Press, 2002.

Siegel, Marcia B. *The Shapes of Change: Images of American Dance*. Boston: Houghton Mifflin, 1979.

Silva, Vanda de Sá. 'Avondano's Lisbon Minuets: The Establishment of a Cosmopolitan Model'. *Ad Parnassum* 8, no. 15 (2010), 79–92.

Silverman, Kaja. *The Miracle of Analogy, or The History of Photography*, vol. 1. Stanford: Stanford University Press, 2015.

Simonson, Mary. *Body Knowledge: Performance, Intermediality, and American Entertainment at the Turn of the Twentieth Century*. Oxford: Oxford University Press, 2013.

Simpson, Claude. *The British Broadside Ballad and Its Music*. New Brunswick: Rutgers University Press, 1966.

Sizer, Sandra S. [Tamar Frankiel]. *Gospel Hymns and Social Religion: the Rhetoric of Nineteenth-Century Revivalism*. Philadelphia: Temple University Press, 1978.

Smart, Mary Ann. 'Mourning the Duc d'Orléans: Donizetti's *Dom Sébastien* and the Social Meanings of Grand Opéra'. In *Reading Critics Reading: Opera and Ballet Criticism in France from the Revolution to 1848*. Edited by Roger Parker and Mary Ann Smart, 188–212. Oxford: Oxford University Press, 2001.

 Mimomania: Music and Gesture in Nineteenth-Century Opera. Berkeley and Los Angeles: University of California Press, 2004.

Smith, Augustine. *Lyric Religion: The Romance of Immortal Hymns*. New York: Century Co., 1931.

Smith, Marian. *Ballet and Opera in the Age of 'Giselle'*. Princeton: Princeton University Press, 2000.

 'Dance and Dancers'. In *The Cambridge Companion to Grand Opera*. Edited by David Charlton, 93–107. Cambridge: Cambridge University Press, 2003.

Snape, Richard. 'Continuity, Change and Performativity in Leisure: English Folk Dance and Modernity 1900–1939'. *Leisure Studies* 28, no. 3 (2009), 297–311.

Sobchack, Vivian. *The Address of the Eye: A Phenomenology of Film Experience*. Princeton: Princeton University Press, 1991.

Sontag, Susan. 'Against Interpretation'. In *Against Interpretation and Other Essays*, 4–14. New York: Farrar, Straus and Giroux, 1966.

Sozen, Joyce Chalcraft. 'Anna Morgan: Reader, Teacher, and Director'. PhD diss., University of Illinois, 1961.

Stebbins, Genevieve. *Society Gymnastics and Voice-Culture; Adapted from the Delsarte System*. 6th edn. New York: E. S. Werner, 1888.

Stein, Louise K. '"La musica de dos obres": A Context for the First Opera of the Americans'. *Opera Quarterly* 22 (2006), 433–58.

Stevens, John. *Words and Music in the Middle Ages: Song, Narrative, Dance and Drama, 1050–1350*. Cambridge: Cambridge University Press, 1986.

Stillwell, Robynn. 'Sense and Sensibility. Form, Genre and Function in the Film Score'. *Acta Musicologica* 72, no. 2 (2000), 219–40.

Stott, Alan, ed. *Bach and the Dance of Heaven and Earth*. Weobley: Anastasi, 2003.

Sulloway, Alison. *Jane Austen and the Province of Womanhood*. Philadelphia: University of Pennsylvania Press, 1989.

Sunday, Billy. 'A Plain Talk to Women'. In William T. Ellis, *Billy Sunday: The Man and His Message*, 223–24. Philadelphia: L. T. Myers, 1914.

Suter, Lisa. 'The Arguments They Wore: The Role of the Neoclassical Toga in American Delsartism'. In *Rhetoric, History, and Women's Oratorical Education: American Women Learn to Speak*. Edited by David Gold and Catherine L. Hobbs, 134–53. New York: Routledge, 2013.

Sutherland, Kathryn. 'Jane Austen on Screen'. In *Cambridge Companion to Jane Austen*. 2nd edn. Edited by Edward Copeland and Juliet McMaster, 215–31. Cambridge: Cambridge University Press, 2011.

Sutton, Julia. 'Late Renaissance Dance.' In *Fabritio Caroso, Nobilità di dame*. Edited by Julia Sutton and F. Marian Walker, 21–30. Oxford: Oxford University Press, 1986.

Svétlow, Valerian. *Le Ballet contemporain*. Paris: Brunoff, 1912.

Tabourot, Jean [Thoinot Arbeau]. *Orchésographie* [1589], réimpression précédée d'une notice sur les danses du XVIe siècle par Laure Fonta. Paris, 1888; Genève: Slatkine Reprints, 1970.

Tanzer, Gerhard. *Spectacle müssen seyn: die Freizeit der Wiener im 18. Jahrhundert*. Vienna: Böhlau, 1992.

Taruskin, Richard. *Oxford History of Western Music*. Oxford: Oxford University Press, 2005.

'Setting Limits'. In *The Danger of Music and Other Anti-Utopian Essays*, 447–66. Berkeley and Los Angeles: University of California Press, 2009.

Tester, Keith. *The Flâneur*. London and New York: Routledge, 1994.

Thomas, Valérie and Jerôme Perrin. *Loïe Fuller, danseuse de l'art nouveau*. Paris: Éditions de la Réunion des Musées Nationaux, 2002.

Thorau, Christian and Hansjakob Ziemer, eds. *The Oxford Handbook of Music Listening in the 19th and 20th Centuries*. Oxford: Oxford University Press, 2018.

Thorp, Jennifer. 'In Defence of Danced Minuets'. *Early Music* 31 (2003), 101–8.

Thurner, Christina. *Beredte Körper – bewegte Seelen: Zum Diskurs der Doppleten Bewegungen in Tanztexten*. Bielefeld: transcript Verlag, 2009.

Tomko, Linda J. *Dancing Class: Gender, Ethnicity, and Social Divides in American Dance, 1890–1920*. Bloomington and Indianapolis: Indiana University Press, 1999.

Tucker, Thomas Deane. *Derridada: Duchamp as Readymade Deconstruction*. Lanham: Lexington, 2009.

van Orden, Kate. *Music, Discipline, and Arms in Early Modern France*. Chicago: University of Chicago Press, 2005.

Wagner, Ann Louise. *Adversaries of Dance: From the Puritans to the Present*. Urbana: University of Illinois Press, 1997.

Wagner, Cosima. *Diaries*, vol. 1, Edited by Martin Gregor-Dellin and Dietrich Mack, translated by Geoffrey Skelton. New York: Harcourt Brace Jovanovich, 1977.

Wagner, Richard. 'A Report on the Production of *Tannhäuser* in Paris'. In *Prose Works. Vol. 3: Theatre*. Edited and translated by W. A. Ellis, 347–60. London: Kegan Paul, Trench, Trübner & Co. Ltd., second impression, 1907.
Gesammelte Schriften und Dichtungen. Leipzig: Breitkopf & Härtel, 1911.
My Life. Translated by Andrew Gray. Cambridge: Cambridge University Press, 1983.
Selected Letters of Richard Wagner. Translated and edited by Stewart Spencer and Barry Millington. New York: W. W. Norton, 1988.
Sämtliche Briefe, vol. 12. Edited by Martin Dürer. Wiesbaden: Breitkopf & Härtel, 2001.
Waite, Philippa and Judith Appleby. *Beauchamp-Feuillet Notation: A Guide for Beginner and Intermediate Baroque Dance Students*. Cardiff: Consort de Danse Baroque, 2008.
Walker, Donald. *Exercise for Ladies: Calculated to Preserve and Improve Beauty*. London: Thomas Hurst, 1836.
Walkowitz, Daniel J. *City Folk: English Country Dance and the Politics of the Folk in Modern America*. New York: New York University Press, 2010.
'Patrolling the Boundaries'. *Radical History Review* 84 (2002), 119–22.
Ward, Andrew. 'Dancing around Meaning (and the Meaning around Dance)'. In *Dance in the City*. Edited by Helen Thomas, 3–20. Basingstoke: Macmillan, 1997.
Ward, J. M. 'And Who But Ladie Greensleeues?' In *The Well Enchanting Skill: Essays in Honour of F. W. Sternfeld*. Edited by J. A. Caldwell, E. D. Olleson and S. Wollenberg, 181–211. Oxford: Oxford University Press, 1990.
Warman, E. B. *How to Read, Recite and Impersonate*. Chicago: M. A. Donohue & Co., 1889.
Watkins, Holly and Melina Esse. 'Down with Disembodiment; or, Musicology and the Material Turn'. *Women and Music: A Journal of Gender and Culture* 19 (2015), 161–8.
Watson, J. R. *The English Hymn: A Critical and Historical Study*. Oxford: Clarendon Press, 1997.
Weatherly, F. E. *The Holy City: Illustrated Pantomimed Hymn*. New York: Edgar S. Werner, 1904.
Wells, Juliette. '"In music she had always used to feel alone in the world": Jane Austen, Solitude, and the Artistic Woman'. *Persuasions* 26 (2004), 98–110.
'A Harpist Arrives at Mansfield Park: Music and the Moral Ambiguity of Mary Crawford'. *Persuasions* 28 (2006), 101–14.
Wenger, Tisa. 'The Practice of Dance for the Future of Christianity: "Eurythmic Worship" in New York's Roaring Twenties'. In *Practicing Protestants: Histories of Christian Life in America, 1630–1965*. Edited by Laurie F. Maffly-Kipp, Leigh E. Schmidt and Mark Valeri, 222–49. Baltimore, MD: Johns Hopkins University Press, 2006.

Wheelock, Gretchen. *Haydn's Ingenious Jesting with Art: Contexts of Musical Wit and Humor*. New York: Schirmer, 1992.

Wiley, Roland John. *Tchaikovsky's Ballets: Swan Lake, Sleeping Beauty, Nutcracker*. Oxford: Clarendon Press, 1985.

Williams, Raymond. *The Country and the City*. Oxford: Oxford University Press, 1973.

Williamson, John. 'The Earliest Completed Works: A Voyage Towards the First Symphony'. In *The Mahler Companion*. Edited by Donald Mitchell and Andrew Nicholson, 39–61. Oxford: Oxford University Press, 1999.

Wilson Kimber, Marian. 'Musical Topics, Historical Styles, and Narrative in Carl Davis's Score for *Pride and Prejudice* (1995)'. *Journal of Adaptation in Film and Performance* 6, no. 2 (2013), 121–35.

The Elocutionists: Women, Music, and the Spoken Word. Urbana: University of Illinois Press, 2017.

Wilson, Alexandra. *The Puccini Problem: Opera, Nationalism and Modernity*. Cambridge: Cambridge University Press, 2002.

Wilson, Cheryl. 'Dance, Physicality, and Social Mobility in Jane Austen's *Persuasion*'. *Persuasions* 25 (2003), 55–75.

Literature and Dance in Nineteenth-Century Britain: Jane Austen to the New Woman. Cambridge: Cambridge University Press, 2009.

Wilson, Thomas. *An Analysis of Country Dancing [. . .]*. 3rd edn. London: J. S. Dickson, 1811.

The Complete System of English Country Dancing [. . .]. London: Sherwood, Neely and Jones, c. 1815.

The Treasures of Terpsichore; or, a Companion for the Ball-room. 2nd edn. London: Sherwood, Neely and Jones, 1816.

Winkler, Amanda Eubanks. 'From Whore to Stuart Ally: Musical Venues on the Early Modern English Stage'. In *Musical Voices of Early Modern Women: Many-Headed Melodies*. Edited by Thomasin La May, 171–85. Aldershot: Ashgate, 2005.

Witzmann, Reingard. *Der Ländler in Wien: ein Beitrag zur Entwicklungsgeschichte des Wiener Walzers bis in die Zeit des Wiener Kongresses*. Vienna: Arbeitsstelle für den Volkskundeatlas in Österreich, 1976.

Wood, Margaret. *Rock of Ages*. New York: Edgar S. Werner, 1903.

Yaraman, Sevin H. *Revolving Embrace: The Waltz as Sex, Steps, and Sound*. Hillsdale, NY: Pendragon, 2002.

Yumibe, Joshua. *Moving Color: Early Film, Mass Culture, Modernism*. New Brunswick: Rutgers University Press, 2012.

Zbikowski, Lawrence M. 'Dance Topoi, Sonic Analogues and Musical Grammar: Communicating with Music in the Eighteenth Century'. In *Communication* in *Eighteenth-Century Music*. Edited by Danuta Mirka and Kofi Agawu, 283–309. Cambridge: Cambridge University Press, 2008.

'Music, Dance, and Meaning in the Early Nineteenth Century'. *Journal of Musicological Research* 31, nos. 2–3 (2012), 147–65.

Zedler, Johann Heinrich. *Grosses vollständiges Universal-Lexicon aller Wissenschafften und Künste*. 64 vols. Halle and Leipzig, 1731–54, www.zedler-lexikon.de.

Index

Abbate, Carolyn, 4, 9, 58, 231, 279
Académie Impériale de Musique. *See* Opéra, Paris
Académie Nationale de Musique. *See* Opéra, Paris
adaptations, 259, 262–3, 268, 269, 270, 279
Adler, Guido, 5
Adorno, Theodor W., 66, 70, 228, 235, 242, 255
Agawu, Kofi, 51, 52
air parlant, 231
Alfano, Franco, *La leggenda di Sakùntala*, 59, 64
Allan, Maude, 148
Allanbrook, Wye J., 6, 10, 264
almées, 60
America. *See* United States
ancien régime, 177, 180, 182, 193, 194, 196
Anderson, Hans Christian, *The Red Shoes*, 70
Anderson, Jack, 245–6, 257
Arbeau, Thoinot, 50, 177
    Orchésographie, 187, 190–1
aristocracy, 14, 180, 203
art, modernist, 207
art, visual, 12, 149, 233
artforms, 56, 207
artwork, total, 13, 122–3, 125, 126, 128, 136, 137, 138, 139, 142, 148, 149, 150, 234
Ashton, Frederick, 251
    Illuminations, 231
Auber, D. F. E.
    La muette de Portici, 59, 127
    opéra comique, 127
Austen, Jane, 259, 262–3, 275, 279
    Crown Inn, 259
    Emma, 15, 259
    love of dance, 259
    Meryton Assembly, 275
    Netherfield ball, 259, 275
    Northanger Abbey, 262
    Pride and Prejudice, 15, 259
Austen-Leigh, James Edward, 266

authenticity, 56, 58, 66
automata, 58, 62
avant-garde, 122, 180, 209, 210

bacchanal, 122, 130, 135, 252, 255. *See* Wagner, Richard: Venusberg Bacchanal
Bacchanale. *See* Saint-Saëns, Camille: 'Bacchanale'
Bach, J. S., 11, 29, 177, 182, 245
    Cantata BWV213, 31
    'Coffee Cantata', BWV211, 31
    copying processes, 21
    English Suite no. 1, BWV806, 30
    French dance suites, 52
    Lute Suite in C minor, BWV997, 30
    Musical Offering, 245
    orchestral overtures, 20
    Passions, 30
    wedding cantata, BWV202, 31
Bakhtin, Mikhail, 4
Bakst, Léon, 149, 209, 210, 223
Balanchine, George, 7
ball, charity, 71
ballet, 69, 126, 150, 174, 176, 180
    as art ('high'), 150
    classical, 95
    homosexual, 245
    modern, 148
    musicological literature on, 116
    popularity of, 181
    preëminence in Paris, 181
    Romantic, 57, 58, 59, 147, 231, 256
    Wagner's opposition to, 122
ballet d'action, 63
ballet-divertissement. *See* divertissements
ballet-pantomime, 6, 63, 124, 126, 130
    Giselle, 66
    La Péri, 61
Ballets Russes, 126, 203, 207
    and burlesque, 148
    and the dance poem, 150
    and Diaghilev, 149
    and Fauré's Pavane, 195

302

scandal of modernism, 148
ballrooms, 72, 263
barrel organ. *See* hurdy-gurdy
Barthes, Roland, 262
Bausch, Pina, 236, 257, 258
   Adagio, 233, 257
   Fritz, 233, 257
Beck, Jill, 212
Béjart, Maurice, 236, 258
   Amor di Poeta, 232
   Ce que l'amour me dit, 244
   Le Chant du compagnon errant, 232, 244–50, 257
   Early Songs, 232
   Mathilde, 232
   Rite of Spring, 245
Benois, Alexandre, 148, 150
Berg, Alban
   Lulu, 62
   Wozzeck, 66
Bertrand, Eugène, 182
Bizet, Georges, *Carmen*, 59, 62, 66, 69
Boccherini, Luigi, 75
Bohemia, 60
Bois de boulogne, 195
Boito, Arrigo, *Mefistofele*, 222
bolero, 67
bourgeoisie, 55, 72
Bournonville, August, 60
bourrée, 11, 20, 26, 31, 74, 202
Boyes, Georgina, 268
Braque, Georges, 208, 210
Brion, Katherine, 1
Britten, Benjamin, *Les Illuminations*, 231
Broadbridge, Aidan, 277
Brooks, Lynne Matluck, 50
Brunold, Paul, 202
Buhlerkünste, 124
burlesque, 148

cachucha, 62
canon, 16, 49, 207
canonicity, 229, 233
Carnival season (*Fasching*), 71
carousel, 58
Carré, Albert, 181
Carter, Alexandra, 54, 56
censorship, 186
Chabrier, Emmanuel, *Dix pièces pittoresques* for piano, 183
Chénier, André, 'Ode à Versailles', 194
Chéret, Jules, 1–4
Chopin, Frédéric, 58, 110

Bolero in A minor, op. 19, 67
churches, 28, 162
clubs, women's, 158, 162
Cole, Jonathan, 89
Comédie-Française, 175, 186, 189
commedia dell'arte, 1–4
commoner, 180
community, 158, 272, 279
   folk, 272
   imagined, 265
   and self, 48
Concerts de l'Opéra, 182, 183
conductors
   Boulez, Pierre, 219
   Jansons, Mariss, 258
   Klenau, Paul, 221
   Munch, Charles, 221
   Pierné, Gabriel, 112, 221
   Rattle, Sir Simon, 258
   Ronald, Sir Landon, 220
   Ruhlmann, Franz, 93
   Solti, Sir Georg, 258
   Stokowski, Leopold, 220
   Welser-Möst, Franz, 258
consciousness, 207
contredanse, 52
Corelli, Arcangelo, 274
Cornazano, Antonio, 54, 65
corps de ballet, 136, 140, 181, 189, 252
costume designs, 62
couleur locale, 60, 187
country dance. *See* dance, English country
Country Dances, The Apted Book of, 269
court, Bourbon, 180
Cox, Arnie, 8
Cranko, John, 251
   Opus 1, 252
Cubism, 208
Cusick, Suzanne, 9

d'Estrée, Jean, 177
   Danseries, 187, 188
dance
   baroque, 190
   'characteristic', 124
   choraic, 24
   English country, 259, 263–7, 274
   German, 71, 72
   Indian, 60
   late baroque, 177
   Lutheran attitudes towards, 24

dance (cont.)
    neo-pavane, 172, 175, 176, 177, 182, 183,
        190, 192, 197, 201, 202
    neo-Renaissance, 175
    Renaissance, 187
    Waffentanz (dance of arms), 129
dance hall, 72, 172, 175, 176, 177, 182, 183, 192,
    197, 201, 202
Dance of the Bee, 61, 64
Dance of the Seven Veils, 61
danses anciennes, 185
danseuse, 62, 70, 97
de Greffulhe, Elisabeth, 194
de Montesquiou, Robert, 193
Debussy, Claude, 15, 110, 150,
    208, 213
    Prélude à l'après-midi d'un faune, 207
    Suite bergamasque, 172, 185–6
Delibes, Léo, 175, 182, 187
    Airs de danse dans le style ancien, 187
    Coppélia, 189
    Pavanne lesquercarde, 189
Delsarte, 13, 152–62, 163
Delsartism, 231
demi coupé, 79–80, 86, 87, 89, 90
Denby, Edwin, 214
Descartes, René, 26
Destouches, André Cardinal, 182
Deutsche Tänze. See dance, German
Diaghilev, Sergei, 149, 196, 207, 208
difference, sexual, 228
divertissements, 15, 122, 124, 127, 144, 175,
    180, 181, 186, 203, 271
Division Violin, The (1686), 53
Donizetti, Gaetano, *La favorite*, 59
Dresden, 128
drills, broom, 157–8
dualism, mind–body, 49
Dujardin, Edouard, 186, 187
Duncan, Isadora, 93, 148, 149, 232

Ecole Niedermeyer, 183
Egypt, 67, 68
Ellis, Katharine, 91, 179
elocutionists, 154, 162
Elssler, Fanny, 62
emotion, 27, 29, 30, 32, 35, 46, 65, 107, 108, 159,
    161, 255, 261, 279
entertainment, popular, 58
entrainment, bodily, 76
eroticism, 62, 67
exoticism, 57, 176
    antique, 14

fandango, 58
Fauré, Gabriel, 172, 176, 182, 183, 193
    'Clair de lune', 195
    Masques et bergamasques, 195
    Pavane, 194, 203
    Pavane in F♯ minor, 174
Featherstone, Simon, 267
Feld, Eliot, 236, 258
    At Midnight, 232, 237–43, 245, 257
Feldtenstein, Carl Joseph von, 76, 79
feminine, 11
fête galante, 195
Filippi, Filippo, 66
Finnegan, Ruth, 49
Flam, Jack, 211
Fokine, Mikhail, 149
folk, 56, 57, 59, 124
Fonta, Laure, 188–9, 202
Forkel, Johann Nikolaus, 19, 20
Foster, Susan Leigh, 59
Foucault, Michel, 95
Framéry, Nicolas Etienne, 265–6
France, 176, 177
    early modern, 50
François, Anne-Lise, 94–5
Freud, Sigmund, 'The Unconscious', 230
Freudian, 208
Friedl, Johann, 71
Fuller, Loie, 12, 95, 148
    Salomé, 116

Gailhard, Pierre, 182
gaillarde, 187
Gallet, Louis, 187
gavotte, 20, 31, 177
Germany, 56, 60
Gesamtkunstwerk. See artwork, total
gesture, pantomimic, 63
gigue, 11, 26
Gilbert, Jeremy, 49
Gilman, Sander, 236
Ginot, Isabelle, 76
Gjerdingen, Robert, 183, 197
Glinka, Mikhail, *Ruslan and Ludmila*, 222
Gluck, Christoph Willibald, 182
Godkin, Paul, 233
Goldmark, Karl, *Die Königen von Saba*,
    59, 61
Goodwin, Noel, 254
Göttin Diana, Die, 146
Gounod, Charles, *Faust*, 222
grand opéra, 59, 63
Greensleeves, 53

Grieg, Edvard, 110
Grover-Friedlander, Michal, 9

habañera, 69
Halévy, Fromental
    La juive, 127
Handel, George Frideric, 177, 182, 274
Hanna, Judith Lynne, 49, 59
Hansen, Joseph, 182
Hasty, Christopher, 85
Haydn, Franz Joseph, 11, 52
    Minuet in D major, Hob. IX/11, No. 1, 73
    String Quartet, Op. 76 No. 4, finale, 74
Hebrew, 61
Heidegger, Martin, 7
Heine, Heinrich, 13, 125, 145–6, 147
    Der Doktor Faust, 146
    Die Göttin Diana, 146
Herbert, Robert L., 4
Hering, Doris, 237
hermeneutics, 10, 51, 94, 95
    of suspicion, 94
Hindustan, 60
historicism, 176
historiography, 91, 207
Hobbs, June Hadden, 164
Hobsbawm, Eric, invented traditions, 16
Hofburg Redoutensäle, 71, 76
Hollins Institute, 161
Holloway, Robin, 70
Holm, Hanya, 233
Hugo, Victor
    Les orientales, 70
    Le roi s'amuse, 175, 182, 186
Hungary, 60
hurdy-gurdy, 58
Hutchinson Guest, Ann, 212, 213
hymns, 13, 152, 162, 163–5, 171

identity, national, 58
Idylle, 183
impresario, 208
Impressionism, 220
industrialization, 57
Italy, fifteenth-century, 50

Jaleo de Jerez, 62
Jeschke, Claudia, 212
Joffrey, Robert, *Remembrances*, 231
Johnson, Julian, 235
Juilliard, 212, 222
July Monarchy, 180

Kelly, Michael, 72
King Wilhelm I of Prussia, 129
kitsch, 70
Knittel, K. M., 236
Koegler, Hörst, 254
Kramer, Lawrence, 9

Labanotation, 212, 213, 221
Lacoste, Louis, 182
Lajarte, Théodore de
    Airs à danser, de Lulli à Méhul, 201
Ländler, 72
laughter, 4, 16
Le Guin, Elisabeth, 9, 12, 75
Lefton, Sue, 272
Leipzig, 21
Lemaire, Gaston, 193
Levine, Lawrence, 159
Lidov, David, 74
Lieder, 231
Litz, Katherine, 233
Locke, Ralph P., 66, 67, 69
Lully, Jean-Baptiste, 182

MacMillan, Kenneth, 258
    Song of the Earth, 232, 250–5, 257
Magdanz, Teresa, 57
Magri, Gennaro, 54
Mahler, Gustav, 15, 232, 233, 234–6, 245, 257
    Kindertotenlieder, 232, 233, 257
    Das Lied von der Erde, 232, 233, 253
    Lieder eines fahrenden Gesellen, 244
    Rückert-Lieder, 232, 237, 240, 244
    Symphony No. 3, 244
    Symphony No. 5, 233, 257, 258
    'Von der Jugend', 253
    'Von der Schönheit', 253
Mahlerites, 258
Mallarmé, Stéphane, 15, 150, 207, 219, 228
    L'après-midi d'un faune, 215
manuals, elocution, 157
march, 67
    'Turkish', 63
Marianelli, Dario, 274
Marschner, Heinrich, 127
    Hans Heiling, 136
Marx, A. B., 65
Mason, Monica, 251
masquerades, 56
Massenet, Jules
    Cléopâtre, 59, 68
    Hérodiade, 59
Massine, Léonide, *Las Meninas*, 195

Matisse, Henri, 210–12
  Le bonheur de vivre, 210
Mattheson, Johann, 24, 27–8
McClary, Susan, 9, 69
McKayle, Donald, *Rainbow 'Round My Shoulder*, 234
McKee, Eric, 52
McLeary, Donald, 254
mechanization, 57
Méhul, Etienne-Nicolas
  Les deux aveugles de Tolède, 67
Mellers, Wilfred, *Bach and the Dance of God*, 19
melody, endless, 122
Merleau-Ponty, Maurice, 7, 11, 21
Messager, André
  La Basoche, 191
  Isoline, 185
Meyerbeer, Giacomo
  L'Africaine, 59
  Les Huguenots, 127
  Robert le diable, 127
middle classes, 73, 203
Milan, 68
mimesis, 234
mind, 3, 10, 16, 35, 49, 53, 58, 65, 155, 159, 236, 261
minuet, 11, 20, 52, 54, 71, 175, 177
  Portugese, 58
  step, 78
Mirka, Danuta, 74
mise en abyme, 279
mise en scène, 60, 149, 268
modernism, 93, 98, 125, 148, 207, 210, 211, 222, 230
modernity, 14, 185
Monplaisir, Hyppolyte, *Le figlie di Chèrope*, 68
Monte Carlo, 209
Montero, Barbara, 89
Montesquiou Robert de, 196
Morley, Thomas, 53
Morris, Mark, 7, 257
Mozart, W. A., *Don Giovanni*, 59
Mulvey, Laura, 2
musette, 194
musical, filmed, 272
musicians, street, 54

nationalism, 14, 57
natural, the, 57
Near East, representations of the, 68
neo-*art nouveau*, 255
Neumeyer, David, 52, 55

New York City, 170
Nietzsche, Friedrich, 121–2
  Nietzsche contra Wagner, 121
Nijinska, Bronislava, 208, 222
Nijinsky, Vaslav, 105, 149, 207, 208, 219
  L'après-midi d'un faune, 15, 150
  Le sacre du printemps, 144
nobility, 54, 72, 73, 180, 193
  French, 180
Noblet, Lise and Félicité, 62
nostalgia, 56, 193, 194, 195, 196, 243, 274, 279
Novak, Jelena, 242

opera, German Romantic, 127
Opéra, Paris, 13, 62, 126, 130, 139, 181, 188, 189, 195
  ballet, 142, 182
  Jockey Club, 140
  library, 202
opéra-ballet, 231
Opéra-Comique, 181
Orchestra, Boston Symphony, 221
Orchestra, Cleveland, 220
Orchestra, English Chamber, 274
Orchestra, Philadelphia, 220
Orchestra, Royal Philharmonic, 221
Orchestre des Concerts Colonne, 221
Orientalism, 51, 63, 67

Painter, Karen, 236
Paladilhe, Émile, 182
  Patrie, 177, 183
  Pavane from *Patrie*, 194
  Pavane in F♯, 177
pantomime, 124, 152, 234
  in Richard Wagner, *Rienzi*, 128
Paris, 130
Paris Conservatoire, 183
Paris World's Fair (1900), 181
Paris, late nineteenth- and early twentieth-century, 92
Paris, nineteenth-century, 91
pas de deux, 225, 232, 240, 241–2, 243, 245, 249, 253, 256
  male-male, 246
Pasch, Johann, 25
Pasler, Jann, 172, 179
passamezzo antico, 53
passepied, 41, 179, 189
passepied de Bretagne, 190
pastoral, 150, 207, 209, 210, 211, 219, 228
pavane, 14, 172–4, 175, 176, 177, 179

Pavane Lesquercarde, 187
Pavlova, Anna, 105
Pearson, Ewan, 49
Percival, John, 244
Petipa, Lucien, 140, 144
Pezzl, Johann, 72
phenomenology, 11, 15, 21, 94
Philistine, 61
Piazzolla, Astor, 58
Picasso, Pablo, 208, 210
   Les demoiselles d'Avignon, 210
Pietism, 22
piva, 54
Playford, John
   country dances, English, 56
   Dancing Master, 259, 265, 269
   'Mr Beveridge's Maggot', 271–4
poetry, 208
Poland, 59, 60
polonaise, 58
polska, 60
prayer, 152
Princess Metternich, 140
projection, metre as, 85
projections, coloured light, 96
prostitution, 124, 125, 145, 155
Proust, Marcel, 193
Prynne, William, 51
psychoanalysis, 230
Puffett, Derek, 66
Purcell, Henry, 16, 172, 274–5, 279
   Rondeau from *Abdelazar*, 277

Rameau, Jean-Philippe, 182
   Les fêtes de Polymnie, 191
Rancière, Jacques, 95–7
Ratner, Leonard, 6, 51
Ravel, Maurice, 172, 176, 193, 222
   Daphnis et Chloé, 150, 222
   Ma mère l'Oye, 197
   'Pavane pour une infante défunte', 183, 193, 199–200
Readymade, the, 110, 116
reel, 261
Regency period, 269
Reihen, 36
religious groups, American, 162
Renaissance, 52
répétition générale, 116
repression, 207, 212, 230
revival, English country dance, 16
rhetoric, 26–7
Riga, 129

Rite of Spring. See Stravinsky, Igor: *Le sacre du printemps*
Roberts, David, 149
Robinson, Paul, 60
Roerich, Nicholas, 149
romanesca, 53
Rosengard Subotnik, Rose, 228
Rossini, Gioachino, *Guillaume Tell*, 59
round-dance, 24
roundelay. *See* round-dance
Royer, Alphonse, 140
Rüetz, Caspar, 28
Russia, 60

Saint-Saëns, Camille, 176, 183, 186
   'Bacchanale', 69
   Etienne Marcel, 175, 186
   pavane from *Etienne Marcel*, 186
   Proserpine, 195
   Samson et Dalila, 59, 61, 62
Sanguinetti, Giorgio, 183
sarabande, 26, 30
Saxony, 27
Schneider, Louis, 214
Schubert, Franz, 110
Schumann, Robert
   Dichterliebe, 232
   Frauenliebe und Leben, 231
Scottish Highlands, 261
seguidilla, 69
Serral, Dolores, 62
Servos, Norbert, 258
Sharp, Cecil, 267, 268, 269
Sheen, Erica, 262
Sicily, 59
Smart, Mary Ann, 6, 91
Smith, Marian, 6
somatics, 7, 76
Sondheim, Stephen, *Gypsy*, 148
song, illustrated, 154, 157
song-ballets, 15, 231–3, 235
Sor, Fernando, 58
soundscape, 275
soundtrack, 111, 275–6, 279
Spain, 59
spirituality, 154, 159
St. Denis, Ruth, 148
Staats, Leo, 105
Stebbins, Genevieve, 156, 157, 159
   Society Gymnastics and Voice Culture, 160
Strauss, Richard, 231, 234
   Elektra, 66
   Elektra's *Totentanz*, 61, 66

Strauss, Richard (cont.)
  Lieder, 232
  Salome, 62, 64, 66, 68
Stravinsky, Igor, 126, 149, 180, 245, 252
  L'oiseau de feu, 149
  Pulcinella, 175
  Le sacre du printemps, 70, 144, 150
Svétlov, Valerian, 93
Symbolists, 234

tableaux mouvants, 166
tableaux vivants, 166, 170
tango, 58
Tantzrei[h]en. *See* round-dance
Tanzpoem. *See* dance poem
Taruskin, Richard, 9, 149, 150, 263
Tchaikovsky, Pyotr
  Eugene Onegin, 222
  Le mariage d'Aurore, 196
  The Queen of Spades, 222
  Sleeping Beauty, 196
Tenroc, Charles, 208
Terry, Walter, 233
Theater, Alvin Ailey City Center Dance, 234
Theatre du Châtelet, 93
Theatre, American Ballet, 232, 237
Theatre, New York State, 237
Third Republic, 181, 183
Thom, Rose Anne, 234
Thurner, Christina, 25
Tmesis, 263
topic, 10, 11, 51, 52
topoi. *See* topic
tragedy, ancient Greek, 123
translation, 207, 208, 222
Trouhanova, Natalia, 93
Tudor, Anthony, 232, 251
  Dark Elegies, 232, 250
  Shadow of the Wind, 232, 233, 250

unconsciousness, 58, 207, 212, 230
United States of America, 13, 154, 156, 159, 162, 232
urns, Grecian, 158

Valencia, Tórtola, 148
van Dantzig, Rudi
  Antwoord gevend, 231
  Lieder, 231
  Vergezicht, 231
  Vier letzte Lieder, 231
Venusberg. *See* Wagner, Richard: Venusberg Bacchanal

Verdi, Giuseppe
  Aida, 59, 60, 62, 64, 66, 67
  Aida, 'Ballabile', 69
  Aida, 'Danza sacra', 68
Verlaine, Paul
  Fêtes galantes, 195
  'Mandoline', 194
Vienna, 11, 71, 73
  eighteenth-century, 73
Villany, Adorée, 148
Volk. *See* folk
volta, 50

Wagner, Cosima, 126, 149
Wagner, Richard, 13, 61, 110
  Artwork of the Future, 122, 123, 125, 129, 145, 146
  Bayreuth Festival, 149
  A Communication to my Friends, 127
  Die Feen, 127
  Der fliegende Holländer, 126, 136
  Die Meistersinger, 127
  Flower Maidens scene, *Parsifal*, 137
  influence in France, 176
  Liebestod from *Tristan und Isolde*, 232
  Das Liebesverbot, 127
  music drama, 127
  'On Conducting', 141
  Opera and Drama, 127
  Paris *Tannhäuser*, 122, 148
  Parsifal, 127, 150
  'Ride of the Valkyries', 112, 116
  Rienzi, 125, 126, 128
  The Ring of the Nibelung, 122
  Tannhäuser, 13, 61, 125, 126, 145, 149
  Tristan und Isolde, 127, 142, 150
  Venusberg Bacchanal, 13, 61, 125, 130–5, 136, 137–47, 149, 150
  Wesendonck-Lieder, 231, 232
Walker, Donald, *Exercise for Ladies*, 65
Walkowitz, Daniel, 269, 274
waltz, 57, 60, 63, 64–5, 125
  as damaging to women, 65
  Elektra's *Totentanz*, 66
  folk, 136
  from *Der Freischütz*, 65
  in Salome's dance, 69–70
war, Franco-Prussian, 177
Warlock, Peter, *Capriol Suite*, 175
Watteau, Jean-Antoine, 1
Weber, Carl Maria von, 65, 127
  Aufforderung zum Tanz, 63

Freischütz, Der, 64
Webern, Anton, 231
   Passacaglia, 252
Werth, Margaret, 212, 228–9
Wheelock, Gretchen, 74
Wiesenthal, Grete, 148
Williamson, John, 247

Willson, Meredith, *The Music Man*, 158
Wilson, Thomas, 265
Wirthschaften, 56
Witzmann, Reingard, 72
Wright, Joe, 276

Zbikowski, Lawrence, 5, 6, 55–6, 57, 74

For EU product safety concerns, contact us at Calle de José Abascal, 56–1°, 28003 Madrid, Spain or eugpsr@cambridge.org.

www.ingramcontent.com/pod-product-compliance
Ingram Content Group UK Ltd.
Pitfield, Milton Keynes, MK11 3LW, UK
UKHW050111230326
469255UK00021B/482